T0254600

Scalable Input/Output

Scientific and Engineering Computation
Janusz Kowalik, editor

Data-Parallel Programming on MIMD Computers, Philip J. Hatcher and Michael J. Quinn, 1991

Unstructured Scientific Computation on Scalable Multiprocessors, edited by Piyush Mehrotra, Joel Saltz, and Robert Voigt, 1992

Parallel Computational Fluid Dynamics: Implementations and Results, edited by Horst D. Simon, 1992

Enterprise Integration Modeling: Proceedings of the First International Conference, edited by Charles J. Petrie, Jr., 1992

The High Performance Fortran Handbook, Charles H. Koelbel, David B. Loveman, Robert S. Schreiber, Guy L. Steele Jr., and Mary E. Zosel, 1994

Using MPI: Portable Parallel Programming with the Message-Passing Interface William Gropp, Ewing Lusk, and Anthony Skjellum, 1994

PVM: Parallel Virtual Machine-A Users' Guide and Tutorial for Networked Parallel Computing, Al Geist, Adam Beguelin, Jack Dongarra, Weicheng Jiang, Robert Manchek, and Vaidy Sunderam, 1994

Enabling Technologies for Petaflops Computing, Thomas Sterling, Paul Messina, and Paul H. Smith, 1995

Practical Parallel Programming, Gregory V. Wilson, 1995

An Introduction to High-Performance Scientific Computing, Lloyd D. Fosdick, Elizabeth R. Jessup, Carolyn J. C. Schauble, and Gitta Domik, 1995

Parallel Programming Using C++, edited by Gregory V. Wilson and Paul Lu, 1996

Using PLAPACK: Parallel Linear Algebra Package, Robert van de Geijn, 1997

Fortran 95 Handbook, Jeanne C. Adams, Walter S. Brainerd, Jeanne T. Martin, Brian T. Smith, and Jerrold L. Wagener, 1997

MPI-The Complete Reference: Volume 1, The MPI Core, second edition, Marc Snir, Steve Otto, Steven Huss-Lederman, David Walker, and Jack Dongarra, 1998

MPI-The Complete Reference: Volume 2, The MPI-2 Extensions, William Gropp, Steven Huss-Lederman, Andrew Lumsdaine, Ewing Lusk, Bill Nitzberg, William Saphir, and Marc Snir, 1998

A Programmer's Guide to ZPL, Lawrence Snyder, 1998

How to Build a Beowulf: A Guide to the Implementation and Application of PC Clusters, Thomas L. Sterling, John Salmon, Donald J. Becker, and Daniel F. Savarese, 1999

Using MPI: Portable Parallel Programming with the Message Passing Interface, second edition, William Gropp, Ewing Lusk, and Anthony Skjellum, 1999

Using MPI 2: Advanced Features of the Message Passing Interface, William Gropp, Ewing Lusk, and Rajeev Thakur, 1999

Beowulf Cluster Computing with Windows, Thomas Sterling, 2001

Beowulf Cluster Computing with Linux, Thomas Sterling, 2001

Beowulf Cluster Computing with Linux, Second Edition, edited by Thomas Sterling, William Gropp and Ewing Lusk, 2003

Scalable Input/Output: Achieving System Balance, Daniel A. Reed, 2004

Scalable Input/Output: Achieving System Balance

edited by
Daniel A. Reed

The MIT Press
Cambridge, Massachusetts
London, England

©2004 Massachusetts Institute of Technology

All rights reserved. No part of this book may be reproduced in any form by any electronic or mechanical means (including photocopying, recording, or information storage and retrieval) without permission in writing from the publisher.

This book was set by the author and was printed and bound in the United States of America.

Library of Congress Cataloging-in-Publication Data

Scalable input/output : achieving system balance / edited by Daniel A. Reed.
    p.   cm. — (Scientific and engineering computation)
  Includes bibliographical references.
  ISBN 978-0-262-68142-1 (pbk.   )
  1. Computer input-output equipment. 2. Parallel computers. 3. Memory management (Computer science). I. Reed, Daniel A. II. Series.

TK7887.5.R43 2003
004.7—dc21   2003051205

The MIT Press is pleased to keep this title available in print by manufacturing single copies, on demand, via digital printing technology.

To Andrea, the love of my life, for her unwavering belief in my dreams.

Also, to the loving memory of my father, now gone but never forgotten.

Contents

**A   Appendix: Proposal for a Common Parallel File   279
         System Programming Interface**
         *Peter F. Corbett,   Jean-Pierre Prost, Chris Demetriou,   Garth
         Gibson, Erik Riedel, Jim Zelenka, Yuqun Chen, Ed Felten, Kai Li,
         John Hartman, Larry Peterson, Brian Bershad, Alec Wolman and
         Ruth Aydt*

Preface

A new generation of scientific instruments, ranging from telescopes to particle accelerators and gene sequencers, is producing prodigious amounts of experimental data. Concurrently, high resolution simulations, executed atop very-high-performance computing systems, are generating ever larger amounts of computational data.

Only a few years ago, a file or data set containing a few gigabytes was considered large. Today, multiple terabyte scientific data sets are common, and petabyte data archives for single scientific experiments are very near. Arguably, we are entering the "decade of data," when large-scale analysis of scientific data via high-performance computing systems can be a major source of new scientific insights.

Rapidly rising disk storage capacities have made it economically feasible to store ever larger scientific data sets. Commodity disks with well over O(100) GB capacity are now widely available, and disks with even larger capacities appear regularly. Consequently, one can now acquire a terabyte of commodity storage for only a few thousand dollars and a petabyte of secondary storage for only millions of dollars.

Unfortunately, disk capacities are rising far more rapidly than data transfer bandwidths. Hence, the ratio of disk bandwidth to capacity is asymptotically approaching zero, making it ever more difficult to access the torrent of emerging scientific data. This input/output (I/O) bottleneck is a major constraint on the effective use of scientific data for leading-edge research.

In addition, rapid increases in computing and communication performance are exacerbating these I/O limitations. Indeed, for many otherwise scalable parallel applications, input/output is emerging as a major performance bottleneck.

The Scalable I/O (SIO) Initiative was launched by Paul Messina, then Director of the Center for Advanced Computing Research (CACR) at the California Institute of Technology to explore software and algorithmic solutions to the I/O bottleneck. SIO Initiative members included Brian Bershad (Washington), Andrew Chien (Illinois, now at UCSD), Alok Choudhary (Syracuse, now at Northwestern), David

DeWitt (Wisconsin), Garth Gibson (Carnegie-Mellon), William Gropp (Argonne), Ken Kennedy (Rice), Kai Li (Princeton), Ewing Lusk (Argonne), Larry Peterson (Arizona, now at Princeton), Jim Poole (Caltech), Joel Saltz (Maryland, now at Ohio State), Dan Reed (Illinois) and Rajeev Thakur (Argonne).

The SIO initiative's technical activities were organized under five working groups: applications, performance evaluation, compilers and languages, operating systems, and integration and testbeds. With funding from the Department of Defense's Advanced Research Projects Agency (DARPA), the National Science Foundation (NSF) via multiple grants, the Department of Energy, and the National Aeronautics and Space Administration, the SIO working groups explored a variety of techniques for I/O optimization:

- I/O characterization to understand application and system I/O patterns,

- system checkpointing strategies to support application recovery and restart,

- collective I/O and parallel database support for scientific applications,

- parallel I/O libraries and strategies for file striping, prefetching and write behind,

- compilation strategies for out-of-core data access,

- scheduling and shared virtual memory alternatives for I/O,

- network support for low-latency data transfer and

- parallel I/O application programming interfaces (APIs).

In addition, a set of application scientists from a variety of institutions collaborated with the initiative's computing researchers to analyze and optimize I/O-intensive applications for parallel systems. Key individuals included Jim Bower, David Curkendall, Robert Ferrarro, Aron Kupperman, Tony Leonard, Vince McKoy, Dan Meiron, Tom Prince, Carl Winstead and Mark Wu. All of the computing research participants are grateful for the time and energy provided by our application partners.

This book is a summary of major research results from the SIO Initiative. I would like to thank all of the authors, Ruth Aydt, Brian Bershad, Bradley Broom, Chailin Chang, Yuqun Chen, Andrew Chien, Alox Choudary, Doug Clark, Peter Corbett, Phyl Crandall, Chris Demetriou, Christos Faloutsos, Ed Felten, Rob Fowler, Garth Gibson, Bill Gropp, John Hartman, Liviu Iftode, Mahmut Kandemir, Ken Kennedy,

Chuck Koelbel, Tahsin Kurc, Kai Li, Ewing Lusk, Tara Madhyastha, Sachin More, Jaechun No, Michael Paleczny, James Plank, Larry Peterson, Jean-Pierre Prost, Erik Riedel, Joel Saltz, Alan Sussman, Rajeev Thakkur, Limin Wang, Alec Wolman, Jim Zelenka and Yuanyuan Zhou. Most importantly, I express special thanks to Paul Messina for his tireless efforts in coordinating the initiative.

At Illinois, preparation of this book was supported in part by NSF grant EIA 99-75248 and cooperative agreement ACI 96-19019.

Finally, this book would not have been completed without the tireless editing of my able research coordinator, Deb Israel, and the persistent nudging of Doug Sery, the MIT Press editor. I can only express my sincere thanks to both for their efforts.

1 I/O Characterization and Analysis

PHYLLIS E. CRANDALL, RUTH A. AYDT, ANDREW A. CHIEN AND DANIEL A.
REED

Recent progress building systems whose aggregate computation and communication performance can be economically scaled across a wide range has encouraged application scientists to pursue computational science models that were heretofore considered intractable. Unfortunately, for many scalable parallel applications, the I/O barrier rivals or exceeds that for computation. In short, high-performance commodity processors and high-speed networks are necessary but not sufficient to solve many national challenge problems — scalable parallel secondary and tertiary storage systems are needed as well.

Distressingly, I/O and file system research on scalable parallel systems is still in its infancy. Moreover, commodity storage technology trends suggest that the disparity between peak processor speeds and disk transfer rates will continue to increase — the commodity disk market favors low cost, low power consumption and high capacity over high data rates. With commodity disks, only disk arrays [47] can provide the requisite peak data transfer rates.

When hundreds or thousands of disks and disk arrays are coupled with tertiary storage devices, a multilevel storage management system (e.g., Unitree), and a broad range of possible parallel file access patterns, the space of potential data management strategies is immense, and identifying optimal or even acceptable operating points becomes problematic. Unfortunately, file system and storage hierarchy designers have little empirical data on parallel I/O access patterns and are often forced to extrapolate from measured access patterns on either traditional vector supercomputers [182, 206, 205] or Unix workstations [202]. Neither of these environments reflects the application usage patterns, diversity of configurations, or economic tradeoffs salient in scalable parallel systems.

The goal of our work is to characterize parallel I/O requirements and access patterns, enabling application developers to achieve a higher fraction of peak I/O performance on existing parallel systems and system software developers to design better parallel file system policies for future generation systems. We analyze the I/O behavior of three parallel applications on the Intel Paragon XP/S: an electron scattering code, a terrain rendering code, and a quantum chemistry code.

These applications represent a snapshot of current I/O practice on scalable parallel machines and reflect the developers' I/O design choices based on perceived and actual limitations of available I/O systems. These codes are but a small part of the Scalable Input/Output Initiative's (SIO) code suite [219], and this characterization is one step in a continuing I/O characterization effort.

Our experimental data show that application I/O signatures differ substantially, with a wide variety of temporal and spatial access patterns, including highly read-intensive and write-intensive phases, extremely large and extremely small request sizes, and both sequential and highly irregular access patterns. This data indicates that parallel I/O systems must deliver high performance across broad diversity in application access patterns. Our preliminary experiences with parallel file systems [119, 132] suggest that supporting robust performance requires tuning file system policies to specific access patterns.

The remainder of this chapter is organized as follows. In §1.1–§1.2, we summarize our approach to I/O performance characterization and its relation to the Scalable I/O Initiative. This is followed in §1.3 by a brief description of the three application codes and their high-level I/O behavior. In §1.4–§1.6 we analyze the temporal and spatial I/O patterns of the applications in detail, followed in §1.7 by discussion of the implications for parallel file system policies. Finally, §1.8 and §1.9 describe, respectively, related work on I/O characterization and a brief summary of our experiences and directions for future research.

1.1 Background

Though the reasons for I/O in high-performance applications are varied, they can be broadly classified as compulsory or out-of-core [182]. As the name suggests, compulsory accesses are unavoidable and arise from reading initialization files, generating application output (e.g., scientific data sets or visualizations), or reading input data sets. A high-performance file system can reduce the time needed for these accesses, but they cannot be eliminated by clever cache or memory management schemes.

Checkpoints are necessary because production runs of scientific codes may span hours or even days, the computing resources are typically shared among a large user base, and standard operating practice dictates regular down time for system maintenance. In addition, users often use computation checkpoints as a basis for parametric studies, repeatedly modifying a subset of the checkpoint data values and restarting the computation. The frequency and size of checkpoints is highly application dependent, but a high-performance file system can reduce the cost of checkpointing by exploiting knowledge of checkpoint I/O characteristics.

Finally, out-of-core I/O is a consequence of limited primary memory. Historically, vector supercomputers have, by design, lacked paged virtual memory, and users have managed the limited primary memory by staging data to and from secondary storage. Even on scalable parallel systems with paged virtual memory, many users eschew the convenience of paging for the tight control possible with user-managed overlays and scratch files. Larger primary memories can reduce the number and size of out-of-core scratch files, but not obviate their need — many important problems have data structures far too large for primary memory storage to be economically viable.

Within these broad I/O classes, there are wide variations in file access patterns, and such variations have deep performance implications for parallel file systems. Moreover, there are circular dependences between parallel file system efficiency and parallel program access patterns. Parallel file systems are designed based on the system developers' knowledge of extant file access patterns. Often, these patterns are historical artifacts, themselves based on application developers' exploitation of the idiosyncrasies of previous generation file systems. Consequently, it is critical to both quantify current access patterns and understand the reasons for these patterns. Simply put, are the observed access patterns intrinsic to the application algorithms, or are they artifacts of the current software environment? While definitive answers may in general be unobtainable, frank conversations with code developers and analyses of similar applications on different parallel platforms provide a good basis for insight.

Understanding extant parallel file access patterns and developing more effective file system policies is the goal of the Scalable I/O Initiative, a broad-based, multi-agency group that involves academic researchers, government laboratories, and parallel system vendors. The initiative seeks to develop the technology base needed to support high-performance parallel I/O on future scalable parallel systems. It includes five research working groups: applications, performance characterization (of which the authors are a part), compiler technology, operating systems, and software integration. The three parallel applications described in §1.3 were obtained from application working group participants.

1.2   Experimental Methodology

An ideal I/O characterization of an application code includes access patterns and performance data from the application, I/O library, file system, and device drivers. Application file accesses are the logical I/O stimuli; their sizes, temporal spacing, and spatial patterns (e.g., sequential or random) constrain possible library and file system optimizations (e.g., by prefetching or caching). The physical patterns of

·

I/O at the storage devices are the ultimate system response. Minimizing their number and maximizing their efficiency (e.g., by disk arm scheduling and request aggregation) is the final responsibility of the file system and device drivers.

Given performance data from the application and all system levels, one can correlate I/O activities at each level and identify bottlenecks. However, a complete I/O instrumentation of all system levels is a major undertaking that requires indepth knowledge of operating system structure and access to operating system source. As a prelude to a more detailed instrumentation of system software as part of the Scalable I/O Initiative, we have developed a suite of application I/O software instrumentation and characterization tools. This suite, an extension of the Pablo performance environment [224, 223], brackets invocations of I/O routines with instrumentation software that captures the parameters and duration of each invocation.

1.2.1   Pablo Input/Output Instrumentation

The Pablo performance environment consists of (a) an extensible performance data metaformat and associated library that separates the structure of performance data records from their semantics, (b) an instrumenting parser capable of generating instrumented SPMD source code, (c) extensible instrumentation libraries that can capture timestamped event traces, counts, or interval times and reduce the captured performance data on the fly, and (d) a group of graphical performance data display and sonification tools, based on the data metaformat and coarse-grain graphical programming, that support rapid prototyping of performance analyses.

To capture and analyze I/O performance data, we have extended the Pablo environment to capture the parameters of application I/O calls on a variety of single processor and parallel systems.[1] To minimize potential I/O perturbations due to performance data extraction, the Pablo instrumentation software supports real-time reduction of I/O performance data in addition to capture of detailed event traces. The former trades computation perturbation for I/O perturbation. Measurements show that the instrumentation overhead is modest for I/O data capture and is largely independent of the choice of real-time data reduction or trace output for post-mortem analysis.

Pablo's real-time I/O performance data reductions include any combination of three summaries: file lifetime, time window, and file region. File lifetime summaries include the number and total duration of file reads, writes, seeks, opens, and closes, as well as the number of bytes accessed for each file, and the total time each file

---

[1]This software is available at http://www-pablo.cs.uiuc.edu.

was open. Time window summaries contain similar data, but allow one to specify a
window of time; this window defines the granularity at which data is summarized.
File region summaries are the spatial analog of time window summaries; they define
a summary over the accesses to a file region. Finally, general I/O statistics computed off-line from event traces provide means, variances, minima, maxima, and
distributions of file operation durations and sizes.

1.2.2   Intel Paragon XP/S

Using the Pablo performance instrumentation software, we measured application
I/O performance on the Intel Paragon XP/S [21] at the Caltech research computing
facility. At the time our experiments were conducted, the system had 512 computation nodes and 16 I/O nodes, each with a RAID-3 disk array composed of five 1.2
GB disks. The software environment consisted of several versions of Intel OSF/1
1.2 with PFS, Intel's parallel file system.

PFS stripes files across the I/O nodes in units of 64 KB, with standard RAID-3
striping on each disk array. In addition to file striping, PFS supports six parallel
file access modes:

- M_UNIX: each node has an independent file pointer,

- M_LOG: all nodes share a file pointer, node accesses are first come first serve,
  and I/O operations are variable length,

- M_SYNC: all nodes share a file pointer and accesses are in node number order,

- M_RECORD: each node has an independent file pointer, access is first come first
  serve and I/O operations are fixed length,

- M_GLOBAL: all nodes share a file pointer, perform the same operations and
  access the same data, and

- M_ASYNC: each node has an independent file pointer, access is unrestricted and
  variable size, and operation atomicity is not preserved.

We will return to these modes in §1.4–§1.6 when discussing their use in application
codes.

1.3   Application Code Suite

As we noted earlier, one of the primary goals of the national Scalable I/O Initiative
was analyzing the I/O patterns present in a large suite of scientific and engineering

codes. These span a broad range of disciplines, including biology, chemistry, earth sciences, engineering, graphics, and physics [219]. Despite large differences in their underlying algorithms, the codes share two features. First, each code runs on one or more scalable parallel systems, permitting cross-machine comparisons of I/O performance. Second, all codes have both high I/O and computational requirements. In short, they typify large-scale scientific and engineering computing.

We selected three codes from this suite as an initial I/O characterization effort. In the following subsections we briefly describe the algorithms underlying the three applications, the code structure, and its I/O organization. In §1.4–§1.6, we examine the I/O patterns in greater detail and discuss their implications for file system design.

1.3.1   Electron Scattering (ESCAT)

The study of low-energy electron-molecule collisions is of interest in many contexts, including aerospace applications, atmospheric studies, and the processing of materials using low-temperature plasmas (e.g., semiconductor fabrication). The Schwinger multichannel (SMC) method is an adaptation of Schwinger's variational principle for the scattering amplitude that makes it suitable for calculating low-energy electron-molecule collisions [281]. The scattering probabilities are obtained by solving linear systems whose terms include a Green's function that has no analytic form and is evaluated by numerical quadrature. Generation of the quadrature data is compute-intensive, and the size of the data set is highly variable depending on the nature of the problem. The quadrature is formulated to be energy independent so it can be used to solve the scattering problem at many energies.

ESCAT is a parallel implementation of the Schwinger multichannel method written in a combination of C, FORTRAN, and assembly language. From an I/O perspective, there are four distinct execution phases. First, a compulsory read loads the problem definition and some initial matrices. Next, all nodes participate in the calculation and storage of the requisite quadrature data set, with each node processing a different set of integrals. This phase is compute-intensive and is composed of a series of compute/write cycles with the write steps synchronized among the nodes. Memory limitations and the desire to checkpoint the quadrature data set for reuse in later executions prompt the writes during this phase. The third phase involves calculations that depend on the collision energy. In it, energy-dependent data structures are generated and combined with the reloaded quadrature data set to form the system of linear equations. In the last phase, the linear system matrices are written to disk for later solution on another machine.

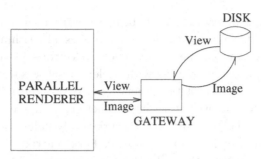

Figure 1.1
Rendering algorithm organization

1.3.2   Terrain Rendering (RENDER)

NASA's deep space imaging and Earth observation satellites have obtained multi-spectral data of Mars and Venus, as well as earth. Combining satellite imagery with terrain elevation data can produce intuitive, three-dimensional perspective views of the planetary surfaces. By generating these views in real-time, it is possible to conduct a "virtual flyby" of the planetary surface where scientists can interactively examine false color terrains from a variety of positions and orientations, supporting rapid exploration of large data sets. A parallel ray-identification algorithm [36] distributes terrain data among processing nodes, decomposing via the natural data parallelism, and exploiting positional derivatives to vary rendering resolution. Together these techniques achieve several frames per second on gigabyte data sets, approaching the ten frames per second needed for real-time animation.

The RENDER code is a hybrid control and data parallel implementation of the ray identification rendering algorithm; Figure 1.1 shows its high-level structure. A single gateway node manages a group of parallel rendering processes and begins by reading the initial data set. The initial read is followed by a read-render-write cycle for each of the subsequent view perspectives (frames). In this loop, the gateway inputs view perspective requests, directs rendering tasks to produce the view, collects rendered views from the group of rendering tasks, and outputs frames to either secondary storage or a HiPPi frame buffer. Thus, RENDER's I/O activity consists of a compulsory read of the initial data set, a series of reads of view coordinates, and corresponding writes of the rendered frames.

1.3.3   Hartree Fock (HTF)

Ab initio chemistry calculations are the key to a detailed understanding of bond strengths and reaction energies for chemical species. Moreover, they allow chemists to study reaction pathways that would be too hazardous or too expensive to explore experimentally. This version of the Hartree Fock algorithm calculates the non-relativistic interactions among atomic nuclei, electrons in the presence of other electrons, and electrons interacting with nuclei. Basis sets derived from the atoms and the relative geometry of the atomic centers are the initial inputs. Atomic integrals are calculated over these basis functions and are used to approximate molecular density. This density and the previously calculated integrals are used to compute the interactions and to form a Fock matrix. A self consistent field (SCF) method is used until the molecular density converges to within an acceptable threshold.

The Hartree Fock implementation we studied consists of three distinct programs totaling roughly 25K lines of Fortran. The three programs operate as a logical pipeline, with the second and third accepting file input from the previous one. The first program, *psetup*, reads the initial input, performs any transformations needed by the later computational phases, and writes its result to disk. The next program, *pargos*, calculates and writes to disk the one and two-electron integrals. The final program, *pscf*, reads the integral files multiple times (they are too large to retain in memory) and solves the SCF equations. In subsequent sections, we refer to these three programs as initialization, integral calculation, and self-consistent field calculations.

With these brief descriptions of the electron scattering, parallel rendering, and Hartree Fock codes, in §1.4–1.6 we examine the detailed patterns of I/O present in each and discuss the implications for file systems design.

1.4   Electron Scattering Behavior

To accurately assess the I/O patterns of the electron scattering code, we used a data set large enough to capture typical behavior but small enough to permit parametric studies of different code versions. On 128 nodes with this data set, the ESCAT code executed for roughly one and three quarter hours. Production data sets generate similar behavior, but with ten to twenty hour executions on 512 processors.

Succinctly, the dominant I/O behavior in the current version of the ESCAT code is small writes, and most of the time is spent computing. During initialization, a single node uses the M_UNIX mode to read the initialization data and broadcast it to the other nodes. In the major execution phase, each node repeatedly seeks and then writes quadrature data to intermediate staging files. Near the end of execution, the nodes reload the previously written data, with each node rereading

Operation	Operation Count	Volume (Bytes)	Node Time (Seconds)	Percentage I/O Time
All I/O	26,418	60,983,136	38,788.95	100.00
Read	560	34,226,048	81.19	0.21
Write	13,330	26,757,088	16,268.50	41.94
Seek	12,034	-	20,884.11	53.84
Open	262	-	1179.06	3.04
Close	262	-	376.06	0.97

Table 1.1
Number, size, and duration of I/O operations (ESCAT)

Operation	Operation Size			
	< 4 KB	< 64 KB	< 256 KB	≥ 256 KB
Read	297	3	260	0
Write	13,330	0	0	0

Table 1.2
Read/write sizes (ESCAT)

the same quadrature data that it wrote. As we shall see in §1.4.2, this software organization is largely due to the constraints system performance places on the application developers — not only would they prefer a different program organization, the problem they wish to solve requires dramatically greater I/O performance.

1.4.1 Experimental Data

Tables 1.1–1.2 are a high-level summary of the I/O behavior of the ESCAT code. During the roughly 6,000 seconds of execution, the total volume of I/O data is only 60M bytes, or 10K bytes/second. Read operations represent 56 percent of the I/O volume, but only two percent of the operations and 0.2 percent of the I/O time. As Figure 1.2 and Table 1.2 show, read sizes are bimodal, with roughly equal numbers of small and large read requests. The overheads for writes and seeks dominate other I/O operations, representing almost 96 percent of the total I/O time.

As we noted earlier, the ESCAT code has four distinct read/write phases. These phases are clearly visible in Figures 1.2–1.3, which show timelines of the ESCAT reads and writes. In the first phase, the initial data is read from three files by node zero and broadcast to the remaining nodes. During the second phase, all nodes repeatedly compute, synchronize, and then write 2 K bytes of quadrature data to two intermediate staging files – one file for each of the two possible collision

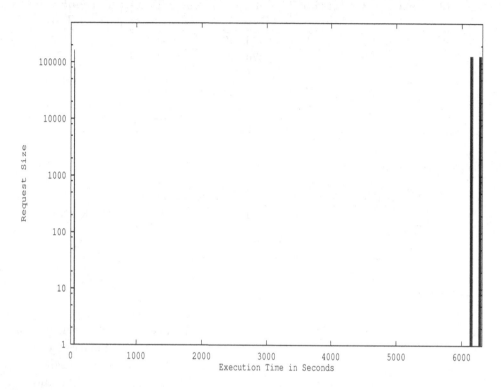

Figure 1.2
Read operation timeline (ESCAT)

outcomes contained in our test data. To simplify reloading of the data in the next phase, each node seeks to a calculated offset dependent on the node number, iteration, and PFS stripe size before writing the data. Intel's M_UNIX file mode is used for these writes.

In the third I/O phase, the previously written quadrature files are read by all the nodes using the Intel M_RECORD mode.[2] Finally, in the last I/O phase, data is sent to node zero by all other nodes and written to three output files.

As can be seen in Figure 1.2, read operations occur only in the first and third phases. The first spike in Figure 1.2 is the initial, compulsory data input; the phase three read operations at the far right of the figure are the staging of the

---

[2]Recall that in this mode each node has a separate file pointer, but the nodes must read fixed size records in first-come-first-serve order.

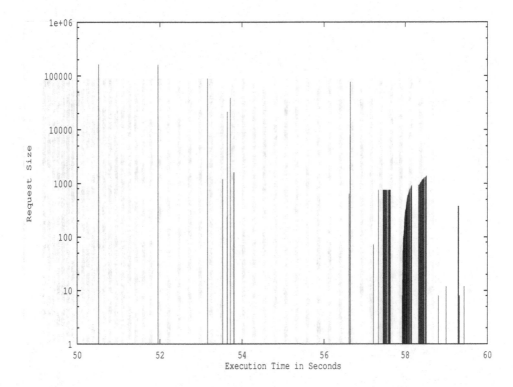

Figure 1.3
Read operation detail (ESCAT)

previously computed quadrature data. Figure 1.3 shows the initial input phase in greater detail, capturing the variety of access sizes and temporal irregularity of the requests.

The tight clustering of the quadrature data writes by all the processors is evident in Figure 1.4. The temporal spacing of the groups decreases as the quadrature calculation phase proceeds, ranging from roughly 160 seconds near the beginning of the phase to half that near the end. Table 1.1 shows that seek overhead is a major contributor to the temporal dispersion of each group.

Finally, Figure 1.5 shows when each of the input and output files was accessed during the ESCAT execution. In the figure, diamonds denote reads, and crosses denote writes. Three files with the identifiers 9, 10, and 11 contain the initial input data, two other files with identifiers 7 and 8 are used for staging the quadrature

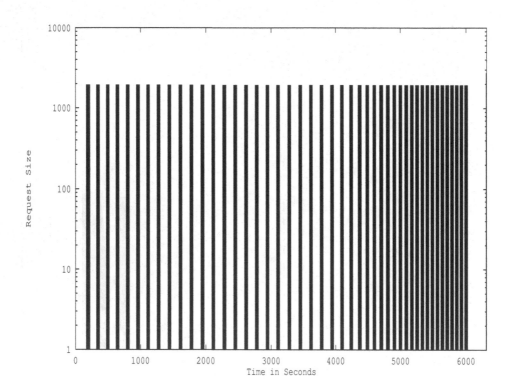

Figure 1.4
Write operation timeline (ESCAT)

data, and the final output is written to the files with identifiers 3, 4, and 5.

1.4.2   Discussion

The implementation and I/O behavior of the ESCAT electron scattering code high-light the disparity between the ideal and current practice. At first glance, it appears that the I/O is inefficient, but seemingly of little import because the code is heavily computation bound. Indeed, for current data sets, this is true. However, the complexity of the quadrature data volume grows as $\mathcal{O}(N^3)$, where N is the number of electron scattering outcomes. Conversations with McKoy *et al* reveal that for current problems, with $N \approx 10$, computation dominates. This reflects their pragmatic need to attack only solvable problems. Their research goal is $N \approx 50$, or two orders of magnitude more data. In short, research practice and the behavior of this code

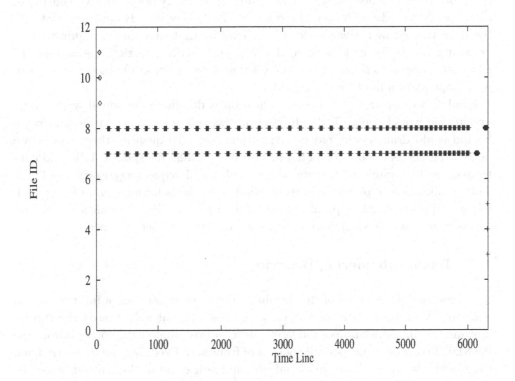

Figure 1.5
File access timeline (ESCAT) (Crosses denote writes; diamonds denote reads)

would change dramatically were higher performance I/O possible.

Not only is the current problem size constrained by I/O limitations, the ESCAT code's I/O behavior is constrained as well. Although the initial data is needed by all processors, the application developers discovered by experimentation that it was more efficient for a single node to read the initial data and then use the communication network to broadcast the data than it was for each node to independently read the initialization data. More efficient support for parallel reading of complete files would simplify the application, eliminating the need to write data distribution code.

The decision to use the Intel M_UNIX mode to write the quadrature data, rather than the M_RECORD mode, was driven by the desire to reduce the time needed to read the data. On writes, the M_RECORD mode generates a sequence of fixed size records that appear to have been written in node order (i.e., for N nodes, the file consists of groups of N records, with each group written in node order). However, in ESCAT, the data written by a given node is later read by that same node, requiring it to be contiguous if the node is to read it efficiently with a single large access. To efficiently support accesses of this type, either a richer set of file modes is needed, or the application must be redesigned.

Finally, because the I/O in this application is dominated by small writes, read prefetching would benefit little. In contrast, write request aggregation and write behind could dramatically reduce the output cost. To quantify these effects, we ported the ESCAT code to PPFS, our portable parallel file system [119], and configured the file system with write behind and global request aggregation policies. This combination of policies effectively eliminated the behavior seen in Figure 1.4. In our experience, this type of optimization (i.e., choosing file policies based on access pattern knowledge), is the key to maximizing I/O performance.

1.5   Terrain Rendering Behavior

To assess the I/O behavior of the terrain rendering code, we used a full production data set (Mars flyby data from the Viking mission), but abbreviated the run by limiting the number of frames rendered. Beyond this point in the computation, the RENDER code performs periodic output of frames, of fixed size and at nearly fixed time intervals. In addition, in actual production use, all of this output would be directed to a HiPPi frame buffer, not the file system. On 128 nodes, the production data set required roughly eight minutes to initialize and output one hundred views (frames). Full production runs consist of 5000 or more frames and execute for approximately thirty minutes. These production runs generate identical initial I/O requirements, extending only the reading of views to render and output views.

Overall, the dominant file I/O requirement of the current version of RENDER is the initial read of a gigabyte data set, followed by compute-limited rendering phases. During initialization, a single node uses the M_UNIX file mode to read the entire data set and broadcast it to the rest of the nodes. During the major computation phase (rendering), view coordinates are retrieved from a control file (small reads), and the rendering of each view produces a single large write of the rendered image to the HiPPi frame buffer. As we shall see in §1.5.2, the I/O structure is the product of restrictions on the file system I/O modes; the developers would like to exploit file system features, but they cannot.

Operation	Operation Count	Volume (Bytes)	Time (Seconds)	Percentage I/O Time
All I/O	1504	979,162,982	164.75	100.00
Read	121	8457	0.17	.10%
AsynchRead	436	880,849,125	4.60	2.79
I/O Wait	436	-	88.44	53.68
Write	300	98,305,400	31.76	19.28
Seek	4	0	.13	0.08
Open	106	-	32.78	19.90
Close	101	-	6.87	4.17

Table 1.3
Number, size, and duration of I/O operations (RENDER)

Operation	Operation Size			
	< 4 KB	< 64 KB	< 256 KB	≥ 256 KB
Read	121	0	0	436
Write	200	0	0	100

Table 1.4
Read and write operation sizes (RENDER)

1.5.1 Experimental Data

Tables 1.3 and 1.4 contain a high-level summary of the I/O behavior of RENDER. Over the 470 seconds of execution, the total volume of I/O is nearly one gigabyte, dominated by the read of the initial data set.

Read operations dominate the I/O, accounting for 89 percent of the I/O volume and 64 percent of the I/O requests. The read traffic is dominated by asynchronous reads both in volume and in the number of requests. However, the read requests take only a small fraction of the I/O time – reads and asynchronous reads account for 0.17 and 4.6 percent of the I/O time respectively. For asynchronous reads, the measured time is only the cost of issuing the read, some of the input time may be overlapped — the part not overlapped appears as iowait time. In this code, the iowait time is the major fraction of the I/O time. Read sizes are again bimodal, clustered below 4K bytes and above 256K bytes. Large reads dominate both in number of requests and in volume. The writes account for nearly 20 percent of the I/O time, though accounting for only a small fraction of the I/O volume.

The RENDER code has two basic phases, initialization and rendering. These

phases are not only distinguished computationally, they have dramatically different
I/O patterns as shown in Figures 1.6 and 1.7, timelines of RENDER read and
write requests. In the first phase, the terrain data is read in from four files by the
gateway node using M_UNIX mode. These requests are extremely large, clustered at
3 megabytes and 1.5 megabytes. The input data is then broadcast to the other 128
nodes which form the renderer, each selecting an appropriate subset of the data.
The initial phase ends around 210 seconds into the run, and the rendering phase
begins. The gateway node reads views from a control file, directing the renderer to
produce the requisite image. The data for each view (640x512 24-bit color image,
approximately one megabyte) is collected by the gateway and output in a single
request. In our runs, this data is written to disk using M_UNIX mode, but in a
production run, this data would be sent directly to a HiPPi frame buffer.

Figure 1.6 clearly shows the large read request sizes generated by the initialization
phase. The first set of read requests are 3 megabytes, then the size decreases to 1.5
megabytes. At 210 seconds, there is a pronounced transition to the render phase,
and the only read requests are small requests to read the view coordinates. Figure
1.7 shows the write behavior of RENDER, and also reflects the phase structure of
the code. There is no write traffic in the initialization phase, and in the rendering
phase, write requests consist exclusively of the writes of the one megabyte color
images.

Figure 1.8 shows the file activity for RENDER, and also clearly reflects the
two phase structure of the RENDER code. The critical read initialization phase
accesses primarily four files (the data set). The control file (views) is accessed in
both phases, but heavily in the rendering phase. The output files are each accessed
only once (written in their entirety) accounting for the staircase structure.

1.5.2   Discussion

The RENDER code illustrates how scalable parallel systems can enable new classes
of applications, which in turn engender new challenges for system designers. Increased computational power and memory capacity enable interactive visualization
of multi-gigabyte data sets, which introduces the complexity of real-time requirements and online output, streaming to a frame buffer. The RENDER I/O pattern
fits a classic scientific computing I/O stereotype: large initial read, followed by the
writing of output results.

The RENDER code and data set described are matched to the capabilities of currently available systems; however, such scientific visualization applications present
much larger computational and I/O challenges. Because RENDER is used for visualizing NASA sensor data, the resolution of input data sets (and their size) is limited

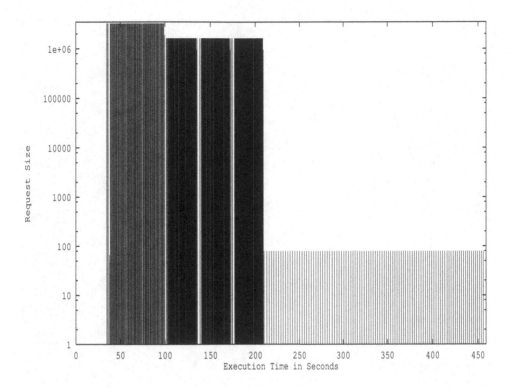

Figure 1.6
Read operation timeline (RENDER)

by sensor resolution and available data base sizes. Examples include LANDSAT, Mars (Viking), and Venus (Magellan). These data sets currently range from 100's of megabytes to 100's of gigabytes, but with increases in sensor resolution and deployment of systems such as the Earth Observation System, much larger data bases (terabytes) are becoming available. Larger data bases increase the size of the input burst for initialization, and terabyte data bases may require the adoption of out-of-core algorithms. Current images are output with a resolution of 640x512 with 24-bit color; with higher resolution data bases and higher output resolutions (3000x2000), corresponding increases in the computation and output are required. Finally, the current system requires several seconds per frame, but higher frame rates (ten or as high as thirty) are desirable. More directly, higher I/O performance is required for larger data sets and higher resolution output with this code.

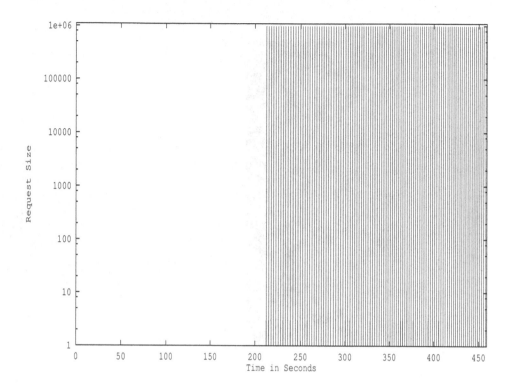

Figure 1.7
Write operation timeline (RENDER)

The RENDER code performs only sequential file access, and all the I/O is mediated by the gateway node. The gateway node reads the data set, then broadcasts it. Although the basic data distribution is block-cyclic, and therefore apparently well-matched to the PFS M_RECORD mode, this mode requires all of the nodes to participate. The code developers eschewed the use of M_RECORD because RENDER uses nodes asymmetrically (gateway and renderer); not all nodes need to participate. Hence, use of M_RECORD mode would require some additional code restructuring and data shuffling regardless.

Using sequential I/O, the code explicitly prefetches initial file data by using asynchronous reads and initiates large read requests, but only achieves a read throughput of approximately 9.5 megabytes/second. Parallel access using the M_UNIX mode was empirically determined not to improve code performance. RENDER would

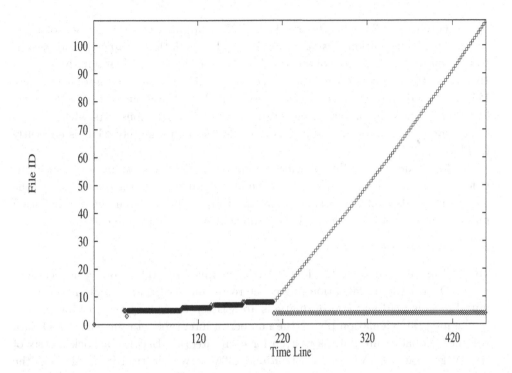

Figure 1.8
File access timeline (RENDER) Cross marks indicate reads and diamonds indicate writes.

benefit from efficient parallel file access modes that allow node subsets to participate without requiring shared file pointers. Another approach, eschewed by the
developers, is the use of separate input files for each node. Though this might
improve input performance, it incurs additional preprocessing steps, expensive for
large data bases, and binds the data base representation to the machine configuration. Efficient parallel access modes that give the effective performance of this
change without requiring logical reorganization across files in the application are
desirable. Finally, while occasionally single frames or collections of frames might
be written to disk, the typical use for RENDER is to write the output data to a
HiPPi frame buffer. This presents another dimension of *streaming* I/O which has
not yet received much attention in the scalable systems community.

1.6   Hartree Fock Behavior

As we noted in §1.3.3, the Hartree Fock (HTF) application is composed of three codes: an initialization (*psetup*), an integral calculation (*pargos*), and a self-consistent field calculation phase (*pscf*). For our rather small input data set of 16 atoms, the respective execution times of the three program components were 127, 1173, and 1008 seconds on 128 nodes of the Intel Paragon XP/S, with slightly less than 20 percent of that time consumed by I/O operations. As with the ESCAT code, we shall see that this is not the desired ratio, merely what is currently feasible.

The first code in the HTF application reads a small initial data file and transforms it for use by the later phases. The second, integral calculation phase creates the files of integrals that are consumed by the third, self-consistent field calculation phase. The Intel M_UNIX file mode is used exclusively in all three codes.

1.6.1   Experimental Data

Tables 1.5–1.6 summarize the I/O behavior of the three HTF application components. During the initialization phase, the reads and writes are small and occur as initial data is read and transformations are written for use by the ensuing phases. In the integral calculation phase, the number of integrals determines the I/O data volume — quadrature data is written for each integral. Because a Fock matrix of size N generates $\mathcal{O}(N^2)$ one electron and $\mathcal{O}(N^4)$ two electron integrals [95], the data volume grows dramatically with matrix size and is substantial even for small matrices. This phase is, therefore, write intensive, which shows clearly in Table 1.6 and Figure 1.12. The final, self-consistent field calculation phase is quite read intensive, with each node repeatedly reading the integral files.

Despite the substantial I/O, the maximum request size is rather small, only four times the Intel PFS striping factor of 64K bytes. Moreover, the number of requests smaller than 4K bytes is non-trivial. In short, the request size distribution of Table 1.6 is bimodal, though skewed toward larger requests, the opposite of the size distribution shown in Table 1.2 for the ESCAT code

Figures 1.9–1.13 and 1.10–1.14 show, respectively, read and write request sizes as a function of time. The write intensities of the integral calculation phase and read intensity of the self-consistent field computation phase are striking on this time scale. With this data set, each of the nodes writes roughly 5M bytes of data during the integral calculation. Figures 1.15–1.17 show that each node writes the integral data to a separate file; the nodes then read this data during the final calculation phase.

Operation	Operation Count	Volume (Bytes)	Node Time (Seconds)	Percentage I/O Time
HTF Initialization				
All I/O	832	7,267,422	55.23	100.00
Read	371	3,522,497	15.34	27.77
Write	452	3,744,872	5.50	9.96
Seek	2	53	0.43	0.78
Open	4	-	31.49	57.02
Close	3	-	2.47	4.47
HTF Integral Calculation				
All I/O	17,854	698,992,502	6,398.03	100.00
Read	145	34,393	0.47	0.00
Write	8,535	698,958,109	1996.4	31.20
Seek	130	0	0.14	0.00
Open	130	-	4056.60	63.40
Close	129	-	11.43	0.18
Lsize	128	-	15.27	0.24
Forflush	8,657	-	317.72	4.98
HTF Self-Consistent Field Calculation				
All I/O	52832	4,205,483,650	32,800.99	100.00
Read	51499	4,201,634,304	32,263.20	98.36
Write	207	3,849,268	5.88	0.02
Seek	813	3,495,198,798	1.67	0.00
Open	157	-	518.74	1.58
Close	156	-	11.50	0.04

Table 1.5
Number, size, and duration of I/O operations (HTF)

1.6.2   Discussion

Quite clearly, the HTF code has substantial I/O requirements even for what is, by current computational chemistry standards, a rather small problem of 16 atoms. In general, though, the I/O pattern in this code is quite regular, with little but sequential accesses except in the final calculation phase.

In conversations with the code developers, we discovered that this is the version of the code they would like to use for larger, more interesting problems. By precomputing the integrals and reusing the quadrature data as needed, the computation requirements can be reduced dramatically. Unfortunately, because the I/O requirements grow as the number of two electron integrals (i.e., as $\mathcal{O}(N^4)$), this is not

Operation	Operation Size			
HTF Initialization				
	< 4 KB	< 64 KB	< 256 KB	≥ 256 KB
Read	151	220	0	0
Write	218	234	0	0
HTF Integral Calculation				
Read	143	2	0	0
Write	2	1	8,532	0
HTF Self-Consistent Field Calculation				
Read	165	109	51225	0
Write	43	158	6	0

Table 1.6
Read/write sizes (HTF)

feasible with current I/O systems. Instead, the integrals are recomputed as needed, substantially increasing the computation requirements but reducing the I/O costs and, with current I/O software, the total execution time.

For integral I/O to be preferable to recomputation, reading an integral from secondary storage must take less than the roughly 500 floating point operations needed for integral calculation. For current systems, this requires a sustained I/O rate of approximately 5–10 Mbytes/second per node. With current and projected disk technology, this implies a system with a disk or disk array directly attached to each processor. Moreover, as processor speeds increase, the I/O rate must increase commensurately, else recomputation becomes the preferred alternative. Simply put, this application requires high storage capacity and high throughput for simple access patterns.

1.7   Parallel File System Implications

The most significant observation from our study is that the I/O requirements of scientific codes (electron scattering, terrain rendering and quantum chemistry) greatly exceed the capabilities of existing scalable systems. Scientific applications have I/O patterns and requirements more complex than simple stereotypes, and these requirements are extremely challenging. The mismatch between desired and currently available I/O performance has two important consequences for application scientists: it complicates application code structure, and it reduces the scope of experiments computationally feasible. For parallel systems vendors and file system

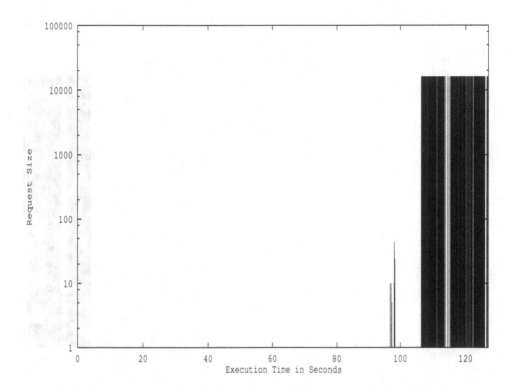

Figure 1.9
Read operation timeline (HTF initialization)

designers, it is clear that improvements in scalable parallel I/O capabilities can enable or even catalyze advances in science and scientific computing.

All three applications that we studied exhibited a wide variety of read/write mixes and request sizes, with the latter ranging from a few bytes to several megabytes. In short, to provide robust performance, parallel file systems must efficiently support a variety of request size and read/write mixes. However, the performance characteristics of current I/O systems favor large requests because high bandwidths are achieved through parallelism. Consequently, achieving good I/O performance for applications that make small requests admits two basic possibilities: programmers can manually aggregate requests or file systems (and user level libraries) can transform request streams via caching or prefetching, serving as impedance matchers between the application access patterns and disk performance characteristics.

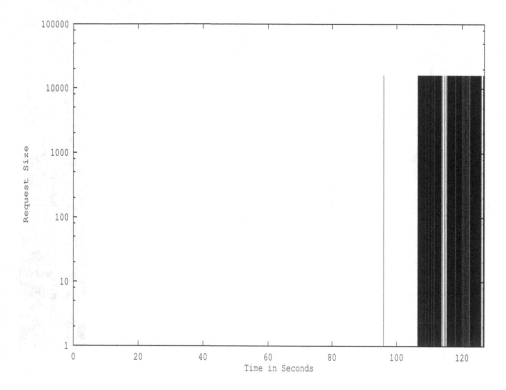

Figure 1.10
Write operation timeline (HTF initialization)

The latter approach is promising, and demonstrations of the effectiveness such approaches are appearing [119].

Even for our set of only three application codes, no simple characterization of I/O request sizes or access patterns is viable. Further, studies show that the detailed spatial and temporal characteristics of the I/O critically affect I/O performance. We believe this indicates that the simple synthetic kernels often used to evaluate new file system ideas may not be good predictors of potential performance on full-scale applications. The impact of file system changes on real applications or application mixes depends on much more complex application structure, suggesting that the development of larger application skeletons and workload mixes are an essential part of developing high performance I/O systems.

One characteristic of all three applications is that data files were generally read

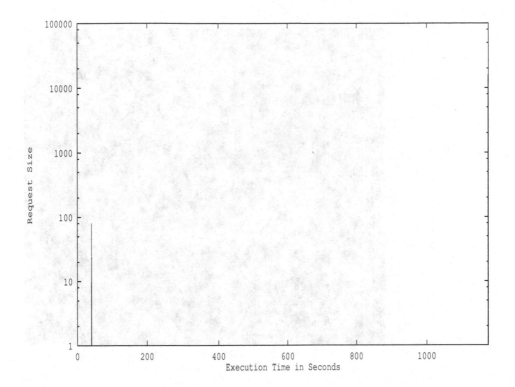

Figure 1.11
Read operation timeline (HTF integral calculation)

or written in their entirety, in many cases by a single node. This reflects the current inclination of application programmers to control the mapping of files to disks (for performance) and express I/O in ways that are independent of parallel file system features (for portability). For example, in several cases, I/O is done by a single node sequentially, followed by data broadcast through the interconnection network. Such I/O patterns could be expressed as collective operations [30, 63, 155] to allow the file system to optimize performance.

In general, these observations point out the importance of developing standard parallel file system API's; not only to provide functional portability, but also to provide performance portability. Being able to run the code on several platforms is not enough, performance optimizations on one platform must be portable to others. This is an important guiding principle for file system implementors, but a difficult

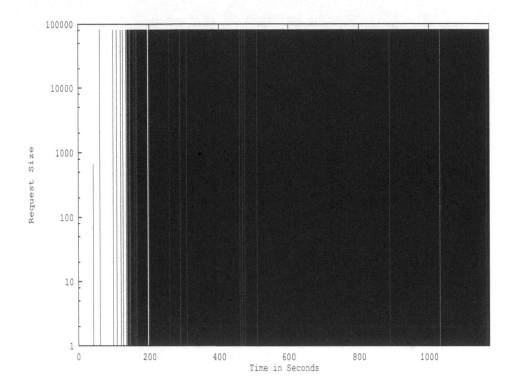

Figure 1.12
Write operation timeline (HTF integral calculation)

challenge in the face of the wealth of possible I/O configurations and the richness
of their performance space. In short, parallel file system interfaces need to become
portable and robust if applications are to adopt and exploit them.

Another common characteristic of the codes is that most of the data written
eventually was propagated to secondary storage. This characteristic has been observed previously on supercomputing systems, and differs markedly from Unix file
systems where statistics generally record many small short-lived temporary files. If
all output data survives to disk, the objective of write caching in the file system
must be to increase the achieved bandwidth of the physical I/O system, not to reduce the I/O volume to disk. For example, aggregation of small request to transfer
sizes efficient for disks (or internally parallel RAID's) is critical to achieving a large
fraction of peak performance. Aggregation is feasible; as an example, the ESCAT

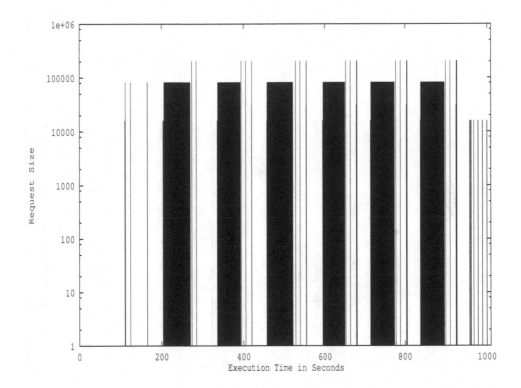

Figure 1.13
Read operation timeline (HTF self-consistent field calculation)

code employs multiple writers into disjoint locations in a shared file. Individually, these requests would utilize a disk poorly, however they can be combined, significantly increasing disk efficiency [119]. This experience suggests that in some cases, two level buffering at compute nodes and I/O nodes can be beneficial.

Characterization studies are by their nature inductive, covering only a small sample of the possibilities and attempting to extract more general patterns. The three applications we have studied represent but a few samples from a large space of parallel applications. We believe they are indicative, though they are by no means an exhaustive description of the parallel I/O requirements or behavior exhibited by scalable parallel applications. In addition, it is always difficult to determine how much a code has been influenced by the available technology. Doubtless our characterization results are conditioned by both the parallel I/O hardware, sys-

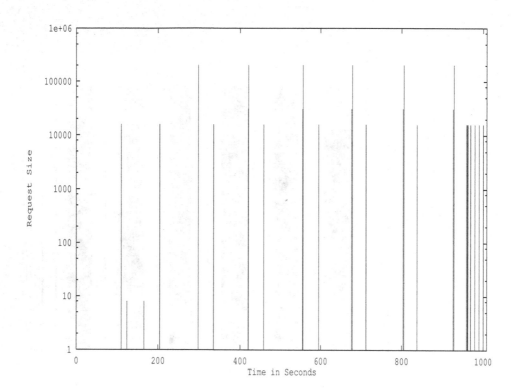

Figure 1.14
Write operation timeline (HTF self-consistent field calculation)

tem software, and even machine configurations available. In an attempt to access
these dependences, we are currently broadening our I/O characterization studies to
applications on other hardware platforms.

1.8   Related Work

The widespread availability of scalable parallel systems has stimulated development of I/O intensive parallel applications and highlighted the critical need for
understanding parallel file access patterns. Though our understanding of I/O parallelism is still in its infancy, there is a long history of file access characterization
for mainframes and vector supercomputers.

Much of the early work considered whole file access characteristics, including file

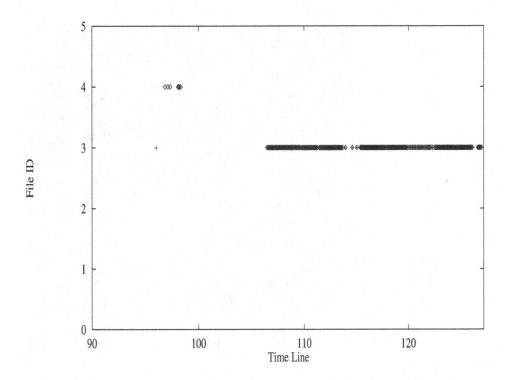

Figure 1.15
File access timeline (HTF initialization)

sizes, lifetimes, and reuse intervals. Notable examples of this work include Lawrie
and Randell's study [169] of automatic file migration algorithms for the CDC Cyber
175, Stritter's analysis [250] of file lifetime distributions, Smith's study [239] of file
access behavior on IBM mainframes, and Reed and Jensen's study [133] of accesses
to NCSA's file archive.

More recently Miller and Katz [182] captured detailed traces of application file
accesses from a suite of Cray applications from the National Center for Atmospheric
Research (NCAR). They observed that many access patterns were sequential and
cyclic and that I/O operations could be classified as compulsory, checkpoint, and
data staging. Pasquale and Polyzos [206, 205] considered the static and dynamic file
access characteristics of production vector workloads at the San Diego Supercomputer Center (SDSC) and concluded that most applications had regular behavior.

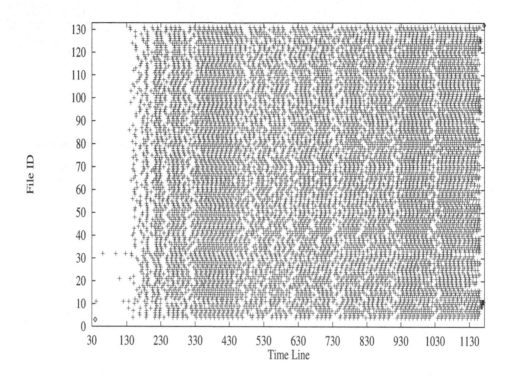

Figure 1.16
File access timeline (HTF integral calculation)

The work by Kotz *et al* [158, 221] is closest in spirit to our characterization effort. Using instrumentation in the I/O libraries of the Intel iPSC/860 and the Thinking Machines CM-5, they captured traces of individual file operations and analyzed the data to extract access patterns. The concluded that file access parallelism was important, file caching was important for certain access patterns, and that contrary to intuition, small requests are quite common in large scientific codes.

Our work differs from all of these in considering traces for individual application programs at the level of individual file accesses, coupled with an analysis of the application source code and conversations with application developers to understand the reasons for the access behavior. Given the limitations of current parallel file systems, extrinsic knowledge is critical to understanding if certain access patterns are inherent or file system artifacts.

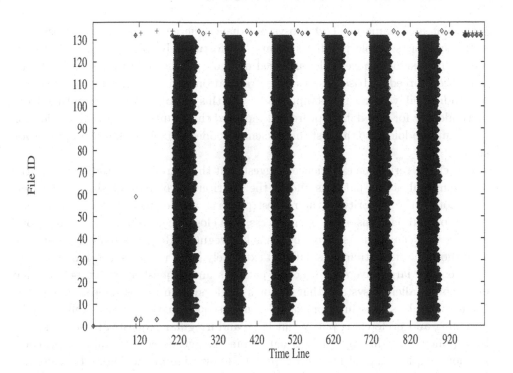

Figure 1.17
File access timeline (HTF self-consistent field calculation)

Several research groups are developing parallel file systems and access policies that can exploit an application developer's knowledge of access patterns. PIOUS [190] is a portable I/O system designed for use with PVM. PASSION [53] supports out-of-core algorithms in a user-level library, but focuses on a high-level array oriented interface. PPFS [119] provides user control of file cache sizes and policies, as well as data placement. Similarly, IBM's Vesta parallel file system [61] allows applications to define logical partitions, data distributions, and some access information. In addition to research efforts, several vendors have developed parallel file systems, including the Thinking Machines CM-5 Scalable Parallel File System [176, 164], the Intel Concurrent File System [96] for the iPSC/2 and iPSC/860 [198], the Intel Parallel File System for the Pargon XP/S [21], and PIOFS for the IBM SP-2.

1.9   Conclusions and Future Directions

Inefficient and immature I/O subsystems have emerged as a major performance bottleneck on scalable parallel systems. Unfortunately, file system and storage hierarchy designers have little empirical data on parallel I/O access patterns and have been forced to base designs on extrapolations from the access patterns seen on traditional vector supercomputers. In this chapter, we have outlined our methodology for I/O data capture and reported the results of an initial application of this methodology to the first three scientific codes from a much larger application suite.

Our characterization experiences suggest that there are large variations in spatial and temporal access patterns and in the distribution of request sizes. As others have noted, the majority of the request patterns are sequential. Cyclic behavior, with repeated patterns of file open, access, and close, occur often, but the temporal spacing between requests across cycles is less regular. Requests tend to be of fixed size, though both extremely small and extremely large requests are common.

Given the large diversity in access patterns and request sizes, we believe that design of parallel file systems that rely on a single, system-imposed file system policy is unlikely to be successful. For example, small sequential requests are well served by a caching and prefetching policy, but large and irregular requests are better served by a policy that directly streams data from storage devices to application code. In short, exploitation of I/O access pattern knowledge in caching and prefetching systems is crucial to obtaining a substantial fraction of peak I/O performance. Inherent in such an adaptive approach is the need to identify access patterns and choose policies based on access pattern characteristics.

Building on I/O characterization experiences, we have also developed a portable parallel file system [119] that allows users to advertise expected file access patterns and to choose file distribution, caching, and prefetch policies. To lessen the cognitive burden of access specification, we have also developed general, adaptive prefetching methods that can learn to hide I/O latency by automatically classifying and predicting access patterns.

Acknowledgments

We thank the members of the Scalable I/O Initiative who provided us with the applications examined in this paper. In particular, the electron scattering code (ESCAT) was provided by Vincent McKoy and Carl Winstead at Caltech, and the terrain rendering code (RENDER) was provided by Peggy Li from the Center for Space Microelectronic Technology at the NASA Jet Propulsion Laboratory. The HTF application was provided by Rick Kendall of the Molecular Science Software (MSS) Group at the Molecular Science Research Center (MSRC) of the Pacific Northwest Laboratory (PNL). All data presented here were obtained from code executions on the Intel Paragon XP/S at the Caltech Concurrent Supercomputing Facility.

This work was supported in part by the National Science Foundation under grant NSF ASC 92-12369, by the National Aeronautics and Space Administration under NASA Contracts NGT-51023, NAG-1-613, and USRA 5555-22 and by the Advanced Research Projects Agency under ARPA contracts DAVT63-91-C-0039 and DABT63-93-C-0040. Andrew Chien was also supported in part by NSF Young Investigator Award CCR-94-57809.

2 Collective I/O and Large-Scale Data Management

ALOK CHOUDHARY, MAHMUT KANDEMIR, SACHIN MORE, JAECHUN NO AND
RAJEEV THAKUR

Many large-scale scientific applications are data intensive, processing data sets ranging from megabytes to terabytes. These include applications from data analysis and
mining, image processing, large archive maintenance, real-time processing, and so
on. As an example, consider a typical computational science analysis cycle, shown
in Figure 2.1. In this cycle several steps are involved. These include mesh generation, domain decomposition, simulation, visualization and interpretation of results,
archival of data and results for post-processing and check-pointing, and adjustment
of parameters. Thus, it is not sufficient to consider simulation alone when determining how to store or access data sets because they are used in other phases.
In addition, these steps may need to be performed in a heterogeneous distributed
environment.

These considerations require storing visualization and data (which can run in the
100s of megabytes to terabytes range) in a canonical form so that other tools can
use them easily without having to re-organize the data. Furthermore, to restart the
computation with a different number of processors, the data storage must be be
independent of number of processors that produced it. Such requirements present
challenging, I/O intensive problems, and an application programmer may be over-
whelmed if required to solve these problems. Designing efficient I/O schemes for
such I/O intensive problems requires expert knowledge. With the increasing number of applications that manipulate huge amounts of data, the effective data management problem is becoming important. Efficient data management should provide query capabilities, high-performance access methods, and optimizations for
accessing the large data sets found in scientific computations.

In our work, we have addressed two related, challenging problems; namely, large-
scale data management for scientific computing and high-performance I/O techniques [74]. We believe that it is important to provide flexible database systems
to manage large-scale data sets that are produced or used in scientific simulations
and experiments while providing a capability to achieve high-performance I/O.

In the world of large-scale data management, high-performance parallel file systems (e.g., Intel's PFS [226] and IBM's Vesta [63]) have been built to exploit the
parallel I/O capabilities provided by modern architectures. However, some serious obstacles prevent such file systems from becoming a real solution to the data
management problem.

First, file system interfaces are low level [154] and programmers cannot specify

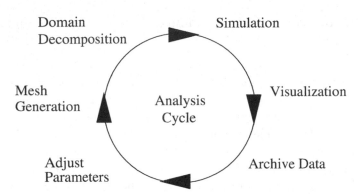

Figure 2.1
A typical computational science analysis cycle.

access application access patterns using a high level description, but instead must explicitly manipulate file pointers. This makes it difficult for the programmers to perform optimizations at the application levels because of the complexities involved in managing buffers and file pointers.

Second, every file system comes with its own set of I/O calls, which renders ensuring program portability a very difficult task. It should be stressed at this point that the hope is that the emerging MPI-IO standard [59, 265] will remedy this problem. However, two observations lead us to think that in reality it may not be so. First, the MPI-IO, like its predecessor parallel file systems and parallel I/O libraries [53, 270], provides a large number of functionalities leaving the user with the difficult task of selecting the appropriate ones for her application's needs. Second, users are unwilling to change their programming practices whose roots can be found in UNIX style I/O programming. A recent paper [264] on the MPI-IO states that unless this programming practice is changed, the MPI-IO will not be able to help much in delivering high levels of I/O performance from large-scale applications. The third problem with the file systems is that the file system policies and optimizations are, in general, hard-coded in it and tuned to work well for a few commonly occurring cases only. As noted by Karpovich et al. [141], even if the programmer has full knowledge of access patterns of her code, it is difficult to convey this information to the file system in a convenient way.

There are many proposed techniques for optimizing I/O accesses, including [154, 53, 265, 82, 155, 265, 229, 141, 74]. Although parallel I/O libraries (e.g., [53]) built atop parallel file systems have the potential to provide both ease-of-use and high performance through the use of advanced I/O optimization techniques, their extensibility is severely limited by the design principles and the programming language used in their implementation [141].

At the other end of the spectrum are databases. They almost eliminate the major problems experienced with file systems. They provide a layer on top of file systems, which is portable, extensible, easy to use and maintain, and that allows a clear and natural interaction with the applications by abstracting out the file names and file offsets. However, these advantages do not come for free. Since their main target is to be general purpose and support transaction processing, they cannot provide high performance on general data management, especially for scientific computing applications. Additionally, data consistence and integrity semantics provided by almost all DBMS further impede high performance. Finally, most DBMS' support only a very limited set of data types and data manipulation models [141].

In this chapter, we first present a new approach to the data management problem, called "MDMS (Meta-Data Management System)". Our approach *combines* the advantages of file systems and databases, while avoiding their respective disadvantages that allows easy application development, code reuse, and portability; at the same time, it extracts high I/O performance from the underlying parallel I/O architecture by employing advanced I/O optimization techniques like data sieving and collective I/O. Next, we present a runtime system that we developed as our recent work, called "PASSION (Parallel and Scalable Software for Input-Output)." *PASSION was the first system to introduce collective I/O and associated mechanisms for high-performance I/O, which are now widely accepted and used in various runtime systems, file systems, and MPI-IO.* It uses a high-level interface that makes it easy for the user to specify the I/O required in the program, and also eliminates the need for the user to make several small requests. PASSION also uses collective I/O in which processors cooperate to perform I/O efficiently in large chunks and in proper order.

The remainder of this chapter is organized as follows. In §2.1 we present the details of the MDMS, which is built using Object-Relational DBMS (OR-DBMS) technology [247]. We also present performance numbers from our initial implementation using several applications. In §2.2 we present an overview of the design and implementation of the various components of PASSION including the performance results. Finally, §2.3 contains a summary.

2.1   Metadata Management System

The overall architecture for large-scale data management proposed by us has three interacting components as illustrated in Figure 2.2. These components are, Metadata Management System (MDMS), the Hierarchical Storage System (HSS), and Applications (which use the client interface of the runtime system in the HSS component). Below, we discuss the MDMS. In the next section, we describe PASSION library.

The main objectives of a MDMS are as follows:

- Metadata design, management, access, update and corresponding interfaces to enable efficient query processing, updates, and interaction. Design, build schemas and catalogs to be used for: (1) managing data generated and used by different applications, and (2) creating and keeping histories, annotations, and trails of data accesses.

- Embed rules for intelligent and informed optimizations such as collective prefetching, pooled striping, and caching; and collective I/O based upon user specified access patterns in the metadata or access patterns learned from historical patterns.

2.1.1   Metadata Management System (MDMS)

The scalable data management system has three components. **(1)** a user program; **(2)** a metadata management system (MDMS); and **(3)** a hierarchical storage system (HSS). These three components can exist in the same site or be fully distributed across distant sites. Currently, we run a parallel volume rendering application on the SP2 at Argonne National Laboratory that interacts with the MDMS located at Northwestern University and accesses its data files using TCP/IP stored on the HPSS (High Performance Storage System) [70] at the San Diego Supercomputer Center. The experimental configuration is depicted in Figure 2.2.

The main functions fulfilled by the MDMS can be summarized as follows:

- It stores information about abstract storage devices (ASDs) that can be accessed by applications. By querying the MDMS, applications can learn where in the HSS their data reside (i.e., in what part of the storage hierarchy) without the need of specifying file names. They can also access the performance characteristics (e.g., speed) of the ASDs and select a suitable ASD (e.g., a disk subsystem consisting of eight separate disk arrays) to store their data sets.

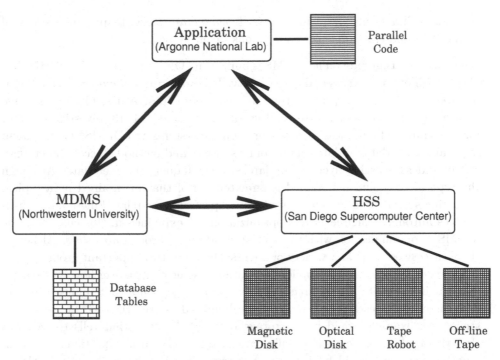

Figure 2.2
Three-tiered architecture (Three sites illustrating setup to evaluate architecture)

- It stores information about the *storage patterns* and *access patterns* of data sets. For example, a specific multidimensional array that is striped across four disk devices in round-robin manner will have an entry in the MDMS. The MDMS utilizes this information in a number of ways. The most important use of this information, however, is to choose a parallel I/O method based on *access pattern* (*hints*) provided by the application. By *comparing* the storage pattern and access pattern of a data set, the MDMS can, for example, advise the HSS to perform collective I/O [74] or prefetching [82] for this data set.

- It stores information about *pending* access patterns. It utilizes this information in making some global decisions (e.g., file migration [275] and staging [275]), possibly involving data sets from multiple applications.

- It keeps metadata specifying access history and a navigation trail.

Notice that the MDMS is not merely a data repository but also an *active* component in the overall data management process. It *communicates* with applications as well as the HSS and can *influence* the decisions taken by both.

Directive Categories   The MDMS is built using ORDBMS technology [247] that allows high expressiveness and extensibility. It keeps both *system-level* [35, 54] and *user-level metadata* [77] about the data sets, data files, ASDs, physical storage devices (PSDs), access patterns, and users. Baru *et al* [14, 13] investigate use of high-level unified interfaces to data stored on file systems and DBMS. Their system maintains metadata for data sets, resources, users, and methods (access functions); and provides the ability to create, update, store, and query this metadata. Although the type of metadata maintained is an extension of that maintained by a typical operating system, our metadata also involves performance-related metadata, which enables automatic high-level I/O optimizations as explained in this chapter. The MDMS's communication with the user application is through *directives*. Although these directives come in a variety of flavors, there are two important groups:

• *Layout Directives*: The application can have some control over how its data are laid out in the HSS. These directives are *strong* in the sense that (unless they are inconsistent with each other) the MDMS should advise the HSS to take necessary steps. An example would be a (storage pattern) directive that tells the MDMS that the application wants a specific data set to be stored in a particular fashion. Another example would be a (usage pattern) directive that tells the MDMS to advise the HSS to migrate a specific data set from disk to tape, probably because it will not be used in the remainder of the application.

• *Access Pattern Directives*: These directives are used as *hints* that indicate that the user's application is about to start a specified sequence of I/O operations on the HSS. In response to such a directive the MDMS can, for example, advise the HSS to perform a specific I/O optimization in accessing the relevant data. These optimizations include prefetching, caching, collective I/O etc., and are *mild* in the sense that they do not imply a major data re-organization on the HSS but rather enable a specific I/O optimization to be performed to reduce I/O latency or increase I/O .

Currently, both types of directives are being implemented using embedded SQL (E-SQL) functions. It should be mentioned that a directive (whether strong or mild) may be rejected at either of two points. First, the MDMS may decline to take the necessary action due, for example, to the fact that the directives used are not consistent with each other. Second, even if the MDMS advises an I/O optimization to the HSS, the HSS may reject it due to the current state (e.g., overload).

One might wonder at this point why, instead of using a MDMS (and incurring its overhead), the application code does not directly negotiate with the HSS. This is not a reasonable solution for at least two reasons. First, the application program does not need to know the details of the HSS. Otherwise, it would be very difficult to decide appropriate I/O optimizations. In the proposed architecture, the user does not need to know where her data sets reside on the HSS or what their storage patterns are, though she can obtain this information by *querying* the MDMS.

The second factor that prevents the user code from communicating directly with the HSS is the fact that a user's code, in general, cannot have a global information about the other applications concurrently using the HSS. To manage overall I/O activity effectively, one must have global knowledge of all users' access patterns and I/O resources; that information is available as *metadata* in the MDMS. We note, however, that the actual data transfer occurs between the application and the HSS *directly* once the appropriate I/O method has been decided.

Individual Directives   Using directives, an application can convey information about its expected I/O activity to the MDMS. As a minimum, we expect the applications' user to know how her data will be used by parallel processors (henceforth we call this information *access pattern*). However, the more information that is provided to the MDMS, the better I/O optimizations can be. Table 2.1.1 shows the types of information that can be provided by applications using directives to the MDMS. These directives can be combined in meaningful ways and can be applied to a number of data sets simultaneously as explained below.

In this environment, an access pattern for a data set is specified by indicating how the data set is to be divided and accessed by parallel processors. For example, an access pattern such as (BLOCK,*) says that the data set in question is divided (logically) into groups of rows and each group of rows will be *mostly* accessed by a single processor. The number of row-groups can also be specified using another directive. Notice that this access pattern information does *not* have to be very accurate, as the processors *may* occasionally access the data elements outside their assigned portions. A few frequently used access patterns are depicted in Figure 2.3(a) for a four processor case. Each processor's portion is shaded using a different style. A (BLOCK,BLOCK) access pattern indicates that each processor will mostly access a rectangular block and a (*,CYCLIC) pattern involving P processors implies that each processor will mostly access every P^{th} column of the data set. A star '*', on the other hand, indicates that the dimension in question is not partitioned across processors.

In our framework, these patterns are also used as storage patterns. For example,

Directive Explanation		Usage
storage pattern directive	Declares a storage pattern for the HSS-resident data set A. Each \<ptrn\> can be BLOCK, CYCLIC, BLOCK-CYCLIC(b), or *	`organize` A(\<ptrn\>,\<ptrn\>,...)
access pattern directive	Declares an access pattern for the HSS-resident data set A each \<ptrn\> can be BLOCK, CYCLIC, BLOCK-CYCLIC(b), or *	`access` A(\<ptrn\>,\<ptrn\>,...)
abstract storage directive	Declares an abstract storage device (ASD) and the number of processors involved e.g. DISK(4,4) indicates a 4 × 4 processor array will access a disk storage.	`storage` D(\<np\>,\<np\>,...)
I/O type directive	Declares the type of I/O that will be performed on data set A \<type\> can be read-only (RO), write-only (WO), or read-write mix (RW)	`iotype` A(\<type\>)
sequentiality directive	Informs about access pattern for each dimension of data set A. Each \<seq,b\> can be (sequential,*), (strided,B), or (variable,*), where B is the stride	`sqntl` A(\<seq,b\>,\<seq,b\>,...)
repetition directive	Informs about how many times data set A will be accessed. \<rep\> can be only-once (OT), or multiple-times (MT)	`repeat` A(\<rep\>)
usage pattern directive	Informs about what to do with data set A *after* this point in program. \<usg\> can be purge (PG) or migrate (MG).	`usage` A(\<usg\>)
association (abstract data set space) directive	Declares that data sets A,B,C,... are associated with T. An association implies that the concerned data sets will be treated similarly.	`associate(A,B,C,...) with T`
data set size directive	Declares an approximate size for data set A, e.g., `size` A(16,777,216) indicates that data set A is approximately 16MB.	`dsize` A(\<size-in-bytes\>)
request size directive	Declares an approximate size for data set A. \<rs\> can be small request (SR), large request (LR), or variable request (VR	`rsize` A(\<rs\>)
metadata query directive	Queries a parameter of an entity (data set, ASD, association, etc.) e.g., query(data set,A,storage-pattern) returns the storage pattern for data set A	`query(entity,name,parameter)`
batch directives	Provide a number of directives as a single block to the MDMS e.g., `begin-directives` `access` A(BLOCK,*); `access` B(*,BLOCK) `end-directives`	`begin-directives` `directive1;` `directive2;` ... `end-directives`

Table 2.1
User data management directives.

a (BLOCK,*) storage pattern corresponds to row-major storage layout (as in C); a (*,BLOCK) storage pattern corresponds to column-major storage layout (as in Fortran), and a (BLOCK,BLOCK) storage pattern corresponds to blocked storage layout which may be very useful for large-scale linear algebra applications whose data sets are amenable to blocking [270].

As an example consider the following scenario. An I/O-intensive application executes in three steps using five, two-dimensional data sets (arrays) P, Q1, Q2, R1 and R2 whose default disk layouts are row-major (BLOCK,*). Step (1) a single processor reads the data set P and broadcasts its contents to other processors. Step (2) the data set Q1 is created by four processors collectively in row-major order (BLOCK,*) on the disk subsystem; also the data set Q2 is created by the same processors in a (BLOCK,BLOCK) manner. Finally, in step (3) two data sets, R1 and R2, are read by four processors collectively in row-major order from the disk sub-system and then the application does some computation and terminates.

For Step (1), the I/O activity can be captured by the directive:

    `access` P(BLOCK,*).

Here it is assumed that the data set P is accessed row-wise; also since no `storage` directive appears, it is assumed to be a single processor.

For the I/O activity of Step (2), we can use

    `organize` Q1(BLOCK,*) `storage` DISK(4)

    `organize` Q2(BLOCK,BLOCK) `storage` DISK(2,2).

The user indicates that four processors will write onto four disjoint parts of Q1 (i.e., four row-blocks). The system now has *several* options in implementing this directive. It can, for example, use four disks and store each processor's portion in a separate disk (as shown in Figure 2.3(b)). This will allow each processor to do I/O independently of others, maximizing the I/O parallelism. Or alternatively, the whole data set Q1 (actually the file containing it) can be striped over four disks (as shown in Figure 2.3(c), assuming that each processor's portion contains four stripe units of data). Although this storage style does not necessarily lead to conflict-free disk accesses, in most practical cases it allows sufficient I/O parallelism. Also, more intelligent striping methods such as the one shown in Figure 2.3(d) can eliminate potential disk conflicts.

As for the directive that involves Q2, again the system has a number of options. The most interesting one, however, is the one that uses collective I/O [74]. Since the default disk layout is row-major (BLOCK,*) and the processors will write data in (BLOCK,BLOCK) fashion, a data re-organization between processors may be necessary for high performance.

Finally, for Step (3) the following directives can be used:

associate (R1,R2) with T

access T(BLOCK,*) storage DISK(4)

First, the associate directive indicates that R1 and R2 will be treated together (i.e., accessed, staged, migrated in similar fashions) as shown in Figure 2.3(e). Then the second directive conveys the access pattern. Note that since the storage pattern and the access pattern are the same, no collective I/O is required. An abstract data set space (T, in our example) is a dummy data set variable that helps specify the desired access pattern of a data set by describing its *relationship* to other data sets. For example, 'associate (A,B,C) with T' implies that whenever the data set A is accessed, the data sets B and C will also likely be accessed. This information can then be used to pre-stage the data sets B and C from tape to disk (if they are not already on disk) whenever A is accessed. The associate directive also provides convenience in specifying the access pattern of data sets with respect to each other as in Step (3) of the scenario discussed above. It implies that the corresponding portions of R1 and R2 will be used (mostly) by the same processor and, therefore, should *preferably* be stored on the same disk.

It should be emphasized that the main idea behind using directives is to help the system *match* the *access pattern* (i.e., how data is accessed) and the *storage pattern* (i.e., how data is stored). When, for example, DISK(4) is entered to the MDMS, what the application program indicates is that four processors will access the data set in question in parallel. Although the best I/O parallelism can be obtained by allocating each processor's portion on a separate disk, the system does not necessarily have to do so. It should be noticed, though, in cases where less than four disks (or I/O nodes) are used, the I/O parallelism will suffer because of disk *contention* (as shown in Figure 2.3(f)). Thus, a DISK(4) directive essentially reveals to the system that, for maximum I/O parallelism, at least four disk devices are needed. It should also be noted that the directives explained above are *high-level* and constructed using the *names* of the data sets used in the application, which are intuitive to the user. Contrast this with a classical high-performance file system interface that boils down everything to linear streams of bytes that do not bear any resemblance to the data sets the user manipulates.

Implementation   Internally the MDMS keeps its metadata in the form of database tables (relations). Figure 2.4 shows the most important parts for each table in our on-going implementation. Using an ORDBMS [247] instead of a pure relational DBMS brings the advantage of using pointers (hence avoiding duplication of metadata in different tables) as well as extending metadata as the need arises (using inheritance and/or collection data types [247]).

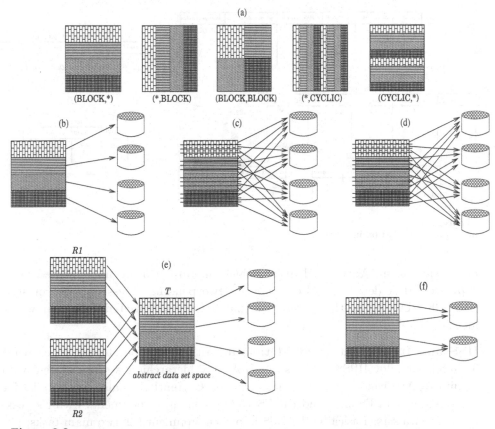

Figure 2.3
(a) Different access patterns. (b-d) Non-striping vs. striping. (e) Abstract data set space. (f) Contention on disks.

Notice that, in almost every table, there is a field (attribute) called *user-level metadata*. Actually, such a field contains a pointer to a table where the MDMS stores the *user-level* metadata (i.e., the metadata that help a user find her data or obtain information and performance characteristics about the storage sub-systems currently available in the HSS). For example, the *user-level metadata* field for a file entity can contain information (metadata) on who created the file, when it was created, what its current size, when it was last modified etc.

The example metadata entries shown in Figure 2.4 indicate that two data sets, P and Q, are associated with an abstract data set space T and are stored as (BLOCK,*) fashion (i.e., row-major) in files file-P and file-Q, respectively. These

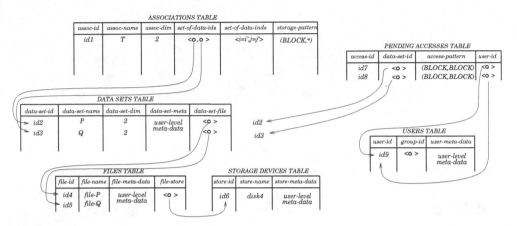

Figure 2.4
Internal representation in MDMS.

files reside on an ASD called disk4 (which, in turn, can be implemented using 4 physical disk devices). Also, there are two pending access patterns of style (BLOCK,BLOCK) on these data sets that have been initiated by a user whose identity is id9.

HSS and Its Utilization of Metadata   Although in our future experiments we intend employ HPSS [70] as our HSS, any hierarchical storage system with a suitable API can be used for that purpose. Currently, we also use parallel file systems such as PFS [226] and PIOFS [58] to conduct experiments with the disk-resident data sets. Basically, the HSS in our environment has two main tasks:

• It keeps the storage related metadata updated in the MDMS. This is important to present the users with accurate information about the available I/O resources. Any data reorganization performed independently by the HSS should be reflected on the MDMS.[1]

• It honors I/O optimization requests from the MDMS and I/O requests from user application, and it returns results to the application.

To exploit the capabilities of modern parallel I/O architectures, it is imperative to use advanced I/O techniques [73]. In principle, these techniques have two main objectives:

• *enhancing I/O parallelism;* that is, maximizing the number of storage units

---

[1] In the future, we intend to use the Data-links software [72] from IBM. This will relieve us from the responsibility of updating independent HSS data re-organizations as all the I/O activity on the data sets registered with the DB2 will be intercepted and checked for security and consistency.

(e.g., disks) that can be kept busy at any given time interval, and

• *improving locality of I/O accesses;* that is, accessing as many consecutive data elements as possible using as few I/O calls as possible (*spatial locality*) *or* maximizing the number of data accesses that can be satisfied from fast components (i.e., higher levels) of the storage hierarchy (*temporal locality*).

Notice that these objectives can be realized only by careful data placement across storage devices and careful computation decomposition across processors. Throughout the years several I/O techniques have been designed and implemented [73]. Table 2.2 briefly summarizes the techniques currently employed by our framework. More detailed descriptions can be found in respective references cited at the end of this Chapter; here we only discuss collective I/O.

In many parallel applications, the storage pattern of a data set is, in general, different from its access pattern. The problem here is that, if each processor attempts to read its portion of data (specified in the access pattern), it may need to issue a large number of I/O calls. Suppose that four processors want to access (read) a two-dimensional array in (BLOCK,BLOCK) fashion. Assuming that the array's storage pattern is (BLOCK,*), each processor will have to issue many I/O calls (to be specific $N/2$ read calls each for $M/2$ consecutive data items, if we assume that the array is $N \times M$). What collective I/O does, instead, is to read the data in (BLOCK,*) fashion (i.e., using minimum number of I/O calls) and then *re-distribute* the data across processors' memories to obtain the desired (BLOCK,BLOCK) pattern. That is, taking advantage of knowing the access and storage pattern of the array, we can realize the desired access pattern in two phases. In the first phase, the processors access the data in a layout conformant way ((BLOCK,*) in our example) and, in the second phase, they re-distribute the data in memory among themselves such that the desired access pattern is obtained. Considering the fact that I/O in large-scale computations is much more costly than communication, huge performance improvements can be achieved through collective I/O.

The last column in Table 2.2 gives the conditions under which the respective optimizations will be suggested by the MDMS to the HSS. For example, collective I/O is considered only if *access pattern $\neq$ storage pattern* and multiple processors are involved (P denotes the number of processors). The symbols $\vee$ and $\wedge$ are used for *logical or* and *logical and* operations, respectively. SQ denotes 'sequential' and 'ST' means 'strided;' other abbreviations are from Table 2.2

User Interface   One of the main problems with current parallel file systems and parallel I/O libraries is the excessive number of functions presented to the user. It becomes the task of the user to choose those that express her access patterns

Optimization	Brief Explanation	Suggested Condition
Parallel I/O	Performing I/O using a number of processors in parallel to improve the bandwidth.	$access\ ptrn \neq (*,*,...,*) \lor P \neq 1$
Data sieving	Instead of reading each noncontiguous piece of data separately, it reads a single contiguous chunk spanning all the data requested the unwanted data are then sieved out.	SR
Collective I/O	Distributing the I/O requests of different processors among them so that each processor accesses as many consecutive data as possible. It involves some extra communication between processors.	$access\ ptrn \neq storage\ ptrn \land P \neq 1$
Sequential prefetching	Bringing consecutive data into higher levels of storage hierarchy before it is needed. It helps to overlap the I/O time and computation time, thus hiding the I/O latency.	SQ ∧ RO ∧ SR
Strided prefetching	Same as sequential prefetching except that data is brought in fixed strides (some elements are skipped).	ST ∧ RO ∧ SR
Caching & replacement policy	Keeping the data to be used in near future in the higher levels of storage hierarchy (currently two replacement policy is used (LRU-least recently used and MRU-most recently used).	SQ ∧ RO ∧ SR ∧ MT → LRU SQ ∧ WO ∧ SR ∧ MT → MRU
Setting striping unit size	To select a striping unit such that as many storage devices (e.g., disks) as possible will be utilized.	dsize used
Data migration	Migrating data from higher levels of storage hierarchy (e.g., disks) to lower levels of storage hierarchy (e.g., tapes).	MG ∧ MT ∧ OT
Data purging	Removing data from the storage hierarchy. Useful for temporal files whose lifetime is over.	PG ∧ MT ∧ OT
Pre-staging	Fetching data from tape sub-system to disk sub-system before it is required	associate used
Disabling cache & prefetch	Used when the benefit of caching or prefetching is not clear.	LR

Table 2.2
I/O optimization techniques and the corresponding trigger rules.

as closely as possible. Even in the latest MPI-IO standard [59], there are over 30 read/write calls alone. This makes selecting the right ones a daunting task. We believe that a majority of these calls can be eliminated if the user is allowed to express access patterns using *directives*.

In our initial implementation (which targets only scientific codes that use large, multidimensional arrays) we support the functions shown in Table 2.1.1. Notice that these are the only commands that can be sent to the HSS directly from the application code. Queries about data sets and storage devices are performed by negotiating with the MDMS through directives. Notice however that the use of directives is optional.

Contrast this with current file system and I/O library interfaces that demand each and every parameter in the parameter-list of the command be supplied by the user. In Table 2.1.1, *name* can be a data set name or name of an abstract data set space, in which case all the associated data sets are opened. The data in memory is specified by *buffer* that can be either a pointer or a multidimensional memory region (e.g., an array). It is assumed that each involved processor will have enough space in their respective *buffer* areas to hold its portion of data accessed. The *portion* parameter, on the other hand, denotes the region of the data set to be accessed; the '*' symbol is used to denote the 'whole data set.'

The *opt* parameter is the *optimization pointer* that is set by the MDMS depending on the directives collected so far from the application. It points to a structure that contains sufficient information to carry out an I/O optimization. Currently we are in the process of implementing these high-level functions on top of MPI-IO [265] and SRB (Storage Resource Broker) [14] from the San Diego Supercomputer Center.

The Storage Resource Broker (SRB) is middleware that provides distributed clients with uniform access to diverse storage resources in a distributed heterogeneous computing environment. Storage systems handled currently include the UNIX file system, hierarchical storage systems such as Unitree [275] and HPSS [70], and database large objects managed by various ORDBMS such as DB2 [72] and Postgres [249]. We are experimenting with the version being built on top of MPI-IO, to evaluate the optimizations involving mainly disk-resident data in parallel file systems, and with the version being built on top of SRB, to evaluate optimizations involving tape-resident data.

Consider the following example.

OpenDataSet(P,*opt*)
access P(*,BLOCK) storage DISK(8)
ReadDataSet(P,*bf*,*,*opt*)

In this example, the application first opens the data set (here the array P). It also gives an optimization pointer *opt* to be used later. Then it sends an `access` directive to the MDMS, which declares that 8 processors will access the data set in a column-major fashion. The MDMS, in turn, compares the storage pattern (the default is (BLOCK,*)) with this access pattern and decides that *collective I/O* needs to be performed. It passes this advice to the HSS by filling out the relevant entries of the data structure indicated by *opt*. Later, when the application issues the `ReadDataSet` command, a collective read operation is performed (considering the contents of the structure indicated by *opt*).

Now suppose that the directive was instead `access` P(BLOCK,*) `storage` DISK(8). In that case, since the access pattern and the storage pattern are the same, the MDMS may advise *prefetching* to the HSS by setting the appropriate entries of the structure indicated by *opt*. Notice that in either case the syntax of the actual read call does not change. The only difference is the contents of the data structure pointed to by *opt*.

Given that a typical, large-scale application will have only a few directives, the function performed by the application in question can be changed by modifying only a few program lines. This helps readability and re-usability as well as program maintainability.

Let us now consider the following example fragment.

```
associate (P,Q) with T
access T(BLOCK,*) storage TAPE(16)
OpenDataSet(P,opt1)
ReadDataSet(P,bf1,*,opt1)
OpenDataSet(Q,opt2)
ReadDataSet(Q,bf2,*,opt2)
```

In this case, the application first associates two tape-resident arrays with an abstract data set space T. Then the `access` directive indicates that 16 processors will access the respective portions of P and Q row-wise. Afterward, the application opens P, an activity that, most probably, forces the HSS to stage the data set P from tape sub-system to disk sub-system. This also triggers the MDMS to advise the HSS to *pre-stage* the data set Q from tape to disk, as this array is associated with P and most probably the two arrays will be used together. Assuming that the default layout is row-major, the MDMS also sets the necessary parameters in the structure pointed to by *opt1* and *opt2* to enable prefetching; no collective I/O is required. Consequently, the two calls to `ReadDataSet` take advantage of prefetching.

Experiments In this section, we present preliminary performance numbers from an on-going implementation. All experiments were run on an IBM SP-2 (at Ar-

Function
OpenDataSet(*name,opt*)
CloseDataSet(*name,opt*)
ReadDataSet(*name,buffer,portion,opt*)
WriteDataSet(*name,buffer,portion,opt*)

Table 2.3
Supported I/O functions.

gonne) and Intel Paragon (at Caltech). Each node of SP-2 is RS/6000 Model 390 with 256 megabytes memory and has an I/O sub-system containing four, 9 gigabyte SSA disks attached to it. The nodes on Paragon (Intel i860 XP), on the other hand, are divided into three groups: compute nodes, HIPPI nodes, and service nodes. The total memory capacity of the compute partition is around 14.4 gigabytes. The platform on which the experiments were conducted has three service nodes, each with a RAID SCSI disk array attached to it.

We use four different applications; three of them to measure the benefits of collective I/O for disk-resident data sets in parallel file systems; the last one to see how pre-staging performs in HPSS [70] for tape-resident data. Tables 2.4(a) and (b) show the total I/O times for a 2-D astrophysics template on the Intel Paragon and the IBM SP-2, respectively. 'Original' refers to the code without collective I/O, and 'Optimized' denotes the code with collective I/O. In all cases, the MDMS is run at Northwestern University. The important point here is that, in both the 'Original' and the 'Optimized' versions, the user code is essentially the same; the only difference is that in the 'Optimized' case, the user code sends directives to the MDMS. The MDMS then automatically determines that collective I/O should be performed; this hint is then sent by the MDMS to the HSS. As a result, impressive reductions in I/O times are observed. Since the number of I/O nodes are fixed on both the Paragon and the SP-2, moving from 64 processors to 128 processors causes, in general, an increase in the I/O times.

Table 2.5-2.6 report similar results for a 3-D astrophysics code and for an unstructured code, respectively. Since these codes have not yet been modified to work through the MDMS, the results reported are obtained by hand. Nevertheless, they indicate the order of potential savings once collective I/O is used.

Our last example is a parallel, volume rendering application. As in previous experiments, the MDMS is run at Northwestern University. On the other hand, the application itself is executed on Argonne National Laboratory's SP-2, and the HPSS at the San Diego Supercomputer Center (SDSC) is used as the HSS. In

	t_{total} (64 procs)	t_{total} (128 procs)
Original	64.95	87.02
Optimized	27.44	49.37

(a) Total I/O time (seconds) on Paragon.

	t_{total} (32 procs)	t_{total} (64 procs)
Original	23.46	39.67
Optimized	14.05	11.23

(b) Total I/O times (seconds) on IBM SP2

Table 2.4
Astro-2D application with 256 MB data size 8192×8192) matrix.

	t_{total} (64 procs)	t_{total} (128 procs)
Original	51.04	81.45
Optimized	36.41	68.02

(a) Total I/O time (seconds) on Paragon.

	t_{total} (32 procs)	t_{total} (64 procs)
Original	109.93	211.47
Optimized	3.33	3.51

(b) Total I/O times (seconds) on IBM SP2

Table 2.5
Astro-3D application: 8 MB data size (128×128×128) matrix with 6 iterations.

the 'Original' code, four data files are opened and parallel volume rendering is performed. In the 'Optimized' code ('Original' code + user directives) the four data sets (corresponding to four data files) are associated with each other and pre-staging (from tape to disk) is applied for these data sets.

Table 2.7 shows the total read times for each of the four files for the 'Original' and 'Optimized' codes. The results reveal that, for both 4 and 8 processor cases, pre-staging reduces I/O times significantly. We need to mention that, in every application we experimented with, the time spent by the application in negotiating with the MDMS is less than 1 second. When considering the fact that, for large-scale applications, I/O times are likely to be huge (even when optimized), overhead in this range is acceptable.

	t_{total} (64 procs)	t_{total} (128 procs)
Original	76.30	142.73
Optimized	1.68	0.94

(a) Total I/O time (seconds) on Paragon.

	t_{total} (32 procs)	t_{total} (64 procs)
Original	547.614	488.133
Optimized	1.25	2.13

(b) Total I/O times (seconds) on IBM SP-2

Table 2.6
Unstructured code: 64 MB data size (1024×1024) matrix.

File No →	1	2	3	4
Original	31.18	19.20	61.86	40.22
Optimized	11.90	11.74	20.10	18.38

(a) Total read time on 4 processors.

File No →	1	2	3	4
Original	18.79	37.69	21.02	14.70
Optimized	10.74	6.23	4.49	6.42

(b) Total read time on 8 processors.

Table 2.7
Volume rendering code on HPSS: 16 MB data size (256×256×256).

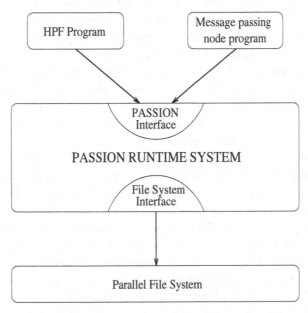

Figure 2.5
PASSION software architecture

2.2 PASSION Runtime System

The PASSION (Parallel and Scalable I/O for Input-Output) runtime system provides functions to efficiently perform the I/O required in parallel programs. PAS-
SION supports a loosely synchronous Single Program Multiple Data (SPMD) model
of computations. It uses a simple high-level interface, which is a level higher than
any of the existing parallel file system interfaces, as illustrated in Figure 2.5.

PASSION is designed to be either directly used by application programmers, or
by compilers translating out-of-core programs written in a high-level data-parallel
language (i.e. High Performance Fortran (HPF) to node programs with calls to the
library for I/O. Since PASSION is used in programs containing arrays, which do

not fit in main memory, data has to be stored in files in some fashions.

2.2.1   Local and Global Placement Model

In the Local Placement Model (LPM), the global array is divided into local arrays belonging to each processor. Since the local arrays are out-of-core, they have to be stored in files on disks. The local array of each processor is stored in a separate file called the *Local Array File (LAF)* of that processor, as shown in Figure 2.6. The node program explicitly reads from and writes to the file when required. The simplest way to view this model is to think of each processor as having another level of memory much slower than main memory.

If the I/O architecture of the system is such that each processor has its own disk, the LAF of each processor will be stored on the disk attached to that processor. If there is a common set of disks for all processors, the LAF will be distributed across one or more of these disks. In other words, we assume that each processor has its own logical disk with the LAF stored on that disk.

The mapping of the logical disk to the physical disks depends on how much control the parallel file system provides the user. At any time, only a portion of the local array is fetched and stored in main memory. The size of this portion depends on the amount of memory available. The portion of the local array that is in main memory is called the *In-Core Local Array (ICLA)*. All computations are performed on the data in the ICLA. Thus, during the course of the program, parts of the LAF are fetched into the ICLA. The new values are computed and, if necessary, the ICLA is stored back into appropriate locations in the LAF.

In the Global Placement Model (GPM), the global array is stored in a single file, called the *Global Array File (GAF)*, as shown in Figure 2.7 and no local array files are created. The global array is logically divided only into local arrays, in keeping with the SPMD programming model. However, there is a single global array on disk. The PASSION runtime system fetches the appropriate portion of each processor's local array from the global array file, as requested by the user.

The advantage of the Global Placement Model is that it saves the initial local array file creation phase in the Local Placement Model. In addition, if the distribution of the array among processors needs to be changed during program execution, an explicit redistribution of the out-of-core data is not required. The disadvantage is that each processor's data may not be stored contiguously in the GAF, resulting in multiple read requests and higher I/O latency time. Also, explicit synchronization is required when a processor needs to access data belonging to another processor.

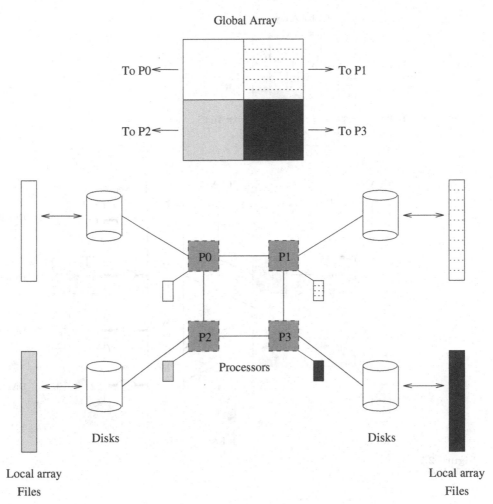

Figure 2.6
Local placement model

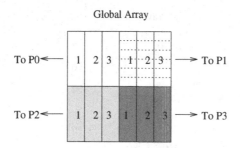

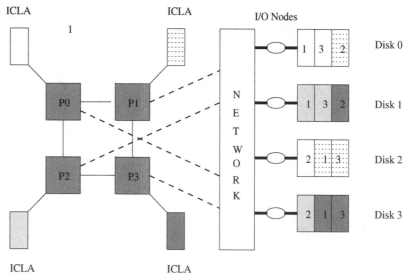

Figure 2.7
Global placement model

```
do n = 1, n_step
    ...
    do i = 1, nedge
        x(edge1(i)) = x(edge1(i)) + y(edge2(i))
        x(edge2(i)) = x(edge2(i)) + y(edge1(i))
    end do
    ...
end do
...
Write the result to a file.
```

Figure 2.8
An example with an irregular loop

2.2.2   Irregular Data Accesses

The computations in which data accesses are performed through a level of indirection are considered irregular computations. Many scientific applications make extensive use of indirection arrays. Examples include Computational Fluid Dynamics Codes (CFD), Particle Codes, Finite Element Codes etc. The domain of these problems is normally irregular, describing for example, a physical structure that is discretized.

Figure 2.8 illustrates an irregular loop [33, 217]. This example shows the code that sweeps over *nedge* mesh edges. Arrays x and y are *data arrays*. Loop iteration *i* carries out a computation involving the edge that connects vertices *edge1(i)* and *edge2(i)*. Arrays such as *edge1* and *edge2*, which are used to index data arrays, are called *indirection arrays*. After the computations are finished, all the results are written to files for further processing such as visualization. The *indirection arrays* determine the data access pattern for each processor during the I/O.

In the application, the data and/or indirection array is divided into smaller partitions that can fit in the main memory of the processors. This is done using a graph partitioning algorithm such as Recursive Coordinate Bisection, to maintain data locality as well as load balance. During the I/O operation in the irregular application, each processor generates a fine-grained access pattern that cannot be expressed using regular section descriptors and that causes significant I/O costs in the I/O subsystem. However, this drawback can be overcome to a large extent by using the Two-Phase Method of PASSION [30, 260].

2.2.3   Implementation Strategy

Many applications require accessing large arrays from disks and distributing them among the processors in some fashion. In those applications, the performance of I/O depends, to a large extent, on the way data is distributed on disks and processors. To obtain better I/O performance, a group of processors need to cooperate in reading or writing data in an efficient manner, which is known as *collective I/O*. Our group has proposed a technique for doing collective I/O, called the two-phase method [30, 260], which is used extensively in the PASSION library. In this subsection, we describe the detailed implementation of PASSION.

Two-Phase Method   Data distribution on disks depends on the data striping method and file storage order (row-major or column-major). The data distribution on the processors is said to be a *conforming* distribution if it results in accessing consecutive data blocks from files. It has been observed that I/O performance is very good in the case of conforming distributions. Other data distributions give much lower performance. To alleviate this problem, the **Two Phase Access Strategy** has been proposed. This strategy is an alternative to accessing data directly according to the data distribution (called **Direct Access Strategy**).

In the two-phase method, I/O is done in two distinct phases. In the first phase, processors read data in large chunks in a manner conforming to the data distribution on disks. In the second phase, data is redistributed among processors using interprocessor communication. The basic principle behind the two phase approach is as follows. Consider the problem is reading an entire array from a file into a distributed array in main memory. In a distributed memory computer with a parallel file system, data is distributed among processors in some fashion and stored in files on disk in some fashion.

For a two-dimensional array, some of the common distributions are row-block, column-block, block-block, row-cyclic, column-cyclic, cyclic-cyclic etc. The file containing the array is typically striped across disks as determined by the striping unit. When data is distributed among processors in such a way that it *conforms* to the way it is stored on disks, *conforming distribution*, each processor can directly read its local array in a single request.

For example, if an array is stored in a file in column-major order, a column-block distribution among processors is the conforming distribution. For any other distribution, a processor's local array will be stored in a non-contiguous manner in the file and, if each processor directly tries to read its local array (called the direct method), it will result in a large number of low-granularity requests. Hence, in the direct method, the I/O performance is best for the conforming distribution, but it

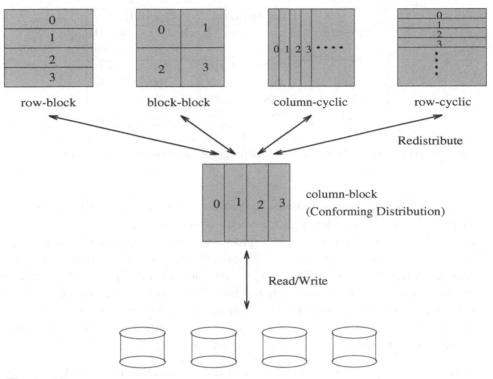

Figure 2.9
Two-phase I/O

degrades drastically for any other distribution.

The two-phase method proposes to read an array from a file into a distributed array in main memory in two phases, as shown in Figure 2.9. In the first phase, processors always read data assuming the conforming distribution, which requires the least I/O time. In the second phase, data is redistributed among processors, using interprocessor communication, to the actual desired distribution. Since the cost of interprocessor communication is orders of magnitude lower than that of I/O, the extra cost of the second phase is negligible. The reverse procedure is used for writing a distributed array to a file. The main advantages of the two-phase method are:

- It results in high granularity data transfer between processors and disks.

- It makes use of the higher bandwidth of the processor interconnection network.

Processors	Unoptimized		Optimized	
	16 I/O nodes	64 I/O nodes	16 I/O nodes	64 I/O nodes
16	2,557	2,546	428	399
32	1,203	1,199	100	97
64	638	628	76	69
128	385	369	86	77

Table 2.8
Execution times (in seconds) for an astrophysics application performing 2.2 GB of I/O.

Table 2.2.3 shows the performance improvement provided by the two-phase I/O strategy for an astrophysics application with a reasonably large input array of size 2K × 2K elements. 16 and 64 I/O nodes are used on the Intel Paragon. The astrophysics application performs I/O for data analysis, check-pointing, and visualization purposes. At every dump point, data for the three purposes are written by the various processors onto a shared file. To be specific, the snapshots of the input array are written to disk at fixed dump points for check-pointing and data analysis. Data are also processed and written out for the purposes of visualization. We compare two different implementations of the code:

(1) *Unoptimized version:* I/O done using the Chameleon library, and

(2) *Optimized version:* I/O done using a run-time system library performing two-phase I/O.

We see a significant performance improvement in the overall execution time in the optimized case due to a huge reduction in the I/O time. The Chameleon library makes I/O in smaller, non-contiguous chunks and has a bottleneck of all I/O performed by a single node. This adds to the I/O time. The two-phase I/O approach, on the other hand, eliminates small I/O requests by performing large chunks of sequential I/O.

The two-phase method can also be performed at the I/O node level. In the first phase, the I/O nodes can read data in a manner that conforms to the distribution on disks and send data directly to the appropriate compute nodes. A similar technique has been proposed recently, called disk-directed I/O [155]. Here a collective request is sent to the I/O nodes, which determine the order and timing of the flow of data.

Accessing Sections of Out-of-Core Arrays   In many out-of-core applications, processors need to access sections of out-of-core arrays stored in files. A two-phase

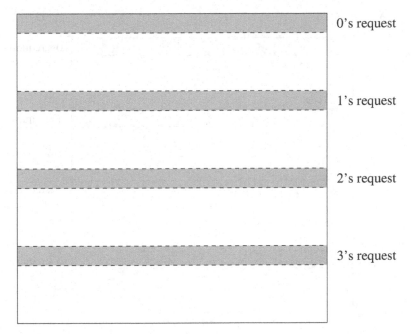

Figure 2.10
Accessing row blocks of a file stored in column-major order

method can be used to access sections of out-of-core arrays as follows [254]. Let us consider the case where each processor needs to read some regular section of a two-dimensional array stored in a file in column-major order. For example, in Figure 2.10, processors need to access row blocks of an array stored in a file in column-major order. The section needed by each processor is represented in terms of its lower-bound, upper-bound, and stride in each dimension $(l_1 : u_1 : s_1, l_2 : u_2 : s_2)$ in global coordinates.

We assign *ownership* to portions of the file such that a processor can directly access only the portion of the file it *owns*. The file is effectively divided into *domains*. The portion of the file that a processor can directly access is called its *file domain*. For a file stored in column-major order, the file domain of each processor is some set of columns of the array. File domains are selected dynamically, depending on the access requests. This results in a dynamic partitioning of the I/O workload among processors. Note that this is just a logical partitioning of the file among processors. The file is not physically divided into separate files. Details about dynamic partitioning of I/O are given in [254].

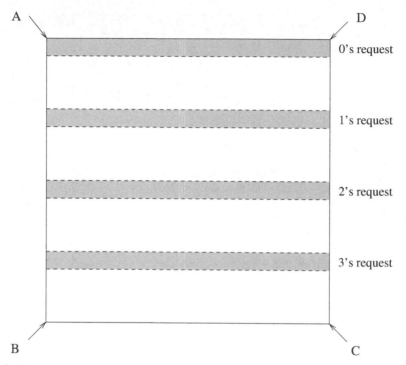

A   D
                                                          0's request
                                                          1's request
                                                          2's request
                                                          3's request
B   C

Figure 2.11
ABCD is the smallest section including all the data that must be read. It is read using data sieving.

Processors first exchange their own access information (the indices $l_1, u_1, s_1, l_2, u_2, s_2$) with other processors so that each processor knows the access requests of other processors. Each processor then calculates what portions of its own request, as well as the requests of other processors, lie in its file domain. For the example access pattern in Figure 2.10, the file domain of processor 0 and the portions of this file domain that have been requested by other processors are shown in Figure 2.11. Each processor must then read all the required data from its file domain.

A simple way of reading would be to read all the data needed by processor 0, followed by that needed by processor 1, and so on, in order of processor number. But in many cases, this method may result in too many small accesses that are not in sequence. For the read to be done efficiently, it is important that the file be accessed in sequence and contiguously.

We use a very general method, as follows. Each processor calculates the minimum of the lower-bounds and the maximum of the upper-bounds of all sections requested from its file domain. This effectively determines the smallest section containing all the data that needs to be read from the file domain (for example, section ABCD in Figure 2.11). This section may also include some data that is not required by any processor.

An optimization known as *data sieving* is used to read the useful data from this section. Basically, large contiguous portions of data are read at a time from the file, the useful data is extracted, and the unwanted portion is discarded. All the required data is read from the file domain in this fashion. This completes the first phase of the two-phase method. The second phase consists of communicating the data read in the first phase to the respective processors. The algorithm for writing sections is essentially the reverse of the algorithm for reading sections [254].

We tested the performance and scalability of this two-phase method extensively and found it to be far superior to the direct method for both reading and writing out-of-core array sections [254]. For example, Figure 2.12 shows the time taken by the two methods, on the Intel Paragon, for reading sections of an out-of-core array of size 16K × 16K single-precision real numbers. Each processor p needs to read a section of this array, specified by $(1+20p:16+20p:1, 4000:12000:1)$. The number of processors is varied from 4 to 128.

We observe that the two-phase method performs considerably better than the direct method. The performance improvement is even better for larger numbers of processors. When the number of processors is doubled, the amount of I/O performed also doubles, but the time taken increases only slightly. Therefore, the I/O bandwidth obtained increases with number of processors.

2.2.4 Optimizations

In addition to the two-phase method, PASSION uses several optimizations:

Data Sieving   All PASSION routines for reading or writing data from/to disks support the reading/writing of regular sections of arrays with strides. Suppose a processor needs to read the section $(l_1 : u_1 : s_1, l_2 : u_2 : s_2)$ of an out-of-core local array from the local array file. Since none of the parallel file system interfaces currently support strided accesses, the only way of reading this array section by using a direct method is to explicitly seek to each element and read it individually.

This requires as many reads as the number of elements in the section. Thus, a major disadvantage of this method is the large number of I/O calls and low granularity of data transfer. Since I/O latency is very high, this method proves to be very expensive. For example, using one processor and one disk on the Intel

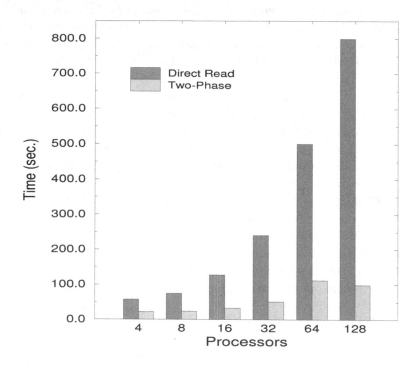

Figure 2.12
A comparison of the two-phase and direct methods for reading sections of an out-of-core array of size 16K × 16K single-precision real numbers (1 GB file) on the Intel Paragon. Each processor p needs to read the section $(1+20p{:}16+20p{:}1, 4000{:}12000{:}1)$. When the number of processors is doubled, the amount of I/O performed also doubles, but the time taken increases only slightly. Hence, the I/O bandwidth obtained increases with number of processors.

Paragon, it takes 16.06 ms to read 1024 integers as one block, whereas it takes 1948 ms to read all of them individually.

PASSION routines use an optimization known as data sieving [257] to read/write strided sections. To read a strided section, a large contiguous portion of data, starting from the first element of the section, is read into a temporary buffer in main memory by using one read call. This may include some unwanted data. The required data is then extracted from the buffer and the unwanted data is dynamically discarded. This process is repeated until the entire section is read. The amount of data read each time depends on the amount of memory available.

Data sieving is a way of combining several small I/O requests into fewer, larger requests to reduce the effect of high I/O latency time. The main advantage of this method is that it requires very few I/O calls and the rest is data transfer within main memory. The disadvantage is that it requires extra memory and it reads more data from disk than is actually required. However, we have found that the reduction in I/O calls increases performance considerably, even though extra data is read.

Data sieving can also be considered from the following perspective. In the direct method, even though a separate read call is required for each individual element, it may not result in a disk access each time. There is usually some form of caching done at the I/O nodes and, if the requested data lies in the cache, it can be read from the cache itself. In spite of this, we find that reading individual elements is a lot more expensive than reading one large chunk. This is because of the overhead of making several requests to the I/O nodes and looking up the software cache at the I/O node each time. Data sieving can be considered a way of doing software caching in user space at the compute node itself. An entire chunk of data, starting from the first element in the section, is effectively cached at the compute node and all the required elements are supplied from this cache. The file system sees only a single request or at most a few requests, depending on the amount of memory available for this cache.

For writing strided sections using data sieving, it is necessary to first read a large chunk of data from the file into a temporary buffer, then store the strided section into the buffer, and finally write the buffer back to the file. If the buffer is not read first, data in the buffer between the strided elements of the section will overwrite the corresponding data elements in the file. Thus, writing strided sections requires twice the amount of I/O required when reading strided sections.

Table 2.9 shows the performance improvement provided by data sieving over the direct method on the Intel Paragon, for both reading and writing array sections. An array of size 2K × 2K single precision real numbers is distributed among 64 processors in one dimension along columns. We observe that data sieving performs considerably better than the direct method in all cases. The reason for this is the large number of I/O requests in the direct method, even though the total amount of data accessed is higher with data sieving.

In data sieving, the total amount of data transferred depends only on the lower and upper bounds of the section and is independent of the stride. Hence the time taken using data sieving does not vary much for all the sections we have considered. However, there is a wide variation in time for the direct method, because only those elements belonging to the section are read. The time is lower for small sections and higher for large sections. We also observe that, for writing array sections, data

Array Section	PASSION_read_section		PASSION_write_section	
	Direct Read	Sieving	Direct Write	Sieving
(1:2048:2, 1:32:2)	52.95	1.970	49.96	5.114
(1:2048:4, 1:32:4)	14.03	1.925	13.71	5.033
(10:1024:3, 3:22:3)	8.070	1.352	7.551	4.825
(100:2048:6, 5:32:4)	7.881	1.606	7.293	4.756
(1024:2048:2, 1:32:3)	18.43	1.745	17.98	5.290

Table 2.9
Performance of direct read/write versus data sieving on 64 processors on the Intel Paragon.
Global array size is 2K × 2K single-precision real numbers. All times are in seconds.

sieving performs better than the direct method even though it requires reading the section before writing.

Data Prefetching   In both the Local and Global Placement Models, program execution proceeds by fetching data from a file, performing the computation on the data, and writing the results back to a file. This process is repeated on other data sets until the end of the program. Thus I/O and computation form distinct phases in the program. A processor has to wait while each data set is being read or written, since there is no overlap between computation and I/O. This is illustrated in Figure 2.13(A), which shows the time taken for computation and I/O on three data sets in sequence. For simplicity reading, writing, and computation are shown to take the same amount of time, although this may not be true in certain cases.

The time taken by the program can be reduced if it is possible to overlap computation with I/O in some fashion. A simple way of achieving this is to issue an asynchronous I/O read request for the next data set immediately after the current data set has been read. This is called *data prefetching*. Since the read request is asynchronous, the reading of the next data set can be overlapped with the computation being performed on the current data set. If the computation time is comparable to the I/O time, this can result in significant performance improvement. Figure 2.13(B) shows how prefetching can reduce the time taken for the example in Figure 2.13(A). Since the computation time is assumed to be the same as the read time, all reads other than the first are overlapped with computation.

We use an out-of-core median filtering program using the Local Placement Model to illustrate the performance of data prefetching. Median filtering is frequently used in computer vision and image processing applications to smooth the input image. Each pixel is assigned the median of the values of its neighbors within a window of a particular size, say 3×3 or 5×5 or even larger. In our implementation, the image

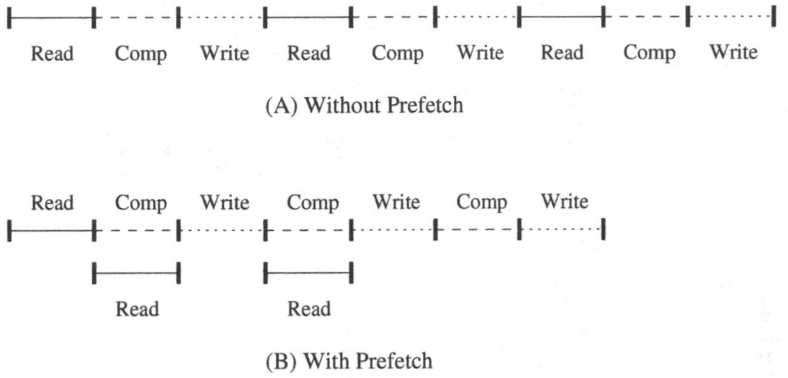

```
├──────┼ - - - ┼ · · · · · ┼──────┼ - - - ┼ · · · · · ┼──────┼ - - - ┼ · · · · · ┤
```
   Read   Comp   Write   Read   Comp   Write   Read   Comp   Write

(A) Without Prefetch

   Read   Comp   Write   Comp   Write   Comp   Write
```
├──────┼ - - - ┼ · · · · · ┼ - - - ┼ · · · · · ┼ - - - ┼ · · · · · ┤
```
```
          ├──────┤          ├──────┤
```
            Read   Read

(B) With Prefetch

Figure 2.13
Data prefetching

was distributed among processors in one dimension along columns and stored in
local array files. Figure 2.14 shows the performance of median filtering on the Intel
Paragon for an image of size 2K × 2K pixels using a 3 × 3 window. We observe that
prefetching improves performance considerably, by as much as 40% in some cases.

2.2.5   Parallel I/O Runtime Support for Irregular Problems

In PASSION, collective I/O for irregular applications has been developed to achieve
three main goals: utilizing the I/O bandwidth as much as possible, reducing
the storage space occupied by the application, and avoiding the post-processing
(sort/merge) step in the computational analysis cycle. To utilize the I/O bandwidth, the design of collective I/O library functions is based on the two-phase I/O
strategy described in subsection 2.2.3. To reduce storage space, compression has
been incorporated as an option in the collective I/O scheme. Using compression in
the library achieves two major goals: reducing disk space requirements [280], and
reducing the total execution time of the applications [231, 193].

The correspondence between compressed chunks and data array is established
using a *chunk index*, persistently stored in an *index file* composed of fixed-length
records. Each record provides information for managing the chunks within the
I/O library, such as chunk identification, length, file offset, compression algorithm,
compressed length, and portion of the array corresponding to the chunk. Finally,
to avoid the post-processing step (sort/merge), the I/O is executed on *global files
canonically ordered*. These files need not be reordered because it is done, on-the-fly,
in the collective I/O functions [199, 41].

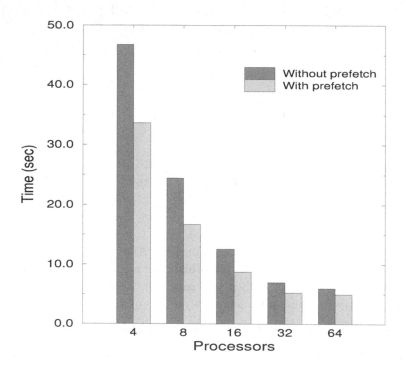

Figure 2.14
Performance of an out-of-core median filtering program on the Intel Paragon

Schedule   Schedule describes the communication and I/O patterns required for each processor participating in the I/O operation. For regular multidimensional arrays, the accesses can be described using regular section descriptors. Access and communication schedules can be built based upon just this information. On the other hand, when indirection arrays are involved to reference data array, the indirection arrays must be scanned to consider each element of the array individually and determine both its place in the global canonical representation and its destination processor for communication. Note that once it is constructed, the schedule information can be used repeatedly by the irregular problems whose access pattern does not change during computation. This amortizes its cost.

I/O Operation   We proposed two collective I/O schemes for irregular applications. In the first scheme, all processors participate in I/O concurrently, making scheduling of I/O requests simpler but creating the possibility of contention at the

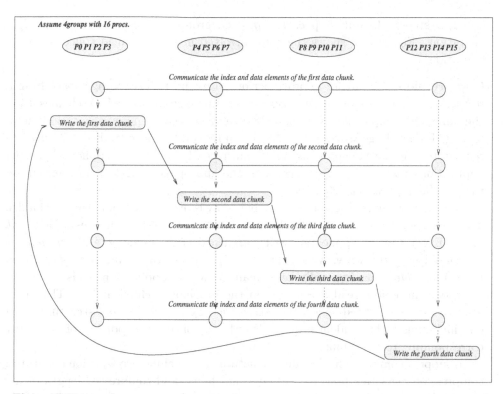

Figure 2.15
Collective write operation

I/O nodes. In this collective I/O scheme, a processor involved in the computation is also responsible for reading data from files or writing data into files. Let D bytes be the total size of data and P be the number of processors. Each processor then reads D/P bytes of data from the file and distributes it among processors based on schedule information. In case of writing, each processor collects D/P bytes of data from other processors and then writes it to the file. By performing I/O this way, the workload can be evenly balanced across processors.

In the second scheme, processors are dynamically organized into several groups and only one group performs I/O at a time, while the other groups perform communication to rearrange data and this entire process is pipelined. The expectation is that while one group of processors is performing an I/O operation, another group performs communication in order to collect(redistribute) data for write(read) operations. Thus, if there are G groups, then there will be G interleaved communication and I/O steps, where in step g, $0 \leq g \leq G$, group g is responsible for the I/O operation. Figure 2.15 shows the steps involved in the pipelined collective write operation.

Compression To further improve performance and reduce storage space from a software point of view, one feasible option is to enhance collective I/O schemes using chunking and compression. Chunking by itself has been proposed as a technique to manage I/O for large arrays [141, 232]. Compression has been traditionally used to reduce storage space requirements [280], but recently it has been applied to parallel applications managing large arrays with the aim of reducing the total execution time of the applications [231, 193].

To provide a chunked scheme, the global array is organized as an array of chunks. The correspondence between chunks and data array is established using a *chunk index*. Every time an application writes an array using chunking, a *chunk index* is associated with the array. When the array is written, the chunk index is written to an *index file* which is usually very small. When an application reads the array, the index file is also read and stored in the in-memory chunk index. The index file is composed of fixed-length records defined by a *chunk_layout* structure, each one including a chunk identification, length, file offset, and portion of the array corresponding to the chunk.

To support compression, the index structure must include two additional features: compression algorithm used to compress the chunk, and compressed length of the chunk. An uncompressed chunk will have NONE in the compression algorithm field and -1 in the compressed length. One major problem of combining chunking and compression, when several processors cooperate to generate a data array, is that it cannot be assumed that all the portions will be of the same length.

Having chunks of different sizes, which is equivalent to having variable-length records [118], does not allow for computing file offsets in advance. Thus, the file offset must be propagated after compressing each local chunk and receiving previous offset. Moreover, compressed chunks do not fit exactly on file system blocks, generally having a portion of the first and last block *partially* rewritten, which may decrease I/O performance. This problem can be avoided by aligning each chunk to the next file system block. Figure 2.16 shows the steps involved in the collective write operation with compression.

Performance Results We evaluated our collective I/O schemes combined with synthetic kernels and an irregular application on ASCI/Red teraflop system, located at Sandia National Laboratory. Each result shows the overall I/O bandwidth observed at the application level. In other words, the bandwidth measure takes

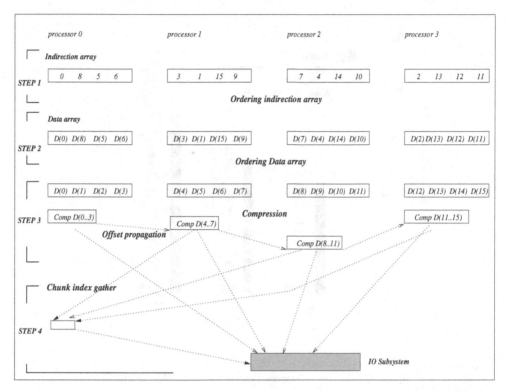

Figure 2.16
A parallel collective write operation with compression

into account communication, computation overhead, and the actual I/O operation. Figures 2.17 and 2.18 show performance results by varying the total size of data, number of processors, and processor groups (Figure 2.18).

In Figure 2.17, as the data size is increased from 256 MB to 512 MB, we noticed slight performance improvement in most cases because, as the number of processors increases, it requires more communication steps to distribute/collect data to/from other processors, even though the size of index and data values becomes smaller, degrading the overall performance. Also, with the same number of processors, we increased the size of data from 512 MB to 1024 MB by using multiple data set (32bytes in this experiment) to be referenced by each index value. We obtained much better performance in this case because the communication overheads to exchange index and data values are amortized over larger data elements.

Figures 2.19 and 2.20 show the overall bandwidth for the collective and pipelined

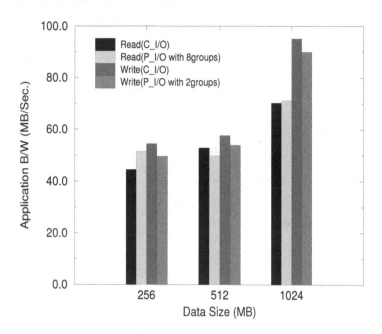

Figure 2.17
Collective and pipelined collective I/O operations on the *ASCI/Red teraflop system* as a
function of data size.

collective I/O using different compression ratios and data sizes. The bandwidth of
the compressed version is higher than the original one (ratio 1:1). For the 1024
MB of data size with a compression ratio of 6:1, the overall bandwidth has been
enhanced by almost 25 percent in both schemes. Moreover, compressing the data
on the ASCI/Red teraflop system generated two new effects which have a negative
influence on the performance:

- *small writes* on the RAIDs (only 3 disks of 6 occupied), and

- compression ratio reduction (6:1 *ASCI/Red*, 8:1 *Intel Paragon*) due to block
  alignment: 256 KB are *wasted* per chunk against the 32 KB on the Paragon.

Both effects could be enhanced by tuning the parallel file system to achieve much
better performance.

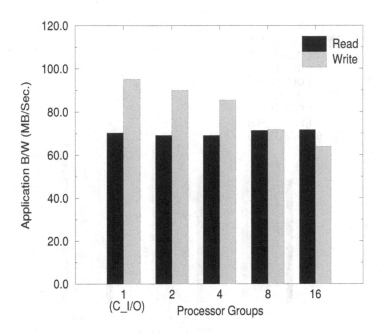

Figure 2.18
Collective and pipelined collective I/O operations on the *ASCI/Red teraflop system* as a
function of processor groups.

2.3 Conclusions

In this chapter, we have presented an architecture for large-scale data management
and collective I/O techniques developed as part of the PASSION project. The
main concept is using the flexibility of a database management system to extract,
analyze, maintain, and transparently use meta-data to achieve I/O optimizations.
This environment consists of a user code, a metadata management system (MDMS),
and a hierarchical storage system (HSS). It provides a seamless data management
and manipulation facility for use by large-scale scientific applications. Its goal
is to combine the advantages of file systems and DBMSs without incurring their
respective disadvantages and to provide access function transparency (through the
automatic invocation of high-level I/O optimizations like collective I/O and data
sieving).

Also, by storing metadata and providing means to manipulate it, our framework

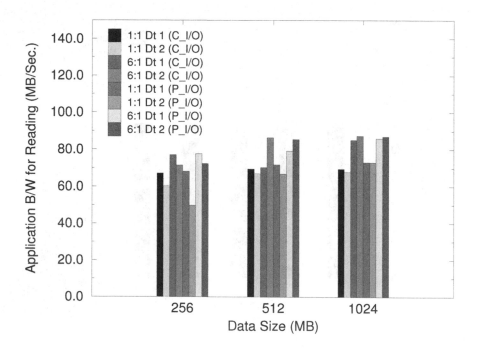

Figure 2.19
Collective and pipelined (two groups) collective read operations on ASCI/Red teraflop system as
a function of data size, compression ratio and data type.

is able to manage distributed resources in a heterogeneous environment. Preliminary results obtained using several applications are encouraging and motivate us
to complete our implementation and make extensive experiments using large-scale,
data intensive applications.

We also presented a description of the PASSION Runtime Library which aims
to improve the I/O performance of applications by providing a set of optimized
functions based on collective I/O. Collective I/O was first proposed in PASSION
as a mechanism to achieve high-performance and has since been adopted in many
runtime systems, file systems, and MPI-IO.

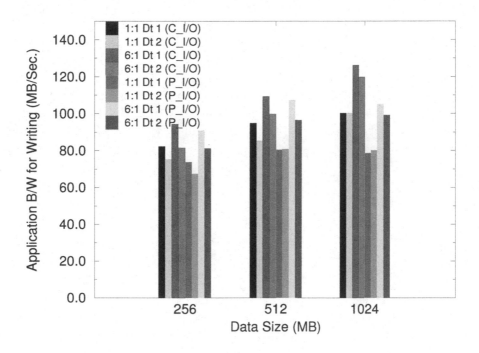

Figure 2.20
Collective and pipelined (two groups) collective write operations on ASCI/Red teraflop system as a function of data size, compression ratio and data type.

3 Building Parallel Database Systems for Multidimensional Data

CHAILIN CHANG, TAHSIN M. KURC, ALAN SUSSMAN AND JOEL SALTZ

As computational power and storage capacity increase, processing and analyzing large volumes of data play an increasingly important part in many domains of scientific research. Typical examples of very large scientific data sets include long running simulations of time-dependent phenomena that periodically generate snapshots of their state, for example:

- hydrodynamics and chemical transport simulation for estimating pollution impact on water bodies [44, 50, 177],

- magnetohydrodynamics simulation of planetary magnetospheres [252],

- simulation of a flame sweeping through a volume [208],

- airplane wake simulations [178]),

- archives of raw and processed remote sensing data (e.g. AVHRR [192], Thematic Mapper [166], MODIS [183]), and

- archives of medical images (e.g., high resolution light microscopy [5], CT imaging, MRI, sonography).

These data sets are usually multidimensional (i.e., each data element in a data set is associated with a point in a multidimensional space defined by the attributes of the data element). The data dimensions can be spatial coordinates, time, or varying experimental conditions such as temperature, velocity, or magnetic field. Access to data elements of such a data set is often described by a *range query*, which retrieves all the data elements whose associated points fall within a given multidimensional box in the underlying attribute space of the data set.

The increasing importance of such data sets has been recognized by several database research groups and multiple systems have been developed for managing and/or visualizing them [16, 75, 129, 175, 207, 246]. In addition, commercial object-relational database systems provide some support for managing multidimensional data sets (e.g., the *SpatialWare DataBlade Module* [241] for the Informix Universal Server and the Oracle 8 *Spatial data cartridge* [201]).

These systems, however, focus on lineage management, retrieval, and visualization of multidimensional data sets. They provide little or no support for analyzing or processing these data sets – the assumption is that this is too application-specific to warrant common support. As a result, applications that process these data sets are usually decoupled from data storage and management, resulting in inefficiency due to copying and loss of locality. Furthermore, every application developer has to implement complex support for managing and scheduling the processing.

Over the past three years, we have been working with several scientific research groups to understand the processing requirements for such applications [2, 45, 50, 93, 103, 174, 184, 185, 208]. Our study of a large set of applications indicates that the processing for such data sets is often highly stylized and shares several important characteristics. Usually, both the input data set as well as the result being computed have underlying multidimensional grids. The basic processing step usually consists of transforming individual input items, mapping the transformed items to the output grid, and computing output items by aggregating, in some way, all the transformed input items mapped to the corresponding grid point. For example, remote-sensing earth images are usually generated by performing atmospheric correction on 10 days of raw telemetry data, mapping all the data to a latitude-longitude grid, and selecting those measurements that provide the clearest view.

As another example, chemical contamination studies simulate circulation patterns in water bodies with an unstructured grid over fine-grain time steps and chemical transport on a different grid over coarse-grain time steps. This is achieved by mapping the fluid velocity information from the circulation grid, possibly averaged over multiple fine-grain time steps, to the chemical transport grid and computing smoothed fluid velocities for the points in the chemical transport grid.

3.1   Active Data Repositories

This chapter presents the *Active Data Repository* (ADR), an infrastructure for building parallel database systems that enables integration of storage, retrieval, and processing of multidimensional data sets on a distributed memory parallel machine. ADR supports common operations including index generation, data retrieval, memory management, scheduling of processing across a parallel machine, and user interaction. It achieves its primary advantage from the ability to integrate data retrieval and processing for a wide variety of applications and from the ability to maintain and jointly process multiple data sets with different underlying attribute spaces.

Several runtime support libraries and file systems have been developed to support efficient I/O in a parallel environment [19, 62, 119, 155, 196, 230, 259, 260, 266]. These systems are analogous to ADR in that (a) they plan data movements in advance to minimize disk access and communication overheads and (b) in some cases, they attempt to optimize I/O performance by masking I/O latency with computation and with interprocessor communication. Also, ADR schedules its operations based on the completion of disk I/O requests, which is similar to the strategy used by disk-directed I/O [155] and server-directed I/O [230].

However, ADR differs from those systems in a number of ways. First, ADR is able to carry out range queries directed at irregular, spatially indexed data sets, such as satellite data consisting of two-dimensional strips embedded in a three-dimensional attribute space, digitized microscopy data stored as heterogeneous collections of spatially registered meshes, and water contamination simulation data represented by unstructured meshes over simulated regions of bays and estuaries.

Second, computation is an integral part of the ADR framework. Users provide ADR with procedures to carry out data preprocessing and analysis, and the required computations are performed while I/O and interprocessor communication is in progress. With the collective I/O interfaces provided by many parallel I/O systems, data processing usually cannot begin until the entire collective I/O operation completes.

Third, data placement algorithms optimized for range queries are integrated as part of the ADR framework. Analytic and simulation studies have shown that these algorithms allow ADR to exploit the disk of the entire system, and evenly partition the workload across all the disks.

ADR has been developed as a set of modular services. Because its structure mirrors that of a wide variety of applications, ADR is easy to customize for different types of processing. To build a version of ADR customized for a particular application, a user must provide functions to pre-process the input data, map input data to elements in the output data, and aggregate multiple input data items that map to the same output element.

Several extensible database systems that can be tailored to support particular applications have also been proposed [15, 39, 110, 148, 248]. In addition to the functionality provided by a general-purpose relational database system, these systems also provide support for adding new storage methods, new data types, new access methods, and new operations. The incorporation of user-defined access methods and operations into a computation model as general as the relational model allows these systems to support a large number of applications. However, it also makes query optimization very difficult. A number of researchers have begun to address this problem [233]. ADR on the other hand, defines a more restrictive processing structure that mirrors the structure of many applications, such as the ones described in Section 3.2. In this processing structure, user-defined functions are

applied to each input data element in a pre-defined order once the data is retrieved
from disks. This processing structure is described in more detail in Section 3.4.7.
Good performance is achieved via careful scheduling of the operations and good
utilization of the system resources, not by rearranging the algebraic operators in a
relational query tree, as is done in relational database systems.

The remainder of this chapter is organized as follows. In §3.2, we present several
motivating applications to illustrate their common structure. In turn, §3.3 presents
an overview of ADR, including its distinguishing features and a running example.
This is followed in §3.4–§3.5, respectively, by detailed descriptions of each service
and techniques for customizing database services. In §3.6, we present performance
results for three motivating applications implemented with ADR. Because ADR
is a system in evolution, we conclude in §3.7 with a description of the current
status of the ADR design and implementation and discuss future directions for
ADR research.

3.2   Motivating Examples

To illustrate the common structure of many scientific data analysis problems, we
begin by reviewing their features.

3.2.1   Satellite Data Processing

Earth scientists study the earth by processing remotely-sensed data continuously
acquired from satellite-based sensors, since a significant amount of earth science research is devoted to developing correlations between sensor radiometry and various
properties of the surface of the earth. A typical analysis [2, 45, 103, 174] processes
satellite data for ten days to a year (for the AVHRR sensor, ten days of data is
about 4 GB) and generates one or more composite images of the area under study.

Generating a composite image requires projection of the globe onto a two-
dimensional grid; each pixel in the composite image is computed by selecting the
"best" sensor value that maps to the associated grid point. A variety of projections
are used by earth scientists – the USGS cartographic transformation package supports 24 different projections [276]. An earth scientist specifies the projection that
best suits her needs, maps the sensor data using the chosen projection, and generates an image by compositing the projected data. Sensor values are pre-processed
to correct the effects of various distortions, such as instrument drift, atmospheric
distortion, and topographic effects, before they are used.

3.2.2   Virtual Microscope and Analysis of Microscopy Data

The Virtual Microscope [5, 93] is an application we have developed to support the need to interactively view and process digitized data arising from tissue specimens. The Virtual Microscope provides a realistic digital emulation of a high power light microscope. The raw data for such a system can be captured by digitally scanning collections of full microscope slides under high power. We estimate that an array of 50x50 photo-micrographs, each about 1000x1000 pixels, is required to cover an entire slide at high resolution, and each pixel is a three byte RGB color value. Under this scenario, one slide image requires over 7 GBytes, uncompressed. However, such an image captures only a single focal plane, and many specimens will require capture of from five to thirty focal planes.

The digitized images from a slide are effectively a three-dimensional data set, since each slide can contain multiple focal planes. At the basic level, the Virtual Microscope can emulate the usual behavior of a physical microscope, including continuously moving the stage and changing magnification and focus. The processing for the Virtual Microscope requires projecting high-resolution data onto a grid of suitable resolution (governed by the desired magnification) and appropriately compositing pixels mapping onto a single grid point, to avoid introducing spurious artifacts into the displayed image. Used in this manner, the Virtual Microscope can support completely digital dynamic telepathology [200, 278, 279]. In addition, it enables new modes of behavior that cannot be achieved with a physical microscope, such as simultaneous viewing and manipulation of a single slide by multiple users.

3.2.3   Water Contamination Studies

Powerful simulation tools are crucial to understanding and predicting transport and reaction of chemicals in bays and estuaries [162]. Such tools include a hydro-dynamics simulator, such as ADCIRC or UTBEST [50, 177], which simulates the flow of water in the domain of interest, and a chemical transport simulator, such as CE-QUAL-ICM [44], which simulates the reactions between chemicals in the bay and transport of these chemicals. For each simulated time step, each simulator generates a grid of data points to represent the current status of the simulated region.

For a complete simulation system for bays and estuaries [162], the hydrodynamics simulator must be coupled to the chemical transport simulator, since the latter uses the output of the former to simulate the transport of chemicals within the domain. As the chemical reactions have little effect on the circulation patterns, the fluid velocity data can be generated once and used for many contamination studies. Whereas the grid data for a single time step may require several megabytes, thousands of time steps may need to be simulated for a particular scenario, leading to very large database storage requirements.

The grids used by the chemical simulator are often different from the grids the hydrodynamic simulator employs, and the chemical simulator usually uses coarser time steps than the hydrodynamics simulator. Therefore, running a chemical transport simulation requires retrieving the hydrodynamics output from the appropriate hydrodynamics data sets stored in the database, averaging the hydrodynamics outputs over time, and projecting them into the grid used by the chemical transport simulator, via a projection method such as UT-PROJ [51] developed at University of Texas at Austin.

3.3   ADR Overview

In this section, we provide an overview of ADR. We describe its distinguishing features and use a database that generates composite images out of raw satellite data as an example to illustrate how ADR would be used.

There are four distinguishing features of ADR. First, it is targeted toward multidimensional data sets – the attributes of each data set form an underlying multidimensional attribute space (e.g., spatial coordinates, time, temperature, velocity, etc.). ADR can simultaneously manage and process multiple data sets with different attribute spaces and different distributions of data within each attribute space. For example, ADR can manage satellite data at multiple stages in a processing chain, ranging from the initial raw data that consists of a two-dimensional strip embedded in a three-dimensional space, to ten day composites that are two-dimensional images in a suitable map projection, to monthly composites that are 360x180 images with one pixel for each longitude-latitude element. ADR uses multidimensional indices (e.g., R^*-trees [17, 109], quad-trees [94]) to manage these data sets.

For a given data set, a separate index is created for every attribute space of interest. For example, the underlying attribute space for AVHRR satellite data has three axes - latitude (in 1/128th of a degree), longitude (in 1/128th of a degree), and time (in seconds). During processing, this attribute space is mapped to another attribute space, which is a grid in the *Interrupted Goodes Homolosine* map projection [243]. ADR allows users to index this data set either on the underlying latitude-longitude-time attribute space or on the attribute space jointly defined by the Goodes map projection and time.

Second, ADR leverages commonality in processing requirements to integrate data retrieval and processing for a wide variety of applications. Software that integrates data retrieval and data processing can exhibit substantial performance advantages compared to a scenario in which data retrieval and data processing are performed by separate processes, which may be running on different machines. First, integration of data retrieval and computations makes it possible to mask I/O latencies. Second, in many cases, large data sets may have to be copied between the data retrieval program and the data processing program. In our motivating applications, the output data set for a query is much smaller than the data sets that need to be retrieved for processing the query. ADR integrates data retrieval and processing by providing support for a variety of common operations such as index generation, data retrieval, memory management, scheduling of processing across the parallel machine, and user interaction.

Third, ADR can be customized for a wide variety of applications without compromising efficiency. To customize ADR, a user has to provide (a) a transformation function to pre-process individual input items, (b) one or more mapping functions to map from input attribute space(s) to the output attribute space, and (c) an aggregation function to compute an output data item given the set of input data items that map to it.

Fourth, ADR leverages the commonality in the structure of data sets and processing to present a uniform interface. Users specify, in an ADR query, the data set(s) of interest, a region of interest within the data set(s), and the desired format, resolution, and destination of the output. In addition, they select the transformation, mapping, and aggregation functions to be used. The output of an ADR query is also multidimensional. The attribute space for the output is specified as a part of the query (by specifying the desired format and resolution). The region of interest can be specified in terms of any attribute space for which the data set has an index. For example, a query to retrieve and process AVHRR data could specify its region of interest in terms of either the latitude-longitude-time attribute space that underlies the AVHRR data set or the attribute space defined by the Goodes map projection and time.

Figures 3.1 and 3.2 show how ADR is used to generate the desired output image from processing raw AVHRR satellite data. Each data item in the AVHRR data set is referred to as an *instantaneous field of view* (IFOV), and consists of eight attributes – three key attributes that specify the spatio-temporal coordinates and five data attributes that contain observations in different parts of the electromagnetic spectrum. IFOVs from multiple orbits are stored in ADR, although Figure 3.1 only shows a strip from a single orbit.

The query region is specified in terms of the latitude-longitude-time attribute

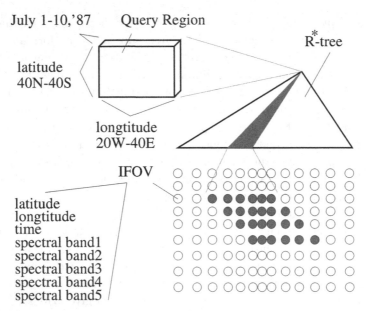

Figure 3.1
ADR query for an AVHRR data set.

space, an R^*-tree indexed over the IFOVs on the same attribute space, is used
to identify the IFOVs of interest. The output is an image in the Goodes map
projection. Each IFOV selected for the query is pre-processed by a transformation
function to correct the effects of various distortions – instrument drift, atmospheric
distortion, and topographic effects. It is then mapped to a pixel in the output
image by a mapping function. Because the query region extends over ten days and
since observations from consecutive orbits overlap spatially, multiple IFOVs can
map to a single output pixel. The aggregation function for an output pixel selects
the "best" corrected IFOV that maps to the output pixel, based on a measure of
the clarity of the sensor readings. Figure 3.2 illustrates these operations.

3.4 ADR System Architecture

Figure 3.3 shows the architecture of ADR. A complete ADR application consists of
a *front-end process*, and a *back-end*. A client program, implemented for a specific
domain, generates requests to the front-end. The front-end translates the requests
into ADR *queries* and sends one or more queries to the back-end, which consists

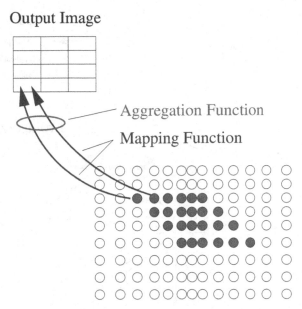

Figure 3.2
AVHRR query output (image in Goodes map projection).

of a set of processing nodes and one or more disks attached to each node. During query processing, the back-end nodes are responsible for retrieving the input data and performing projection and aggregation operations over the data items retrieved to generate the output products as defined by the range query.

ADR has been developed as a set of modular services in C++. In this section, we first describe the attribute space service, the data loading service, the indexing service, and the data aggregation service, which are the back-end services that the user would customize for a particular application. We then describe the query interface service, which is provided by ADR to receive queries from clients and relay them to the back-end nodes. Finally, we describe the query planning service and the query execution service, which are the internal back-end services provided by ADR for query processing. Some of the functions provided by these services, such as the indexing service, correspond directly to those provided by object-relational database systems; other functions are provided to support the stylized processing required by our target applications. ADR services have been implemented as C++ classes. Customization for each application is done through the use of inheritance and virtual functions.

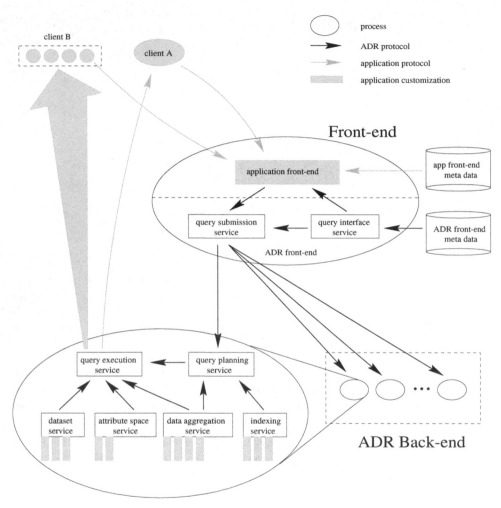

Figure 3.3
ADR architecture.

3.4.1 Attribute Space Service

The attribute space service manages the registration and use of attribute spaces and mapping functions. Mapping functions are used to map either individual points between previously registered attribute spaces or to map points from a registered attribute space to define a new attribute space. In this section, we describe how attribute spaces and mapping functions are specified and maintained.

Multidimensional attribute spaces are the central structures in ADR. All other structures and operations are specified in terms of these attribute spaces. An attribute space is specified by the number of dimensions and the range of values in each dimension. For user convenience, additional information can be stored with an attribute space. For example, a name and the resolution of the values in a dimension can be specified (e.g., for the latitude-longitude-time attribute space from §3.3, the resolution of the latitude dimension is 1/128-th of a degree).

ADR supports two kinds of attribute spaces: *base* and *derived*. *Base* attribute spaces are explicitly specified by the user and are persistent, so can be identified by names that are visible to users. A *derived* attribute space is specified as a (*base* attribute space, mapping function) pair. Logically, a *derived* space is defined as the space generated by mapping every point in the *base* space using the mapping function.

Mapping functions are specified by the domain and range attribute spaces and an algorithm for the mapping between them. The attribute space service manages the namespace of attribute spaces and mapping functions and allows users to browse the sets of available attribute spaces and mapping functions via the query interface service. Currently, mapping functions are statically linked; we plan to provide dynamic linking in the near future.

3.4.2 Data Loading Service

The data loading service manages the process of loading new data sets into ADR. To achieve low-latency retrieval of data, a data set is partitioned into a set of chunks, each of which consists of one or more data items. A chunk is the unit of I/O and communication in ADR. That is, a chunk is retrieved as a whole during query processing. As every data item is associated with a point in a multidimensional attribute space, every chunk is associated with a minimum bounding rectangle (MBR) that encompasses the coordinates (in the associated attribute space) of all the items in the chunk. Since data is accessed through range queries, it is desirable to have data items that are close to each other in the multidimensional space in the same data chunk. Data chunks are declustered across the disks attached to

back-end nodes to achieve I/O parallelism during query processing. Data chunks
on a single disk are clustered to obtain high bandwidth from each disk. An index,
constructed from the MBRs of the chunks, is used to find the chunks that intersect
a query window during query processing. Thus, a data set in ADR is identified by
its name, its multidimensional attribute space, a list of data files that contain the
data chunks, and a list of index files that contain the index information.

Loading a data set into ADR is accomplished in four steps:

- partition a data set into data chunks,

- compute placement information,

- create an index, and

- move data chunks to the disks according to placement information.

The placement information describes how data chunks are declustered and clustered
across the disk farm. After data chunks are stored in the disk farm, data set catalogs
are updated to register the new data set in ADR.

A data set to be loaded into ADR is specified as a list of data files that contain
the data items, along with metadata information. The metadata consists of a set of
files that contain placement and index information for data chunks. For the purpose
of loading data sets, we categorize them into three classes depending on the type
of metadata information available and the structure of the data set. A *fully cooked*
data set is already partitioned into data chunks, and its metadata contains pre-
computed placement information and a corresponding index (e.g., an R-tree [109]).
Only the fourth step must be executed for fully cooked data sets.

A *half cooked* data set is also already partitioned into data chunks. However, no
placement information has been pre-computed. The metadata files must contain a
MBR for every data chunk, and a start and end position for the data chunk in the
data files. The ADR data loading service uses MBRs to compute the placement of
data chunks, and build an index. The third class of data sets is *raw* data sets. In a
raw data set, no placement information is pre-computed, and the data set has not
been partitioned into data chunks.

The data loading service currently provides support for fully cooked and half
cooked data sets. We are designing an interface for raw data sets. This interface
will allow users of raw data sets to incorporate user-defined partitioning methods
into the data loading service.

The data loading service consists of a *master manager* and *data movers*. The
master manager reads the metadata for the data set, and computes placement

information for the data chunks if it has not been pre-computed. ADR provides two default methods to compute the placement information.

The first method uses the *minimax* algorithm [184, 185] to assign the data chunks to individual disks, and the Short Spanning Path (SSP) algorithm [88] to place the set of chunks assigned to the same disk. The placement decisions for the data chunks in a data set determine the amount of disk that can be exploited by ADR for data retrieval. The minimax and SSP algorithms have been shown to outperform other declustering and clustering schemes, such as disk modulo [78], fieldwise xor (FX) [147] and Hilbert curves [87], for range queries into a multidimensional space via both analytic and simulation studies [185]. However, the runtime complexity of the minimax algorithm is $O(N^2)$, where N is the number of data chunks. Therefore, its execution time may be prohibitively long for large numbers of chunks.

The second declustering method provided by ADR uses *Hilbert curve methods* [87] for fast declustering and clustering of large data sets. A fast placement method is especially useful when data sets are permanently stored in archival (i.e. tertiary) storage devices, so that ADR must use its local disks as a cache to load data sets on demand.

Data movers are responsible for actually copying the data chunks onto disks in the ADR back-end. The data mover running on each of the back-end nodes is responsible for storing the data chunks to the disks attached to that node. After the master manager computes the placement information, it broadcasts the information to the data movers. Each data mover extracts placement information for data chunks that must be placed on its local disks. Each mover accesses the data files for the data set and copies the required data chunks onto its local disks. After all data chunks are copied, each data mover builds an index on its local data chunks using the indexing service. The index is used by the back-end process running on that node during query execution. The ADR indexing service uses a variant of R*-trees as the default indexing structure.

The current implementation of the data loading service requires that each mover be able to access all the data files of the data set to be loaded. In addition, the data loader does not perform subsetting of a large data set so that only a portion of the data set is loaded into ADR. In another project we have been developing an infrastructure, called ADR′ (since it is based on a subset of ADR functionality), to access very large data sets stored in tertiary storage systems, such as IBM's high-performance storage system (HPSS) [121]. ADR′ allows users to submit range queries into a data set, retrieve portions of the data set that satisfy the range query, and perform user-defined filtering operations on those portions of the data set before sending them to the requester. The ADR data set service will employ

ADR′ to load portions of data sets stored in tertiary and remote storage systems on demand, in systems where data movers cannot directly access all data files. ADR′ is also being deployed within the NSF National Partnership for Advanced Computational Infrastructure (NPACI), to extend the capabilities of Storage Resource Brokers (SRBs) [14] to allow access to subsets of large data sets. SRBs provide location-independent access to data sets stored on multiple, heterogeneous, high-performance platforms in a distributed computational grid environment.

3.4.3   Indexing Service

The indexing service creates an index for a given (data set, attribute space) pair. An attribute space can be used for indexing a data set if and only if it is either the *native* attribute space of the data set or the target of a chain of mapping functions that maps the *native* attribute space to the new attribute space. ADR allows users to optionally specify an indexing algorithm; by default it uses a variant of R^*-trees.

An index can be created at any time, although it is expected that most indices will be created as a part of the data loading operation. To create an index, the indexing service uses information about the *MBR* for each chunk in the data set and about the physical location of each chunk on disk. It obtains this information from the data loading service. For *derived* attribute spaces, the indexing service uses the associated mapping function to first map the *MBR* for each chunk into the *derived* attribute space.[1]

3.4.4   Data Aggregation Service

The data aggregation service manages both the user-provided functions for aggregation operations and the data types of the intermediate results used by these functions. It manages the namespace of these functions and data types, and performs type checking both when the functions and data types are registered (as a part of customization) and when they are used in response to a query.

An intermediate data structure, referred to as an *accumulator*, may be used during query processing to hold partial results generated by the aggregation functions. An accumulator is associated with a data type that provides functions to iterate through its constituent data items, which are called *accumulator elements*. Functions are provided to access the attributes of the individual elements. As for input and output data sets, an accumulator has an underlying attribute space, and each of its elements is associated with a range of coordinates for each dimension of the

---

[1]Recall that a *derived* attribute space is specified as a (*base* attribute space, mapping function) pair.

attribute space. The accumulator data type provides a navigation function that, given a point in the underlying attribute space, returns references to the accumulator elements (there may be more than one) that contain that point.

Mapping functions registered with the attribute space service, discussed in §3.4.1, are used together with the navigation function to associate data items from input data sets with accumulator elements. The coordinates of an input data item are first mapped by a chain of mapping functions from the native attribute space of the input data set to the attribute space for the accumulator, and the navigation function is then used to locate the matching accumulator elements. In addition, an accumulator data type provides the information required by the query planning service, to be described in more detail in Section 3.4.6. ADR currently provides implementations of these functions for accumulators consisting of regular dense arrays with elements evenly spaced in an attribute space, such as raster images. Users, however, can replace these functions with their own implementations.

The data aggregation service also manages functions that implement various aggregation operations. In particular, it manages two kinds of functions: (a) *transformation functions* that take one data item as input and generate another data item as output; and (b) *aggregation functions* that are used to merge the value of an input data item with matching accumulator elements. Transformation functions are used to pre-process data items before aggregation. Aggregation functions are assumed to be commutative and associative and can be applied to individual data items in parallel and in any order. ADR is able to deal with both *distributive* and *algebraic* aggregation functions as defined by Gray *et. al.* [104].

An ADR aggregation function is associated with an accumulator data type, and actually consists of several functions. These include a *data aggregation function* that takes an input data item and a matching accumulator element and aggregates the value of the input data item into the accumulator element. An *initialization function* is used to properly initialize the individual accumulator elements before any aggregation takes place (e.g., with the identity value for the data aggregation function). A *finalization function* postprocesses the accumulator into the desired final output after all the data aggregation is complete. To allow for efficient parallel execution of the aggregation operations, an aggregation function can optionally provide an *accumulator aggregation function*, which merges the values of a set of accumulator elements with another matching set of accumulator elements (e.g., to merge accumulators located on different processors). Such a function allows additional flexibility for the query planning service to generate efficient query execution plans.

Currently, aggregation functions are statically linked. We plan to provide dynamic linking facilities in the future. Functions are specified by a (function name, object file name) pair. The query interface service uses namespace information from the data aggregation service to allow the user to find the set of transformation functions and aggregation functions that can be applied to a given data set.

3.4.5   Query Interface Service

The query interface service has two functions. First, it allows clients to find out what data sets are available and what functions and indices are associated with each data set. Second, it allows clients to formulate and present valid queries.

As a part of the first function, the query interface service allows clients to browse all the namespaces in ADR:

- attribute spaces,

- data sets,

- indices,

- placement algorithms,

- mapping functions,

- transformation functions, and

- aggregation functions.

As part of the second function, the query interface service ensures that for each query:

- the domain of the transformation function selected is the same as that of the input data set (i.e. the types are the same),

- the range of the transformation function has the same type as the domain of the aggregation function, and

- the chain of mapping functions is consistent (that is, all the types and shapes match) and the input attribute space of the first mapping function matches the native attribute space of the data set selected.

Metadata necessary for ADR to perform the two functions is managed by the database system administrator and maintained by the query interface service.

3.4.6 Query Planning Service

To efficiently integrate data retrieval and processing on a parallel machine, ADR manages the allocation and scheduling of all resources, including processor, memory, disk and network . The main goals of query planning in ADR are (a) to ensure that main memory is used effectively, so that paging never occurs (which could interfere with explicit ADR I/O requests) and (b) to balance the workload effectively, so that all resources (processors, disks, network) are kept busy as much as possible.

The task of the query planning service is to determine a schedule for the use of the available resources to satisfy a set of queries. Given the stylized nature of the computations supported by ADR, use of several of these resources is not independent (e.g., it is not possible to use disk without having memory to store the data being transferred from disk). In addition, the associative and commutative nature of the aggregation operations must be leveraged to form loosely synchronized schedules – the schedules for individual processors need not proceed in lock-step and only need to synchronize infrequently.

The ADR query planning service creates schedules based on requirements for memory, processor, and network . The input to the planning service consists of: (a) the list of *chunks* that need to be processed, their locations on disk, and the region of the output attribute space that each of them maps to, (b) the dependencies between *chunks* – dependencies may occur when multiple data sets are being processed simultaneously, (c) a description of the accumulator, including its size in the underlying attribute space and the extent of each accumulator element in the attribute space, and (d) the amount of memory available on each processor.

Query planning occurs in two steps; *tiling* and *workload partitioning*, described below. A query plan specifies how parts of the final output are computed and the order the input data chunks are retrieved for processing. The output of the planning service consists of a set of ordered lists of *chunks*, one list per disk in the machine configuration. Each list consists of a sequence of sublists separated by synchronization markers. The operations in each sublist can be performed in any order; all operations in a sublist must be completed before any operation in the subsequent sublist can be initiated. This restriction is enforced to ensure schedulability.

We now briefly describe how these resources are considered during query planning, assuming a shared-nothing database architecture.

Tiling – Optimizing Memory Usage. ADR uses memory for three purposes – to hold the data read from disk or received from the network, to hold the accumulators for the aggregation operations, and to hold the final output data set.

If enough memory is available for all three purposes, operations for all *chunks* in a sublist are scheduled together. Otherwise, memory is first allocated to hold the buffers needed for incoming input data and the remaining memory is partitioned between the other two uses.

ADR manages the memory allocated for input and accumulator (output) chunks by executing a tiling step before query execution. In this step either input chunks or accumulator chunks are partitioned into tiles, so that the total size of the chunks in a tile fits into the main memory in each processor. Thus, the planning service can generate a plan that retrieves each input data chunk request just once and bring into memory on demand the required portion of the matching accumulator. When the system runs out of memory during query processing, accumulator elements with partial results must be written back to disk. The advantage of this approach is that all processing for a data chunk can be performed while the chunk is in memory.

Alternatively, the planning service can partition the accumulator into chunks that are small enough to fit entirely in memory, and have all the processors work on each accumulator chunk in turn. This approach computes the final output one chunk at a time, and avoids the disk writes generated by the previous approach. However, input data chunks that intersect with multiple accumulator chunks must be retrieved multiple times. These memory management strategies are similar to the strip-mining and/or blocking operations performed for optimizing cache usage for matrix operations [76, 152, 188].

Workload Partitioning – Load Balancing   The query planning service considers two strategies for workload partitioning for each accumulator tile. The first strategy, referred to as *input partitioning*, requires each processor to generate an independent intermediate result in an accumulator using the data aggregation function, based on the chunks that are stored on its local disks. The accumulators are merged using the accumulator aggregation function to obtain the final output. This yields correct results due to the order-independent nature of the processing. The second strategy, referred to as *output partitioning*, partitions the final output; the data needed to compute the portion of the output assigned to a processor is forwarded to it by all the other processors in the machine configuration.

The choice between these approaches is based on several factors, including the distribution of the data in the output attribute space, the placement of the input data chunks needed to answer the query on disk, and the machine characteristics (i.e. the relative costs of computation, interprocessor communication and disk accesses). Input partitioning is only possible if the aggregation function selected by the query provides an accumulator aggregation function. However, this strategy may generate less interprocessor communication than output partitioning, since only the accumulators are communicated among the processors, whereas the input data set must be communicated for output partitioning.

For the applications targeted by ADR, accumulators are often much smaller than the input data required to satisfy a query. Output partitioning, on the other hand, has a smaller memory requirement than input partitioning, since the accumulators are effectively partitioned among the memories of all processors. Selecting between the two strategies for a given query requires evaluating the tradeoff between communication costs and memory usage.

3.4.7   Query Execution Service

The query execution service manages all the resources in the system using the schedule created by the planning service. The primary feature of the ADR query execution service is its ability to integrate data retrieval and processing for a wide variety of applications. It achieves this in two ways. First, it creates a *query environment* consisting of the set of functions that capture application-specific aspects of the processing. The query environment includes: (1) the access functions for individual input data items; (2) the iterator to iterate over the input data items in a chunk; (3) the transformation function; (4) the sequence of mapping functions that are to be applied to map each input data item to the corresponding accumulator elements; and (5) the aggregation functions needed to compute the output.

In effect, explicitly maintaining this environment allows the query execution service to push the processing operations into the storage manager and allows processing operations to be performed directly on the buffer used to hold data arriving from disk. This avoids one or more levels of copying that would be needed in a layered architecture where the storage manager and the processing belonged to different layers.

Second, this service overlaps the disk operations, network operations and the actual processing as much as possible. It does this by maintaining explicit queues for each kind of operation (data retrieval, message sends and receives, processing) and switching between them as required. Appropriate functions are invoked whenever a chunk arrives, either from the local disks or from the network interface. These functions iterate through the data items in a chunk, apply the transformation function to each data item, map the transformed data items to accumulator elements using the mapping function, and finally aggregate the data items that map to each accumulator element. This approach has the advantage of being able to fully overlap the I/O, communication, and processing operations even for applications where the amount of work applied to each retrieved data chunk varies widely.

The processing of a query on a back-end processor progresses through the following phases for each tile:

- **Initialization**. Accumulator chunks in the current tile are allocated space in memory and initialized. If an existing output data set is required to initialize accumulator elements, an output chunk is retrieved by the processor that has the chunk on its local disk, and the chunk is forwarded to the processors that require it.

- **Local Reduction**. Input data chunks on the local disks of each back-end processor are retrieved and aggregated into the accumulator chunks allocated in each processor's memory in phase 1.

- **Global Combine**. Partial results computed in each processor in phase 2 are combined across all processors to compute final results.

- **Output Handling**. The final output chunks for the current tile are computed from the corresponding accumulator chunks computed in phase three. If the query creates a new data set, output chunks are declustered across the available disks, and each output chunk is written to the assigned disk. If the query updates an already existing data set, the updated output chunks are written back to their original locations on the disks.

A query iterates through these phases repeatedly until all tiles have been processed and the entire output data set is handled. When multiple queries are processed simultaneously by the ADR back-end, each query independently progresses through the four query execution phases.

The query execution service performs two kinds of synchronization. First, it enforces the synchronization indicated by the synchronization markers in the list of chunks to be retrieved from every disk (computed by the planning service). That is, the operations between a pair of markers can be performed in any order; all operations before a marker must be completed before any operation after the marker can be initiated. This restriction is used to avoid deadlocks.

The second type of synchronization attempts to preserve load balance by reordering operations. If a particular processor is unable to keep up with its peers, the other processors reorder their operations to reduce the amount of data that is sent to that processor. This mechanism can be used only between synchronization markers.

3.5   Customization Examples

To illustrate ADR's customization features, we use three application examples. First, we show customization for the AVHRR satellite database described in §3.3. This example is loosely based on Titan [45, 234], a prototype data server capable of producing composite images out of raw remotely-sensed data.

The second customization example is for the Virtual Microscope [5, 93], a system for serving digitized high-power light microscope data. The final example is a system for storing data produced as part of a complete simulation of bay and estuary hydrodynamics and chemistry [162]. In this example, the ADR database stores the output from a hydrodynamics simulation, which can then be used multiple times to perform various simulations of chemical transport and reactions in the bay/estuary, for example to study pollution or oil spill scenarios.

3.5.1   AVHRR Database

The AVHRR data set is partitioned into IFOV chunks based on the geometry of the IFOVs and the performance characteristics of the disks used to store the data. On the machine used for Titan, one reasonable partitioning creates chunks of 204x204 IFOVs – the size of each chunk is 187 KB. The format of the chunk is specified using an iterator that understands the multi-spectral nature of the values.

The three-dimensional latitude-longitude-time attribute space that underlies the IFOVs is registered as a *base* attribute space with the attribute space service. An access function is used to extract the coordinate attributes from an IFOV, and the coordinates of the four corner IFOVs are used to compute, for each chunk, a minimum bounding rectangle in the latitude-longitude-time attribute space.

The default ADR declustering and clustering algorithms described in §3.4.2 can be used to assign disk locations for the IFOV chunks. The data loading service records all the relevant information about the AVHRR data set, and moves the IFOV chunks to their assigned disk locations. A simplified R^*-tree suffices for indexing this data set, and uses the spatio-temporal bounds of the IFOV chunks as access keys. The spatio-temporal bounds are specified as a region in the latitude-longitude-time attribute space. The R^*-tree, as shown in Figure 3.1, indexes over the IFOV chunks, not the individual IFOVs.

Because the standard AVHRR data product is presented in the Goodes map projection, a three-dimensional attribute space jointly defined by the Goodes map projection and time is registered with the attribute space service as another *base* attribute space, and a mapping function is defined accordingly to map points from the latitude-longitude-time attribute space to this attribute space. This allows the indexing service to map the *MBR* of each IFOV chunk from the latitude-longitude-time attribute space to the Goodes time attribute space, and build an index for the AVHRR data set on the Goodes time attribute space. With this additional index, a query region then can be specified in terms of the Goodes map projection. A two-dimensional spatial attribute space can be derived from either of the three-dimensional spatio-temporal attribute spaces, with a mapping function that discards the temporal coordinate. This derived spatial attribute space is used for the standard AVHRR data product.

As described in §3.3, the transformation function registered with the data aggregation service performs a sequence of corrections to each IFOV. In addition, it also computes the Normalized Difference Vegetation Index (NDVI) [135] for each IFOV, using corrected values from the first two bands of each IFOV. A registered aggregation function selects the NDVI value with the "best" IFOV among all IFOVs that map to a single output pixel, based on the clarity of the IFOV and the angular position of the satellite when the observation was made.

A typical query specifies an area of interest, usually corresponding to a geopolitical area of world, and a temporal bound, which gets translated into a query region in either of the two *base* attribute spaces. The query chooses the AVHRR-correction/NDVI-generation algorithm as the transformation function, and the previously described NDVI aggregation algorithm as the aggregation function. The query also specifies the desired resolution of and where to send the output image (e.g., to disk or to another program for further processing).

The query interface service validates the received query, and the query planning service generates an efficient schedule by taking into account the available machine resources. The query execution service carries out data retrieval and processing according to the generated schedule, and sends the output image to the desired destination.

3.5.2   Virtual Microscope

The Virtual Microscope data set for a slide is a three-dimensional image consisting of an array of RGB pixel values, with two dimensions (x and y) representing a focal plane within a slide, and the third dimension (z) representing multiple focal planes. The data set for a slide is partitioned into rectangular chunks of pixels, with each chunk containing about 100K pixels on the machine where the high-performance implementation of the Virtual Microscope currently executes. The format of an RGB chunk is specified with a simple iterator that allows access to the pixels in raster order, and also understands the layout of the RGB data.

The three-dimensional attribute space underlying the data (effectively a 3-D regular grid, with the resolution of the grid determined by the magnification of the digitized microscope image) is registered as an ADR base attribute space. The *MBR* of an RGB chunk is computed based on the magnification of the image. The default ADR declustering and clustering algorithms can be used to assign disk locations for the RGB chunks. The data loading service records all the relevant information about the data set for a slide, and builds an index for the data set. The index is a table that is accessed by the (**x,y,z**) location of a data chunk within the slide via a simple computation, and returns the disk location for a given RGB chunk.

The output image for a Virtual Microscope query is a subset of the data for a given slide, at a requested magnification less than or equal to that of the stored data (in powers of two down from the stored image). Therefore, three-dimensional attribute spaces for all the lower magnifications are also registered with the attribute space service as derived attribute spaces.

A query region can be specified as a subset of the base attribute space for the slide, and the corresponding regions of either the base attribute space or one of the derived spaces for lower magnifications is specified for the output of the query. The mapping function between the base and derived attribute spaces is a straightforward computation to map a region of the higher magnification space to the corresponding pixel in the lower magnification space.

No transformation function for the raw digitized image data is currently required. If some correction to the raw data were desired, it could be specified as a transformation function. A registered aggregation function currently performs subsampling to produce a lower magnification image from the stored high magnification data, although a weighted average of all the pixels that map to the same output pixel could also be used.

We are also considering aggregation functions that reconstruct portions of the slide that cut through multiple focal planes, to look at features that cross focal planes. This form of image reconstruction would treat the slide data as a true three-dimensional data set, allowing better visualization of the data. The cost, on the other hand, is the computation required to perform the computational geometry determining the data that has to be accessed and to produce the output image from the stored data.

A typical query specifies a region of the slide in one focal plane at the desired magnification, which gets translated into a query region in the base attribute space. The query chooses the aggregation function (e.g., subsampling or weighted average), and also specifies where to send the output image (e.g., back into ADR on disk, or to a client program). As in the AVHRR database example, the internal ADR services (query interface, query planning, and query execution) are then performed to generate the output image that is sent to the desired destination.

The above description of the Virtual Microscope services in ADR assumes that the RGB slide image data is stored in an uncompressed format. The current implementation of the Virtual Microscope also allows data to be stored in a JPEG compressed format, while still allowing direct indexing of data chunks via their location on the slide. In addition, after the data chunks are uncompressed to perform aggregation to generate the desired magnification image, the chunks are again compressed before being sent over the (potentially wide-area) network to a client. This scheme minimizes network and disk bandwidth requirements, potentially improving client response time, at the expense of extra work for compression and decompression at the server and client.

3.5.3   Bay and Estuary Simulation

For this application, the hydrodynamics simulation is used to generate water flow output (e.g., velocity and elevation values at the grid nodes). The output of the hydrodynamics simulation is partitioned into chunks, each containing velocity and elevation values over a set of time steps at a subset of the grid points. These outputs are stored into the ADR database using the data loading service.

The chemical transport simulator requests hydrodynamics data from ADR to compute transport of the various chemicals being simulated. ADR performs the data retrieval of the hydrodynamics simulation output and the post-processing required to generate the input data for the chemical transport code, using the UT-PROJ [51] projection code for the aggregation service first mentioned in §3.2. UT-PROJ also provides the mapping function for the attribute space service, for mapping between the hydrodynamics grid and the chemistry grid. The role of ADR in coupling the hydrodynamics and chemical transport simulators is shown in Figures 3.4–3.5.

The hydrodynamics simulator simulates circulation patterns in coastal shelves and estuaries with an unstructured grid. The elements of the grid are two-dimensional triangles, or three-dimensional tetrahedra. The elevations and the velocities at all vertices of the grid are computed every time step, and must be written into ADR. The attribute space for this data to be written into ADR is therefore a three-dimensional spatial grid, with an additional dimension for simulation time. This attribute space must be registered with ADR as a base attribute space.

Data blocks are the basic unit for data storage and retrieval in ADR. Thus, the data generated by the hydrodynamics module must be partitioned into blocks using an unstructured grid partitioning algorithm (e.g., recursive coordinate bisec-

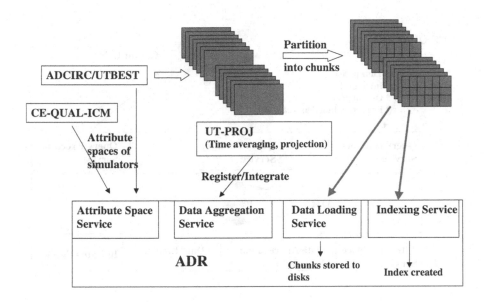

Figure 3.4
ADR hydrodynamics simulation data input.

tion [20]). To allow data blocks to be accessed by their spatio-temporal attributes, an index (e.g., an R-tree) is created, with a bounding box for each data block used as the access key. The bounding boxes are also used by the default ADR declustering and clustering algorithms in the data loading service, which determines the location on the disk farm to which each data block is assigned.

The hydrodynamics inputs required by a chemistry code, such as CE-QUAL-ICM [44], are the fluid depths, flow rates and turbulent eddy viscosity coefficients. CE-QUAL-ICM also uses a (two- or) three-dimensional unstructured grid, but the grid consists of hexahedral elements, as compared to the triangular elements used by the hydrodynamics code. Since CE-QUAL-ICM is a finite-volume algorithm, the data is required at the midpoints of cell edges. Due to differences in the time scales of interest, the simulation time steps used by CE-QUAL-ICM are usually much larger than those used by hydrodynamics simulators such as ADCIRC and

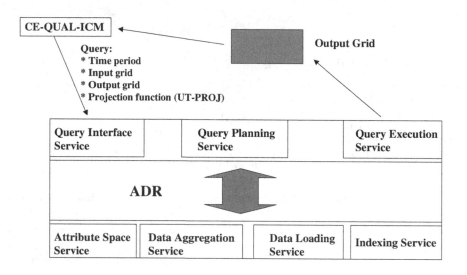

Figure 3.5
ADR chemical transport simulation data retrieval.

UTBEST [50, 177]. This implies that it is not sufficient to access one time step
of the hydrodynamics data from ADR, so the aggregation function in ADR must
perform time averaging.

In addition, because the unstructured grid used by CE-QUAL-ICM is not the
same as the one used in the hydrodynamics code, the hydrodynamics data has to
be projected onto the grid for CE-QUAL-ICM. Therefore, the unstructured grid
for CE-QUAL-ICM must also be registered as a base attribute space with the ADR
attribute space service. The functions for performing the projection, both the ADR
mapping function in the attribute space service and the aggregation function for
the data aggregation service, are provided by the UT-PROJ code. A typical query
from CE-QUAL-ICM specifies

- the hydrodynamics grid of interest,

- the chemistry grid that the output will be computed into,

- the mapping function and aggregation function to use (e.g., from UT-PROJ), and

- the time period of interest in the hydrodynamics simulation.

No transformation function is currently required for this application.

The query also specifies where to send the output data (wherever CE-QUAL-ICM is running). For this application, it is desirable to allow one query to specify multiple sets of time steps to be aggregated, because CE-QUAL-ICM will otherwise send multiple queries to ADR that are identical except for the time period specified. Again, as for the AVHRR database example, the internal ADR services (query interface, query planning, and query execution) are then performed to generate the output grid data that is sent to the desired destination.

Because ADR and both the hydrodynamics and chemistry simulations are parallel programs, an efficient mechanism for moving large amounts of data between parallel programs is required. The data transport mechanism could be implemented directly by completely specifying the communication between all source and destination processes individually, or more conveniently can be performed using the Maryland Meta-Chaos library [81]. Meta-Chaos is a runtime library that has been developed to facilitate exchange of distributed data structures between two parallel programs, and generates the required communication between pairs of processes from a high-level specification.

3.6 Experimental Results

The ADR services have been implemented and tested on an IBM SP-2 at the University of Maryland. The Maryland SP-2 consists of 16 RS6000/390 processing nodes, running AIX 4.2, with six disks (IBM Starfire 7200) attached to each processing node. The ADR is implemented in C++ and is compiled with the IBM C/C++ compiler. For portability, the ADR query execution service uses the POSIX lio_listio interface for its non-blocking I/O operation, and MPI [240] as its underlying inter-processor communication layer.

To show the effectiveness of ADR, we have customized the various ADR services to provide the functionality of the three applications described in §3.2. In this section, we present preliminary performance results, including comparisons of the original custom-built systems for Titan and the Virtual Microscope with their respective counterparts implemented in ADR. In these experiments, we focus on the performance of the query execution service. Therefore, the execution times given in this section only show the query processing time in the query execution service. They do not include the time to send the output to clients.

3.6.1 Satellite Data Processing: Titan

Titan [45, 234] is a custom-built image database for storing remotely sensed data, and is currently operational on the Maryland SP-2, containing about 24 GB of data from the AVHRR sensor on the National Oceanic and Atmospheric Administration NOAA-7 satellite. Titan dedicates one of the sixteen SP-2 processing nodes as a front-end node, which interacts with Java GUI client programs, and uses the other fifteen nodes as the back-end processing and data retrieval nodes. Four disks on each of the back-end nodes are used to store the AVHRR data set, and the same declustering and clustering algorithms provided by ADR (see Section 3.4.2) are used for placing the data chunks onto the sixty disks.

Each data item in the AVHRR data set is referred to as an *instantaneous field of view* (IFOV), and consists of eight attributes – three key attributes that specify spatio-temporal coordinates and five data attributes that contain observations in different parts of the electromagnetic spectrum. An AVHRR data chunk consists of 204×204 IFOVs. In prior work [45], we showed that Titan delivers good performance for both small and large queries. ADR is customized by implementing wrapper functions that directly call the computational kernel of Titan. This includes customizing the default ADR back-end function that is responsible for invoking the projection function and aggregation function for each data chunk.

Several sample queries were used to evaluate the performance of the ADR implementation against that of Titan. These queries select IFOVs that correspond to various areas of the world over a ten day period and each generates a composite image. The values of the output pixels are obtained by first computing the Normalized Difference Vegetation Index (NDVI) [135] for each IFOV, using corrected values from the first two bands of each IFOV, and then selecting the "best" IFOV among all IFOVs that map to the same output pixel, based on the clarity of the IFOV and the angular position of the satellite when the observation was made.

Table 3.1 shows the total amount of data read from disk to resolve the sample queries, and Table 3.2 shows the query processing time for both Titan and the ADR implementation. Note that one of the SP-2 nodes (and its four disks) was not available at the time the experiments were conducted, so all results reported for this application were obtained using fourteen back-end processes.

The results show that ADR performance is very close to that of Titan. Table 3.3 shows the time both implementations spent processing the data chunks (the

Query	Australia	Africa	S. America	N. America	Global
Input Size	65 MB	191 MB	155 MB	375 MB	1.6 GB

Table 3.1
Data volume read for Titan query resolution.

System	Australia	iAfrica	S. America	N. America	Global
Titan	3.8	11.0	8.5	22.3	107.5
ADR	3.9	10.7	8.4	23.5	113.1

Table 3.2
Titan and ADR query processing times (seconds).

computation column), communicating and merging the accumulator elements (the *communication* column), and the time spent for submitting and polling the disk reads plus other software overhead (the *others* column).

The table shows that both implementations spent most of their time processing the data chunks. ADR, however, incurs more overhead in the computation and the communication than Titan. The computation overhead is caused by the wrapper functions, which in turn invoke the Titan computation functions. The communication overhead comes from each Titan back-end process only handling one query at a time, so is therefore able to estimate the sizes of all incoming messages to be received, whereas an ADR back-end process may receive messages from multiple simultaneous queries so cannot accurately predict message sizes.

As a result, each Titan processor can post a non-blocking receive as early as possible, while the current implementation of the ADR back-end probes for the size of an incoming message before posting a corresponding receive. We are redesigning the communication subsystem of ADR to reduce the communication overhead.

The query processing time does not include the time for generating the query plan. In both implementations, generating a query plan after the index is read from disk takes less than a second. However, Titan uses the front-end to generate a query plan and distributes the plan to all the back-end nodes, whereas ADR has

System	Total Time	Computation	Communication	Others
Titan	107.5	104.3	1.3	1.9
ADR	113.1	107.9	3.9	1.3

Table 3.3
Titan and ADR global query processing times (seconds).

System	Total Query Time	Computation	Others
VM	1.74	0.36	1.38
ADR	3.22	1.39	1.86

Table 3.4
VM and ADR query processing times (seconds).

all back-end nodes generate their own query plans. Because there is only one index defined in Titan and the index is shared by all Titan queries, the Titan front-end is able to load the index from disk once and keep it in memory.

ADR, on the other hand, reads the index into memory for each query and discards it after locating all the data chunk of interest. This is because there might be multiple indices in the ADR system, and caching multiple indices in memory may significantly reduce the amount of memory available on the back-end nodes for query processing. The index for the AVHRR data set is about 11 MB, and takes about 3.5 seconds to load into memory for both implementations.

3.6.2   Virtual Microscope

The Virtual Microscope (VM) system [5, 93] provides the ability to access high-power, high-resolution digital images of entire pathology slides, and sample the images for display via a local or remote client. Each data chunk consists of about 67500 pixels and is of size 202 KB. For this experiment, the data chunks are distributed across eight of the Maryland SP-2 nodes by the ADR default declustering/clustering algorithm, using one disk per node.

A VM query specifies a high-power digitized microscopy image, the region of interest and the desired magnification for display. An output image is computed by subsampling the high-power input image. No interprocessor communication between server processes is required in the current implementation of the Virtual Microscope. A sample query that retrieves 374 data chunks in total (75 MB) is used to evaluate the performance of the two implementations.

As shown in Table 3.4, the query processing time for ADR is about 85 percent slower than that of VM. Because the Virtual Microscope currently uses a very simple subsampling algorithm, little computation is performed on the data chunks. In fact, a large percentage of the query execution time for VM is spent waiting for its disk requests to complete. With so little computation actually taking place within the system's main loop, high overhead due to excess virtual function invocation is incurred by the ADR implementation.

To reduce the overhead for applications that require little computation on each data block, such as the current implementation of the Virtual Microscope, the ADR aggregation base class from the data aggregation service allows the user to overload its default data chunk processing function. The default data chunk processing function invokes the appropriate user-defined functions from various services for every input element to properly aggregate the input elements with the accumulator. It is general enough to handle all data sets and functions registered with ADR, but the disadvantage is extra overhead for invoking the virtual functions. To avoid the overhead for function invocation, the user can optionally provide a more efficient implementation of the data chunk processing function while customizing the ADR aggregation base class.

The Virtual Microscope implementation uses this optimized interface to ADR, which improved performance significantly. An early implementation in ADR that used the original interface was almost three times slower than the current implementation. We are still reducing functional call overhead in the implementation. If an application requires large amounts of computation to answer queries, the ADR function call overhead would be insignificant. Since this is not the case for the Virtual Microscope, the overhead becomes a performance bottleneck, when compared to a fully custom implementation. The experience with the Virtual Microscope shows that sophisticated compiler optimizations (inter-procedural analysis) may be very useful in optimizing the performance of the customized processing functions required by ADR applications.

The functionality of the Virtual Microscope will not be limited to simply serving microscopy images at various magnification. Current and future projects that use the Virtual Microscope server infrastructure involve image compression/decompression, three-dimensional image reconstruction, and other complex image processing operations, hence require more computation to be performed on the data chunks. This offsets the seemingly high cost observed by the current VM implementation with ADR.

3.6.3   Water Contamination Studies

In this application, we have used ADR to couple a hydrodynamics simulator to a chemical transport simulator. In our implementation of the coupled simulation system, we use a hydrodynamics simulator, called ADCIRC [177], developed by the US Army Corps of Engineers to model circulation patterns in coastal seas, bays, and estuaries, and a chemical transport simulator, called UT-TRANS, developed at the Texas Institute for Computational and Applied Mathematics (TICAM) at the University of Texas at Austin.

The hydrodynamics simulator simulates the flow of water in a bay, modeled by a

2-D unstructured grid, and the chemical transport simulator simulates the transport of a chemical (e.g., oil) on the same grid. The chemical transport simulator uses the output of the hydrodynamics simulator to simulate the transport of the chemical. Because transport of chemicals does not affect the computed hydrodynamics values, the flow values can be generated once and stored, and used later by the chemical transport simulator for different simulations.

The chemical transport simulator uses coarser time steps than the hydrodynamics simulator. Thus, velocity and elevation values over several time steps of the hydrodynamics simulation need to be averaged to generate initial values for each time step in the chemical transport simulation. This averaging operation involves computation of gradients of elevations and weighted averaging of velocity values at each time step. The averaged velocity and elevation values at the grid points are then converted into fluxes, used for computing the transport of the chemical at a simulation step, on the edges of the grid by the chemical transport simulator using a projection code (UT-PROJ, also developed at TICAM).

We have customized ADR to store, retrieve, and process the outputs of the hydrodynamics simulator as needed by the chemical transport simulator. The output from the hydrodynamics simulator was partitioned into chunks. A chunk contains velocity and elevation values over a set of time steps at a subset of the grid points. In the experiments, we used a grid that models Galveston bay with 2113 grid points. Each chunk is 128 KB, and contains 33 grid points and 323 time steps for the hydrodynamics simulator. The chunks were distributed across disks using an application-specific algorithm. First, chunks were sorted with respect to the minimum time step values in each chunk in ascending order, then each chunk was assigned to a disk in round-robin fashion so that each disk attached to a processor has an almost equal number of chunks covering almost the same set of time steps. A spatial index, containing a bounding box for each chunk and the locations of the chunks on the disks, is created for each processor.

The query from the chemical transport code specifies the time period of interest, and the hydrodynamics data set of interest. ADR performs the retrieval and averaging of velocity and elevation values (from the data set of interest) over the time steps that fall into the time period of interest. Each processor retrieves the chunks stored on its local disks and creates partial results. The partial results are then exchanged between processors to create the final values. Finally, the results are sent to the chemical transport simulator.

Table 3.5 shows the query processing time for the ADR query execution service. The ADR back-end was run on eight processors using two disks on each processor and on sixteen processors using one disk per processor. The chemical transport

P	Period	Total	Computation	Communication	Other
8	360 secs	2.00	1.45	0.18	0.37
16	360 secs	1.54	0.91	0.24	0.39
8	7200 secs	20.84	20.17	0.17	0.50
16	7200 secs	10.96	10.24	0.21	0.51

Table 3.5
ADR water contamination query processing times (seconds).

simulator is a sequential program and was run on the host processor of the IBM SP-2. The timing results do not include the time to send the results to the chemical transport code. Two queries were used for each configuration; one with a time period of interest of 360 seconds (24 time steps of the hydrodynamics simulator) and the other over 7200 seconds (480 time steps).

As the table shows, when the number of processors increases, the total query processing time decreases. However, this decrease is small for small queries for two reasons. First, the computation time does not decrease linearly due to the overhead of initializing the accumulator array. In the current implementation the accumulator array is replicated across all processors. Each processor has to create the full accumulator array and initialize it. Second, the overheads from inter-processor communication (the *communication* column), and the time spent for submitting and polling disk reads and other system overheads (the *others* column) take a larger percent of total execution time for small queries than for larger queries.

3.7 Current Status and Future Work

In this chapter, we described the Active Data Repository, a customizable parallel database system that integrates storage, retrieval, and processing of multidimensional data sets. We summarized the services provided by ADR and illustrated customization of those services for a particular application. We have also provided performance results showing that the satellite data processing and Virtual Microscope applications implemented with the ADR services perform almost as well as custom implementations, and that the bay/estuary simulation system implemented in ADR scales well up to 16 processors.

We are optimizing ADR services and exploring planning algorithms and cost models for the query planning service. As part of that investigation, we are also characterizing the scalability of the ADR algorithms, with the goal of showing that the ADR design and implementation scales both to large numbers of processors (and disks) and to very large disk-based data sets. We are also investigating techniques for extending ADR to tertiary storage, to efficiently store and process data sets that are too large to fit into secondary storage.

Finally, we are beginning to investigate how the ADR services for multidimensional data sets can be integrated with services provided by more general purpose databases (e.g., relational or object-relational commercial databases). Our goal in that research is to define standard ways of integrating ADR services into existing database systems. That would allow, for instance, the ability to do a join between data stored in a relational database and multidimensional data stored in ADR and perform the join efficiently.

4 ADIO: A Framework for High-Performance, Portable Parallel I/O

Rajeev Thakur, William Gropp and Ewing Lusk

Parallel computers are being used increasingly to solve large, I/O intensive applications in many different disciplines. A limiting factor, however, has been the lack of a standard, portable application programming interface (API) for parallel I/O. Rather than a single, standard API, multiple APIs are supported by different vendors and research projects.

Many commercial parallel file systems (e.g., IBM PIOFS [120] and Intel PFS [128]) and research parallel file systems (e.g., PPFS [119], Galley [196], HFS [160], Scotch [100], and PIOUS [189]) provide their own APIs. In addition, several I/O libraries with special APIs have been developed (e.g., PASSION [260], Panda [230], Chameleon I/O [98], SOLAR [270], Jovian [19], and ChemIO [195]). Moreover different APIs are used by systems that support persistent objects (e.g., Ptool [108], ELFS [141], and SHORE [38]). Only recently has MPI-IO [180] emerged as the standard interface for parallel I/O.

In this chapter, we describe the design of ADIO, an abstract device interface for parallel I/O. ADIO serves as a mechanism for implementing any parallel I/O API portably and efficiently on multiple file systems. Any API can be implemented portably atop ADIO, and only ADIO need be implemented separately on each different file system.

We developed ADIO before MPI-IO emerged as a standard, as a means to implement commonly used I/O APIs on different machines, enabling applications written to those APIs to run portably. We also felt that the resulting experience users gained with different APIs would help in the definition of a standard. Hence, we used ADIO to implement the Intel PFS interface and subsets of MPI-IO and IBM PIOFS interfaces on PFS, PIOFS, Unix, and NFS file systems. We were able to run applications that use these interfaces portably on the IBM SP, Intel Paragon, and networks of workstations.

Now that MPI-IO is the standard API, we are using ADIO to implement MPI-IO. We stress that ADIO is not intended to be a new API itself (i.e., it is not intended to be used directly by application programmers). Instead, it is a strategy for implementing other APIs portably.

The remainder of this chapter is organized as follows. We first discuss the role of ADIO in the Scalable I/O Project in §4.1. In §4.2 we explain the ADIO concept. We describe the design of ADIO in §4.3 and discuss its use in implementing APIs such as the MPI-IO, PFS, PIOFS, PASSION, and Panda interfaces in §4.4. This is followed by performance results in §4.5. Finally, we describe the evolution of

MPI-IO and the role of ADIO in the implementation of MPI-IO in §4.6.

4.1   The Role of ADIO in the SIO Project

As the Scalable I/O project began, many experimental parallel I/O systems were being investigated, and the vendors of the projects' testbed systems, Intel and IBM, offered incompatible parallel file system interfaces. A pressing need existed for a way to execute existing parallel applications on both testbed systems and also to support experimentation with alternate APIs. These considerations led to our decision to design an intermediate layer between the vendor-supported file systems (both parallel and otherwise) and the application layer. This portability layer would translate the high-level calls made by any of a potentially large number of both experimental and vendor-supplied APIs into the lower-level calls of a relatively small number of APIs supported by vendor file systems.

The APIs supported initially were the two APIs offered by the testbed vendors: IBM's PIOFS and Intel's PFS. Successful implementation of ADIO permitted existing applications, written for either of the testbeds, to execute on both. The overhead introduced by the intermediate layer could be precisely measured by an application written for, say, PIOFS, in two ways:

- calling PIOFS directly, and

- calling the PIOFS interface implemented atop ADIO, which then called native PIOFS routines in response.

The overhead so measured was small [261].

In the long run, ADIO proved most useful as an implementation technique for a third API, the MPI-IO interface, which was being developed during the same period. The low-level systems supported initially were the parallel file systems PFS and PIOFS, the Unix file system, and NFS. During the project, this collection was extended to include other vendors' high-performance file systems, and the low-level application programming interface (LLAPI) that was developed by other groups in the SIO project [60].

4.2   The ADIO Concept

The main goal of ADIO is to facilitate a high-performance implementation of any existing or new parallel I/O API on any existing or new file system, as illustrated in Figure 4.1. ADIO consists of a small set of basic functions for performing parallel

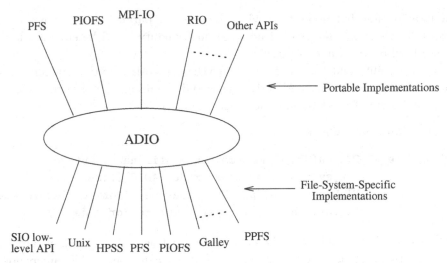

Figure 4.1
ADIO design concept.

I/O. Any parallel I/O API (including a file system interface) can be implemented in a portable fashion atop ADIO. ADIO in turn must be implemented in an optimized manner on each different file system separately. In other words, ADIO separates the machine-dependent and machine-independent aspects involved in implementing an API. The machine-independent part can be implemented portably atop ADIO. The machine-dependent part is ADIO itself, which must be implemented separately on each different system.

ADIO enables users to experiment with new APIs and new low-level file system interfaces. Once a new API is implemented atop ADIO, it becomes available to all file systems on which ADIO has been implemented. Similarly, once ADIO is implemented on a new file system, all APIs implemented atop ADIO become available on the new file system. This approach enables users to run applications on a wide range of platforms, regardless of the parallel I/O API used in the applications. A similar abstract device interface approach for communication has been used very successfully in the MPICH implementation of MPI [107].

4.3   ADIO Design

ADIO was designed to exploit the high-performance features of any file system, and any API can be expressed in terms of ADIO. We designed ADIO by first studying the interface and functionality provided by different parallel file systems and high-level libraries and then deciding how the functionality could be supported at the ADIO level portably and efficiently.

For portability and high performance, ADIO uses MPI [181] wherever possible. Hence, ADIO routines have MPI datatypes and communicators as arguments. Below, we describe the ADIO interface in more detail.

4.3.1 Open and Close

```
ADIO_File ADIO_Open(MPI_Comm comm, char *filename, int
          file_system, int access_mode, ADIO_Offset disp,
          MPI_Datatype etype, MPI_Datatype filetype, int iomode,
          MPI_Info *hints, int perm, int *error_code)
```

All opens are considered to be collective operations. The communicator `comm` specifies the participating processes. A process can open a file independently by using `MPI_COMM_SELF` as the communicator. The `file_system` parameter indicates the type of file system used. The `access_mode` parameter specifies the file access mode, which can be either `ADIO_CREATE`, `ADIO_RDONLY`, `ADIO_WRONLY`, `ADIO_RDWR`, `ADIO_DELETE_ON_CLOSE`, `ADIO_UNIQUE_OPEN`, `ADIO_EXCL`, `ADIO_APPEND`, or `ADIO_SEQUENTIAL`. These modes may be combined by using the bitwise-or operator.

The `disp`, `etype`, and `filetype` parameters are provided for supporting displacements, etypes, and filetypes as defined in MPI-IO's file view [180]. The `iomode` parameter is provided for supporting the I/O modes of Intel PFS [128]. The `MPI_Info` structure may be used to pass hints to the ADIO implementation for potential performance improvement. Examples of hints include file-layout specification, prefetching/caching information, file-access style, data-partitioning pattern, and information required for use on heterogeneous systems. Hints are purely optional; the calling program need not provide any hints, in which case ADIO uses default values. Similarly, the ADIO implementation is not obligated to use the specified hints. The `perm` parameter specifies the access permissions for the file. The success or failure of the open operation is returned in `error_code`. The ADIO_Open routine returns a file descriptor that must be used to perform all subsequent operations on the file.

Note that the displacement, etype, filetype, iomode, access mode, and hints associated with an open file can be changed by using the routine ADIO_Fcntl.

```
void ADIO_Close(ADIO_File fd, int *error_code)
```

The close operation is also collective — all tasks that opened the file must close it.

4.3.2   Contiguous Reads and Writes

void ADIO_ReadContig(ADIO_File fd, void *buf, int len, int file_ptr_type, ADIO_Offset offset, ADIO_Status *status, int *error_code)

Similarly ADIO_WriteContig.

ADIO provides separate routines for contiguous and noncontiguous accesses. The contiguous read/write routines are used when data to be read or written is contiguous in both memory and file. ADIO_ReadContig and ADIO_WriteContig are independent and blocking versions of the contiguous read and write calls. Independent means that a process may call the routine independent of other processes; blocking means that the resources specified in the call, such as buffers, may be reused after the routine returns. Nonblocking and collective versions of the contiguous read/write calls are described in §4.3.4 and §4.3.5, respectively.

For ADIO_ReadContig, buf is the address of the buffer in memory into which len contiguous bytes of data must be read from the file. The location in the file from which to read can be specified either in terms of an explicit offset from the start of the file or from the current location of the file pointer. ADIO supports individual file pointers for each process; shared file pointers are not directly supported for performance reasons. Shared file pointers can be implemented atop ADIO if necessary. The file_ptr_type parameter indicates whether the routine should use an explicit offset or individual file pointer. If file_ptr_type specifies the use of explicit offset, the offset itself is provided in the offset parameter. The offset parameter is ignored when file_ptr_type specifies the use of an individual file pointer. The file pointer can be moved by using the ADIO_SeekIndividual function, described in §4.3.6. The status parameter returns information about the operation, such as the amount of data actually read or written.

4.3.3   Noncontiguous Reads and Writes

void ADIO_ReadStrided(ADIO_File fd, void *buf, int count, MPI_Datatype datatype, int file_ptr_type, ADIO_Offset offset, ADIO_Status *status, int *error_code)

Similarly ADIO_WriteStrided.

Parallel applications often need to read or write data that is located in a noncontiguous fashion in files and even in memory. ADIO provides routines for specifying noncontiguous accesses with a single call. Noncontiguous access patterns can be represented in many ways, e.g., [197]; we chose to use MPI derived datatypes because they are very general and have been standardized as part of MPI. `ADIO_ReadStrided` and `ADIO_WriteStrided` are independent and blocking versions of the noncontiguous read and write calls; nonblocking and collective versions are described in §4.3.4 and §4.3.5, respectively. Note that these routines support all types of noncontiguous accesses that can be expressed in terms of MPI derived datatypes, not just simple uniform strides.

For `ADIO_ReadStrided`, `buf` is the address of the buffer in memory into which `count` items of type `datatype` (an MPI derived datatype) must be read from the file. The starting location in the file may be specified by using an explicit offset or individual file pointer. The noncontiguous storage pattern in the file is indicated by the `filetype` (an MPI derived datatype) specified in `ADIO_Open` or `ADIO_Fcntl`.

Note that `ADIO_ReadContig` and `ADIO_WriteContig` are special cases of `ADIO_ReadStrided` and `ADIO_WriteStrided`. We consider contiguous accesses separately, however, because they are directly supported by all file systems and may therefore be implemented efficiently.

4.3.4 Nonblocking Reads and Writes

```
void ADIO_IreadContig(ADIO_File fd, void *buf, int len, int
file_ptr_type, ADIO_Offset offset, ADIO_Request *request, int
*error_code)
```

```
void ADIO_IreadStrided(ADIO_File fd, void *buf, int count,
MPI_Datatype datatype, int file_ptr_type, ADIO_Offset offset,
ADIO_Request *request, int *error_code)
```

Similarly `ADIO_IwriteContig`, `ADIO_IwriteStrided`.

ADIO provides nonblocking versions of all read and write calls. A nonblocking routine may return before the read/write operation completes. Therefore, the resources specified in the call, such as buffers, may not be reused before testing for completion of the operation. Nonblocking routines return a `request` object that must be used to test for completion of the operation. The ADIO routines for testing the completion of a nonblocking operation are described in §4.3.7.

4.3.5 Collective Reads and Writes

```
void ADIO_ReadContigColl(ADIO_File fd, void *buf, int len, int
file_ptr_type, ADIO_Offset offset, ADIO_Status *status, int
*error_code)
```

```
void ADIO_ReadStridedColl(ADIO_File fd, void *buf, int count,
MPI_Datatype datatype, int file_ptr_type, ADIO_Offset offset,
ADIO_Status *status, int *error_code)
```

```
void ADIO_IreadContigColl(ADIO_File fd, void *buf, int len, int
file_ptr_type, ADIO_Offset offset, ADIO_Request *request, int
*error_code)
```

```
void ADIO_IreadStridedColl(ADIO_File fd, void *buf, int count,
MPI_Datatype datatype, int file_ptr_type, ADIO_Offset offset,
ADIO_Request *request, int *error_code)
```

`ADIO_WriteContigColl`, `ADIO_WriteStridedColl`, `ADIO_IwriteStridedColl` are analogous.

Several researchers have demonstrated that, for many common access patterns, collective I/O can greatly improve performance [74, 155, 230, 259].

To enable the use of collective I/O, ADIO provides collective versions of all read/write routines. A collective routine must be called by all processes in the group that opened the file. A collective routine, however, does not necessarily imply a barrier synchronization.

4.3.6   Seek

```
ADIO_Offset ADIO_SeekIndividual(ADIO_File fd, ADIO_Offset offset,
int whence, int *error_code)
```
This function can be used to change the position of the individual file pointer. The file pointer is set according to the value supplied for **whence**, which could be `ADIO_SEEK_SET`, `ADIO_SEEK_CUR`, or `ADIO_SEEK_END`. If **whence** is `ADIO_SEEK_SET`, the file pointer is set to `offset` bytes from the start of the file. If **whence** is `ADIO_SEEK_CUR`, the file pointer is set to `offset` bytes after its current location. If **whence** is `ADIO_SEEK_END`, the file pointer is set to `offset` bytes after the end of the file.

4.3.7   Test and Wait

It is necessary to test the completion of nonblocking operations before any of the resources specified in the nonblocking routine can be reused. ADIO provides three kinds of routines for this purpose: a quick test for completion that requires no further action (`ADIO_xxxxDone`), a test-and-complete (`ADIO_xxxxIcomplete`), and a wait-for-completion (`ADIO_xxxxComplete`). Separate routines exist for read and write operations.

```
int ADIO_ReadDone(ADIO_Request *request, ADIO_Status *status, int
error_code)
```

Similarly `ADIO_WriteDone`.

These routines check the **request** handle to determine whether the operation is complete and requires no further action. They return true if complete, and false otherwise.

```
int ADIO_ReadIcomplete(ADIO_Request *request, ADIO_Status *status,
int *error_code)
```

Similarly `ADIO_WriteIcomplete`.

If an operation is not complete, the above routines can be used. Note that these routines do not block waiting for the operation to complete. Instead, they perform some additional processing necessary to complete the operation. If the operation is completed, they return true and set the **status** variable; otherwise, they return false. If an error is detected, they return true and set the **error_code** appropriately.

```
void ADIO_ReadComplete(ADIO_Request *request, ADIO_Status *status,
int *error_code).
```

Similarly `ADIO_WriteComplete`.

These routines block until the specified operation is completed and set the **status** variable. If an error is detected, they set the **error_code** appropriately and return.

4.3.8 File Control

```
void ADIO_Fcntl(ADIO_File fd, int flag, ADIO_Fcntl_t *fcntl, int
error_code)
```

This routine can be used to set or get information about an open file, such as displacement, etype, filetype, iomode, access mode, and atomicity.

4.3.9 Miscellaneous

ADIO also provides routines for purposes such as determining the type of file system, setting and querying hints, deleting files, resizing files, flushing cached data to disks, and initializing and terminating ADIO.

```
void ADIO_FileSysType(char *filename, int *fstype, int *error_code)
```

```
void ADIO_SetInfo(ADIO_File fd, MPI_Info users_info, int *error_code)
```

```
void ADIO_Delete(char *filename, int *error_code)

void ADIO_Resize(ADIO_File fd, ADIO_Offset size, int *error_code)

void ADIO_Flush(ADIO_File fd, int *error_code)

void ADIO_Init(int *argc, char ***argv, int *error_code)

void ADIO_End(int *error_code)
```

4.4 Implementation

Two aspects are involved in implementing ADIO: implementing an API atop ADIO and implementing ADIO on a file system.

4.4.1 Implementing an API Atop ADIO

Here we explain how some of the different parallel I/O APIs can be implemented by using ADIO routines. In particular, we explain how the main features of the API map to some feature of ADIO.

MPI-IO   MPI-IO [180] maps quite naturally to ADIO because both MPI-IO and ADIO use MPI to a large extent. In addition, we included a number of features in ADIO specifically to enable the implementation of MPI-IO: displacement, etype, filetype, the ability to use explicit offsets as well as file pointers, and file delete-on-close. We have implemented all of MPI-IO atop ADIO.

Intel PFS   For the Intel PFS [128] parallel file system on the Intel Paragon, in addition to a Unix-like read/write interface, one also needs to support several file-pointer modes that specify the semantics of concurrent file access. The Unix-like interface is straightforward to implement atop ADIO. The ADIO_Open function has an argument iomode intended for supporting PFS file-pointer modes. The file-pointer modes, therefore, are implemented by the ADIO implementation.

IBM PIOFS   For the PIOFS [120] parallel file system on the IBM SP-2, in addition to a Unix-like read/write interface, one also needs to support logical partitioning of files. A process can independently specify a logical view of the data in a file, called a subfile, and then read/write that subfile with a single call. It is straightforward to implement the Unix-like interface of PIOFS atop ADIO. The logical file views of PIOFS can be mapped to appropriate MPI derived datatypes and accessed by using the noncontiguous read/write calls of ADIO. We have implemented the Unix-like portion of PIOFS, but not the logical views.

PASSION and Panda   PASSION [260] and Panda [230] are libraries that support input/output of distributed multidimensional arrays. I/O of this type involves collective access to (potentially) noncontiguous data. ADIO supports both collective I/O and noncontiguous accesses; therefore, PASSION and Panda can be implemented by using appropriate ADIO routines. We have not implemented the PASSION and Panda interfaces, however.

4.4.2   Implementing ADIO on a File System

Here we explain how we implemented ADIO on PFS, PIOFS, Unix, and NFS file systems.

ADIO on PFS   Some ADIO functions, such as blocking and nonblocking versions of contiguous reads and writes, are implemented by using their PFS counterparts directly. For functions not directly supported by PFS, however, the ADIO implementation must express the ADIO functions in terms of available PFS calls. For example, noncontiguous requests can be translated either into several contiguous requests separated by seeks or implemented using optimizations such as data sieving [260]. Collective operations can be implemented by using optimizations such as two-phase I/O [74, 259]. Our implementation uses both data sieving and two-phase collective I/O.

ADIO on PIOFS   As in the case of PFS, blocking versions of contiguous reads and writes are implemented by using their PIOFS counterparts directly. Since PIOFS does not support nonblocking I/O, we implemented the nonblocking ADIO functions by using blocking PIOFS functions. In other words, the nonblocking ADIO functions actually block on PIOFS. Since the logical views supported by PIOFS are not general enough to represent any ADIO file view, we do not use the logical-views feature; instead, we use data sieving. Similarly, since PIOFS does not directly support collective I/O, the ADIO implementation performs two-phase I/O atop PIOFS.

ADIO on Unix and NFS   ADIO can be implemented easily on a Unix file system that supports all Unix semantics, such as atomicity and concurrent accesses from multiple processes to a file. However, the Network File System (NFS), which is widely used in a workstation environment, does not guarantee consistency when multiple processes write to a file concurrently (even to distinct locations in the file), because it performs client-side caching [245]. To overcome this problem, we implemented ADIO on NFS by using *file locking* with the `fcntl` system call, which disables client-side caching. As a result, all requests from clients always go to the server, and consistency is maintained. Disabling client-side caching decreases the overall performance of NFS, but nevertheless, it is necessary to ensure correctness of the result in the case of concurrent writes.

4.4.3   Optimizations

An ADIO implementation can perform certain optimizations that are not usually performed by the underlying file system. For example, high-level interfaces like MPI-IO allow the user to specify complete (potentially noncontiguous) access information in a single function call. In addition, the user can specify the collective access information of a group of processes. Most file system interfaces like Unix, on the other hand, allow the user to access only a single, contiguous piece of data at a time. Our ADIO implementation takes advantage of the "global" access information provided by high-level interfaces and performs optimizations such as data sieving and collective I/O [263]. These optimizations improve performance enormously [263].

4.5   Performance

We first present performance results illustrating that the overhead of using ADIO as a portability layer is low. We then present the performance of some optimizations ADIO performs, namely data sieving and collective I/O, which file systems typically do not perform.

For our experiments, we used the two SIO testbeds: IBM SP at Argonne and the Intel Paragon at Caltech. The parallel I/O systems on these two machines were configured as follows during our experiments. On the SP, there were eight I/O server nodes for PIOFS, each with 3 GB of local SCSI disks. The operating system was AIX 3.2.5. On the Paragon, there were 16 I/O nodes for PFS, each connected to a 4.8 GB RAID-3 disk array. The operating system was Paragon/OSF R1.3.3. On both machines, users were not allowed to run compute jobs on the I/O nodes.

We studied the performance overhead of ADIO on PIOFS and PFS by using two test programs and one real production parallel application.

4.5.1   Test Programs

In the first program, called Program I, each process accesses its own independent file. Each process writes 1 MB of data to its local file and reads it back. This writing and reading procedure is performed ten times. We wrote three different versions of this program: for PFS, PIOFS, and MPI-IO.

Program	PIOFS Time	PIOFS–ADIO Time	PIOFS–ADIO Overhead	MPI-IO–ADIO Time	MPI-IO–ADIO Overhead
I	7.42	7.44	0.27%	7.44	0.27%
II	8.44	8.69	2.96%	8.67	2.72%

Table 4.1
I/O time (16 processor IBM SP (seconds)).

The second program, called Program II, is similar to Program I except that all processes access a common file. The data from different processes is stored in the file in order of process rank. Each process writes 1 MB of data to a common file and reads it back, and this writing and reading procedure is performed ten times. We also wrote three different versions of this program: for PFS, PIOFS, and MPI-IO.

To determine the overhead due to ADIO, we ran three cases of each program on the SP and Paragon. The three cases run on the SP were as follows:

1. The PIOFS version run directly on PIOFS.

2. The PIOFS version run through ADIO on PIOFS (PIOFS -> ADIO -> PIOFS). This case shows the overhead due to ADIO.

3. The MPI-IO version run through ADIO on PIOFS (MPI-IO -> ADIO -> PIOFS). This case shows the overhead of using the MPI-IO interface along with ADIO.

Table 4.1 shows the I/O time for all three cases of the two test programs, run on 16 processors on the SP. Clearly, the overhead of using ADIO was negligible.

The three cases run on the Paragon were as follows:

1. The PFS version run directly on PFS.

2. The PFS version run through ADIO on PFS (PFS -> ADIO -> PFS).

3. The MPI-IO version run through ADIO on PFS (MPI-IO -> ADIO -> PFS).

Table 4.2 shows the I/O time for all three cases of the two test programs, run on 16 processors on the Paragon. The overhead of using ADIO was negligible on the Paragon as well. For both test programs, the overhead of using MPI-IO through ADIO was slightly lower than that of PFS through ADIO, possibly because the MPI-IO versions had fewer I/O function calls than the PFS versions. The MPI-IO versions did not use any explicit seek functions. Instead, they used

Program	PFS Time	PFS–ADIO Time	PFS–ADIO Overhead	MPI-IO–ADIO Time	MPI-IO–ADIO Overhead
I	14.03	14.43	2.85%	14.41	2.78%
II	12.19	12.38	1.56%	12.31	0.98%

Table 4.2
I/O time (16 Processor Intel Paragon (seconds).

`MPI_File_read_at` and `MPI_File_write_at` functions that use an offset to indicate the location in the file for reading or writing. The PFS versions, however, used seek calls in addition to the read and write calls.

4.5.2   Production Application

The application we used is a parallel production code developed at the University of Chicago to study the gravitational collapse of self-gravitating gaseous clouds. Details about the application and its I/O characteristics can be found in [262].

The application uses several three-dimensional arrays that are distributed in a (block, block, block) fashion. The algorithm is iterative and, every few iterations, several arrays are written to files for three purposes: data analysis, checkpointing and visualization. The storage order of data in files is required to be the same as it would be if the program were run on a single processor. The application uses two-phase I/O for reading and writing distributed arrays, with I/O routines optimized separately for PFS and PIOFS [262]. I/O is performed by all processors in parallel.

We ran three cases of the application on the SP and Paragon. The three cases on the SP were as follows:

1. The PIOFS version run directly.

2. The PIOFS version run through ADIO on PIOFS (PIOFS –> ADIO –> PIOFS).

3. The Intel PFS version run through ADIO on PIOFS (PFS –> ADIO –> PIOFS).

The three cases on the Paragon were as follows:

1. The PFS version run directly.

2. The PFS version run through ADIO on PFS (PFS –> ADIO –> PFS).

3. The IBM PIOFS version run through ADIO on PFS (PIOFS –> ADIO –> PFS).

PIOFS	PIOFS–ADIO		PFS–ADIO	
Time	Time	Overhead	Time	Overhead
11.22	11.47	2.23%	11.68	4.10%

Table 4.3
I/O time for the production application on 16 processors on the IBM SP. The three cases are:
PIOFS version run directly, PIOFS version run through ADIO on PIOFS, and the Intel PFS
version run through ADIO on PIOFS. Times are in seconds.

We could not run an MPI-IO version, because the application had not yet been
ported to MPI-IO.

On both machines, we ran the application on 16 processors using a mesh of size
$128 \times 128 \times 128$ grid points. The application started by reading a restart file and ran
for ten iterations, dumping arrays every five iterations. A total of 50 MB of data
was read at the start, and around 100 MB of data was written every five iterations.
The sizes of individual read/write operations were as follows: there was one small
read of 24 bytes and several large reads of 512 KB; there were a few small writes of
24 bytes and several large writes of 128 MB and 512 KB.

Tables 4.3 and 4.4 show the I/O time taken by the application on the SP and
Paragon, respectively. The overhead due to ADIO was very small on both systems.
In addition, ADIO allowed us to run the SP version of the application on the
Paragon and the Paragon version on the SP, both with very low overhead.

4.5.3   Data Sieving and Collective I/O

As mentioned in §4.4.3, ADIO optimizes noncontiguous accesses by performing data
sieving for independent requests and collective I/O for collective requests. These
optimizations improve performance considerably compared with regular Unix-style
independent I/O. Details of the data sieving and collective I/O implementation
and detailed performance results can be found in [263]. Here we show a few Upshot
plots that illustrate the reduction in time obtained by using data sieving and collective I/O instead of Unix-style independent I/O for writing a three-dimensional
distributed array of size $128 \times 128 \times 128$ on the Intel Paragon.

We instrumented the ADIO code to measure the time taken for each file system
call made by ADIO and also the computation and communication required for
collective I/O. The instrumented code created trace files, which we visualized by
using Upshot [114].

Figure 4.2 shows the Upshot plot for Unix-style independent I/O; that is, each
process makes a separate write function call to write each row of its local array. The

PFS	PFS–ADIO		PIOFS–ADIO	
Time	Time	Overhead	Time	Overhead
22.28	22.78	2.24%	22.92	2.87%

Table 4.4
I/O time for the production application on 16 processors on the Intel Paragon. The three cases are: PFS version run directly, PFS version run through ADIO on PFS, and the IBM PIOFS version run through ADIO on PFS. Times are in seconds.

numerous dark bands represent the numerous writes in the program, as a result of which, the total time taken is about 125 seconds. (The large white portions are actually lots of writes clustered together, which become visible when you zoom in to the region using Upshot.)

Instead of writing each row of the local array separately, if the user expresses the entire noncontiguous access pattern of a process by using MPI's derived datatypes and then calls independent I/O functions, ADIO performs data sieving. Data sieving is an optimization in which the ADIO implementation always makes large file accesses, extracts the data actually needed by the user, and discards the rest. In the case of writing with data sieving, the process must perform a read-modify-write and also lock the region of the file being written.

Figure 4.3 shows the Upshot plot for data sieving, in which the implementation performs data sieving in chunks of 4 MB. Note that the total time decreased to about 16 seconds compared with 125 seconds for Unix-style independent I/O. Because of the need for file locking and a buffer size of 4 MB, many processes remain idle waiting to acquire locks. Therefore, only a few write operations take place concurrently. It should be possible to increase parallelism, however, by decreasing the size of the buffer used for data sieving. Figure 4.4 shows the results for a buffer size of 512 KB. Since more I/O operations take place in parallel, the total time decreased to 10.5 seconds. A further reduction in buffer size to 64 KB (Figure 4.5 resulted in even greater parallelism, but the I/O time went up because of the smaller granularity of each I/O operation.) The performance of data sieving can thus be tuned by varying the size of the buffer used for data sieving. The user can vary the size via ADIO's hints mechanism.

If the user describes the entire noncontiguous access information and uses ADIO's *collective* I/O functions, ADIO performs collective I/O. In collective I/O, the access requests of different processes are merged into larger requests to the file system. Since the accesses of different processes are often interleaved in the file, such merging of requests leads to large, contiguous requests and, unlike in data sieving, none of the data accessed needs to be discarded. Figure 4.6 shows the Upshot plot for

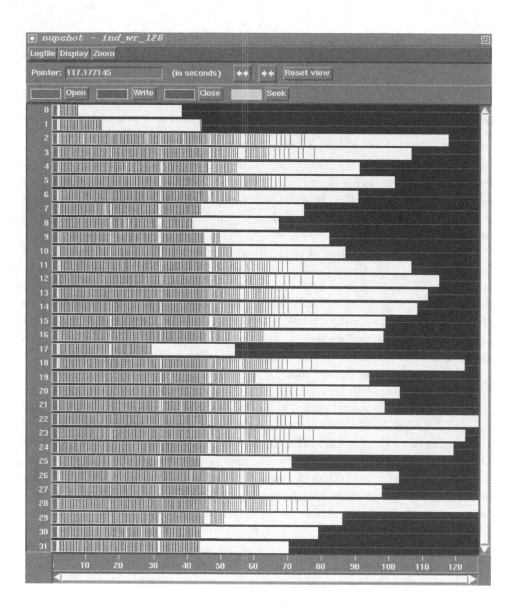

Figure 4.2
Writing a $128 \times 128 \times 128$ distributed array on the Intel Paragon by using Unix-style
independent writes. The elapsed time is 125 seconds.

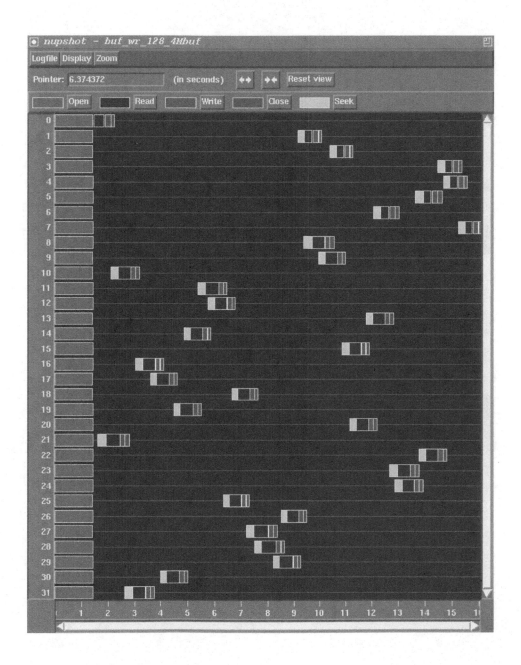

Figure 4.3
Writing a $128 \times 128 \times 128$ distributed array on the Intel Paragon by using data sieving with buffer size 4 MB. The elapsed time is 16 seconds.

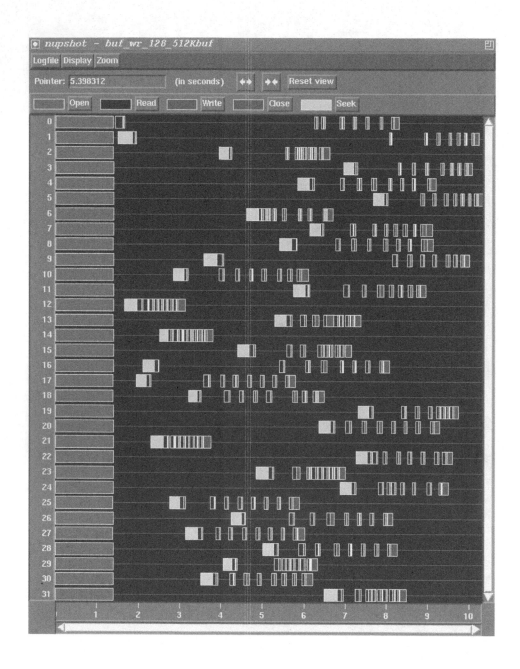

Figure 4.4
Writing a 128 × 128 × 128 distributed array on the Intel Paragon by using data sieving with buffer size 512 KB. The elapsed time is 10.5 seconds.

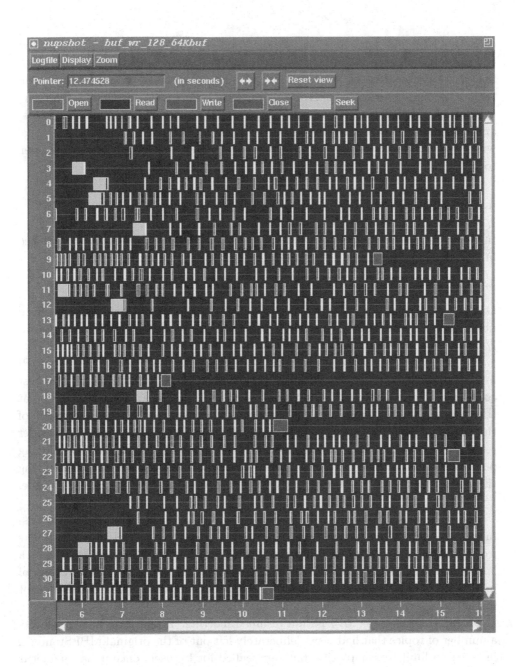

Figure 4.5
Writing a $128 \times 128 \times 128$ distributed array on the Intel Paragon by using data sieving with buffer size 64 KB. The elapsed time is 20 seconds.

collective I/O. The total time decreased to about 2.75 seconds, which means that collective I/O was about 45 times faster than Unix-style independent I/O and about four times faster than the best data sieving time. The reason for the improvement is that the numerous writes of each process have been coalesced into a *single* write at the expense of some computation (to figure how to merge the write requests) and communication (to actually move the data). With collective I/O, the actual write time was only a small fraction of the total I/O time; for example, file open took longer than the write.

4.6 MPI-IO

In this section we describe the evolution of MPI-IO and the role ADIO has played in the implementation and adoption of the new MPI standard for I/O.

4.6.1 Background

One of the original goals of the SIO project was to propose to vendors a standard library interface for parallel I/O. As the SIO project was starting, two other relevant I/O interface developments were under way.

The first was the effort begun at IBM to investigate the impact of the new MPI message passing standard on the topic of parallel I/O. The MPI forum had just completed its work, deliberately not addressing the issue of parallel I/O. A group at IBM wrote an important paper [220], which one can interpret as an exploration of the analogy between message-passing and I/O. Roughly speaking, one can consider reads and writes to a file system as receives and sends. This paper was the starting point of MPI-IO in that it was the first attempt to exploit this analogy by applying the (then relatively new) MPI concepts for message passing to the realm of parallel I/O.

The idea of using message-passing concepts in an I/O library appeared successful and the effort was expanded into a collaboration with parallel-I/O researchers from NASA Ames. The resulting specification appeared in [57]. At this point a large email discussion group was formed, with participation from a wide variety of institutions. This group, calling itself the MPI-IO Committee, pushed the concept further in a series of proposals, culminating in [268].

During this time, the MPI Forum resumed meeting. Its purpose was to address a number of topics that had been deliberately left out of the original MPI Standard in order to limit its complexity, but were called for by users once it became clear that the MPI standard was being widely adopted. It was recognized that the

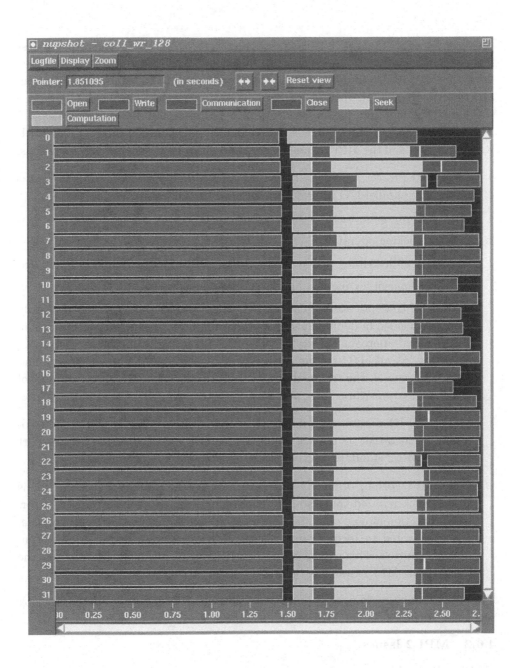

Figure 4.6
Writing a 128 × 128 × 128 distributed array on the Intel Paragon by using collective I/O. The elapsed time is 2.75 seconds.

three major areas that MPI-1 had postponed were parallel I/O, dynamic process
management, and one-sided operations. Initially, the MPI Forum recognized that
both the MPI-IO Committee, led by members of the IBM-NASA collaboration,
and the Scalable I/O Project represented efforts to develop a parallel I/O interface
standard. Therefore the forum decided not to address I/O in its deliberations.

In the long run the three threads of development—by the SIO Project, the MPI-
IO Committee, and the MPI Forum—merged because of a number of considerations:

- The SIO Project, originally conceived independently of MPI, came to realize
  that any parallel-I/O interface would need the following:

  - collective operations,

  - nonblocking operations,

  - a way of describing noncontiguous data, both in memory and in a file, and

  - a mechanism for passing hints to the implementation.

  All these concepts are present in MPI, where considerable effort had already
  been expended in defining and implementing them. This realization made an
  MPI-based approach attractive. The SIO Project did undertake a study of
  existing, parallel I/O-system features and application requirements and found
  that, in general, the still-evolving MPI-IO specification incorporated most of
  the necessary features for a parallel I/O system capable of high performance.

- The MPI-IO committee, originally conceived independently of the MPI Forum, decided that its impact would be greater if its specification became part
  of the MPI-2 standard and petitioned to become part of the MPI-2 effort.

- The MPI Forum, originally intending to leave I/O out of its deliberations
  on MPI-2, realized that the MPI-IO Committee had evolved from a narrow
  collaboration into an open discussion group containing considerable expertise.
  It then voted to incorporate the MPI-IO design group as an MPI Forum
  subcommittee. This expansion of the MPI Forum membership benefited the
  rest of the MPI-2 design as well.

The result was that, from the summer of 1996, the MPI-IO design activities took
place in the context of the MPI Forum meetings.

4.6.2   MPI-2 Issues

MPI-2, which addressed many communication issues outside of I/O, proved to be
good home for the MPI-IO design effort.

MPI and MPI-IO   Application of the analogy between message-passing and I/O turned out to be fruitful. MPI datatypes proved adequate to the task of defining noncontiguous layouts in files as well as in memory. In fact, I/O considerations (e.g., for input/output of distributed arrays) motivated the definition of new MPI derived datatypes that are now available in MPI-2 for message-passing as well. The use of datatypes for all data in memory enabled the definition of portable file formats, using the mechanism that was originally designed for message-passing on homogeneous networks. MPI's communicators turned out to be suitable for simultaneously describing a set of processes participating in file operations and acting as a protected layer of the message-passing space to separate I/O-related message-passing from application-level message passing.

MPI External Interfaces   Part of the MPI-2 specification was a collection of functions designed to expose parts of an MPI implementation's internal data structures in a portable way. A typical example is the set of functions for deconstructing an MPI datatype. The purpose of these functions is to allow libraries that use MPI functionality to do so more efficiently.

In the case of MPI-IO, a small number of these MPI-2 external interface functions allow the implementation of MPI-IO in terms of other MPI-1 functions and simple, possibly nonportable but highly efficient, read and write functions for contiguous data. This feature has caused MPI-IO to be the first part of MPI-2 to appear in implementations.

4.6.3   Implementation

Here we discuss implementation issues particular to the use of ADIO in the implementation of the MPI-IO interface.

ROMIO   The ADIO implementation described above evolved into a more specialized design that supported only the MPI-IO interface. This system is called ROMIO [267]. It supports most of the I/O part of the MPI-2 Standard. It is implemented in terms of multiple, low-level file-system interfaces for doing the actual I/O and MPI itself for the associated message passing. Basically, MPI is used to assemble/disassemble large blocks and a variety of both portable and nonportable I/O systems are used to move large blocks to and from secondary storage. The MPI "hints" mechanism is used to allow the application to take advantage of file-system-dependent features in a semi-portable way.

Layerability via the MPI External Interface   In the deliberations of the MPI-2 Forum, care was taken to make the MPI-IO specification layerable on other parts of the MPI specification to the extent possible. Simultaneously, functions were being defined that would expose some internals of an MPI implementation in a portable way, to encourage layerability of other libraries besides I/O. As a result, it is possible to provide an MPI-IO implementation in terms of MPI-1 and a small number of MPI-2 external-interface functions.

This architecture has greatly accelerated the development of MPI-IO implementations, including ROMIO. Some vendors supplied us with versions of the necessary MPI-2 functions, thus enabling ROMIO to use the vendors' native MPI for its internal message passing. ROMIO is also distributed as a part of MPICH [107], and, as a result, ROMIO is available (with MPICH message passing) for a wide variety of environments. Vendors such as HP, SGI, NEC, and Compaq have incorporated ROMIO into their MPI implementations. ROMIO, and therefore MPI-IO, has been implemented atop the PVFS parallel file system, providing MPI-IO on Linux clusters, and it is delivered as part of both the MPICH and LAM implementations of MPI. There is a web site for ROMIO at http://www.mcs.anl.gov/romio.

4.7   Conclusions

The abstract-device interface for I/O was not part of the original SIO proposal. As the project begain, however, its uses became apparent. Its first use was as an integration tool for the SIO project itself, allowing multiple applications to be automatically ported to both testbed systems. It was further developed as a tool for enabling experimentation with application-level parallel I/O interfaces. Finally it evolved into the foundation of a production-quality implementation of the MPI-IO standard.

Acknowledgments

This work was supported by the Mathematical, Information, and Computational Sciences Division subprogram of the Office of Computational and Technology Research, U.S. Department of Energy, under Contract W-31-109-Eng-38; and by the Scalable I/O Initiative, a multiagency project funded by the Defense Advanced Research Projects Agency (contract number DABT63-94-C-0049), the Department of Energy, the National Aeronautics and Space Administration, and the National Science Foundation.

5 Informed Prefetching of Collective Input/Output Requests

TARA M. MADHYASTHA, GARTH A. GIBSON AND CHRISTOS FALOUTSOS

Poor I/O performance is one of the primary obstacles to effective use of high-performance multiprocessor systems. In an effort to provide high throughput commensurate with compute power, current multiprocessor systems provide multiple disks or disk arrays attached to I/O processors that communicate with compute processors through a fast network (see Figure 5.1). A parallel file system manages parallel files that are declustered across multiple I/O processors. Unfortunately, parallel file systems have been unable to consistently deliver peak hardware performance to applications with widely varying I/O requirements. I/O remains a critical bottleneck for a large class of important scientific applications.

Many studies have shown that parallel I/O performance is extremely sensitive to the file access pattern, which can be extremely complex. Each thread of a parallel application accesses a portion of a parallel file, declustered over multiple disks, with a local access pattern. The temporal and spatial interleaving of the local access patterns is the global access pattern. To optimize application throughput, it often helps to have information about the global access pattern; thus, an important research area in parallel file system design is determining what access pattern information needs to be specified by an application to provide good performance.

One important class of access patterns is collective I/O. Suppose the threads of a parallel application simultaneously access portions of a shared file, and no thread can proceed until all have completed their I/O. If the threads use a UNIX-style interface, a separate system call is required for each disjoint portion. This can result in non-sequential accesses and, consequently, poor performance at the I/O processors. Providing high-level access pattern information to the file system through an application programming interface (API) allows disks to reorder requests, servicing them to maximize throughput. This motivates optimizations such as two-phase [74] and disk-directed I/O [156]; given global, high-level knowledge that some data must be read or written before all the processors can proceed, the I/O operations can be reordered to occur as an efficient collective. In recognition of its importance to high-performance I/O, an interface for collective I/O is specified as an extension to the Scalable Input/Output (SIO) initiative low-level API [60].

A more general technique for improving performance provides access pattern information to a file system through informed prefetching. The application constructs hints, describing future accesses, that a prefetcher uses to issue I/O requests in advance of the demand fetch stream. Although a main advantage of prefetching is its ability to overlap I/O with computation, deep prefetching enables better disk

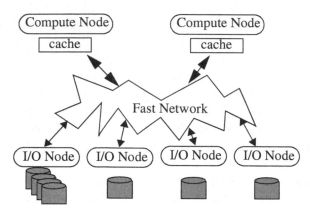

Figure 5.1
System architecture where compute nodes and input/output nodes (each of which manages a disk or disk array) communicate through a fast network interconnect.

scheduling, improving throughput analogously to a collective I/O implementation that sorts disk requests. Unlike an efficient collective I/O implementation, the quality of disk scheduling is a function of the prefetch depth.

Given that a parallel application needs to perform a collective read and provided that each processor has sufficient time to overlap the I/O with computation and some amount of memory to issue prefetch requests, we investigate how to utilize this memory using general informed prefetching techniques to achieve throughput similar to an efficient implementation of collective I/O. We derive models for expected throughput using prefetching and validate these experimentally. We show that with only a small amount of additional memory that scales with the number of disks, informed prefetching can outperform an efficient collective I/O implementation.

There is nevertheless a strong rationale for an application-level interface that expresses I/O request parallelism. If we take the ability to reorder requests to its limit, we allow the application to specify that it would like to access any block that has not yet been accessed, with no regard for order. These relaxed semantics allow an I/O node to dynamically reorder requests using much less memory. If the application can be structured so that it can compute on any portion of the data, we can dynamically reorder I/O requests at the I/O nodes, obtaining the full benefit of request reordering and prefetching. We call this novel interface a *set collective* interface.

The remainder of this chapter is organized as follows. We describe the complexities of collective access patterns and our target application in §5.1. In §5.2 we present the state of the art optimizations for collective I/O. In §5.3 we discuss

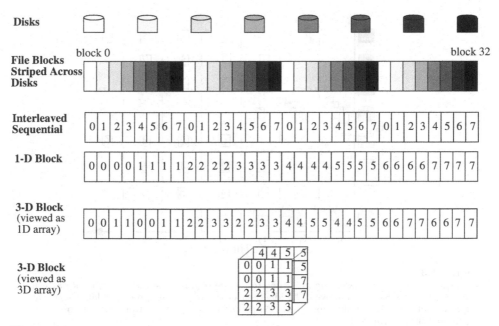

Figure 5.2
Three examples of logical file views. A file, viewed as an array of blocks, may be allocated to processors many ways. The diagrams above show three such logical file views. The numbers identify processors that access the denoted file regions and processors access blocks in logically increasing order. For example, in the interleaved sequential access pattern, each processor will access all the blocks stored on a single disk.

prefetching as an alternative to a collective I/O interface and describe models for prefetching throughput based on the available memory. We present our experimental evaluation of prefetching and collective I/O using a simulation infrastructure in §5.4. In §5.5 we describe and evaluate a set collective interface. In §5.6 we survey related work, and we conclude with directions for future research in §5.7.

5.1   Problem Specification: Collective Access Patterns

We define a collective access pattern to be a special global access pattern where processors simultaneously access portions of a parallel file. A parallel file has several layers of abstraction. At the application level, processors may impose some structure on the logical file to determine how to partition it among themselves. At the system level, there is usually a canonical order for logical file blocks or records. These units are in turn stored on disk drives according to some distribution. Fi-

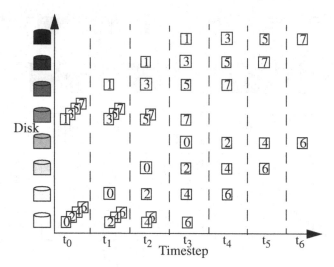

Figure 5.3
Disk queues over time. Assuming unit time to service disk requests, the 1-D block pattern evolves over time as shown above. The identifier of the requesting processor labels each block request. Note that disk utilization is only 50 percent. Ideally this set of accesses could be completed in four timesteps.

nally, the placement of blocks on a single drive may vary from sequential to random, depending on the placement strategy.

Depending on how the logical file blocks are stored on disk and distributed among processors, the global access pattern and consequently queues at each drive, can vary dramatically. Figure 5.2 illustrates how logical file blocks may be striped, round-robin, across drives and distributed among processors according to three different logical file views (interleaved sequential, 1-D block, and 3-D block) that have been used in scientific applications.

Using a UNIX-style interface, processors must at least issue a separate request for each contiguous portion. We assume that in a collective read, processors synchronize and each processor begins reading its portion, block by block, in increasing logical block order. Figure 5.3 depicts an abstraction of how the 1-D block decomposition of Figure 5.2 evolves over time. We can see that disk utilization and, consequently, throughput is poor. This example is very small, so individual drive accesses are still sequential. However, when processors simultaneously access different locations of a larger parallel file, it becomes difficult to exploit sequentiality at the drives.

5.2   Collective I/O Implementations

As we have described, collective access to parallel files is often inefficient from an I/O performance standpoint. Each process accesses its own disjoint portion but, to fully exploit disk , the file system must have knowledge of the global, coordinated access pattern. If the application can specify that the component transfers of the collective operation may be executed in any order, because the application will not progress until the entire operation has been completed, the file system can minimize disk transfer time by reordering requests to match the file layout.

The SIO low-level API [60] includes an extension interface for collective I/O. One task of the application creates a collective I/O, specifying the number of participants, whether the operation is a read or write, the number of iterations, and (optionally) what portions will be operated on. Participating application tasks issue calls to join the collective; each specifies a list of corresponding file regions and memory locations that will be involved in the transfer. The transfer is asynchronous; the file system can either wait for all participants to join the collective before initiating the transfer, or service each request immediately.

There are several implementation alternatives for collective I/O that can be categorized as user-level or system-level. User-level libraries to support collective I/O, such as two-phase I/O [74] have processors access files in long contiguous portions and permute the data among themselves to correspond to the processor data decomposition. Two major performance problems with this approach are that the user-level library cannot exploit information about the physical disk layout and the permutation phase is not overlapped with I/O. System-level implementation approaches provide system support for collective operations; one approach that addresses these problems is disk-directed I/O [156]. Disk-directed I/O allows the I/O processors to sort the physical block requests and transfer the requested blocks directly to the requesting processors. Aside from application buffer space, to receive the outstanding request, no additional memory is necessary.

5.3   Proposed Method: Informed Prefetching

The confluence of application-specified information and system-level support allows optimal scheduling of collective I/O requests. However, the underlying principle (gathering and sorting requests from processors in a globally optimal manner) can improve the performance of many parallel I/O access patterns. Prefetching can provide these benefits for collective I/O using a more general framework that does

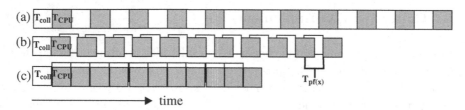

Figure 5.4
Collective input/output benchmark. We consider a benchmark which iteratively reads data (the collective operation) and computes on it (a). Read time and compute time are balanced so that all read time can be partially (b) or fully (c) overlapped with computation.

not rely on specialized system optimizations.

5.3.1   Overview

Prefetching is a general technique that improves I/O performance by reading data into cache before it is requested, overlapping I/O with computation. Although much research has focussed on anticipating data requests based on access history, informed prefetching advocates using application-supplied hints to inform the file system of future requests [209].

Unlike a collective API, using hints to expose future requests to the file system does not explicitly give the system the ability to reorder them. However, deep prefetching promotes deep disk queues, enabling implicit request reordering. The deeper the queues, the more reordering is possible, and the higher the throughput. In a spectrum where demand fetching is at one extreme (no reordering) and collective I/O is at the other (perfect reordering), prefetching with gradually increasing depths describes the performance points in between. In other words, an informed prefetching system permits more flexible use of memory; if there is not enough memory to fully optimize the transaction, the system can still obtain partial benefits, degrading gracefully.

Thus, prefetching improvements have two components; I/O is overlapped with computation, and deep prefetch queues allow the disk to reorder requests dynamically, improving throughput. Collective I/O is an optimization that relies solely upon request reordering. One can overlap I/O with computation by issuing collective I/O calls asynchronously; however, this approach requires allocating enough memory to hold both the collective in progress and the collective in memory.

To formalize this intuition, we consider a parallel benchmark that iteratively performs collective I/O operations and computes on the data. A parallel application must read and process some number of files, each with B blocks. The files are striped round-robin, across D disks; this aspect of the layout is not under application control. There are P processors, each with finite buffer space, and the disks and processors are connected with a zero latency network. For each file, the processors synchronize, each processor reads a disjoint portion of the current file (P/B blocks), and when all processors have completed the read, they begin to compute on the data. Figure 5.4a shows this I/O-compute cycle. Each processor has x blocks available for prefetching, called the prefetch depth (or prefetch horizon), and may issue up to x prefetch requests in advance of the demand fetch stream, to overlap I/O and computation as shown in Figure 5.4b. This functionality might be provided by a very basic prefetching system that could be implemented at the application level using asynchronous I/O.

Drawing from terminology set forth in [209], we describe the elapsed time T for such a benchmark as

$$T = N_{coll}(T_{CPU} + T_{coll}) \tag{5.3.1}$$

where N_{coll} is the number of collective I/O accesses, T_{CPU} is the CPU time between collective operations, and T_{coll} is the time to perform a collective I/O access.

By default, T_{coll} is not overlapped with T_{CPU}; the application sees all I/O time (Figure 5.4a). We define $T_{pf(x)}$ as the time to perform a hinted collective I/O with some per-processor prefetch depth x. In other words, we can overlap some fraction of the I/Os in the collective with compute time (T_{CPU}) to improve performance, as shown in Figure 5.4b. Prefetching will outperform non-overlapped collective I/O if

$$T_{pf(x)} \leq T_{CPU} + T_{coll} \tag{5.3.2}$$

At this point, we make an important observation. $T_{pf(x)}$ is highly dependent both on the global access pattern (the temporal and spatial interleaving of each processor's logical access pattern) and on the disk allocation strategy (the mapping of logical blocks to physical disk locations). Therefore, the choice of prefetch depth will change the time necessary to service the collective using prefetching. We investigate the impact of the global access pattern on prefetch horizon in §5.4.3.

We use memory as the common currency to compare performance of collective I/O and informed prefetching. A collective operation requires B blocks without overlapping, and $2B$ blocks with potentially full overlap of I/O and computation. In contrast, informed prefetching can utilize any available memory between B to $2B$ blocks. To outperform non-overlapped collective I/O using B blocks, prefetching will require $B + x$ blocks, where x is the prefetch depth. We determine bounds on x in §5.3.3.

Parameter	Value
Sector size	512 bytes
Cylinders	1962
Revolution speed	4002 RPM
Transfer time (8 KB)	3.3316 ms
Rotational latency	14.992 ms/revolution
Seek time (C cylinders)	if C < 383, $3.24 + .4\sqrt{C}$ else $8.00 + 0.008C$

Table 5.1
HP 97560 disk parameters.

Symbol	Meaning
T_{cycle}	read/compute cycle time
B	number 8 KB blocks
P	number processors (equal to number of disks)
T_d	time to service block read
T_C	compute time per block
x	per-processor prefetch horizon
M	number tracks in desired horizon
r	prefetch requests per disk

Table 5.2
Symbol definitions.

5.3.2   Performance Model

We consider the throughput of an application with the read/compute cycle of collective operations shown in Figure 5.4 as a function of the prefetch depth x. Assume that disk block placement is random, so the global access pattern, determined by the distribution of blocks to processors, does not significantly affect overall throughput.

The time for each read/compute cycle is the time to service $(B/P) - x$ I/O requests, plus the compute time for the collective, or $(B/P)T_C$. We assume that the initial x prefetch requests are fully overlapped with the previous cycle compute time. Equation (3) expresses the time for a single read/compute cycle.

$$T_{cycle} = (\frac{B}{P} - x) \cdot T_d + (\frac{B}{P}) \cdot T_C \qquad (5.3.3)$$

The time T_d to service a single block varies with the prefetch depth x. We can model the disk service time more accurately with (4), as the sum of the independent variables for the expected transfer time, rotational latency, and seek time as a function of the per-processor prefetch depth x.

$$T_d = E[TransferTime] + E[RotationalLatency] + E[SeekTime(x)] \quad (5.3.4)$$

We can calculate T_d for the HP97560 disk drive (see Table 5.3), used in our experimental evaluation, as follows. The expected transfer time is a constant for 8 KB blocks, expected rotational latency is equal to one half a rotation, and the expected seek time is formulated in (5). If a processor has a prefetch depth of x, it may have at most x outstanding prefetch requests. Although these prefetch requests are issued in logical order within the file, the physical disk blocks will be randomly distributed and reordered at the disk queues. A processor with x outstanding requests cannot prefetch another block until its first prefetch request has been demand fetched. On average, with random placement, the first request will be in the middle of some disk queue, so half of the requests must be serviced before the processor can issue more prefetches. Consequently, on average, only $x/2$ requests are in the queue at any time. We count the current disk position as an additional request. The average seek distance, in cylinders C, between r uniformly distributed requests is given by $C/(r+1)$; thus, our model approximates the average seek distance as $C/((x/2) + 2)$.

$$E[SeekTime(x)] = 3.24 + .04\left(\sqrt{\frac{1962}{\frac{x}{2} + 2}}\right) \quad (5.3.5)$$

For sequential disk placement, it is more difficult to estimate T_d, because it is dependent upon both the prefetch depth x and the access pattern. We simplify the access pattern variations by modeling a global sequential access pattern created by allocating each block in the file to a processor drawn from a uniform distribution. Our intuition is as follows: the optimal schedule for each drive is to read file blocks sequentially, which means that, ideally, each drive should know which processors require the blocks they are reading. Within a particular file region, each disk will have partial information about which processors require which blocks, through prefetch requests. As the prefetch depth x increases, the probability of having complete information for this region increases. Within each track, requests are sequential, but the cost to access a different track incurs rotational latency plus transfer time.

The size of the file region we consider is $2P$ blocks, expressed as tracks in (6). This is two times the prefetch depth necessary for theoretical sequentiality on the drives, as we will show in §5.3.3, and is a good estimate of the practical bound for sequential access (as we show experimentally in §5.4.4).

$$M = \frac{2 \cdot P \cdot sectorsPerBlock}{sectorsPerTrack} \tag{5.3.6}$$

We estimate the average number of tracks hit ($\overline{tracks}$) by r requests using Cardenas's formula [37] in (7). The number of requests at each disk, r, is related to the prefetch depth x by the relationship $r = (Px)/D$. Since the number of drives and processors are the same, r is equal to x.

$$\overline{tracks} = (1 - (1 - \frac{1}{M})^r) \cdot M \tag{5.3.7}$$

Thus, we have $frac_{rand} = (M - \overline{tracks})/M$, and the formula for T_d is given by (8), where T_{seq} is the time to service a sequential disk request. From (8) and (3) we can calculate the throughput for sequential disk layout for a global sequential access pattern.

$$T_d = frac_{rand} \cdot (E[TransferTime] + E[RotationalLatency]) + (1 - frac_{rand}) \cdot T_{seq} \tag{5.3.8}$$

5.3.3   Determining the Prefetch Depth

Collective I/O implementations optimize collective access patterns by requiring each processor to disclose all intended accesses in advance and globally sorting this request list for optimal throughput. It might seem that informed prefetching is incapable of generating this optimal I/O request schedule for any file size and access pattern, because the amount of reordering possible is bounded by the size of each processor's prefetch horizon.

However, we can show that independent of file size and access pattern, with certain disk placement assumptions, the prefetch depth necessary to generate an optimal schedule for collective accesses in an ideal system is theoretically bounded and is equal to D, the number of drives. Figure 5.5 encapsulates our assumptions and sketches a proof of this bound. Blocks of a file are striped, round-robin, across D drives (8 in this figure). Within a drive, logically increasing file blocks are placed sequentially. Each column represents a logical file block, and each row represents a single processor's logical block allocations, or ownerships. Every block is owned by exactly one processor; ownership is represented by an **x** in the row/column intersection. Each processor requests its blocks in increasing order. We assume I/O requests are perfectly synchronized at the disks and occur in unit time. We also assume the rest of our system is infinitely fast, so that the instant a block has been prefetched, the processor that owns that block can issue a new prefetch request.

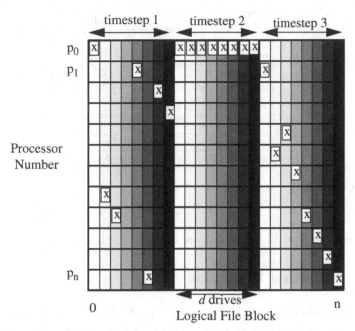

Figure 5.5
Bounding the prefetch depth for collective access patterns. If the network is infinitely fast and disk access occur in unit time, a prefetch depth per processor equal to the number of disks is sufficient to ensure sequential accesses at each drive.

The optimal schedule is predetermined by the file layout; at timestep 1, blocks 0 through $D - 1$ must be serviced, then in the next timestep, blocks D through $2D - 1$, and so on. At each timestep, the disks need to know which processor owns each block (i.e., the processor must have prefetched that block). As shown in Figure 5.5, at any timestep t a prefetch depth of D at each processor will convey this information. This is because all the prefetches for earlier blocks have been serviced, so to service the next D blocks it is sufficient for each processor to reveal its next D requests. For example, in timestep 2, processor p_0 owns all the D blocks that will be accessed; it must have prefetched these blocks.

Intuitively, as requests for blocks in the beginning of the file are serviced, the processors that were waiting on those blocks issue more prefetch requests for the next requests in sequence. In this way, the scheduling algorithm at each drive can dynamically translate an arbitrary decomposition into sequential accesses. Note that the assumption that all blocks of a file will be accessed is crucial to this result, but not necessarily true of collective access patterns in general. For the rest of this

Parameter	Value
Number of disks	8
Disk type	HP 97560
Disk capacity	1.3 GB
Disk transfer rate	2.11 MB/sec
File system block size	8 KB
Number of processors	8
Network latency	25 ns
Network bandwidth	400 MB/sec

Table 5.3
Simulator parameters.

chapter, we consider only files that are accessed in their entirety.

5.4   Experimental Evaluation

In the previous sections, we introduced a model for prefetching throughput and proposed a theoretical bound on the prefetch depth necessary to obtain sequential disk request scheduling. We expect that with equal amounts of memory, informed prefetching should behave slightly worse than a collective interface. However, performance of informed prefetching will increase gracefully as additional prefetch buffers are available, quickly surpassing an efficient collective I/O implementation. In this section we compare collective I/O and informed prefetching experimentally via simulation and measure the accuracy of our model.

5.4.1   Simulator Architecture

We simulated a simple parallel file system for the system architecture shown in Figure 5.1 that supports disk-directed I/O and informed prefetching. The major components of our system are processors, the network, and I/O nodes. Our emphasis is on I/O and queueing effects. Files are striped, block by block, across the I/O nodes and each I/O node services one disk. The network model has point-to-point communication with a fixed startup overhead and a per-byte transfer cost; we assume a very fast interconnect. Each processor has its own cache and prefetcher; we assume no overhead for memory copies incurred by cache hits. The I/O nodes have no cache beyond the disk cache. The disk model we have used is Kotz's reimplementation of Ruemmler and Wilkes' HP 97560 model [159, 225]. Table 5.3 lists the significant simulator parameters. Although this disk is not modern, advances in disk technology do not qualitatively affect the queuing effects we are addressing and this particular model has been well tested and validated.

There are several possible implementation strategies for collective I/O; we limit our comparison to disk-directed I/O, which generally outperforms application-level collective implementations such as two-phase collective I/O [74]. In our simulation of disk-directed I/O, the processors synchronize at a barrier, issue a collective call, and submit the collective requests to the I/O nodes. Each I/O node then knows what blocks it must read and which processors have requested those blocks. The I/O nodes sort the block lists to minimize transfer time and send each block to the requesting processor as it is read from disk. Throughput for the collective using disk-directed I/O is optimal.

Using informed prefetching, each processor constructs a hint containing the list of blocks that it intends to read using a standard UNIX-style interface. A hint contains a flag indicating whether it is a read or a write and an ordered sequence of blocks to be accessed. This matches the specification in the SIO low-level API [60]. A prefetching thread associated with each processor issues up to x outstanding prefetches, to be cached at the processor, where x is the prefetch horizon. This approach allows us to hide network latency as well as disk latency. For fair comparison with disk-directed I/O, processors issue a barrier before reading the file.

One of the advantages of deep disk queues created by prefetch requests is the ability to reorder requests, thereby improving throughput. To this end, we use a shortest-seek time first algorithm to schedule physical I/O requests.

5.4.2 Collective Input/Output Benchmark

Studies of application-level I/O access patterns reveal that iterative I/O compute loops, where processors collaborate to read or write and process multiple data sets over the course of execution, are quite common [71, 238]. In our experiments, we consider a hypothetical application with a read/compute loop that can be restructured to read (and process) files of varying sizes, maintaining a fixed ratio of compute time to I/O volume, as illustrated in Figure 5.4. The compute time for each collective read is equal to the time required to read the file at the throughput obtained with a 4 MB disk-directed I/O operation, ensuring that I/O can be completely overlapped with computation. There is enough lead compute time to fully overlap the initial collective. We describe results from experiments where files are striped over 8 disks and accessed by 8 processors. We obtained qualitatively identical results with larger balanced systems (larger numbers of disks and processors, and larger file sizes) the smaller configuration size was chosen to limit simulation time.

Access Pattern	File Size (MB)	Prefetch Throughput		Collective Throughput	Crossover Prefetch Depth
		Min	Max		
Interleaved Sequential	4	9.018	17.988	9.066	1
	8	9.286	18.132	9.314	1
	32	9.505	18.132	9.509	1
	64	9.534	18.132	9.541	2
	128	9.555	18.132	9.558	2
	256	9.564	18.132	9.566	2
1D Block Sequential	4	3.091	16.894	9.066	16
	32	2.411	18.132	9.509	16
	256	2.344	18.132	9.566	16
3D Block Sequential	4	2.584	17.198	9.066	8
	32	2.708	18.132	9.509	16
	256	2.473	18.132	9.566	16
Global Sequential	4	3.123	16.145	9.066	7
	32	2.623	18.132	9.509	10
	256	2.408	18.132	9.566	14

Table 5.4
Sequential disk block placement.

File Size (MB)	Prefetch Throughput		Collective Throughput	Crossover Prefetch Depth	
	Min	Max		Unsorted	Sorted
4	1.264	2.926	1.551	16	2
8	1.314	3.033	1.593	32	2
32	1.336	3.036	1.642	56	2
64	1.303	3.036	1.643	88	2
128	1.323	3.036	1.660	136	6
256	1.332	3.069	1.697	296	1

Table 5.5
Random disk block placement for interleaved sequential access pattern.

for N iterations:	for N iterations:
1. one processor defines the collective request, describing data to be read by all processors	1. barrier synchronization
	2. each processor reads its portion of the data, one block at a time
2. barrier synchronization	3. each processor gives the prefetcher hints for the next iteration read, begin prefetching with available memory
3. each processor joins collective, reading its portion of data	
4. compute on data	4. compute on data
(a)	(b)

Figure 5.6
Collective input/output pseudocode. Processors collectively read and process N different data files one at a time, using a collective input/output interface (a) and informed prefetching (b).

Figure 5.6 shows the psuedocode for this benchmark using a collective I/O interface and informed prefetching. With a collective interface, processors request all their assigned blocks at once in step 3. Using prefetching, each processor requests its portion, a block at a time, with no interrequest latency. We consider only 8 KB transfers, a common file system block size. Larger requests increase the degree of sequentiality, and are subsumed by access patterns with larger sequential runs. We do not consider collective writes or the additional caching and prefetching issues involved in clustering extremely small, noncontiguous requests.

5.4.3 The Significance of Global Access Patterns

We have explained that throughput using informed prefetching is dependent upon the global access pattern. A collective API allows disks to sort the total amount of work in advance, fully exploiting physical sequentiality. In contrast, the amount of reordering possible through informed prefetching depends upon the prefetch depth.

To illustrate this, we compare disk service times for a file accessed with two different global access patterns: one which results in balanced sequential disk accesses and one where the prefetch depth determines the length of globally sequential runs. Clients issue prefetches; we vary the number of simultaneously outstanding prefetches per client, but the client cache size is large enough that demand fetches do not flush prefetched buffers. In this experiment, a 4 MB file is striped over 8 disks, and blocks are contiguous on each disk.

Our first access pattern is a simple interleaved sequential pattern. There are 8 processors; each processor, p, reads every 8th block beginning with block p. This processor decomposition corresponds perfectly to the disk decomposition; unfortunately, such a perfect data decomposition is relatively unusual. In contrast, we also

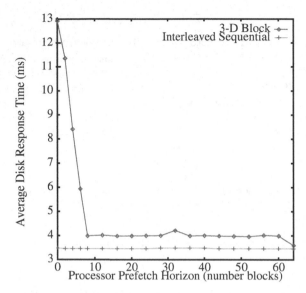

Figure 5.7
Selection of prefetch depth. Average disk response time at different prefetch horizons for
different access patterns varies substantially due to queue reordering.

consider a 3-D block decomposition. Figure 5.7 compares the average disk response
time for these access patterns at different prefetch horizons. Disk response times
for the interleaved sequential access pattern are uniformly good because the stream
of accesses to each disk is already sequential. Therefore, deeper prefetch queues
cannot further improve performance by enabling request reordering; the only benefit of prefetching is overlapping of I/O and computation. In contrast, for the 3-D
block decomposition, larger per-processor prefetch-horizons increase queue depths
and allow reordering for improved performance.

5.4.4   A Comparison of Informed Prefetching and Collective I/O

As described in §5.3, we compare performance of informed prefetching and disk-
directed I/O (an efficient implementation of collective I/O) with respect to their
memory requirements. Both approaches improve throughput through request reordering. Collective I/O does this with a minimal amount of memory using a specialized API and disk request sorting (collective throughput is independent of access
pattern). Prefetching requires additional buffers to store outstanding prefetched
blocks until they are fetched; the exact number of buffers varies with the access
pattern and the physical block layout. At the same time, these additional prefetch

Access Pattern	File Size (MB)	Crossover Prefetch Depth
Interleaved Sequential	256	1
1-D Block	256	96
3-D Block	256	32

Table 5.6
Random disk block placement with sorted block allocation.

buffers allow I/O to be overlapped with computation, further improving performance. Collective I/O can only utilize memory in multiples of the collective file size.

Thus, the comparison is one of determining how much additional memory (in prefetch buffers) is required to equal or surpass the performance of a collective interface through these two factors: improved I/O throughput because of request reordering, and overlapping of I/O and computation. In this section we show that prefetching with only a modest per-processor prefetch depth enables disk scheduling optimizations similar to a specialized collective I/O interface.

A Memory-Based Comparison   We compare the throughput of our benchmark using different I/O techniques with varying amounts of memory. For each collective read size B, there are two data points for collective I/O throughput; either the application allocates just enough memory to read the file (B), leaving no room for overlapping I/O and computation, or it allocates twice as much memory ($2B$), permitting potentially full overlap. In contrast, using prefetching, we obtain a full throughput curve as we vary the amount of memory allocated to prefetch buffers from B to $2B$.

Figure 5.8a shows application throughput for sequentially allocated files accessed using an interleaved sequential access pattern and the 3-D block decomposition illustrated in Figure 5.2. The total memory available for prefetching varies from one to two times the file size (4 MB to 8 MB) divided among the 8 processors. With prefetching, we can gradually increase the per-processor prefetch horizon, utilizing available extra memory to improve performance. With a collective interface, either none of the I/O can be overlapped with compute time, or the collective operation can be performed asynchronously with twice as much total memory. Thus, there are only two points (circled) for collective throughput. The choice of access pattern does not affect collective throughput, because blocks are optimally sorted.

The interleaved sequential access pattern matches the file layout perfectly; ad-

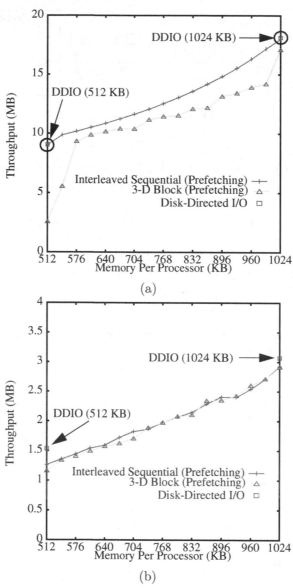

(a)

(b)

Figure 5.8
Throughput versus memory using collective input/output and prefetching. A 4 MB file is striped across 8 disks and accessed by 8 processors using different access patterns. In (a), block allocation is sequential and in (b) it is random. With sequential allocation, only a modest amount of additional memory per processor suffices to surpass the throughput obtained using a collective input/output interface. With random allocation, all access patterns exhibit similar behavior because the correlation between logical sequentiality and physical sequentiality is lost. Prefetch depths must be larger to surpass collective input/output throughput.

ditional memory improves throughput only because prefetching overlaps I/O with computation. In the 3-D block access pattern, additional prefetch buffers not only overlap I/O and computation, but improve throughput by reordering disk requests and balancing disk load, resulting in sharp performance improvements that level off. Performance of the 3-D block access pattern is not as good as the interleaved sequential pattern, even with deep prefetch queues. This is because SSTF scheduling does not reorder requests to be perfectly sequential, and a single stall can have a cascading effect on throughput when it causes other prefetches not to be issued.

Figure 5.8b shows the same throughput curves for a file with random block allocation. In this extreme, the application access pattern has little bearing upon the shape of the prefetch horizon curve; deeper prefetch queues improve throughput according to the same function, regardless of access pattern, as long as the I/O load is balanced among disks. We also observe that, because request reordering is so important to optimize random access patterns, collective I/O always provides higher throughput than prefetching with the same amount of memory. Recall that using disk-directed I/O we sort the disk blocks and with prefetching we use a shortest seek time first (SSTF) scheduling algorithm. Even when each processor prefetches its entire portion, SSTF does not perform as well as sorting the list and making a single disk sweep.

Table 5.4 summarizes throughput for different file sizes, allocated sequentially, using from one to two times the file size total memory for prefetching. The crossover prefetch depth is the number of outstanding prefetch requests per processor (in 8 KB blocks) necessary to surpass throughput obtained using a synchronous collective I/O interface and disk-directed I/O. In addition to the access patterns shown in Figure 5.2, we also evaluated a "global sequential" access pattern, created by assigning each logical file block a processor, drawn from a uniform distribution, until each processor has been assigned its share of the file. As processors read their allocated file blocks, the global access pattern is sequential but it does not correspond to any standard decomposition.

Table 5.5 summarizes throughput for an interleaved sequential collective access for a randomly allocated file; other access patterns have similar characteristics. The crossover prefetch depth increases linearly with the file size. It is clear that to exploit the high bandwidth afforded by multiple disks, file blocks that will be accessed together should be stored sequentially.

5.4.5 Selecting the Prefetch Depth

We proved in §5.3.3 that, for a theoretical system, if logical sequentiality is preserved in the physical sequentiality of the block layout and file blocks are striped, round robin across D disks, a per-processor prefetch depth of D suffices to permit optimal disk scheduling. However, real systems are not infinitely fast, nor do I/O requests occur in constant time, so we should expect the actual crossover prefetch depth, x, to increase depending on network speed, disk placement, and interrequest latency.

In our experiments, interrequest latency of blocks within the collective is zero and, therefore, not an issue. Our network is fast enough that the turnaround time for a prefetched block to be returned to the requesting processor and a new prefetch issued is much smaller than the nearly constant cost of a sequential I/O; however, it is not instantaneous. Thus, we observe in Table 5.4 that the maximum crossover prefetch depth for sequential block placement is $2 - D$; the extra factor of D allows processors to indicate which blocks they own far enough in advance that, at each timestep, the drives will have complete information for the next timestamp without instantaneous turnaround.

In a real file system, block placement is usually somewhere between sequential and random. We noted from Table 5.5 that the crossover prefetch depth increases linearly with the file size; our prefetch depth bound does not apply because the physical disk layout does not reflect the logical block order. However, even if physical blocks are not sequential, as long as they are consecutive (there may be gaps between them) and they are stored on disk in increasing logical order, a limited prefetch buffer depth will suffice to obtain maximum throughput. We demonstrate this by sorting the randomly allocated blocks used to determine the default crossover prefetch depths of Table 5.4 (so that logically increasing blocks are physically increasing on disk) and recomputing throughput. The new depths, shown in the final column of Table 5.5 and, for large files, in Table 5.6 are significantly smaller.

Note that the optimal depths are not bounded by the $2D$ threshold as they are for sequential access; this is because disk service times for randomly allocated blocks are irregular and processors must issue more outstanding prefetches to compensate for the lack of synchronicity.

Finally, although we present results only from a balanced system $(P = D)$, simulation shows that the dependence of prefetch threshold on D also holds when the number of processors and disks are different.

5.4.6   Model Accuracy

We have demonstrated that one of the benefits of informed prefetching is its ability to provide throughput improvements that increase gradually with additional memory. In §5.3.2 we described models for the throughput of informed prefetching as a function of the per-processor prefetch depth. In this section we assess the accuracy of these models compared to our simulation.

Throughput predictions provided by the model for random block placement described in §5.3.2 are accurate to within 5%, as shown in Figure 5.9. Throughput predictions provided by the model for sequential block placement are accurate to within 20% for prefetch depths greater than two. Predictions for very small depths are inaccurate because requests are so scattered that the expected rotational latency will be one revolution, as opposed to the half revolution used to calculate in the model. The model also loses accuracy at larger depths for the same reason. The curve for the 3-D block access pattern in Figure 5.8a is lower than for the interleaved sequential access pattern; the model assumes perfect sequentiality with high prefetch depths, but SSTF scheduling does not reorder requests to be perfectly sequential. The model is more accurate for larger files, when the effect of a single poor scheduling decision is smaller.

5.5 Collective Sets

We have shown that we can obtain better performance for collective operations than disk-directed I/O by prefetching if there is enough compute time to hide the additional I/O latency.

However, applications can only express their access patterns in terms of the application-level I/O interface. A traditional byte stream or record-based interface prevents many parallel applications from completely specifying the inherent parallelism of their I/O requirements. Many applications process disjoint portions of data and the order in which they process these portions is unimportant. The ability to reorder these I/O requests is a basic principle behind improving performance. If the application itself can utilize records in any order, it can give the parallel file system control over request reordering. The difference between such an approach and a collective operation is that the application does not need to consume all the data at once; it can utilize one record at a time.

We call this approach "collective set input/output" because, although like collective interfaces, the file system is given complete global access pattern information, disk accesses can be deferred until the application requires data.

In this section we evaluate this approach in comparison to hinting and disk-directed I/O.

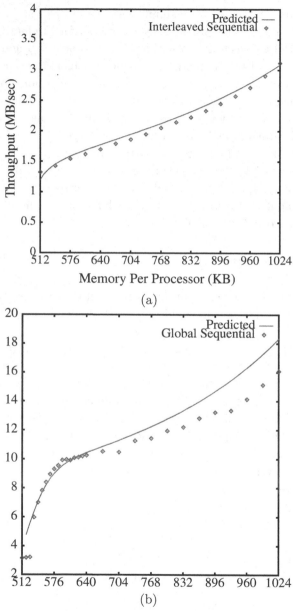

(a)

(b)

Figure 5.9
Predicted throughput versus experimental throughput. Our model for random disk placement
(a) is accurate to within 5 percent. The model for sequential disk placement (b) is accurate to
within 20 percent for prefetch depths greater than two.

5.5.1   Motivation

A large class of scientific applications are more naturally written using a file interface that does not enforce a linear byte order. For example, the Needleman, Wunch and Sellers (NWS) [194] dynamic programming algorithm for parallel gene sequence matching is implemented so that each processor independently compares a test genome sequence against disjoint portions of the sequence database. Significant speedups can be obtained by structuring this database so that processors can access any record that has not yet been requested, without regard to byte ordering and by exploiting this information before issuing physical I/O requests [119].

In general, an unordered file representation is useful for any application with high I/O requirements that can process data records (possibly tagged with metadata) in many possible orders. For example, many Grand Challenge applications (e.g., global climate modeling, modeling of the Earth's interior) periodically output large three-dimensional grids with many variables calculated for each grid point. These grids are partitioned (sometimes using complicated algorithms) among processors in disjoint chunks. At each output phase, data must be flushed as quickly as possible before computation can proceed. However, as long as each file portion is tagged with the grid points it contains, the order in which they are output is irrelevant.

The challenge in implementing collective sets is that disks must maintain additional state for each file accessed in this way. This means maintaining the mapping of logical file blocks to physical disk blocks and keeping track of which blocks have been accessed by a particular application. Such intelligence is not beyond the scope of modern file systems. An important trend in storage architecture is towards network attached disks, with more memory and processing capacity. Network Attached Secure Disks (NASD) [101] export a high-level interface to applications that allows more efficient device operation. It is feasible to extend such an interface to allow an application to specify an application-specific file structure and a corresponding set iterator.

5.5.2   Experimental Results

To evaluate the performance of a collective set interface, we repeat the experiment of §5.4, assuming that the application can read a single 8 KB block at a time. Table 5.7 shows the results of this evaluation. We compare throughput for two file sizes (4 MB and 128 MB) using disk-directed I/O and collective set I/O. The sequence of accesses on each disk is identical (perfectly sorted) for both interfaces. Collective set throughput is slightly lower than collective throughput because network transfer time is not overlapped with I/O. However, a specialized collective

Block Placement	Collective Set Throughput (MB/sec)		Collective Throughput (MB/sec)	
	4 MB	128 MB	4 MB	128 MB
Random	1.522	1.794	1.535	1.796
Sequential	8.949	9.553	9.061	9.553

Table 5.7
Collective set performance. Collective sets achieve throughput comparable to a collective I/O interface for applications that can be restructured to use them, with less application memory.

set interface achieves performance similar to collective I/O with less memory and can provide this performance over a much greater variety of global access patterns. In other words, processors do not need to be synchronized to reap disk scheduling benefits.

5.6   Related Work

Several implementations of collective I/O have been proposed. Two of the most popular are two-phase I/O [74] and disk-directed I/O [156]. In two-phase I/O, the application uses a particular interface to alert the file system to a collective operation. In a two-phase read, for example, data is read from disks sequentially and redistributed to the processors involved in the collective. A variation of two-phase I/O called extended two-phase I/O [259] uses collective I/O in conjunction with dynamic partitioning of the I/O workload among processors to balance load and improve performance. As we have described, disk-directed I/O is another method for optimizing collective requests, where the complete request is passed to the I/O processors to be sorted and transferred to application memory.

Many I/O libraries have been developed that rely upon collective I/O optimizations to improve performance of multiprocessor I/O systems. Jovian [19] is a runtime library for Single Process Multiple Data (SPMD) codes (processors execute the same code on different data). The programmer chooses the appropriate data distribution and I/O operations are implicitly collective. A variable number of coalescing processes aggregate the requests to perform them efficiently under the chosen distribution. PASSION [53, 260, 254] (Parallel And Scalable Software for Input-Output) is another runtime library targeted for SPMD applications with routines to efficiently perform out-of-core operations. The Panda [230, 48] library utilizes server-directed I/O, a variation of disk-directed I/O, and a high-level collective interface to achieve high performance on array accesses.

Patterson *et al* [209] demonstrated the potential of hinting accesses to guide prefetching and caching of files that will be accessed in the future. A cost-benefit analysis evaluates the reduction in I/O service time per buffer access to decide when to allocate buffers. This is an elegant approach for dealing with multiple applications that compete for shared caching and prefetching buffers. Kimbrel *et al* [149] and Tomkins *et al* compare several integrated caching and prefetching policies using hints for systems with multiple disks. However, these approaches do not take into account the effects of disk queue reordering that are essential to prefetching collective I/O operations.

The idea of collective sets is an extension of the Read Any mode of the Portable Parallel File System (PPFS) [119]. Using this mode, an application specifies that the processors want to collectively read disjoint records of the entire file, but in no particular order and without synchronization. This idea has also been exploited in the context of the World Wide Web to create the concept of a dynamic set, an unordered collection of objects used to support searches [242]. The file system can retrieve the set elements in the most efficient order.

5.7   Conclusions and Future Directions

We have demonstrated that informed prefetching is a viable alternative to a specialized collective I/O interface for a large class of access patterns. Unlike an efficient collective I/O implementation, informed prefetching requires limited system support beyond the ability to use memory to store asynchronous reads until they are demand fetched. It may be a more natural programming interface for a parallel application programmer who is accustomed to sequential I/O. While performance of informed prefetching improves as additional buffer space becomes available, a collective I/O interface cannot exploit additional memory unless there is enough to hold the subsequent collective read.

The main perceived advantage to a collective I/O interface over prefetching is the ability to sort the collective request pool for optimal throughput. We have proven that a bounded prefetch horizon will suffice to permit global request reordering similar to a collective interface, regardless of access pattern, assuming logical file sequentiality is preserved in physical block layout. We have validated these theoretical results with simulated experiments. Finally, we have developed and validated analytical models that match our experiments to within 20%, while reflecting the important trends and discontinuities.

While we believe the request reordering facilitated with a collective I/O API can be accomplished more generally, the idea of a specialized API to express request parallelism is important. For this reason, we propose a collective set interface that allows an application to request any block of a file that has not yet been requested. This defers scheduling decisions and results in optimal disk throughput using less memory than either informed prefetching or collective I/O.

This research leaves many directions for future work. We intend to investigate how hints can be used to tailor write policies to similarly improve performance of collective writes.

Acknowledgments

We would like to thank Steven Rudich for his help proving a bound on the prefetch depth. Also, thanks to Khalil Amiri, Mike Bigrigg, Joan Digney, Tom Kroeger, David Petrou, and David Rochberg for their detailed comments on the text. This research was partially funded by the National Science Foundation CISE Postdoctoral Research Associate Award CDA-9704704, by DARPA/ITO Order D306 issued by Indian Head Division, NSWC, under contract N00174-96-0002, by NSF ERC grant ECD-8907068, by NSF Grants No. IRI-9625428 and DMS-9873442, and by the NSF, ARPA and NASA under NSF Cooperative Agreement No. IRI-9411299. Also, by generous contributions from the member companies of the Parallel Data Consortium, including: Hewlett-Packard Laboratories, Intel, Quantum, Seagate Technology, Storage Technology, Wind River Systems, 3Com Corporation, Compaq, Data General/Clariion, and Symbios Logic.

6 Compiler Support for Out-of-Core Arrays on Parallel Machines

BRADLEY BROOM, ROB FOWLER, KEN KENNEDY, CHARLES KOELBEL AND
MICHAEL PALECZNY

Significant improvements in processor performance have greatly increased the scale of applications that can be solved using modern high-performance computing systems. However, applications at the computational limits of current systems often require internal data representations that are far bigger than can be contained in the main memory of any affordable computer. For these applications, most of the data must reside on secondary storage (disk) during execution. Such *out-of-core* applications must repeatedly move data between main memory and secondary storage during processing. Since improvements in disk I/O performance have not kept pace with processor developments, the performance impact of this data shuffling between main memory and secondary storage has become a significant limit factor for many applications.

A naive approach to the implementation of out-of-core applications is simply to rely on the virtual memory system, if one is available. Although this is a suitable technique in some cases, many out-of-core scientific and engineering applications perform quite poorly in a virtual memory environment. There are several reasons for these performance problems. First, no virtual memory page replacement policy can work well for all access patterns over a large data set, so an arbitrary computation order may result in many more I/O operations per block than an optimal computation order. Second, the size of individual paging operations can be limited to the memory subsystem's page or cluster size, which is too small for efficient transfer of large amounts of data. Third, the I/O transfer is often not initiated until the application references the memory location concerned, thus preventing overlap of computation and I/O. These observations on performance are borne out by experience. For example, Cormen and Nicol [67] have shown that, for large FFT computations, explicit out-of-core algorithms can perform more than two orders of magnitude better than an in-core algorithm using virtual memory. Although some operating systems allow an application to indicate, in advance, its memory access pattern and hence mitigate to some extent the above concerns, substantive implementation of these advisory interfaces is discretionary and, where implemented, vary widely in their effectiveness. For these reasons, the implicit virtual memory model is not ideal for many out-of-core computations.

As of today, the only alternative to using virtual memory is to implement out-of-core applications by hand. However, this shifts a substantial programming burden to the application developer. To achieve acceptable performance, such out-of-core applications must be tiled; that is, transformed to operate on subsections of the data at one time. Tiling transformations also improve the performance of programs that rely on virtual memory, but significant additional performance improvement can be obtained by using explicit, preferably asynchronous, I/O operations when moving subsections between main memory and secondary storage [283]. Such transformations require significant programmer effort and result in a much larger, more complex program that is substantially more difficult to maintain.

The amount of computation required to solve a particular problem usually grows at least as fast as the size of the data, so parallel computing systems are particularly attractive for very large problems. Even though the total amount of memory in a parallel system typically grows with the number of processors, memory is still a major capital expense, so the amount of memory per node is often limited. Furthermore, parallel systems leave a smaller fraction of memory available to application data because some part of the operating system and application code and data are replicated on every node. In addition, communication buffers are major consumers of physical memory. Parallelism will not completely remove the need for out-of-core programs. Unfortunately, parallel programming is also complex on current machines and out-of-core issues only make the problem worse. Work at Sandia National Laboratory [283] on parallel out-of-core programs showed that low-level I/O optimization is also important, but requires significant programmer effort.

In this chapter, we describe a compiler-based method for semi-automatically constructing out-of-core programs that can help relieve programmers of the burden of explicit and tedious out-of-core coding. We first describe a general approach used in research at Rice University [27, 145, 203]. We then fill in detail by describing the actions taken by a prototype compiler and how these affect runtime performance.

Our general approach is intended to reduce the burden of implementing the details of optimized out-of-core applications for parallel machines. The fundamental strategy is to allow the user to specify that some arrays are to be implemented as out-of-core data structures, along with their distribution on disk, and to have the compiler and run-time system optimize the application for efficient execution on the target machine and disk configuration. Although the context for these strategies is the High Performance Fortran programming language, the methods described herein could be used on uniprocessors and in other parallel programming languages, as well as in automatic parallelization systems. We address three major technical issues: computation order and partitioning, the size of I/O requests, and overlap of computation and I/O.

This and related research [29, 31, 34, 32, 256, 255, 258] suggest that the development and maintenance of out-of-core applications can be considerably simplified by using compiler technology to automate many of the low-level transformations required. Programmer effort is still required, but is now focused on strategic issues, such as the desired organization of out-of-core data structures, not on low level code manipulation.

The following section §6.1 describes our high-level out-of-core model and the language directives available for describing out-of-core arrays. Section §6.2 comments on the properties desired of an underlying parallel file system model and access library, and it describes the relationship between the compilation techniques and the I/O system. In section §6.3 we briefly describe the general compiler methods we use to transform the program into explicit out-of-core form and choreograph the required I/O. Section §6.4 describes how a prototype compiler using our approach transforms two regular scientific applications from dense, annotated source codes into efficient out-of-core implementations. Section §6.5 illustrates the potential performance impact of using explicit out-of-core programs using experimental performance results obtained on an Intel Paragon. Section §6.6 discusses related research, and we make some final comments in §6.7.

6.1 Annotations for Specifying Out-of-Core Data Structures

As indicated in the introduction, our approach is to have the programmer declare that an array is to be implemented as an out-of-core data structure. As a part of that declaration, the programmer should also provide the desired decomposition of out-of-core arrays. Our work has been grounded in the parallel programming language HPF, so the decomposition specifications are similar to the parallel data decomposition directives in that language. These directives allow a high-level description of the relationship between an array and its use in the computation.

Specifically, we introduce a new directive for specifying an I/O system:

```
CSIO$   IOSYSTEM IOD (16)
```

which is analogous to the HPF PROCESSORS directive for specifying parallel processors. This directive specifies an I/O system consisting of sixteen components. An array can then be distributed over the I/O system:

```
CSIO$   DISTRIBUTE A(*,BLOCK) ONTO IOD
```

This directive specifies that the array A is segmented by columns into out-of-core blocks. As in HPF, an array distribution can also be specified indirectly using the TEMPLATE and ALIGN directives.

The compiler then uses this information and static program analysis to segment the computation, construct appropriate I/O statements, and insert them in the program. Since only part of the data set is in memory at one time, computations that require nonresident data are deferred until the data is resident. We call these groupings of computations "deferred routines." By making data accesses explicit, the compiler can also perform additional optimizations which include overlapping I/O with computation.

The similarity between the I/O directives and those used to express data-parallel computation in HPF presents a consistent framework to the programmer. Both are used to describe an organization of data that will allow efficient execution.

However, data parallelism and out-of-core execution are separate issues. The directives allow the programmer to consider each issue separately and distribute an array for out-of-core, for parallelism, or for both. An array distributed for both will be partitioned in the syntactic order of the distribution statements. (Due to a current limitation of the Rice D compiler, however, an array cannot be distributed for both out-of-core and parallelism along the same dimension. We are working on removing this limitation.)

The I/O and data-parallel directives used in our sample applications are included at the beginning of the untransformed source codes presented in Figures 6.1 and 6.2.

6.2   The I/O System

In our model, a high-performance out-of-core application consists of two components. The first is an application that is optimized to minimize the cost of data transfer between in-core and out-of-core storage, to overlap such transfers with computation, and so on. The principal focus of our research is the automation of transformations for deriving such optimized applications from annotated, dense source codes.

The second component is equally vital: an efficient, runtime file access system. Although discussion of file system implementations is generally beyond the scope of this chapter, we make two remarks.

First, in parallel systems, efficient run-time libraries exist for coordinating file system accesses from all nodes. Two alternatives for efficient parallel disk access are the two-phase access strategy [74] and disk-directed I/O [156]. For instance, Bordawekar, del Rosario, and Choudhary [30] designed a library of user-accessible primitives which are configured at runtime to the desired memory and disk distribu-

```
            program oocRB
            double precision a(0:319,0:319,0:319)

CHPF$ processors        p(16)
CHPF$ template          d( 320, 320, 320 )
CHPF$ align             a(i,j,k) with d(i+1,j+1,k+1)
CHPF$ distribute        d( * , block, * ) onto p
C
CSIO$ iosystem          pio(32)
CSIO$ template          iod( 320, 320, 320)
CSIO$ align             a(i,j,k) with iod(i+1,j+1,k+1)
CSIO$ distribute        iod( * , * , block ) onto pio
C

C     Open the file and read data from disk
C     ********** iterate red-black computation. **********
            do  n  = 1, 5
C     Compute red points
          do  k  = 2, 316, 2
            do  j  = 2, 316, 2
              do  i  = 2, 316, 2
                a(i,j,k)    = (a(i+1,j,k) + a(i-1,j,k)
     *              + a(i,j+1,k) + a(i,j-1,k)
     *              + a(i,j,k+1) + a(i,j,k-1) )/6
                a(i+1,j+1,k)= (a(i+2,j+1,k) + a(i,j+1,k)
     *              + a(i+1,j+2,k) + a(i+1,j,k)
     *              + a(i+1,j+1,k+1) + a(i+1,j+1,k-1) )/6
                a(i,j+1,k+1)= (a(i+1,j+1,k+1) + a(i-1,j+1,k+1)
     *              + a(i,j+2,k+1) + a(i,j,k+1)
     *              + a(i,j+1,k+2) + a(i,j+1,k))/6
                a(i+1,j,k+1)= (a(i+2,j,k+1) + a(i,j,k+1)
     *              + a(i+1,j+1,k+1) + a(i+1,j-1,k+1)
     *              + a(i+1,j,k+2) + a(i+1,j,k) )/6
              enddo
            enddo
          enddo
C     Compute black points
          do  k  = 2, 316, 2
            do  j  = 2, 316, 2
              do  i  = 2, 316, 2
                a(i,j,k+1)    = (a(i+1,j,k+1) + a(i-1,j,k+1)
     *              + a(i,j+1,k+1) + a(i,j-1,k+1)
     *              + a(i,j,k+2) + a(i,j,k) )/6
                a(i+1,j+1,k+1)= (a(i+2,j+1,k+1) + a(i,j+1,k+1)
     *              + a(i+1,j+2,k+1) + a(i+1,j,k+1)
     *              + a(i+1,j+1,k+2) + a(i+1,j+1,k) )/6
                a(i,j+1,k)    = (a(i+1,j+1,k) + a(i-1,j+1,k)
     *              + a(i,j+2,k) + a(i,j,k)
     *              + a(i,j+1,k+1) + a(i,j+1,k-1) )/6
                a(i+1,j,k)    = (a(i+2,j,k) + a(i,j,k)
     *              + a(i+1,j+1,k) + a(i+1,j-1,k)
     *              + a(i+1,j,k+1) + a(i+1,j,k-1) )/6
              enddo
            enddo
          enddo
        enddo
        end
```

Figure 6.1
Sequential red-black relaxation program.

```
      program oocLU
      double precision a(6401,6400),row1(6400),row2(6400)
      integer          pivotrow

CHPF$ processors       p (4)
CHPF$ template         d( 6401, 6400 )
CHPF$ align            a(i,j) with d(i,j)
CHPF$ distribute       d( block, *  ) onto p
CSIO$ iosystem         pio(100)
CSIO$ template         iod( 6401,  6400  )
CSIO$ align            a(i,j) with iod(i,j)
CSIO$ distribute       iod( * , block ) onto pio

      do j = 1, 6400
         pivotEntry = 0.0
C        Find pivot row
         do i = j, 6400
            if( a(i,j) .GT. pivotEntry ) then
               pivotEntry = a(i,j)
               pivotRow   = i
            endif
         enddo
         a( 6401, j) = pivotRow

C        Scale pivot row
         scale =  1.0/pivotEntry
         do i = j, 6400
            a( i, j ) = scale * a( i, j )
         enddo
         a(pivotRow, j) = pivotEntry

         if( j .ne. pivotRow ) then
            do i = j, 6400
               row1(i) = a( j, i )
            enddo
         endif

C        Copy the pivot row
         do i = j, 6400
            row2(i) = a( pivotRow, i )
         enddo

C        If pivot row is not diagonal, swap rows.
         if( pivotRow .NE. j ) then
C           DCOPY((6400-j)+1,row1(1),1,a(pivotRow,j),6400)
            do i = j, 6400
               a( pivotRow, i ) = row1(i)
            enddo
C           DCOPY((6400-j)+1,row2(1),1,a(j,j),6400)
            do i = j, 6400
               a( j, i ) = row2(i)
            enddo
         endif

         do i = j+1, 6400
C           DAXPY(6400-j,-row2(i),a(j+1,j),1,a(j+1,i),1)
            do k = j+1, 6400
               a( k, i ) = a( k, i ) - row2(i) * a( k, j )
            enddo
         enddo
      enddo
      end
```

Figure 6.2
Sequential LU factorization program.

tions of the data. The Passion library [260] efficiently reads and writes entire arrays or sections of arrays in parallel. The more recent MPI-2 standard includes similar capabilities (for instance, see [263]). Such I/O libraries provide efficient access to out-of-core arrays [259] and can, and should, be used effectively by out-of-core compilation strategies. In general, developments in such libraries are complementary to the techniques described in this chapter.

Second, file system access in a parallel environment requires a model for specifying which compute nodes can access which parts of the file system. Thakur *et al* [260] describe three such models. In the *Local Placement Model*, the out-of-core array is partitioned across the available processors, and the data for each processor is then stored on a file system local to that processor. Read access to remote data requires cooperation from its owning processor. In the *Global Placement Model*, the out-of-core array is partitioned across the available processors, but the data for all processors is stored in a global file system. A processor is able to read data owned by another directly from the file system. In the *Partitioned In-core Model*, the data is again stored in a global file system, but subdivided into large partitions each equal in size to the total available in-core memory of all processors. Each out-of-core partition is accessed collectively, with I/O not required during its processing.

6.3   Compiling for Out-of-Core Execution

Our strategy for out-of-core compilation consists of three phases: program analysis, I/O insertion and optimization, and parallelization and communication optimization. This design allows us to use components of the Fortran D system at Rice University in our implementation of an out-of-core compiler.

6.3.1   Program Analysis

The program analysis phase uses both traditional and new compiler techniques to discover patterns of data use within the program. Interprocedural data-flow analysis propagates the user out-of-core directives in the same way that the HPF data mapping directives are handled. The code sections that use the annotated arrays are marked as using out-of-core data and their data use is summarized using Regular Section Descriptors (RSDs) [111]. Again, this analysis is similar to the communications analysis performed by the Fortran D compiler. In addition, data and control dependences are needed to determine when data reuse and overlapping I/O and computation are legal.

The computation should be reordered for maximum reuse. This is important in any memory hierarchy, but for out-of-core transformations more extreme transformations, including redundant computation, must be considered.

6.3.2 I/O Insertion and Optimization

The I/O insertion phase uses the analysis results to partition the computation among tiles and to determine, for each tile, which section of data is needed and which should be stored to disk. The techniques used are similar to the "owner-computes" rule, which assigns computation to the processor owning a particular datum. In the I/O arena, computation (often in the form of loop iterations) is split into code sections that process individual out-of-core tiles. These code sections constitute the "data-deferred routines" since their computation must often be deferred until data is read from disk. Generally, the compiler must insert I/O statements to read the appropriate out-of-core tile into memory and write modified data to disk when finished. USE analysis in the deferred routine determines if data may be required from other out-of-core tiles, in which case additional I/O statements and control-flow are inserted. Next, the compiler inserts the control flow to process out-of-core tiles.

In general, data flow inter-tile dependences determine the ordering of tile computations. If the tiles are independent, any order can be used; initially, we use the execution order of the original program. We implemented this by adding a loop around the deferred-routines to iterate through the out-of-core tiles. More complex orderings, which may be more efficient, could require a more general methodology.

For example, the red and black computation routines in red-black relaxation (see section 6.4.1) exemplify the different effect of global operations on in-core data-parallel versus out-of-core compilation. On a distributed memory machine, with all data in-core, it is reasonable to compute all the red points then compute the interspersed black points. For an out-of-core problem, this approach requires two complete scans of the entire data set. When transforming red-black relaxation, we align the loop, which accesses out-of-core tiles for the black computation, with respect to that for the red, to allow the black computation for tile N to execute after the red computation for tile $N+1$. This requires that sufficient memory is available in-core for two tiles. If insufficient memory is available for a profitable transformation, the compiler can provide feedback to the programmer. This transformation is similar to alignment of vector operations to allow reuse [8].

In the next phase, the compiler optimizes the inserted I/O statements. Dependence analysis results determine when it is safe to overlap computation and I/O. A cost model must also be applied to determine that this is profitable, as the overlapping may require more main memory. Computing which data in a tile will be needed while processing the next tile is handled by intersecting the two sets as summarized by their RSDs. This is easily done using the integer set framework that underlies our current compiler [4].

When the initial or final data layout is not compatible with the temporary storage distribution, or the programmer requests a redistribution during execution, the data must be remapped. This can be done with run-time routines extended for out-of-core data [30, 257] or, when the source and destination distribution are known at compile time, by generating explicit I/O operations interleaved with computation.

6.3.3 Parallelization and Communication Optimization

Finally, a parallelization phase compiles the transformed program for parallel machines. This uses the regular Fortran D compilation process, with extensions to allow I/O access. In particular, we assume either of Thakur's local or global placement models. When parallelizing the out-of-core I/O using the local placement model, each processor executes the I/O statements restricted to the values it "owns." Each processor opens a separate file and does its reads and writes to that file. When a processor needs data it does not own, the owner performs the I/O and sends the data in a message. When parallelizing the out-of-core I/O using the global placement model, all processors open a common global file, and perform reads directly from that file. Each processor is still restricted to only writing values that it "owns."

One important interaction of this phase with the I/O insertion concerns the in-core overlap regions generated by the compiler. These may be interleaved in memory with the addresses available to hold an out-of-core tile. Although the prototype uses the simplest solution—each processor reads and writes the boundary data along with the original—a better solution would be to reorder the computation to isolate accesses to the border area and store the border in a separate buffer. This preserves the connectedness of the out-of-core tile and allows some overlap of the computation with I/O for the border.

6.4 Experience with a Prototype Compiler

We implemented a restricted prototype of the general strategy discussed above as an extension to the Rice Fortran D compiler. This section describes the transformation, by that prototype, of two regular scientific applications into explicit out-of-core form. In §6.5, we discuss the impact of these transformations on performance.

6.4.1 Transforming Red-Black Relaxation

Our first example is red-black relaxation on a $320 \times 320 \times 320$ Cartesian mesh. This is representative of many scientific algorithms on large 3-dimensional domains. The program is shown in Figure 6.1.

The intuitive meaning of the out-of-core annotations used in this program is that one out-of-core tile is a $320 \times 320 \times 10$ block. Orthogonal to the out-of-core distribution, the HPF directives specify blocking among parallel processors in the second dimension. Because the out-of-core and processor distributions are in orthogonal dimensions, each out-of-core tile is distributed across the processors such that each processor operates on a $320 \times 20 \times 10$ tile. The combined out-of-core and parallel distribution of data for one in-core plane of the array is illustrated in Figure 6.3.

In this application, each tile required extra communication only at the boundaries. (This is handled by small overlap regions, well-known from data-parallel compilers.) Inter-tile dependence edges show that the deferred black computation for tile N depends upon the red computation for tiles $N - 1$, N, and $N + 1$. Skewing the tiling loop for the black computation by one iteration, plus peeling the first iteration from the front of the red loop and the last iteration from the black loop, allows the two loops to be fused.

The boundary data also affects a read of the next tile, as the first plane of the next tile is already in-core. We identify this by intersecting the summary RSD, representing data in-core for computation, on the current tile with the RSD for data used by the next tile. The two planes of data adjacent to the next tile are in the intersection and thus are available for reuse. The I/O request for the next tile is reduced in size. After these optimizations are performed, no duplicate I/O occurs within an iteration of red-black relaxation.

6.4.2 Transforming LU Factorization

Our second example is LU factorization with pivoting, a method for solving dense linear systems. Our program is based on one provided by David Womble at Sandia National Laboratory [283, 284]. Since his program is out-of-core and parallel, we started by serializing the computation and then used the compiler to rediscover the original implementation. The sequential code is shown in Figure 6.2.

In this case, the out-of-core annotations specify blocks of columns, while the parallel annotations specify blocks of rows, giving the combined I/O and parallel distribution of data shown in Figure 6.4.

Again, the compilation follows the outline of §6.3. Since an in-core tile consists of

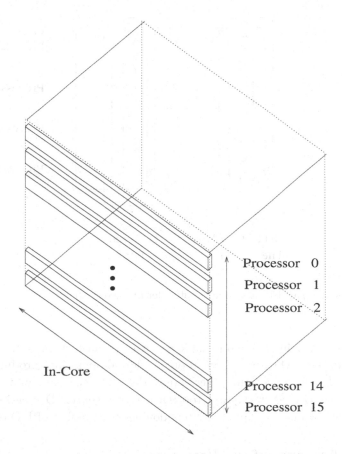

Figure 6.3
One out-of-core tile distributed to processors for red-black relaxation.

a group of columns, a pivot operation spans all tiles to the right of the one containing the current diagonal element. The pivot operation is split into computation on the data currently in memory and deferred pivot operations which apply to tiles to the right. The outer-product operation is likewise divided into current and deferred computations. The deferred pivot and outer-product operations execute in their original order when a tile is brought into memory. The deferred code is essentially a node program from which operations performing computations owned by other tiles are elided or deferred.

The inter-tile communication for the outer-product is more complex than in red-black relaxation, requiring data from all previously computed tiles. Since not

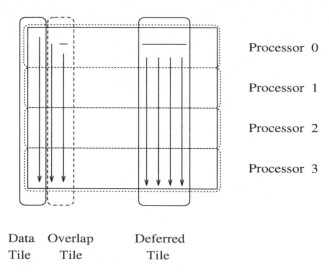

Processor 0

Processor 1

Processor 2

Processor 3

Data   Overlap   Deferred
Tile   Tile   Tile

Figure 6.4
Interaction of data-parallel and I/O distribution for LU factorization.

all these tiles can fit in memory at once, a loop must stage data into memory. Overlapping this I/O with the execution of deferred operations produces significant savings for LU factorization. Overlapping the I/O necessary for the outer loop, however, does not, as it requires too much buffer space. Decreasing the size of deferred tiles by one half approximately doubles the number of I/O operations.

6.5   Performance of the Prototype

To illustrate the effect of the transformations described above, we ran multiple versions of the applications on the Intel Paragon located at Rice University. We used OSF/1 release 1.0.4 version 1.2.3, which supports asynchronous file I/O. All of the file-I/O results were obtained performing I/O to one parallel file system (PFS) using two I/O nodes and two RAID disk systems, each connected using a SCSI-1 interface. The RAIDs are configured with 64K disk blocks and memory is divided into 8K pages.

The local placement model was implemented on the Paragon by creating a separate file for each processor within a parallel file system. This file system is striped onto one RAID device and accessed through one I/O node. The virtual memory system uses both RAID systems for paging.

The performance graphs plot total execution time versus the number of processors. The total execution time includes the time spent reading initial data from files and the final writing of results. The distribution of initial data into files matches the distribution of the array.

The graphs compare the performance of implicit I/O (virtual memory) with explicit I/O and synchronous file I/O with asynchronous I/O. They show that, for these applications, compiler management of I/O is more than two times faster then relying on virtual memory, even when more than half of the data fits in main memory. Testing using different I/O request sizes indicates that much of this improvement is due to the larger requests made by the explicit I/O calls.

The graphs also show that asynchronous I/O consistently performs better than synchronous I/O.

6.5.1   Red-Black Relaxation

The red-black relaxation code was run on nodes with 32 MB of main memory. Our results for virtual memory, synchronous I/O, and overlapped I/O with computation are shown in Figure 6.5. In addition, two different tiling strategies are compared.

The solid line shows the virtual memory performance for 1 to 32 nodes. The performance improvement at 16 nodes occurs when all the data is retained in memory.

Comparing the virtual memory performance to synchronous I/O shows that even at 8 processors, when more than half of the data fits in memory, our approach for compiler management of I/O is more than two times faster than relying on virtual memory. (We believe this result will still hold for larger out-of-core problems run on larger numbers of processors.)

As shown in Table 6.1, overlapping I/O and computation in red-black relaxation further improves performance an average of 17.4 percent for small tiles, and 14.9 percent for large tiles, on 1 to 8 processors. This behavior does not scale to larger numbers of processors for the small-tile version due to the small ratio of computation to I/O and communication at each node. A modified program that performs only I/O shows similar increases in execution time.

Figure 6.5 also shows the effect on performance of varying the tile size. The *large tile* version (shown as dashed lines) uses a tile size containing 10 planes of data. Although this version kept all data in memory when using 16 processors, the large interprocessor messages generated by the compiler crashed the application. The *small tile* version (shown as dotted lines) keeps exactly two tiles of the matrix in memory at any given time, each small tile holds two planes of data. This does not make full use of available memory, but is useful as a comparison to the large-tile

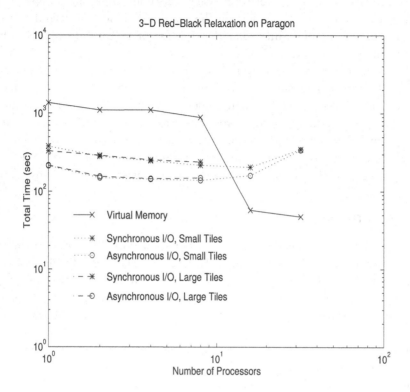

Figure 6.5
Execution time for red-black relaxation.

version. The small size of the tiles avoided the large message problem described above.

6.5.2 LU Factorization

Figure 6.6 shows our results for LU factorization. One set of results used nodes with 16 MB of memory. The other used nodes with 32 MB of memory. The memory available for program text and data on each node was approximately 5 MB and 21 MB, respectively. The graph compares the performance using synchronous file I/O operations (○ data points) with the performance using asynchronous file I/O (∗ data points) for a 6400 × 6400 matrix using each class of node. Table 6.2 shows a consistent improvement obtained by overlapping I/O with computation while

Tile Size	Number of Processors			
	1	2	4	8
Small Tiles	12.3%	20.3%	27.0%	10.1%
Large Tiles	7.4%	19.4%	16.2%	16.7%

Table 6.1
Percent improvement in execution time between synchronous and asynchronous I/O for red-black relaxation.

Memory Size	Number of Processors					
	1	2	4	8	16	32
16 MB	24.4%	22.4%	23.8%	24.4%	19.3%	13.4%
32 MB	10.9%	7.5%	7.4%	5.8%	10.0%	*

Table 6.2
Percent improvement in execution time between synchronous and asynchronous I/O for LU factorization. (* Result unavailable)

varying the number of processors.

The virtual memory version of this program did not complete execution at this problem size. The results of previous tests with a smaller data set are summarized in Table 6.3. The Initial Program/Virtual Memory case used a version of the program with very poor locality. That program was transformed by tiling so that operations were performed in the same order as for the earlier tests. This tiling gives a factor of 200 speedup from improved locality at the memory to disk interface. Further improvements were obtained by using file I/O instead of virtual memory and from overlapping I/O and computation by using asynchronous I/O.

6.5.3   Discussion

Synchronous file I/O performs better than virtual memory on the Intel Paragon, and much of this improvement derives from the compiler's requests for large blocks of data and the large block-size of the RAID I/O devices.

Increasing the system's page size should significantly improve the performance of the virtual memory system on the large sequential accesses in our applications. However, this could adversely affect the performance of applications with different paging requirements. More modern operating systems may achieve most of the gains, due to large page sizes, but not their drawbacks by paging in several sequential pages at a time, perhaps a result of earlier system calls advising on memory usage.

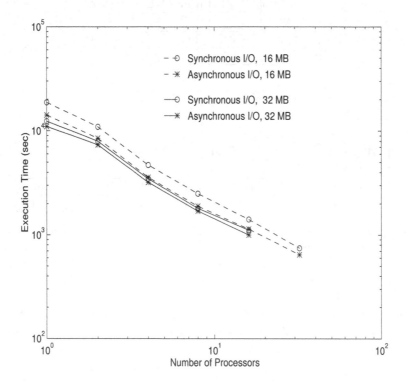

Figure 6.6
Execution times for LU factorization.

Virtual memory systems automatically use the available amount of physical memory. In contrast, we had to explicitly scale the size of the out-of-core tiles to take advantage of the additional main memory available as the number processors increased. However, computations relying on virtual memory are limited by the virtual memory size, whereas those using explicit I/O are not.

Because the I/O is visible to the compiler, overlapping I/O with computation provides further improvements. In this sense, the original insertion is an enabling transformation, allowing the compiler to generate code that utilizes the parallelism both within the I/O system and between it and computation. Explicit I/O, via an optimizing runtime library such as Passion [260], also enables the parallel processors to cooperate when concurrently accessing adjacent and/or overlapping sections of an out-of-core data structure. An additional benefit is the separation of data into

Matrix	Total Execution Time (seconds)			
Size	Initial Program	Tiled Program, after I/O distribution		
	Virtual Memory	Virtual Memory	Synchronous I/O	Overlapped I/O
100x100	0.08	0.09	0.11	0.14
800x800	33.3	33.3	21.4	20.5
1200x1200	2270	178	120	98.4
1600x1600	82587	399	268	234

Table 6.3
Comparison of explicit I/O to virtual memory for small problem sizes on 1 processor with 16 MB memory.

distinct files by the compiler. This makes it simple to distribute data used by different processors onto the available I/O devices.

An important question is whether these applications will exhibit similar performance characteristics when scaled to larger data sets, more processors, and additional I/O nodes. In red-black relaxation, the amount of both computation and I/O scale linearly with the number of data points. Executing a program ten times larger on a system that has been scaled by a factor of ten (processors and I/O nodes) will produce similar results. This is not the case for LU factorization. Computation and I/O increase faster than the size of the data set. Although scaling problem size, processors, and I/O nodes by a factor of ten will result in significantly longer execution times than for our example, the improvements from overlapping I/O and computation should remain similar. They depend upon the ratio of problem size to available memory. This ratio determines the amount of I/O which will be performed but does not affect the amount of computation.

6.6   Related Work

Compiler-based transformations for generating out-of-core programs are closely related to compilation strategies for improving virtual memory performance. Abu-Sufah [1] examined the application of loop distribution followed by loop fusion to improve locality. Trivedi [273] examined the potential benefits of programmer-inserted prefetching directives for matrix multiplication on the STAR computer and compiler support for demand prepaging on sequential machines [274]. A growing body of work [165, 40, 186] examines similar concerns for cache memories.

Bordawekar, Choudhary, Kandemir, and Thakur [256, 137, 139, 136, 138] have also developed compiler methods for out-of-core HPF programs. Since they collaborated with us on the Scalable I/O initiative, their work has many similarities to ours although we believe that our use of explicit I/O directives to specify out-of-core tilings provides useful information to the compiler, while the automatic discovery of which is still a significant research problem. This allows our work to focus on generating efficient code.

Brezany [32] has developed language extensions for describing out-of-core data structures within Vienna Fortran and has developed supporting compilation methods and run-time libraries.

Cormen [64] has developed efficient out-of-core permutation algorithms and examined their I/O requirements within a data-parallel virtual memory system (VM-DP). He has also developed language and compiler techniques for parallel out-of-core I/O using the ViC* language [66, 65, 55].

Mowry, Demke, and Krieger [187] have developed a compiler for aggressively inserting non-binding prefetch and release hints for I/O, enabling a runtime system and the operating system to cooperatively accelerate I/O performance.

Agrawal [7] has described a general interprocedural framework for the placement of split-phase, large latency operations such as I/O.

Despite the significant work in optimizing out-of-core applications described above, substantial research problems remain.

The optimization strategies described above are based on similar strategies used for improving memory-hierarchy performance and automatic parallelization. Although many of these strategies are also appropriate for out-of-core transformations, I/O has its unique characteristics, in particular large seek penalties for non-contiguous data accesses.

The transformations presented in this chapter are only applicable to regular scientific applications. Discovering efficient out-of-core transformations for irregular scientific codes is still a significant research problem, although Brezany [34] has proposed some methods.

Programs implementing large scale computations requiring out-of-core data structures are also likely to have other significant I/O requirements, such as the snapshoting and checkpointing of key data structures. The I/O optimization techniques developed for out-of-core execution can also be applied to scheduling these I/O operations. In addition, the data sets involved in these operations are likely to overlap and performance improvements can be gained by using a single I/O for each such data element. Research into language extensions, runtime systems, and compilation techniques for such optimizations is underway.

Perhaps most interesting is the question of optimizing tile shape and size. In this work, the programmer provides explicit annotations describing the tiling. However in a large program, with several out-of-core data structures, each used in a number of different multiple loop nests, the optimum way of assigning tile shapes and sizes to each array is by no means obvious. A completely automatic system would have to balance considerations of available memory, disk contention, comparative computation and communication rates, and parallel execution across all data structures and loop nests to choose optimal parameters, which is probably impossible. A more plausible scenario is an interactive programming environment that can analyze the performance implications of programmer selected distributions and provide appropriate realtime feedback to the programmer.

6.7   Conclusions

Efficient out-of-core applications are very difficult to write and maintain by hand. In large part, this is because of the lack of appropriate language and system support.

This chapter has described a prototype, compiler-based approach to solving these problems. Using a few, high-level directives like those in data-parallel languages, the programmer can indicate how to subdivide a problem into out-of-core subsets. Using this information, the compiler will then insert and optimize input and output statements to convert the program into an efficient, out-of-core form. The techniques for doing this are based on previous work on parallelizing compilers such as the Fortran D compiler.

To demonstrate the effectiveness and feasibility of this approach, the transformation of two sample scientific applications into out-of-core form was described and their performance evaluated. The results, although not as good as in-core performance, are significantly better than a naive, virtual memory implementation and are very encouraging.

In particular, they show that tiling is appropriate for virtual memory systems and can substantially increase performance. They also show that using explicit I/O requests for managing out-of-core data structures enables the compiler to aggregate I/O into larger requests and to overlap computation and I/O, resulting in significant further performance improvements.

A successful out-of-core compiler will allow the comparatively easy conversion of standard algorithms to efficient out-of-core forms. It will, therefore, also enable the source code to remain in a dense, high-level notation, which is much easier to develop, understand, debug, port, and maintain. The benefits for advanced applications, requiring very large data structures, should be obvious.

Much work, however, remains to be done. We see the area of out-of-core computations as an excellent area of continuing research with practical applications. [130]

Acknowledgments

This research was supported in part by The Center for Research on Parallel Computation (CRPC) at Rice University, under NFS Cooperative Agreement Number CCR-9120008; and by the Scalable I/O Initiative, a multiagency project funded by the Advanced Research Projects Agency, the Department of Energy, the National Aeronautics and Space Administration, and the National Science Foundation.

7 CLIP: A Checkpointing Tool for Message Passing Parallel Programs

Yuqun Chen, James S. Plank and Kai Li

Fault tolerance is very important for large-scale parallel computers. Typically, such machines have more hardware components than their workstation counterparts; their software is more complex and less tested. This results in a smaller mean time before failure. Since most applications for these computers are long-running and CPU-intensive, the ability to tolerate failures is of great importance.

Checkpointing is a useful technique for providing applications with *rollback recovery*. A checkpointing operation stores the execution state of a running program on stable storage. After a system restarts from a crash, the state of the application can be recovered from (or rolled back to) its most recent checkpoint and the program execution resumes as if the crash had never occurred.

This chapter describes CLIP(**C**heckpointing **L**ibraries for the **I**ntel **P**aragon), a semi-transparent checkpointer for the Intel Paragon. CLIP can checkpoint programs written in either NX or MPI; both are *de facto* message-passing platforms for high-performance computing. To use CLIP, a user must link the CLIP library with his or her application program. Additionally, the user must place one or more subroutine calls in his or her code that specify when checkpoints can occur. When the code is executed, CLIP takes periodic checkpoints of the program's state to disk. If for some reason (hardware or software failure) the program is terminated prematurely, it may be restarted from the checkpoint file.

We call CLIP *semi-transparent* because the user must perform minor code modifications to define the checkpointing locations. This is more cumbersome than using a *totally transparent* checkpointer that can checkpoint any running application (but often requires operating system modifications). However, it is more transparent than many checkpointing tools [18, 117, 236], which require the user to rebuild the program state (i.e. the stack frames), the message state and the file system upon recovery. These tasks are handled automatically by CLIP.

The Intel Paragon was designed for high performance. Specifically, there is much custom hardware and specialized software designed to make network and file I/O extremely efficient. This complexity has many ramifications on the design of a checkpointing system. The bulk of this chapter describes the design of CLIP, concentrating on five basic issues: (1) the degree of transparency, (2) checkpoint consistency, (3) protected message state, (4) efficient file I/O and (5) performance optimizations. For each issue, we detail the way in which CLIP inter-operates with the complex hardware and software of the Paragon to balance ease-of-use, correctness, and high performance. Although the discussion is specific to the Paragon, most details are relevant to all multicomputer systems, and even some distributed systems.

The remainder of the chapter assesses the performance of CLIP on several long-running applications on a large (128-node) Paragon installation. The conclusion that we draw is that CLIP is an effective tool for fault-tolerance on the Paragon, providing efficient checkpointing with a minimum of programmer effort.

7.1   Intel Paragon

The Intel Paragon is a MIMD-style distributed-memory multicomputer. A parallel application on Paragon consists of multiple instances (or processes) of the program, each running on a distinct *processing node*. The number of processing nodes in a Paragon can scale up to 1000. A Paragon node is composed of one or two *compute* processors and a *communication* processor. The processors share access to the node-private memory via a cache-coherent bus. The application process runs on the compute processor(s) in user mode. The communication processor runs the system-dependent layer of the message-passing protocol in protected kernel mode. The processors share memory so that communication may proceed in an extremely efficient manner without requiring the application to make costly system calls. This is described in greater detail in section 7.3.3.

The Paragon nodes are connected by a high-speed *mesh routing backplane* capable of 200 MB/sec node-to-node communication bandwidth. Processes of a program communicate with each other using either Intel's NX message-passing protocol [211] or MPI [181]. Both NX and MPI consist of three parts: user-level code linked with the application program, kernel-level code executing on the compute processors, and kernel-level code executing on the communication processor. This design enables users to use the raw power of the message-passing substrate while absorbing a minimum of software overhead.

A number of nodes in a Paragon are reserved as dedicated I/O nodes. They do not execute application processes, but instead cooperate to compose the *Parallel File System (PFS)*. Each has a hard disk attached to it. PFS is optimized for parallel I/O, performing striping across all the I/O nodes at a large granularity. In other words, large data reads and writes are efficient.

Thus, the Paragon is configured to provide a high-performance computing environment for application programmers. The challenge in writing a checkpointer for the Paragon is to enable fault-tolerance in a convenient manner for application users, while maintaining the high-performance of the computing environment.

7.2   CLIP Programming Interface

CLIP consists of two user-level libraries, `libNXckpt.a` and `libMPIckpt.a`, for NX and MPI programs respectively. Both libraries are semi-transparent, meaning the programmer must slightly modify his or her code to enable checkpointing. Specifically, the programmer must insert the procedure call `checkpoint_here()` at code locations where he or she desires checkpoints to be taken. Then, the programmer recompiles the modified modules, and re-links the program with the proper checkpointing library.

Upon instantiation, the user may set runtime parameters via command line arguments or via a control file. The startup portion of CLIP reads these parameters and acts accordingly. Examples of runtime parameters that the user may set are whether to checkpoint or recover from a checkpoint, the minimum interval between checkpoints, and which optimizations to employ.

While CLIP is less transparent than checkpointers that require no code modification [150, 167, 227, 253], it imposes minimal effort on the part of the user. There are several more cumbersome tasks that non-transparent checkpointers [11, 18, 117, 235, 236] force the user to do that are totally automated in CLIP.

First and foremost is stack reconstruction. Non-transparent checkpointers provide the programmer with a convenient interface for saving/restoring critical data, but the user must rebuild the execution state of the program by hand. This means that if checkpointing occurs within one or more levels of procedure calls, the user must somehow re-instantiate those procedures upon recovery. Programming in such a way often results in awkward programs that are hard to read and maintain, and can be less efficient than they would be in the absence of checkpointing. CLIP saves the stack and registers as part of the checkpoint, meaning that the execution state is automatically restored upon recovery. This allows the programmer to insert `checkpoint_here()` calls anywhere in his or her code, regardless of the level of subroutine nesting.

Second is checkpoint consistency. As will be described in §7.3.2, the state of the network must be considered when taking a checkpoint of a parallel machine. If checkpoints are taken at the wrong times, it may be impossible to recover from a stored checkpoint. Non-transparent checkpointers deal with this issue by requiring the programmers to ensure that their checkpoints are consistent. In contrast, CLIP performs the task of assuring that checkpoints are consistent, thus relieving the programmer of that burden.

Third is the communication state of the processor. On the Paragon, a message may be buffered by a receiving node until the application asks for it. Thus, although

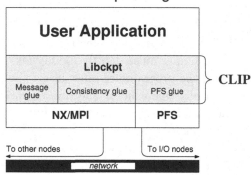

Figure 7.1
Structure of CLIP.

it is not in the network, it is hidden from the application program until needed. If buffered messages are not stored with checkpoints, they will be lost on recovery. A non-transparent solution addressing communication state is to assume that there is none when checkpoints are being stored. In other words, the programmer must assure that all sent messages have been received by the application program before a checkpoint is taken. CLIP handles this problem by making sure that the buffers are stored as part of the checkpoint and then making them available on recovery.

Thus, although CLIP is not totally transparent, it achieves an ease-of-use that is far beyond non-transparent checkpointers.

7.3   The Design of CLIP

CLIP's ancestors are the checkpointers `libckpt` [214] and **ickp** [216]. Libckpt is a checkpointer for uniprocessor systems that will be discussed in detail in §7.3.5. **Ickp** is a checkpointer for the Intel iPSC/860 multicomputer. Because of `libckpt`'s implementation of effective checkpointing optimizations, and because the iPSC/860 is a much simpler machine than the Paragon, `libckpt` was chosen as the basic building block. **Ickp** was employed more as a "study guide" for dealing with consistency and message state.

The conceptual structure of CLIP is depicted in Figure 7.1. Without checkpointing, the user's application is linked with libraries for NX or MPI, and for PFS. These libraries handle communication and file I/O respectively. With checkpointing, the CLIP code acts as middleware between the user's application and the Paragon libraries. The main interface to checkpointing is the interface of `libckpt` [214]. However, there are three important issues on the Paragon that are not relevant for a uniprocessor checkpointer like `libckpt`. These are dealing with message state, processor consistency, and the parallel file system. CLIP integrates these issues with conceptual layers of glue between `libckpt` and the respective Paragon libraries.

The composite view of CLIP is thus as an implementation of `libckpt` with enhancements for working on the Paragon. The benefits of this approach are twofold. First, `libckpt`'s interface was designed to work hand-in-hand with several performance optimizations. These are described below in §7.3.5. By using `libckpt` as a building block for CLIP, we were able to incorporate a majority of `libckpt`'s optimization techniques. Second, application programmers who are familiar with `libckpt`'s approach will have an easy time adapting to CLIP.

In the remainder of this section, we discuss the main design decisions in the implementation of CLIP.

7.3.1 The Degree of Transparency

Ideally, checkpointing should be totally transparent to an application, implemented either in the operating system, or by an external program that can attach to a running executable and checkpoint its state without programmer or user intervention. However, the design of the Paragon precludes either of these approaches, leaving a checkpointing library as the most viable option.

Our initial desire was to make CLIP totally transparent, checkpoints being initiated by timer interrupts and signals. However, this approach was rejected because of its implications on correctness and performance. Instead, we opted for *semi-transparency*, where the programmer must place `checkpoint_here()` calls into his or her code. While this does place a burden on the programmer, it is a slight one compared to non-transparent approaches (discussed above in §7.2).

Below we detail the reasons why total transparency compromises both correctness and performance of the Paragon, and how the semi-transparency alleviates both of these problems.[1]

First, message-passing on the Paragon consists of three parts – the user-level library, the compute processors' kernels, and the communication processor's kernel. All three contain data structures that reflect the current state of the network and communication system. With a totally transparent checkpointer, a checkpoint can occur anywhere in application code, including the message-passing or PFS library.

---

[1] Implicit in this discussion is that we are unable to modify the kernel of the Paragon. This is because it is unreasonable to expect users to be able to install new kernels on the machines that they are using.

This presents a problem because the kernel-level data structures cannot be check-pointed, whereas the user-level data structures can. This means if all three parts of the message-passing system rely upon one another, their states at the time of checkpointing cannot be saved and restored in their entirety.

The best solution to this problem is not to save any of the user-level data structures for the message system. Thus, upon recovery, the Paragon is assumed to be in a "clean" state: no messages are in transit or in the message buffers. If in fact the Paragon was not in a clean state upon checkpointing, we attempt to rebuild it on recovery by re-sending messages and creating a user-level message buffer. A subtle implication of this is that the checkpoint *cannot* occur in the middle of a message-sending procedure. This is because the message-sending procedure may rely on data structures that *will not be restored* when the system recovers from a checkpoint. By forcing the programmer to define the points at which the program can checkpoint, CLIP ensures that checkpointing never occurs in the middle of message-passing or PFS procedures.

Second, the MPI and PFS libraries both make heavy use of "system type" messages. These are messages that cannot be detected using the standard message-probing mechanism of NX. System type messages cause problems for the check-pointer when it goes through its consistency checks because the checkpointer can-not make determinations about the state of the network using standard message-probing. This problem is fixed in CLIP by once again ensuring that a checkpoint cannot be taken in the middle of a Paragon library call.

Finally, taking transparent checkpoints means that blocking message-passing primitives (like `crecv()`, the synchronous message receiving subroutine in NX) should be interruptible. This is sometimes necessary to assure consistency of the checkpointed states. The only way to make blocking calls interruptible is to imple-ment them with non-blocking calls, and "block" by polling until the operation is finished. Unfortunately, the synchronous message sending and receiving calls have been highly optimized in NX and MPI, and implementing them with their asyn-chronous counterparts imposes a significant amount of overhead in many cases. By employing semi-transparent checkpointing, the programmer assures that blocking calls do not have to be interrupted, and thus can utilize the higher performance synchronous messages passing primitives.

Thus, the decision to implement semi-transparent checkpointing simplifies the task of assuring both correctness and high performance. However, the burden on the programmer is small. In our experience, inserting the `checkpoint_here()` calls was straightforward even for complex applications that we did not write.

7.3.2   Checkpoint Consistency

When creating a checkpoint of a parallel program on a message-passing platform, *checkpoint consistency* is a fundamental problem. Simply stated, a checkpoint of a parallel program consists of a *processor state* and a *message state*. The processor state is composed of individual checkpoints for each processor in the system. The message state contains each message m such that m was sent by processor p_i before p_i's checkpoint, and received by p_j after p_j's checkpoint. There may be no messages m such that m is sent by processor p_i after p_i's checkpoint, and received by p_j before p_j's checkpoint. Otherwise, the checkpoint is inconsistent, and the checkpoint is unrecoverable.

Checkpoint consistency has been well-studied (see [84] for a thorough discussion of the area), and implementations have shown that a simple two-phased commit called "sync-and-stop" (SNS) exhibits performance on par with more complex algorithms [216]. Moreover, it is quite simple to implement. For these reasons, the SNS algorithm is implemented in the *consistency glue* module of CLIP.

When a `checkpoint_here()` call is reached and the minimum interval of checkpointing has passed, CLIP freezes the calling processor, and waits for all processors to call `checkpoint_here()`. At this point, any messages that have been sent prior to the `checkpoint_here()` call either have been received or are buffered in the kernel of the sender or receiver. Thus, the message state is well defined, and since all processors are frozen, there can be no messages sent after checkpointing that cause inconsistency.

Thus, when checkpointing, CLIP enforces a barrier synchronization. This barrier is implicit — the programmer need not perform a barrier in order to checkpoint. It simply occurs as a result of checkpointing. Since most programs for the Paragon follow a SPMD methodology, enforcing barrier synchronization should not be a problem. It is anticipated that most calls to `checkpoint_here()` will be made in places where synchronization occurs anyway, such as at the end of coarse-grained iterations, just before or after a natural communication phase of the program. In all of the applications that we instrumented for checkpointing, this was the case.

7.3.3   Protected Message State

The high-level communication structure of a Paragon node is diagrammed in Figure 7.2. The application process on the compute processor(s) shares memory with the kernel of the communication processor. Specifically, they share a *system message buffer* for incoming messages, and a *post-page* as a communication buffer between the processors. By sharing memory, the communication processor can direct

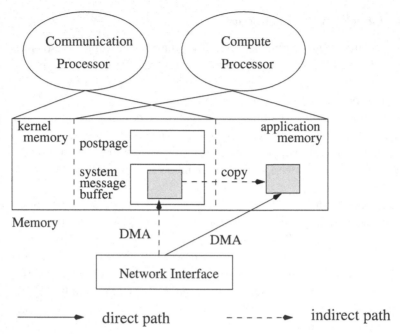

Figure 7.2
Communication structure of a Paragon node.

the communication to and from the network, and the application can access the results without absorbing any system call overhead.

There are two paths that a message can take when it arrives at its destination node: a *direct* path and an *indirect* path. If the user has already posted a receive for the message, then the communication processor instructs the network interface to perform DMA directly to the user's receive buffer. This, the direct path, is the fastest way for the message to arrive at the proper destination. If the user has not posted a receive for the message, then the the communication processor instructs the network interface to perform DMA into the system message buffer. When the user subsequently goes to receive the message, it is copied from the system buffer to the user's buffer by the compute processor. Since the system buffer is shared, this activity involves no system call overhead.

The message-sending primitives on the Paragon may be either synchronous (blocking), or asynchronous (non-blocking). When an asynchronous send or receive call is made, the communication processor ensures that the action is performed, and sets flags in the post-page to store the result. To complete the asynchronous operation, the application checks the post-page, and clears the flags. Again the fact that communication processor shares memory with the application allows all of this to occur without system call overhead.

When checkpointing an application, the buffered messages and the state of asynchronous communication must be stored with the checkpoint. A major design decision of CLIP is how this should be done. A natural and efficient way to store this information would be to simply checkpoint the post-page and system message buffer. However, this solution requires the communication processor to be aware of checkpointing so that it does not modify the shared memory while a checkpoint is being stored. Moreover, upon recovery, the internal data structures of the communication processor would have to be rebuilt to reflect the communication state of the node. Since one of our goals was not to modify the kernel code of the Paragon, we had to reject this solution.

Instead, when a checkpoint is being taken, CLIP "probes" the message buffer using an NX primitive, and extracts messages from the system buffer by calling the synchronous receive operation. These messages are stored in non-shared memory within the *Message Glue* module of CLIP, which gets checkpointed with the application. The shared state between the communication and compute processors is *not* stored as part of the checkpoint. Thus, whenever the application makes a message receive call, the CLIP buffer is first scanned. If the message is found in CLIP's buffer, then it is copied to the application's buffer and the receive is marked as complete. Otherwise, the appropriate Paragon receive primitive is called.

This is the same solution to message buffering as used by **ickp** on the Intel iPSC/860 [216]. Note that it adds an extra level of message copying to the indirect path of message receiving. However, the faster, direct path is unaltered, because the semi-transparent nature of CLIP combined with the SNS checkpointing algorithm insure that the DMA from the network interface can not be interrupted by checkpointing.

Asynchronous operations are dealt with in a similar manner. Before checkpointing, for each outstanding asynchronous operation, CLIP tests the operation for completion. If the operation is complete, then nothing need be done except store the result for when the application tests for completion. If the operation is not complete, then the parameters of the original operation are stored in the checkpoint so that it may be re-executed upon recovery. Again, semi-transparency and the SNS algorithm assure that the state of asynchronous operations will not change during checkpointing, insuring the integrity of the tests for completion in CLIP.

There are a few more details concerning the Message Glue module, such as dealing with certain MPI calls and maintaining the correctness of the core communication state upon recovery. However, these details are omitted for brevity.

7.3.4   Efficient File I/O

Earlier experimental research in checkpointing parallel and uniprocessor programs
have pointed out that the major source of checkpointing overhead comes from
committing the checkpoints to the stable storage. The PFS Glue in CLIP attempts
to reduce this overhead in two ways:

- smart layout of the checkpoint file and

- efficient use of PFS.

Because CLIP implicitly excludes some runtime data (e.g. shared communication
state) and the application may exclude some application data from checkpointing,
CLIP often has to checkpoint a fragmented data space. Each contiguous segment of
the data needs a small header to identify its size and location. The original version
of `libckpt` interleaves the segment headers with the contents of the segment in the
checkpoint file. On the Paragon, this results in frequent small write requests to the
I/O nodes which are optimized for handling large-size I/O requests. Instead, CLIP
adopts a different layout of the checkpoint which coalesces all segment headers in
a large buffer and writes it out to the disk in one operation.

Figure 7.3 depicts the file layout of checkpoint data for a single process. The
checkpoint header, whose size is aligned to the file system block size, contains
general information about the checkpointed program followed by a sequence of
segment headers. The actual contents of the segments are stored contiguously after
the checkpoint header. The stack is stored as the last segment, and the processor
context, including the program counter and the register file, is stored in a global
data structure in the heap.

CLIP allows checkpoints to be stored in Unix files or in PFS files. Obviously,
PFS allows CLIP to achieve better performance. When each process writes its
checkpoint data to a PFS file, PFS automatically *stripes* the data at a fixed striping
unit size. For optimal performance, the striping unit size should be a multiple of
the file block size. This is 64 KB each on Paragon to optimize large I/O requests.
For peak performance, CLIP attempts to output checkpoint data in multiples of
optimal PFS striping unit, using a large internal buffer to gather segments smaller
than the striping unit.

Opening a PFS file on the Paragon is an expensive operation, because it involves
Mach IPC communication with all the I/O nodes in the parallel file system. To
avoid the high cost of opening multiple checkpoint files, such as would happen if

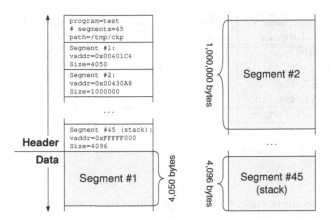

Figure 7.3
Layout of checkpoint file.

every node opened its own checkpoint file, CLIP opens just two large PFS files, one for the current checkpoint, and one for the previous checkpoint. This is made possible by the M_ASYNC access mode, which lets a collection of compute nodes read and write different portions of a large file simultaneously without interprocess coordination. The checkpoint file is partitioned into a number of subregions (or *subfiles*), each of which stores the checkpoint data for a distinct process. The checkpoint headers from all processes are grouped together at the beginning of the checkpoint file. In addition to high throughput for writing checkpoints to the disks, the subfile organization also simplifies the management of checkpoint files.

7.3.5 Performance Optimizations

One of the main strengths of `libckpt` as a checkpointing library is its implementation of performance optimizations. Since CLIP is built on top of `libckpt`, it too benefits from several performance optimizations.

First is *incremental* checkpointing [90], which employs virtual memory primitives so that only pages that have been modified since the previous checkpoint are written to the checkpoint file. If a program contains a significant amount of *read-only* data from checkpoint to checkpoint, incremental checkpointing can improve the performance of checkpointing.

Second is *programmer-directed memory exclusion* [215]. Since the programmer knows where checkpoints will occur, he or she can identify parts of the program that may not need to be checkpointed. For example, at the end of an iteration or subcomputation, there may be temporary arrays whose values are not used any

Name	Language & Library	Time mm:ss	Memory (MB) Node	Memory (MB) Total	Size MB	Interval min	Overhead sec	Overhead %
CFD	MPI/Fortran	66:44	10.3	1320	1303	15	27.5	3.7
PRISM	NX/C	78:04	22.6	2895	421	18	22.0	1.9
RENDER	NX/C	56:00	14.3	1849	137	14	9.3	1.1
PSTSWM	NX/Fortran	53:60	9.0	1153	509	14	9.3	1.2
CFD256	MPI/Fortran	36:29	6.3	1620	1604	9	18.0	3.3

Table 7.1
Basic performance for test applications.

further in the computation. Libckpt provides two procedures exclude_bytes() and include_bytes() that enable programmers to specify when not to include regions of memory in a checkpoint, and when to re-include them if necessary. For many programs, a few memory exclusion calls can yield huge savings in the size and overhead of checkpointing [214]. Memory exclusion as defined by libckpt is included as a part of CLIP.

Third is *implicit memory exclusion*. If the programmer is using a memory allocator (such as malloc() in C), there may be large blocks of memory on the allocator's free list that do not need to be checkpointed. In CLIP, the standard Paragon allocator has been modified to exclude any memory on the free list. This simple tweak can be responsible for large savings in checkpoint size and overhead because the Paragon's allocator uses the *buddy system*. In the buddy system, all memory requests are rounded up to the nearest power of two. This leads to a fast allocation algorithm that returns page-aligned addresses for large requests. The problem with the buddy system is that if the large requests are not powers of two, then much of the allocated memory is unused. Performance-wise, this is not a big problem because the Paragon only maps a page to physical memory if the page is actually used. However, if the checkpointer is unaware of this fact, it can severely degrade performance because it will attempt to checkpoint these unused pages, which results in their being mapped and then written to disk. In extreme cases, this could cause a program that runs correctly in the absence of checkpointing to run out of memory when checkpointing is enabled. CLIP solves this problem by ensuring that both free memory and unused allocated memory are excluded from checkpoint files.

The only optimization implemented by libckpt but omitted from CLIP is the copy-on-write optimization, because it is rare for a Paragon application have the free memory necessary to buffer checkpoints and write them asynchronously.

7.4   Performance

This section presents the performance of CLIP when checkpointing and recovering several large-scale parallel applications. The purpose of this section is to assess the performance of CLIP, a real checkpointer for a commercial machine, on several real-world applications so that the efficacy of CLIP can be gauged. This section is *not* meant to evaluate different performance optimizations, since such work has been performed many times in the past (e.g. [52, 85, 212, 214]).

7.4.1   Applications

We chose several NX and MPI applications to test the performance of CLIP. These applications are written in C or Fortran, and have been chosen from various sources. They are either real applications used to solve large engineering problems or parallel benchmark programs that closely mimic real and complex parallel programs. Table 7.1 summarizes the applications and their basic performance under CLIP. We briefly describe them below.

- *CFD* is the "LU" program from the NASA Parallel Benchmark Suite NPB2.1[9]. It is a three dimensional computational fluid dynamics simulation.

- *PRISM* is a three-dimensional Navier-Stokes turbulence simulation program written at Caltech [113].

- *RENDER* is a program from JPL that combines satellite imagery with terrain elevation to produce three-dimensional perspective views of Mars and Venus surfaces [49].

- *PSTSWM* is a benchmark program from Oak Ridge National Laboratory[285] that performs the core part of many weather modelling programs.

- As detailed below, we executed all of the above applications on 128 nodes. In Table 7.1, we also present the performance of a 256-node configuration for CFD. This is labelled *CFD256*. Due to time and system constraints, we were not able to get 256-node performance data for other applications.

All of the programs besides *RENDER* work in globally synchronized iterations. Thus it is straightforward to insert `checkpoint_here()` calls at the end of iterations, and then set a runtime parameter to force checkpointing at a desired interval. *RENDER* works in a master/slave fashion, where one master node allocates tasks to the other slave nodes. As such, there is no natural synchronization point to insert `checkpoint_here()` calls directly. Nonetheless, it was trivial for us to add a new message type to the program that the master process broadcasts to all slaves when it decides on an appropriate time to checkpoint. Upon receiving the checkpoint message, all processes immediately call the `checkpoint_here()` routine to initiate checkpointing.

7.4.2   Experiment Methodology

We used a 512-node Intel Paragon at Caltech. Each node contains one compute processor and one communication processor, plus 32 MB of memory. The PFS subsystem has 64 I/O nodes, each of which is attached to a disk drive and contains 64 MB of memory. The Caltech Paragon is a production-level system that experiences heavy use daily. As such, we were able to run the applications on only 128 nodes (for *RENDER*, we use 128 slaves and one master node). The heavy use of the Caltech Paragon introduces a small amount of fluctuation into our performance measurements, because other applications can use the parallel file system at the same time as our program. To combat this, we ran each test three or more times to get an average measurement.

The data set for each application is chosen so that the application runs in a normal manner for approximately one hour. This lets us approximate long-running applications without artificially increasing loop iterations. For each application we produced two versions of executables: a *pure* version with the original compilation configuration and a *checkpointed* version that has `checkpoint_here()` inserted and is linked with CLIP. We set the checkpointing interval to 15 minutes, which results in 4 checkpoints for each run.

Where possible, we performed programmer-directed memory exclusion, and combined it with implicit memory exclusion and incremental checkpointing.

7.4.3   Checkpoint Sizes

Figure 7.4 shows the average size of the checkpoint files for each application when using (1) no optimization, (2) implicit memory exclusion, (3) implicit and programmer-directed memory exclusion, and (4) all of the above plus incremental checkpointing. Note that case (1) is equivalent to the "Memory" column in Table 7.1, and that case (4) is equivalent to the "Size" column.

As other optimization studies have shown, the degree of space optimization varies from program to program. Some, such as *CFD*, can not be optimized by these techniques. Incremental checkpointing shrinks the checkpoints of *PRISM* from a

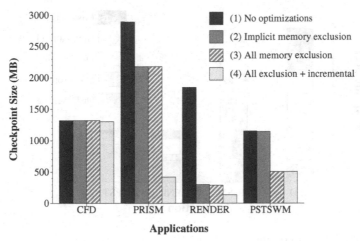

Figure 7.4
Checkpoint sizes.

size of 2.9 GB to 421 MB. Implicit memory exclusion reduces the size of *RENDER* checkpoints from 1.8 GB to 137 MB, and programmer-directed memory exclusion cuts the size of *PSTSWM* checkpoints roughly in half.

For each application, the results that follow use the combination of optimization techniques that performs the best for that application.

7.4.4 Failure-Free Overhead

The *failure-free overhead* introduced by a checkpointer is the additional time it takes a checkpointed application to run from start to completion without encountering any failures. It is a comprehensive measure of the impact of storing checkpoints as well as the overhead introduced into message passing and other parts of the program.

We measure the failure-free overhead for each application by subtracting the running time of the pure version of the program from the running time of the checkpointed version. This overhead is tabulated in the last two columns of Table 7.1. The overhead per checkpoint is the total overhead divided by the number of checkpoints (four), and the percent overhead is the total overhead divided by the running time of the pure version of the program.

The major conclusion to draw from this data is that the overhead of checkpointing is extremely small considering the size of the programs. Most checkpointers target 10 percent overhead as their desired upper limit, and CLIP's performance is far better than that. This is mainly the result of three factors: the aggregate

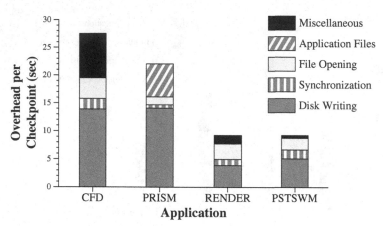

Figure 7.5
Composition of checkpoint overhead.

of disk writing with PFS, the design of CLIP that gets maximal performance from PFS, and the checkpointing optimizations.

In Figure 7.5, we break down the average overhead per checkpoint into its constituent parts. These are as follows:

- *Disk Writing*: This is the time spent performing actual disk writes. Typically, this is the major portion of overhead, and Figure 7.5 shows this to be the case.

- *Synchronization*: This is the time spent ensuring that all of the nodes are in a consistent state before checkpointing. As shown previously [86, 216], this is not a significant portion of checkpointing overhead.

- *File Opening*: As stated above, opening large files in PFS is a very expensive operation. CLIP opens two checkpoint files upon instantiation, and then uses those for all checkpointing. In Figure 7.5, this overhead is amortized over four checkpoints. As more checkpoints are taken, this portion of overhead will become negligible.

- *Application Files*: If the application has opened files, CLIP flushes their state to disk and checkpoints the file pointers. Like file opening, this is an expensive operation, and is the cause of a significant portion of the overhead in *PRISM*. It is not a factor in the other applications.

- *Miscellaneous Overhead*: This accounts for the remaining overhead, which includes managing the memory exclusion, catching page faults for incremental checkpointing, extracting messages from the system buffer, etc.

Name	Recovery Time (seconds)
CFD	36.0
PRISM	33.4
RENDER	22.5
PSTSWM	19.0

Table 7.2
Performance of recovery.

Checkpointing Method	Overhead (seconds)	Checkpoint Size (MB)	Percent Overhead
Native	43	77	0.9
CLIP	89	421	1.9

Table 7.3
Native checkpointing versus CLIP in *PRISM*.

While we expect disk writing to compose the most significant portion of checkpointing, we note that other factors, most notably the overhead of opening files are significant as well. This is an important observation for the fact that most checkpointing research focuses on either minimizing the number of disk writes, or minimizing the messages in the consistency protocol.

7.4.5 Recovery

Table 7.2 shows the time that it takes each application to recover from a checkpoint and to begin executing the application again. Note that recovery times are larger than the average checkpoint times for each application. This is mainly for two reasons. First, while the overhead of opening files is amortized over all checkpoints, it is included in its entirety in the recovery time. Second, if a program contains a lot of read-only data, then with incremental checkpointing the first checkpoint is large, and successive checkpoints are small, improving the average checkpoint size and overhead. However, recovery involves restoring all data (read-only and not read-only), and therefore can exhibit much more overhead than during checkpointing.

Since recovery is a less frequent operation than checkpointing, the higher recovery times are permissible. It should be noted that in no case is the recovery time greater than 10 percent of the application's running time.

7.4.6   Comparison with Non-transparent Checkpointing

The *PRISM* application has its own checkpointing and restart mechanism coded in the program which can be enabled or disabled via a runtime option. This non-transparent checkpointing mechanism saves critical application data into a file at certain loop iterations. To recover, *PRISM* is invoked with a different runtime option which reads the critical data and restarts from the middle of the computation.

It is interesting to compare the performance of CLIP with PRISM's non-transparent checkpointing mechanism. The relevant data is in Table 7.3. The native checkpointer's files are smaller by a factor of 5.5, but the overhead is only a factor of 2 faster. CLIP's better performance per megabyte is due to its optimized use of PFS. Considering the fact that checkpointing with CLIP is far easier than coding checkpointing and recovery explicitly into the application, the extra 1% overhead that CLIP adds to checkpointing seems minor indeed.

7.5   Related Work

Issues in checkpointing for parallel and distributed systems has been a well-studied field of research. A survey paper by Elnozahy, Alvisi, Wang and Johnson [83] provides an excellent background on algorithms and frameworks for checkpoint consistency in message-passing systems. Issues in uniprocessor checkpointing systems are covered in papers on Condor [253] and libckpt [214]. Many performance optimizations are discussed in a paper by Plank [212].

There have been a few implementations of generic checkpointers for message-passing systems. Ickp [216] was implemented on the iPSC/860, and Fail-Safe PVM [172], MIST [43], CoCheck [244], and Starfish [6] have been implemented for PVM/MPI-based systems. There have been transparent checkpointers developed for distributed shared memory platforms [68, 131, 251, 146], and non-transparent checkpointing libraries have been employed for various message-passing platforms [236, 235, 191, 117].

7.6   Conclusions

This paper has described CLIP, a semi-transparent tool for checkpointing parallel programs on the Intel Paragon. There have been checkpointing tools previously released for uniprocessors [214, 253], distributed systems [43, 244, 6], and even multicomputers [216], but none for a machine with the size, performance and complexity of the Paragon. Although CLIP runs only on Intel Paragon, its design techniques may apply to other multicomputer platforms.

Writing a checkpointing tool for a machine such as the Paragon is more difficult than taking a simple core dump. There are many tradeoffs in performance, functionality and ease-of-use that must be addressed in the design stages. This paper details several of these issues and should be valuable to anyone who designs and implements tools for complex machines such as the Paragon.

The performance of CLIP is excellent, mainly due to the efficient distributed I/O of PFS. The bottom line is that with a tool like CLIP, a large application for a massively parallel machine such as the Paragon can be instrumented for fault-tolerance with little burden on the programmer or on the performance of the application.

The memory exclusion technique (*both programmer-directed and implicit exclusion*) can be effective in reducing the checkpointing overhead. In our experiments, memory exclusion reduced checkpoint size by between 25% and 90% for three out of four applications. Furthermore, compilers can also take advantage of the memory exclusion interface to *automatically* exclude certain application data from checkpoints [213].

Acknowledgments

This project is supported in part by the Scalable I/O project under the DARPA grant DABT63-94-C-0049 and by the National Science Foundation under grants CCR-9409496, CCR-9703390 and ACI-9876895. We would like to thank the members of the Scalable I/O Initiative for providing us with the applications used in this study. Ronald D. Henderson at Caltech and Patrick Worley at Oak Ridge National Laboratory gave us insightful suggestions for instrumenting their programs. We also would like thank Sharon Brunett and Heidi Lorenz-Wirzba at Caltech for helping us with running our experiments on the Caltech Paragon.

8 Learning to Classify Parallel I/O Access Patterns

Tara M. Madhyastha and Daniel A. Reed

Input/output is a critical bottleneck for many important scientific applications. One reason is that performance of extant parallel file systems is particularly sensitive to file access patterns. Often the application programmer must match application input/output requirements to the capabilities of the file system. Because this match is so critical, many studies have demonstrated how a file system can exploit knowledge of application access patterns to provide higher performance than is possible with general file system policies [106, 157, 209].

Ideally, the file system should be able to perform this match of access patterns to file system policies automatically. To this end, we investigate automatic input/output access pattern classification techniques that drive adaptive file system policies. Automatic classification can reduce an application developer's input/output optimization effort and increase performance portability across file systems and system architectures by isolating input/output optimization decisions within a retargetable file system infrastructure.

We describe two complementary techniques that use learning algorithms to classify input/output access patterns. The first method uses an artificial neural network (ANN) trained on access pattern benchmarks to recognize access patterns as belonging to one of a set of qualitative categories. The second approach uses hidden Markov models (HMMs) [222, 46] for modeling input/output access patterns, using training data from previous application executions. The two classification methods are complementary. ANN classification can efficiently and dynamically recognize a pattern as one of several known qualitative selections throughout execution, but cannot offer accurate predictions of future accesses. HMM classification builds a model of accesses from one or more previous executions, creating a representation suitable for more precise caching and prefetching control.

Both of these methods classify input/output behavior from a single application thread. Although local (per thread) access pattern information is crucial for improving application performance, a description of the global interleaving of accesses is necessary for optimal policy control. We propose a method for combining these local classifications to make global ones, thereby exploiting this additional information to improve performance.

The remainder of this chapter is organized as follows. We describe the access pattern classification problem in §8.1. In §8.2, we describe our experimental testbed, based on extensions to our Portable Parallel File System (PPFS), and present our methodology for intelligent classification and policy selection. We present results of local classification and policy control on sequential applications in §8.3. Access patterns exist both locally and globally within the context of a parallel program; we describe this distinction and global classification in §8.4. In §8.5, we present experimental data to evaluate global classification on parallel applications. Finally, §8.6-§8.7 place this work in context and summarize our results.

8.1 Access Pattern Classification

Applications often have certain common qualitative input/output access patterns (e.g., 'read-only sequential with large request sizes,' or 'write-only strided.') for which file system policies are normally optimized. When other access patterns occur, performance can be much poorer than that achievable using advance knowledge of the unusual requests. For example, a cache optimized for a read-only sequential access pattern might employ the space-efficient MRU (Most Recently Used) cache block replacement policy. Such a policy is inappropriate for random access requests that exhibit locality; an LRU (Least Recently Used) pattern would be more suitable. These decisions are impossible without access pattern information and the ability to use it to control file system behavior.

An access pattern classification is a qualitative statement that can be used to select and tune file system policies. It need not be a perfect predictor of future accesses to improve file system performance. For example, one might classify an input/output pattern as "sequential" even if a few bytes are skipped, and elect to use an MRU cache replacement policy. However, if the number of bytes skipped is large and regular, the access pattern might be strided. If we expect the skipped bytes to be reread on subsequent strides, an LRU replacement policy may be more suitable.

Such a qualitative description is difficult to obtain on the basis of heuristics alone (e.g., the access pattern is sequential if over 90 percent of the bytes are accessed in increasing order). Many alternate heuristic descriptions using a variety of statistics could be proposed and there would inevitably be exceptions to each one. For example, is an access pattern that reads every file block twice in increasing order also sequential? Although it does not satisfy the above heuristic, for purposes of policy selection it is useful to treat it as a sequential access pattern. We require a classification methodology that can adapt to such exceptions when they occur. Our research investigates automatic learning mechanisms that periodically produce file access pattern classifications. The file system uses these classifications to dynamically tune caching and prefetching policies throughout program execution.

Within a parallel application, there are two levels at which input/output access patterns can be observed. The first is at the local (e.g., per thread) level, and the second is at the global (e.g., per parallel program) level. For example, each thread of a parallel program might access a file locally with a strided access pattern, but the interleaved access stream is globally sequential. Global classification is especially important because optimal policies for the local access patterns can be different from those that would benefit the file access stream as a whole.

8.1.1   Access Pattern Classification Model

Access patterns are closely tied to both the application programming interface (API) used to generate input/output requests, and the underlying file structure. For example, a record-based file that can only be read or written in fixed size records will never have unpredictable request sizes. Small requests generated by calls to the UNIX standard buffered input/output library are translated into fixed size input/output calls to the underlying file system.

In our classification approach, we attempt to divorce the access pattern description from the application input/output programming interface (API). To accommodate a variety of high-level interfaces and underlying file structures, we describe access patterns assuming a byte stream file representation. File accesses are made using UNIX style *read*, *write*, and *seek* operations, and access patterns are determined at the application level. Using this representation, an input/output trace of file accesses may be represented as a stream of tuples of the form

$< byte\ offset, request\ size, read/write >.$

This approach is portable, because both local and global classifications are independent of API, file structure or layout. Input/output requests made using any API can be translated into UNIX style operations, although information might be lost. By classifying accesses at the application level, classifications are completely independent of file system policies. For example, the file system might choose the same policies to optimize a strided access pattern as a sequential access pattern if the stride granularity is small compared to the underlying file system block size.

Access patterns exist within a three-dimensional access pattern space, pictured in Figure 8.1. Each dimension corresponds to patterns observed in the time-varying values of the trace tuple components, and each point in the three-dimensional space represents a unique access pattern. This ternary partition is not unique; we have selected these axes because they are the architecture-independent categories most commonly used to describe access patterns at a small scale (i.e. from observing a small window of accesses). Other useful categories can be added (e.g., file reuse). Relaxing our desire for architecture independence opens additional possibilities, such as interaccess latency. However, these axes embrace a wide range of common

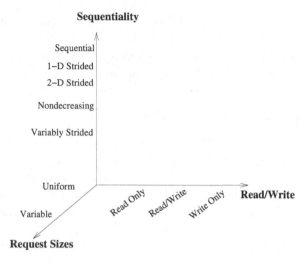

Figure 8.1
Access pattern space.

scientific access patterns, and, as we shall see in §8.3, suffice to effectively select and tune several file policies.

Many functions can be computed on the trace tuple components to yield identifiable features with which to label the three-dimensional access pattern space. However, access patterns that are predictive, can be determined from a small window of accesses, and can be used to influence file system policy selection are the most interesting to identify. The three axes of Figure 8.1 are labeled with certain features meeting these criteria that can be used to classify all points in the access pattern space. Additional features can be added as necessary to each axis to further refine the access pattern space.

The set of classifications on each axis $C = a, b, \dots$ is a partially ordered set $< C, \subseteq >$, where $\subseteq$ is the relationship "is a less precise predictor." For example, a classification of "Read/Write" is a less precise predictor than either a "Read Only" or "Write Only" classification. Figure 8.2 shows the Hasse diagrams for local classifications.

Each category of local classifications forms a lattice, because every pair of elements $a, b \in C$ has a greatest lower bound and a least upper bound. The greatest lower bound, or *meet* operator is denoted by $a \otimes b$ and the least upper bound, or *join*, by $a \oplus b$. For example, if there are two access patterns, read only and write only, from Figure 8.2 the greatest lower bound of the two is a read/write access

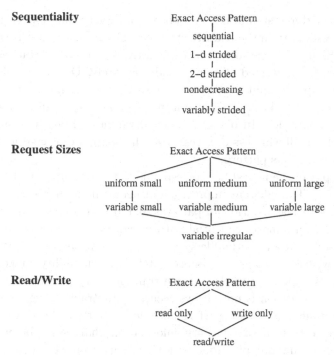

Figure 8.2
Hasse diagrams for local classifications.

pattern. The least upper bound of the two classifications is the exact access pattern, or the precise description of the accesses themselves. This ordering helps us to combine multiple classifications to form global classifications.

8.1.2   Neural Network Classification

Our first classification approach is to train a feedforward artificial neural network [97] to classify patterns. Although neural networks are expensive to train initially, once training is complete, classification is very efficient. Neural networks are particularly suited to classification problems where training data is readily available and some degree of imprecision must be tolerated. Ultimately, qualitative classifications are supplemented by quantitative access statistics to guide policy control (e.g., to provide the quantitative stride length for a qualitative strided access pattern).

Our neural network configuration is a small feedforward network with thirteen input units, ten output units, and one hidden layer consisting of twelve units. The training algorithm is standard backpropagation, a very common learning algorithm.

To successfully train the neural net to recognize access patterns within the space shown in Figure 8.1, we must process the trace of input/output accesses so that training can be performed efficiently and accurately. Our approach is to compute normalized input/output statistics on a small fixed number of accesses. These statistics represent the access pattern in a compact, normalized form suitable for input to a neural net. In our experiments, we have chosen to compute statistics on relatively small windows of accesses, so that periodic reclassification can detect changes in the access pattern.

The output of the neural net corresponds to the presence or absence of features in Figure 8.1. The inherent imprecision of neural nets allows us to train a net to produce a useful classification for patterns that are "very close" to some well-defined pattern (e.g., an almost sequential pattern can be classified as sequential). This is an advantage; it allows the file system to learn, through training, how it should classify new access patterns. Unfortunately, this flexibility makes training very difficult. It is impossible to classify and train on every possible trace subsequence; therefore, classification is not always accurate. In practice, we have observed that incorrect classification yields performance no worse than the system defaults.

However, certain access pattern information that could be used to improve performance is unavailable from periodic observation of short sequences of input/output requests. Not all access patterns are amenable to brief, qualitative descriptions (e.g., sequential, random). For example, an irregular read-only access pattern might be repeatable or truly unpredictable. Metadata accesses to structured data files often have highly irregular patterns, but they are caused by library calls and are repeatable across program executions.

A simple qualitative classification could specify only that an access pattern is highly irregular or random, and an intelligent prefetcher might use this knowledge to disable prefetching. However, when the pattern has a complex, repeatable and detectable structure, a prefetcher could exploit this knowledge to automatically issue prefetch requests for specific file blocks and make intelligent cache replacement decisions based on expected future usage patterns. This motivates us to investigate other classification methodologies.

8.1.3 Hidden Markov Model Classification

A model that allows one to calculate and express the probability of accessing a given portion of a file in the future, having observed some access sequence, can supply more complex access pattern information for caching and prefetching policy decisions. While a neural network might be trained to do this, it is not a very efficient approach. We know precisely the function that we want to compute: the probability distribution function of future accesses, having already observed some access sequence. This knowledge allows us to choose a learning method more appropriate to the problem: Markov models.

A discrete-time Markov process [151] is a system that at any time is in one of N distinct states. At discrete times, the system changes states, or makes a transition, according to a set of probabilities associated with each state. Each state corresponds to a single observable event, or an observation symbol.

In a discrete Markov process, the observation symbol uniquely determines the next state. A hidden Markov process is a generalization of a discrete Markov process where a given state may have several exiting transitions, all corresponding to the same observation symbol. In other words, the "hidden" nature of a hidden Markov process represents the fact that the observation sequence does not uniquely determine the state sequence.

For example, suppose someone tosses two possibly biased coins, one at a time, in the next room. Our observation sequence is a stream of heads and tails, and from that information we attempt to determine the coin selection process and the bias of each coin.

Although discrete Markov models are sufficient to accurately represent many important input/output access patterns, the memoryless property limits their ability to model more complicated application behaviors. Hidden Markov models can "learn" the hidden behavior of the application that generates input/output requests from observation of the request stream. Efficient algorithms exist to train the model on observed sequences and calculate the probability of future sequences.

Modeling Input/Output Patterns There are many possible ways to model access patterns using hidden Markov models; the choice of model description is critical to its predictive ability. One must determine what application behavior corresponds to a state, the number of states in the model, and the allowed observations. Our approach is to construct a hidden Markov model where each state corresponds to a segment of the file.

Segments are contiguous file regions of fixed or variable size. Ideally, segment size is chosen to correspond to an underlying file system caching unit or the application request size. Within a segment, the access pattern is assumed to be sequential. For the purposes of this paper, we assume that a segment is the same as a fixed size file block, and each state corresponds to a block. For example, a 10 MB file has 1280 8 KB file blocks, and accesses to this file could be modeled by an HMM with 1280 states.

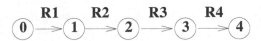

Figure 8.3
Markov model describing sequential reads.

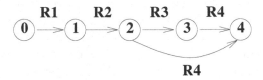

Figure 8.4
Degenerate HMM describing two possible control paths.

Observations are reads or writes that change the current state with some probability to a new state (a new current file block). For example, Figure 8.3 illustrates an HMM that models a sequential read pattern for a file with five blocks. Application requests can be smaller than the block size; we process a trace of input/output requests so that consecutive reads or consecutive writes that access the current block do not incur reflexive transitions.

We prevent state space explosion by consolidating sequential accesses into a single state and pruning unlikely transitions. In practice, we have observed HMM memory requirements for regular access patterns to grow at most linearly with file size. For example, the HMM for a 238 MB strided file used in the Pathfinder application (described in 8.3.3) is less than 61 KB without any state space compression.

In Figure 8.3, the file access pattern is deterministic. Figure 8.4 illustrates a pattern where there is a conditional branch in the underlying program. Suppose that based on data read from block 0, the program either reads the rest of the file sequentially or skips block 3. Trained on previous executions, the HMM computes the probabilities of each transition, information that can help the file system determine if it should prefetch block 3.

In the above examples, the Markov model is completely observable (i.e., given an observation sequence the system can be in only one state), and the only issue for complete specification is to determine, at each state, the probabilities of a read or a write to every other file block. Thus, the HMM is degenerate and can be expressed as a Markov chain.

Markov chains are sufficient to model many scientific input/output file access patterns; however, they fail when several predictable patterns are possible for a single file. For example, consider the case where the application may access a file

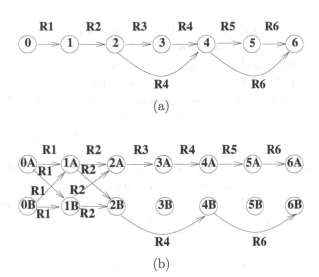

Figure 8.5
Two HMMs for modeling conditional access patterns.

with either a sequential or a mixed sequential and strided access pattern, depending on program input.

Figures 8.5a and 8.5b illustrate two possible models of this behavior. The HMM in Figure 8.5a is a poor predictor because it does not remember the path it took to reach each even-numbered block. Figure 8.5b shows a trained HMM that accurately models the two threads of control. Before training, all transitions are possible. We create two states for each file block, one each in groups A and B, noting that now many state sequences are possible given an observation sequence. At each state, an additional, unspecified parameter determines whether a read or write to a particular file block causes transition to a state in group A or group B. state 2A or 2B, with the next access being a read of block 3 or 4. The probabilities of the transitions determine which of these is more likely. Figure 8.5 can also be viewed as a composite of two individual HMMs.

Training Hidden Markov Models Each application has one hidden Markov model per file; these models are trained online by running an application executable that has been linked with a training module. The HMM segment size is selected in advance based on the underlying cache block size, and the training module maintains counts of all block read or write transitions. Most files involve only a single access pattern[1]; in this case, a degenerate HMM with one state per file block suffices to model them and training is a trivial calculation. The probabilities for each transition are calculated by dividing the number of occurrences of the transition by the total number of transitions from each block, and only a single training execution is required. All examples in this paper utilize this training algorithm.

When a file has several significantly different access patterns (e.g., Figure 8.5), the training process is more complicated. Although we have not observed this to be common in practice, HMMs elegantly model this uncertainty. To reflect the multiple threads of control, we construct a composite HMM from the HMMs trained on each unique access pattern. In essence, HMM construction is a clustering algorithm that assumes the number of clusters (i.e., unique access patterns) is known in advance, the user must provide this. For example, for two threads of control, the HMM structure would resemble Figure 8.5b. For details of the training process see [179].

Classification and Policy Control   Hidden Markov models use data from previous executions to model access patterns probabilistically. A trained hidden Markov model with one state per file block learns the probability distribution function of accessing the next block given the current block. We have written a library of functions that uses an HMM, together with quantitative information computed from the input/output accesses, to estimate the probability of observing patterns within the access pattern space until the next classification.

For example, request size variability is determined heuristically from examining the number of unique request sizes in a recent window of accesses. On the other hand, the probability of sequentiality is estimated from the HMM by multiplying the probability of transitions between consecutive blocks for some number of accesses from the starting position. If the probability exceeds some threshold (e.g., 0.9) we adopt the corresponding policy.

HMM functionality is not limited to choosing among qualitative categories. For example, an HMM can be used to estimate a working set size by determining the minimum number of cache blocks that can capture cyclic access (e.g. multiple file reads, nested strided accesses). Figure 8.6 illustrates the heuristic. Intuitively, as the cache size increases, the application will be able to access more blocks without replacement. This is shown by the curve labeled "Number of Accesses." If there is locality, a small number of blocks suffices to capture the working set. The curve labeled "Unique Cache Blocks" denotes the number of unique blocks accessed as

---

[1]Characterization studies of applications from the SIO initiative suite reveal no files that are accessed throughout an application lifetime with more than one unique access pattern [71, 238, 218].

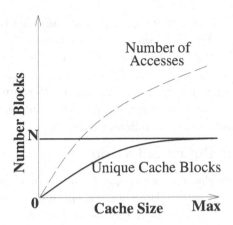

Figure 8.6
Allocating cache space.

cache size increases. The maximum number of unique cache blocks accessed is a good estimate for minimal cache space allocation (N cache blocks). An HMM can be used to compute estimates of these curves by taking the most probable transitions through the states from any starting position within the file and recording the total number of block accesses and the number of unique blocks accessed for a range of hypothetical cache sizes.

An HMM can also be used to control classification frequency. Ideally classification need occur only when the access pattern changes. Neural network classification periodically reclassifies an access pattern; reclassification frequency is a user-specified parameter that must be carefully chosen to balance classification overhead and responsiveness to pattern changes. In contrast, using an HMM, a pattern change is possible only when the probability of accessing the next anticipated block using the current pattern falls below some specified threshold. Thus, the HMM can be used to monitor the input/output request stream, automatically recognizing access pattern changes.

Finally, the availability of data from previous executions can be used to make classifications for better policy selection at file open. In parallel applications involving many processors and large, disjoint, input/output operations, early access pattern classification and policy selection can make a significant difference in overall input/output performance.

HMM classification offers many advantages over ANN classification; however, the cost is the overhead of executing the application once or more to train the HMMs.

This cost must be amortized over the performance improvements of subsequent program executions. For this approach to be profitable, we need to execute an application multiple times on the same data files (or the data files need to have similar structure and access patterns). In practice, this is a common mode of usage. Frequently, scientists rerun applications on the same data set, changing the algorithm slightly without changing the input/output access pattern. Often the access pattern is identical across different data sets.

8.2   Intelligent Policy Selection

A file access pattern classification is platform-independent and unique to a particular application execution. However, an optimal choice of file system policies for a particular access pattern is system-dependent. By using the classification to tune file system policies for each input/output platform, not only is input/output performance portable over a variety of platforms, but the file system can provide better performance over a range of applications than it could by enforcing a single system-wide policy. This adaptivity occurs transparently, without application hints or optimizations.

To provide a framework for experiments involving automatic local and global policy control, we have extended the Portable Parallel File System (PPFS), a flexible file system testbed, as described in §8.2.1. In §8.2.2 we describe a simple algorithm for policy control.

8.2.1   Portable Parallel File System

The Portable Parallel File System (PPFS)[119] is a user-level input/output library designed to be an extensible testbed for file system policies. It has a rich interface for control of data placement and file system policies that can be manipulated by the application or by an automatic classifier.

Figure 8.7 shows the PPFS components and their interactions. Application clients initiate input/output via invocation of PPFS interface functions. To open a file, the application first contacts the metadata server, which stores or creates information about the file layout on remote disk servers (input/output nodes). With this information, the application can issue input/output requests and specify caching and prefetching polices for all levels of the system. Clients either satisfy the requests locally or forward them to servers (abstractions of remote input/output devices). Clients and servers each have their own caches and prefetch engines. All "physical" input/output is performed through an underlying UNIX file system.

To provide automatic policy control based on local and global classification, we extended the basic PPFS design. Each client has a local classification module that

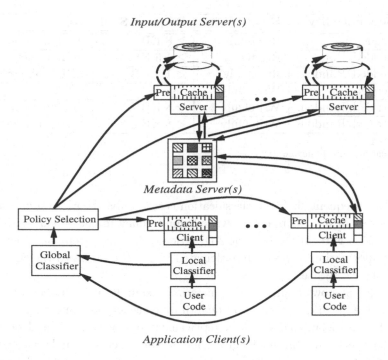

Figure 8.7
PPFS with global classification.

generates qualitative and quantitative information used to control local caching and prefetching policies.

To support global classification, we added a global classification server to consolidate local classifications and necessary access statistics, as described in §8.4. When the global server classifies an access pattern, it updates policies accordingly on the input/output servers and the clients. Under HMM classification, clients can also consult the global classifier at file open for an initial global policy based on previous execution data.

8.2.2 A Simple Algorithm for Policy Control

PPFS provides the necessary framework for using classifications to tune file system policies. Abstractly, the file system continuously monitors and classifies the input/output request stream. This classification is passed to the user policy suite for file policy selection and configuration. For example, when the access pattern classification is sequential, the file system can assume that file accesses will con-

Sequentiality	Read/Write	Request Size	Action
Sequential	ReadOnly	≥ 8 KB	disable cache
Strided/Random	ReadOnly	≥ 1.5 KB	disable cache
Strided/Random	ReadOnly	< 1.5 KB	LRU, enlarge cache
Sequential	WriteOnly	any	MRU
Strided/Random	WriteOnly	≥ 8 KB	disable cache
Strided/Random	WriteOnly	< 8 KB	LRU, enlarge cache

Table 8.1
Classifications and policy control.

tinue to be sequential. If the classification is read only, the file system can prefetch aggressively; if it is write only a write-behind policy might be efficient. When the classification is regularly (1-D or 2-D) strided, the file system can take advantage of this information to prefetch anticipated blocks according to the stride size and adjust the cache size.

Figure 8.8 shows a simple, parameterized example of the policy decisions that are possible given qualitative and quantitative access pattern information. In this example, the default cache block replacement policy is LRU, and default cache and block sizes are chosen to give good performance on small sequential reads. Policy parameters are adjusted whenever they potentially might yield performance improvements given the access pattern classification. Quantitative values for the parameters of Figure 8.8 depend on the particular hardware configuration and are determined experimentally.

8.3 Local Classification Experiments

To compare ANN and HMM local classification, we conducted a series of uniprocessor performance studies using both access pattern benchmarks and an input/output intensive satellite data processing application. The experimental platform is PPFS on a Sun SparcServer 670 running SunOS 4.1.3, with 64 MB of physical memory and a local SCSI disk. Local classification guides policy control, as described in §8.4. Table 8.1, a parameterized version of the algorithm of Figure 8.8, shows how access patterns are matched to policies. The average request size thresholds, default cache block size (32 KB), and large and small cache sizes were determined through experimentation and are platform-dependent.

```
if (sequential) {
    if (write only) {
       enable caching
       use MRU replacement policy
    } else if (read only && average request size > LARGE_REQUEST)
       disable caching
    } else {
       enable caching
       use LRU replacement policy
    }
}

if (variably strided || 1-D  strided || 2-D strided) {
    if (regular request sizes) {
       if (average request size > SMALL_REQUEST) {
           disable caching
       } else {
          enable caching
          increase cache size to MAX_CACHE_SIZE
          use LRU replacement policy
       }
    } else {
       enable caching
       use LRU replacement policy
    }
}
```

Figure 8.8
Dynamic file system policy selection example.

8.3.1   Dynamic Access Patterns

One of the main advantages of dynamic classification is the ability to refine policy selections as the access pattern changes. In this section, we describe the performance of a benchmark that reads the first half of a 40 million byte file sequentially and the second half pseudorandomly. For both access patterns, the request size is 2000 bytes. We executed this benchmark three times using PPFS, twice with adaptive file system policies guided by neural network based classification and hidden Markov model based classification, and once with a single, default system policy.

Figure 8.9 shows the throughput (computed every 10 accesses) for the bench-

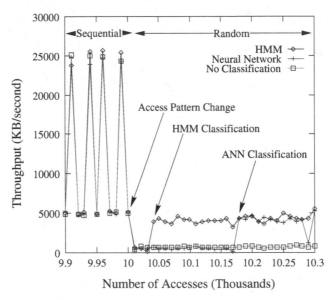

Figure 8.9
Adapting to a changing access pattern.

mark. The periodic dips in throughput before the access pattern change are caused by cache misses. When the access pattern changes from sequential to random, the policy selection of Table 8.1 is to disable caching, reducing the byte volume of physical input/output calls and improving throughput for the random access pattern.

Because the frequency of ANN classification is a user-specified parameter, responsiveness of the ANN classifier is limited by the selected classification frequency. In this PPFS configuration, the HMM classifier is able to detect this access pattern shift sooner than the ANN method. The ANN classifier automatically reclassifies the pattern every 640 KB, so it begins to reclassify the random access pattern after reading 20316160 bytes (i.e., 31 640 KB blocks). Figure 8.10 illustrates the portion of the HMM where the access pattern changes; the symbol **R** denotes a read of the block indicated by the arrow. After detecting a sequential access pattern, the HMM classifier computes the probability that the sequential access pattern will continue. At block 611 the probability of accessing block 612 is 0.0, so the access pattern can no longer be sequential. Because blocks are 32 KB, reclassification occurs after reading 20021248 bytes, the last byte in the block that marks the end of the sequential run.

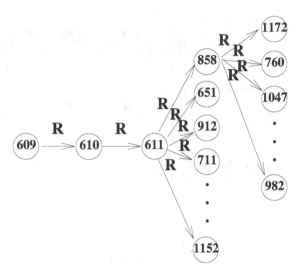

Figure 8.10
HMM at access pattern change.

8.3.2 Sequential File Reuse

In many cases, an application reads a file repeatedly. A common optimization for this access pattern is to retain as many of the file blocks in cache as possible to avoid rereading them. Both ANN and HMM classifiers can recognize sequentiality, but because it classifies access patterns on a much larger scale, the HMM classifier can also predict reuse of sequentially accessed blocks and determine an appropriate cache size, using the method described in §8.1.3.

To illustrate the potential performance improvement, consider a benchmark that reads a 20 million byte file five times sequentially. The request size is 2000 bytes, and classifications occur every ten thousand accesses. Both ANN and HMM classifiers detect that the access pattern is read-only and sequential. The HMM classifier recognizes that the file will be re-read (because the access pattern is sequential and the transition from the last block is a read of the first block) and that a cache size of 20021248 bytes (611 cache blocks of size 32 KB) can retain the file in memory, so the cache is resized.

Figure 8.11 shows the throughput (computed over every 100 accesses) for the benchmark executing with both classification methods. During the initial file read, throughput using both classification methods is roughly equivalent (minor performance variations are due to system level cache effects). After the file is read once,

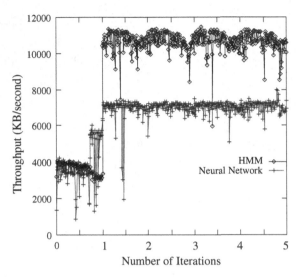

Figure 8.11
Detection of file reuse.

throughput using both classification methods increases because the file is in the
UNIX file system cache. However, under HMM classification the file is also retained in the PPFS user-level cache, further improving throughput.

8.3.3 Pathfinder Satellite Data Processing

Reprocessing large multi-year data sets derived from satellite instrument measurements is a particularly input/output intensive problem. Five years from now, the
typical satellite might collect 100 gigabytes per day, and processed data products
might require a total storage volume of a terabyte/day. Furthermore, the desire to
store data products in a portable format, enabling scientists to access them from
different computers over the Internet, generates a variety of complicated access
patterns for which UNIX file systems are not optimized.

In this section, we explore the performance of Pathfinder, a typical sequential
UNIX application used to process low-level satellite data. Pathfinder is from the
NOAA/NASA Pathfinder AVHRR (Advanced Very High Resolution Radiometer)
data processing project. Our analysis focuses on the generation of daily data sets,
created from fourteen files of AVHRR orbital data (approximately 42 MB each)
processed to produce an output data set that is approximately 228 MB in NCSA's
Hierarchical Data Format (HDF).

Experimental Environment	Total Time
UNIX	4299.3
PPFS (ANN)	2452.0
PPFS (ANN, split cache)	2174.4
PPFS (HMM)	1891.6

Table 8.2
Pathfinder execution times (seconds).

Pathfinder Description   During program execution, ancillary data files and the orbital data files are opened, and each orbit is processed sequentially. The access patterns for ancillary files range from sequential to irregularly strided. The result of this processing is written to a temporary output file using a combination of sequential and two-dimensionally strided accesses. Finally, the temporary file is re-written in HDF format. Because they are processed in a main program loop, we focus on the processing of only one of the fourteen orbital data files.

One of the problems with automatic policy selection using the algorithm of Table 8.1 is that limited physical memory prohibits indiscriminately enlarging file caches. Two Pathfinder files are accessed with small, strided requests; one must decide how to allocate the available cache space between these files. The ANN classifier cannot predict working set sizes, so one can either allocate space to one file, or split it evenly. The HMM classifier can generate a working set size prediction that one can use to allocate cache space.

Pathfinder Experimental Results   Table 8.2 shows the execution times for Pathfinder using UNIX buffered input/output and PPFS using ANN and HMM classification and different cache allocation strategies. When the ANN classifier detects that the output file is accessed with small strided accesses, the output file cache is enlarged. Without enough memory to enlarge the cache for small strided reads, caching is disabled for the input file accessed with that pattern. This policy selection achieves a speedup of approximately 1.75.

Another solution to the problem of limited cache space is to partition space evenly between the two files. In this example, this approach is superior, producing a two-fold improvement in performance over the original execution time. Using HMM classification and the cache space allocation heuristic described in §8.1.3, we can estimate the cache space needed for the input file and allocate the remaining memory to the output file. This strategy yields the best performance, a speedup of 2.27.

| Experimental | Read | | Write | | Lseek |
Environment	Count	Bytes	Count	Bytes	Count
UNIX	3,030,382	2.48247e+10	4,077,265	625,698,239	10,961,293
PPFS (ANN)	3,669,087	1,098,883,277	27,102	888,014,784	3,640,123
PPFS (ANN, split cache)	58,582	1,595,272,028	41,562	1,361,840,064	71,307
PPFS (HMM)	44,134	1,121,577,820	27,102	888,014,784	43,279

Table 8.3
Pathfinder operation counts and bytes accessed.

Table 8.3 shows the UNIX system level input/output operation counts and bytes for Pathfinder using both classification methods. PPFS with ANN classification enlarges the file cache to 25 MB for small, strided writes, and disables caching for small variably strided reads. This contributes to the reduction in number of bytes read while causing an increase in the read count. The write count is reduced by two orders of magnitude, although the total write volume increases because of the larger cache block size (32 KB vs. 8 KB for buffered UNIX input/output). When the cache is evenly split, there are fewer physical reads, but the additional block replacements necessitated by reducing the cache space available to the output file increase the number of writes and the read and write volume.

With the usage prediction provided by the HMM classification, 4 MB is allocated to the input file and the remaining 21 MB to the output file. The number and volume of writes is identical to that obtained by allocating the entire 25 MB cache to the output file, so write performance has not been sacrificed by increasing the input file cache. However, the number of physical reads decreases, and due to block replacements, the total read volume is only slightly greater than when input file caching is disabled.

8.4 Global Classification

Until now, we have described modeling a single input/output access stream; this is local classification, or classification per parallel program thread. Though sufficient for controlling uniprocessor caching and prefetching policies, local classification is a small part of a larger classification problem. The local access patterns within each thread of a parallel program merge during execution, creating a global access pattern.

Global knowledge is especially important for tuning file system policies, because coordinated access patterns cannot be detected with only local information. For example, consider a globally interleaved access pattern; each processor accesses a file by strides but the global pattern is sequential. A sequential prefetching policy at the storage devices can improve performance.

8.4.1 Global Classification Methodology

To create global classifications, we combine local classifications and other local data. However, merging this information is difficult because local information must be coordinated in time and space. Simply put, each processor's local access pattern classifications must overlap in time and space to identify the global file access pattern at a given point in time. Although we can ignore temporal coordination when combining local information to make global classifications, the classifications will not be very useful in guiding file system policies.

Local and global classifications are valid during a specific time interval corresponding to the duration between the first and last accesses within the observation period. We represent the valid time interval of a local classification as (t_s, t_e), where t_s is the start time and t_e is the end time. A global classification is valid for $(max(t_s), min(t_e))$ over all p local classifications. If $max(t_s) \geq min(t_e)$, the local classifications do not all overlap, so we cannot make a global classification with cardinality p. This implies that either multiple access patterns are present, or the local classification windows are too small and are staggered in time.

It is difficult to predict the appropriate duration of local classification windows to ensure a global classification window, because it is dependent upon the dynamic input/output rates of the individual processors. These rates change between and during program executions, varying with input data and system configuration. If the local classification windows are too short to make a global classification, our approach is to extend the local window size to include time between identical local classifications.

When classification windows are large enough that local classifications overlap in time, we form the global access pattern classification by combining local classifications. Each category of the classification (i.e., each axis of Figure 8.1) except for sequentiality can be determined as the meet of the local classifications for that category. For example, the read/write global classifications are straightforward; if each local access pattern is read only, the global access pattern is read only. If the local access patterns collectively involve reading and writing, the strongest global classification is read/write.

In addition, to identify global sequentiality, quantitative information about the input/output access stream is used to "correlate" the local classifications within the global file context. For example, if every local access pattern is sequential, the

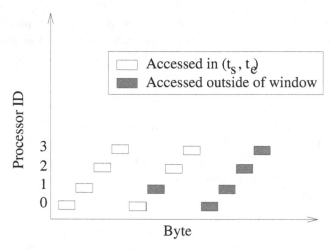

Figure 8.12
Global interleaved sequential classification.

beginning and end of every sequential stream is used to determine whether the global pattern is *global sequential* (every process reads the entire file sequentially) or *partitioned sequential* (the entire file is read in disjoint, sequential segments). As an example, we formulate a classification for a global interleaved sequential access pattern below, assuming a nonzero range $(max(t_s), min(t_e))$.

Interleaved sequential *Processors each access the entire file in strided patterns which interleave to form a global sequential pattern.*

As an example, Figure 8.12 shows byte ranges accessed by each of four processors during an interleaved sequential access pattern. We view the access pattern through a time window; the white regions are accesses used to make a global classification and the shaded accesses have not yet occurred.

We classify this pattern as interleaved sequential under the following conditions:

- $max(t_s) < min(t_e)$

- $\otimes L =$ 1-D strided

- $\cap$ bytes accessed $= \emptyset$

- If we merge the input/output requests from the different processors by file position, there should be at least p contiguous requests, where p is the number of processes involved in the classification. In Figure 8.12, the first 5 requests are contiguous, satisfying this requirement.

8.5 Global Classification Experiments

To demonstrate the performance improvements from global classification, we show results from parallel applications from the Scalable I/O Initiative application suite on the Intel Paragon XP/S.

8.5.1 Intel PFS

In our experiments, we used PPFS as an intermediary between the application requests and the underlying Intel PFS file system [127]. PFS is a parallel file system that stripes data over disks on input/output nodes using a default 64 KB stripe size. In normal usage, applications provide access pattern information by specifying PFS modes and have limited control over input/output node buffering. In our hybrid system, our access pattern classification toolkit identifies access patterns and automatically chooses appropriate PFS file modes and buffering strategies.

The PFS modes we manipulate below are M_UNIX (the default, atomic UNIX style input/output), M_RECORD (efficient access for interleaved sequential accesses), M_ASYNC (which does not preserve input/output atomicity) and M_GLOBAL (for global access patterns, where all processors read the same file bytes). Despite recommendations for matching PFS mode to pattern, identification of the best PFS mode depends upon other factors, such as request size, input/output configuration, and the number of processors doing input/output.

PFS also supports buffering on the input/output nodes. The default buffering strategy, intended for requests larger than 64 KB, is to disable buffering. However, buffering can be enabled on a per file basis to improve performance for smaller input/output requests.

Using global classification, we automatically select optimal PFS input/output modes and buffering strategies and compare performance to the default mode. Our motivation for this approach is not to optimize PFS performance, but rather to demonstrate the feasibility and importance of timely access pattern detection in conjunction with the well-defined set of policies. Emerging APIs like the high-level MPI-IO interface and the Scalable I/O low-level interface provide a much richer set of controls, enabling a larger set of future optimizations using access pattern classifications.

8.5.2 QCRD

The first application we analyzed is QCRD [286, 287], a quantum chemical reaction dynamics code used to study elementary chemical reactions. The code uses the method of symmetrical hyperspherical coordinates and local hyperspherical surface functions to solve the Schrödinger equation for the cross sections of the scattering of an atom by a diatomic molecule. Parallelization is accomplished by data decomposition; all processors execute the same code on different portions of the global matrices. The matrices are large enough to necessitate an out-of-core solution; the chosen data decomposition results in strided and cyclic input/output access patterns.

QCRD has five qualitatively similar phases; we limit our analysis to the second phase of QCRD, using a moderately sized data set. In phase two, 64 processors collectively read 13 matrices (written in phase one). All processors read the first 2412 bytes of each matrix and coordinate to read the remainder with a global interleaved sequential access pattern (i.e., each local pattern is strided, but the global interleaving of accesses is sequential). Most matrices are read twice without reopening. The output of this phase is 12 smaller matrices, written using a global interleaved access pattern.

Because of the initial global reads, mode M_ASYNC, which has performance comparable to mode M_RECORD, is the best mode for all file access patterns. Furthermore, because the request sizes are small (2400 bytes), enabling I/O server buffering further improves performance.

We executed this application on a 64 node partition of a 512 node Intel Paragon XP/S. Output was to a parallel file system with 16 input/output nodes, each controlling a 4 GB Seagate disk.

Figure 8.13 shows the total throughput, calculated every 128 KB, for one of the input matrices. Using artificial neural network (ANN) and hidden Markov model (HMM) classifications, we obtain classifications for each file and change policies as soon as the classification is available. With ANN classification, each processor must locally classify a window of ten accesses before the global classifier can determine that the pattern is globally interleaved. Using HMM classification, the global classification determined from previous execution data is available at file open.

Throughput using mode M_UNIX (no classification) is poor because file operations are serialized. The ANN classifier switches to mode M_ASYNC approximately halfway through execution, dramatically improving throughput. The lag between the policy change and the performance improvement is due to the synchronization

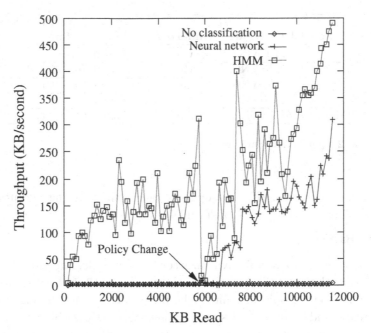

Figure 8.13
QCRD phase two throughput.

overhead of resetting the input/output mode. The HMM classifier can obtain a
better initial default policy from the global classifier at file open, improving performance throughout the file lifetime. However, throughput even with improved
initial policies dips briefly midway through file lifetime, corresponding to when the
file is rewound and reread.

Table 8.4 shows the input/output and execution times for this phase of QCRD.
The most substantial performance improvement is obtained by recognizing that the
global file access pattern is interleaved and selecting mode M_ASYNC. A secondary
performance improvement is possible using the observation that the global average
request size is small. A global interleaved sequential pattern with requests smaller
than the stripe unit size will benefit from caching at the input/output nodes, because several processors will request disjoint segments from the same block.

Early classification, exploiting the fact that input/output access patterns in this
application are the same across program executions, affords the best performance.
There are too few accesses to each output file to classify their patterns using our
implementation of ANN classification, and the ability to select the optimal policies

Classification	PFS Mode	Buffering	Read Time	Write Time	Execution Time
None	M_UNIX	Off	51810.79	4908.84	1144.42
ANN	M_ASYNC	Off	42717.46	5664.19	996.15
ANN	M_ASYNC	On	34503.84	5150.02	858.35
HMM	M_ASYNC	Off	2478.51	433.31	284.20
HMM	M_ASYNC	On	1558.31	286.05	263.92

Table 8.4
QCRD phase 2 input/output times (seconds).

for the input files when they are opened, rather than during execution, reduces total read time by an order of magnitude.

8.5.3   PRISM

PRISM, a computational fluid dynamics code, is a parallel implementation of a 3-D numerical simulation of the Navier-Stokes equations [112, 113]. It is parallelized by apportioning the periodic domain to the processors, with a combination of spectral elements and Fourier modes used to investigate the dynamics and transport properties of turbulent flow. We focus on the first phase, in which every processor reads three initialization files. One of these files is read twice sequentially during startup by each processor. ANN and HMM classification detect that the access pattern is global sequential. There are two optimizations PPFS supports given this classification.

The first possible policy selection is to select PFS mode M_GLOBAL, in which synchronizing processors making identical input/output requests, internally issuing only one request for all processors and broadcasting the result to the others. Because the initialization file is read using UNIX buffered input/output, the input/output request size is 8 KB and synchronization occurs at every global read.

Another common global optimization to improve read performance of small initialization files is to have one processor read the entire file when it is opened and broadcast it to the others. We implemented this policy in conjunction with a local default policy selection of caching with 2 64 KB blocks, sufficient to retain the 127394 byte file. The block size is selected for input/output efficiency (it is the PFS stripe unit size). User-level buffering eliminates the synchronization overhead of M_GLOBAL and provides the best performance, however, this optimization can be selected only if the classification is known at file open.

Figure 8.14 shows average per processor throughput, calculated per 8 KB block. Throughput using the default mode M_UNIX is very poor; in the PFS implemen-

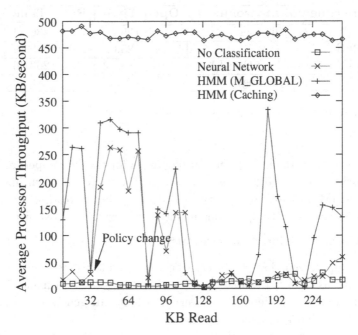

Figure 8.14
PRISM initialization file throughput.

tation of this mode nodes may not read the file in parallel. The ANN classifier improves performance by recognizing, after the first ten accesses, that the access pattern on each processor is sequential and read-only. It sends this information (along with the byte ranges accessed) to the global classifier. The global classifier determines from the sequential classifications and overlapping byte streams that the pattern is global sequential, and recommends each processor select mode M_GLOBAL. Because the call to reset the input/output mode is synchronizing, and it must be issued when all processors are at the same file position, there is some synchronization overhead for a policy change. This accounts for the low throughput at the first measurement under the new policy. The policy change occurs approximately two seconds into input/output execution.

In contrast, the HMM classifier queries the global classifier for a recommended mode at file open. The global classifier computes an initial policy recommendation based on the classifications of previous executions. We use this classification to select mode M_GLOBAL or have one processor read the file and broadcast it to the others. Throughput is greatest using the second approach.

Experimental Environment	Open Time	Read Time	Total
PPFS (no classification)	129.18	430.24	559.43
PPFS (ANN)	25.02	339.89	364.91
PPFS (HMM-M_GLOBAL)	28.32	263.36	291.68
PPFS (HMM-Caching)	238.56	8.42	246.97

Table 8.5
PRISM input/output times (seconds) for one initialization file.

Table 8.5 shows the total input/output times for the four experiments. There is a large variance in the total open time because the open call is synchronizing. However, when HMM classification is used to select a policy of reading and broadcasting the initialization file, the open time includes this significant overhead.

8.5.4   Complex Global Access Patterns

We have emphasized that HMM classification is able to classify a wider range of access patterns than is possible by ANN classification. This makes it particularly useful for guiding a prefetcher; at every access it can generate the probability of the most likely block to be accessed next.

In this experiment we consider a benchmark based on file access patterns exhibited by applications from Caltech for global climate modeling and modeling of the earth's interior [36]. These applications read and write data from a two or three dimensional grid, partitioning data in blocks of contiguous particles among the processors.

Figure 8.15 shows an example of such a partitioning on a two dimensional grid; each numbered block contains cs^2 elements allocated to the processor with that number. Processors simultaneously read their allocated chunks in segments of the particle size. Therefore, each processor exhibits a one-dimensionally strided access pattern. Globally, they coordinate to read the entire file, but the global access pattern is not interleaved sequential nor is it partitioned sequential; it is a mix of these that is unrecognizable as any predefined global pattern. The programmer cannot simply optimize this input/output pattern by changing the file layout so the matrix is accessed globally sequentially, because the allocations of particles to processors might change and can be quite complex.[2]

Prefetching can improve read performance by overlapping input/output latency with computation, but prefetching must correspond to the access pattern. Because

---

[2]Ultimately an application of this kind will prove an excellent candidate for testing the efficacy of HMMs trained on multiple access patterns.

Experimental Environment	Read	Seek	I/O Wait	Execution
PPFS (prefetch disabled)	266.47	0.21	N/A	23.14
PPFS (prefetch depth=1)	11.74	0.21	142.05	24.67
PPFS (prefetch depth=4)	14.58	22.35	6.85	13.43

Table 8.6
Input/output times for prefetching according to a block-block distribution (seconds).

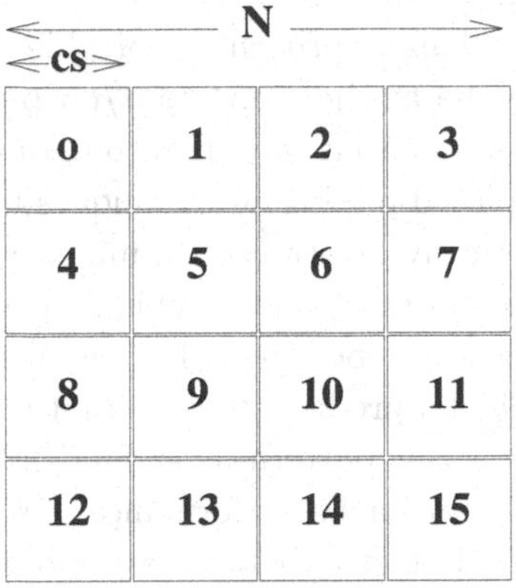

Figure 8.15
Block-block matrix partitioning.

HMMs can be trained to recognize any arbitrary repeatable access patterns, the locally trained HMMs are useful for guiding prefetching.

To demonstrate this capability, our benchmark distributes a 64×64 matrix of 64 KB blocks across 64 processors according to the the block-block distribution shown in Figure 8.15. Each processor reads a block in row major order, and "computes" for 100 ms before continuing to the next block. The input file is striped on 12 input/output nodes, each controlling a Seagate drive. PPFS implements prefetching by using asynchronous PFS reads to initiate fetches for some number of blocks in advance of the access stream (the prefetch depth). Table 8.6 shows the input/output times for PFS operations for this benchmark. Prefetching one block ahead is not enough to keep up with the request stream, and has no significant effect on overall execution time. However, prefetching four blocks ahead significantly reduces read time and improves performance.

8.6   Related Work

Because performance of parallel input/output systems is extremely sensitive to access pattern characteristics, tailoring file system policies to application requirements is a natural approach to improving performance. One system-independent way of specifying application requirements is to provide hints (possibly inaccurate access information) to guide a proactive file system. Patterson *et al* demonstrate the success of providing hints to guide prefetching of files that will be accessed in the future [209, 271]. This approach is portable, but requires the application programmer to describe the application input/output behavior. We view access pattern classification as a potential way to automatically provide these hints.

Many groups have explored intelligent techniques to construct higher level models of file access automatically. Kotz has examined automatic detection of global sequentiality to guide non-sequential prefetching within a file [157].

Exploitation of relationships between files has also been a significant research topic. Fido is an example of a predictive cache that prefetches by using an associative memory to recognize access patterns over time [204]. Knowledge based caching has been proposed to enhance cache performance of remote file servers [153]. Some approaches use probabilistic methods to create models of user behavior to guide prefetching [170, 105, 161]. This work is similar in spirit to our HMM classification methodology. The difficulty with modeling user behavior probabilistically is that recently accessed files are more likely to be re-accessed than frequently accessed files. Access patterns within files are usually highly regular.

8.7   Conclusions

We have shown that automatic classification of common access patterns is possible, both locally and globally. Because parallel input/output performance is a function of the access pattern, we can dynamically tune file system performance by mapping regions in the delimited space of access patterns to suitable, system-dependent policies, freeing the programmer from supplying this information.

The two proposed classification methods differ in approach, and have complementary properties. Neural network classification rapidly identifies known patterns within small, periodic windows of accesses, while hidden Markov models can be trained on one or more executions of an application, creating probabalistic models of irregular but repeatable patterns. Experiments with benchmarks and sequential and parallel applications demonstrate that the HMM approach offers more precise control over caching and prefetching policies than neural network access pattern classification, but has a greater overall cost.

Acknowledgments

We wish to thank J. Michael Lake for his helpful discussions and for suggesting the use of hidden Markov models. Evgenia Smirni also provided many useful comments and suggestions.

This work was supported in part by the National Science Foundation under grant NSF ASC 92-12369 and by a joint Grand Challenge grant with Caltech, by the National Aeronautics and Space Administration under NASA Contracts NGT-S1399, NAG-1-613, and USRA 5555-22 and by the Defense Advanced Research Projects Agency under ARPA contracts DAVT63-91-C-0029, DABT63-93-C-0040 and DABT63-94-C-0049 (SIO Initiative)

9 Thread Scheduling for Out-of-Core Applications with a Memory Server

YUANYUAN ZHOU, LIMIN WANG, DOUGLAS W. CLARK AND KAI LI

Although scalable multicomputers can provide very high performance for many in-core applications, they offer poor performance when an application's working set cannot fit in main memory. For example, many astrophysics, computational biology and engineering problems involve large data sets [71, 73, 219]. Performance for such applications is limited by disk accesses and I/O performance .

One straightforward approach to avoid paging is to run the application on a larger number of multicomputer nodes so that its data set can fit into the memory. This can be useful for parallel applications with low communication overhead and even data partitioning. However, it may not be a viable solution for applications in the following categories:

- *Sequential applications.* Some applications (e.g., hardware simulators) involve large data sets and are very difficult to parallelize. Although these applications cannot run on multiple nodes, it is very useful to exploit the total memory capacity of multicomputers to minimize the amount of disk I/O caused by virtual memory paging. For example, the Intel Paragon at Caltech has 512 computational nodes, each of which has 64 MB of memory. Hence, the total memory capacity is 32 GB. The challenge is to run a sequential application with a data set close to 32 GB on this system efficiently.

- *Parallel applications with limited scalability.* Many applications may have a high communication-to-computation ratio; they cannot scale well to large numbers of nodes. If an application with a data set of size n running on p nodes has linear computation complexity but np communication complexity, running on more nodes may degrade the performance when the communication overhead dominates the execution time.

- *Message-passing parallel applications with uneven data partitions.* Many applications are parallelized for an even distribution of workload rather than data. As a result, when the amount of work associated with a data partition is not proportional to the size of the data partition, application parallelization will yield an uneven data distribution. For such an application, paging may occur even though the size of its working set is less than the total memory capacity of all the participating nodes. N-body applications are one such case.

Earlier studies showed that a *memory server* can reduce the number of disk accesses for some out-of-core applications [123]. This method extends the multi-

computer memory hierarchy by using remote memory servers as distributed caches
for disk backing stores.

However, this approach has several limitations. First, it uses dedicated nodes
to service memory requests from the computation nodes. Therefore, it requires
extra nodes to help parallel applications with irregular data partitions. Second, the
paging overhead in the memory server system is still significant, up to 50 percent
of the total execution time for some applications with poor data locality. Hence, it
is important to improve data locality to reduce page misses.

A recent study proposed a method to improve the cache locality of sequential
programs by scheduling fine-grained threads [210]. The scheduling algorithm relies
on hints provided at thread creation to determine thread execution order to improve
data locality. This method can reduce second level cache misses and consequently
improves the performance of some untiled sequential applications. But the study
only treats independent threads.

In this chapter, we explore use of fine-grained thread scheduling to reduce page
misses for out-of-core applications with a memory server on a multicomputer. We
have extended the thread system and the scheduling algorithm to support applications with dependencies among threads. We have also extended the memory server
model to support both dedicated and non-dedicated memory server nodes. We
have implemented the memory server model and the fine-grained thread system
on an Intel Paragon. Our results with seven applications show that the memory server system outperforms traditional virtual memory (VM) by 90 percent for
sequential applications, 70 percent for parallel applications and 35 percent for irregular applications with uneven data partitions. Fine-grained threading further
improves memory server performance by 40-80 percent for six applications. Using
fine-grained threading with a memory server, the paging overhead requires less than
10 percent of the total execution time for all applications.

9.1   The Memory Server Model

As we noted earlier, the memory server model is a virtual memory management
technique that reduces the number of disk accesses for out-of-core applications on
multicomputers [123]. Iftode demonstrated that this model can improve performance up to a factor of three for some sequential, out-of-core applications. Although this prior work discussed many design issues, the memory server model was
designed to use dedicated memory server nodes, and the prototype implementation
supported only sequential applications.

In this chapter, we assume large-scale distributed memory multicomputers as
the architectural framework. Each node consists of a processor, a local memory

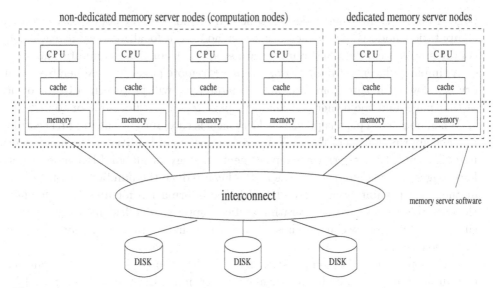

Figure 9.1
The memory server model.

unit, and a network interface. Nodes in the system are interconnected through a
scalable, high-bandwidth routing network. Disks are attached only to some nodes.
The Intel Paragon, the nCUBE series, the TMC CM-5 and the Princeton SHRIMP
are examples of such an architecture [80, 126, 115, 25], as are more recent Linux
clusters.

Our memory server supports both dedicated and non-dedicated memory server
nodes. User can specify the number of dedicated memory server nodes and the
number of computation nodes (non-dedicated memory server nodes) when an application starts.

Dedicated memory server nodes are used only for servicing remote memory requests. Non-dedicated memory server nodes also serve as computation nodes. In
other words, all the physical memory in all computation nodes is managed as a
whole. By doing this, we can reduce the number of page transfers to disks for
message-passing parallel applications with uneven data partitions. For sequential
applications, we use dedicated memory server nodes since only one node is used
for computation. Figure 9.1 shows an example of our memory server model with
four computation nodes (non-dedicated memory server nodes) and two dedicated
memory server nodes.

When a computation node exhausts its local memory, it will swap some victim pages to other computing nodes or dedicated memory server nodes. Because each computation node is also a memory server node, the local memory at each node contains both local data and remote data swapped from other computation nodes.

A simple replacement policy always replaces remote pages first. When free memory is below some threshold, the oldest remote page will be returned to the owner of that page, and the owner can send this page to some other node or to disk.

When no remote page is present, a local page is chosen to be the victim according to some approximation of the LRU algorithm, just as in traditional virtual memory management. One alternative replacement strategy is global LRU among both local pages and remote pages. This method can reduce the number of disk accesses at the cost of maintaining some global timing information for memory references. Because this would involve operating system support to collect memory reference timing information, we have chosen to use the first approach in our prototype implementation.

On a page miss, the computation node fetches the page from either another computation node or a dedicated memory server node. Each node has a page table that records the status and current location for each local page. When a remote page is sent back to the owner, it is removed from the memory server's memory.

In the memory server model, there is always at most one copy in memory for any page. The main advantage of this approach is that it can save memory space; the drawback is that clean pages also need to be transferred to new locations when swapping.

Figure 9.2 shows a simple example of the memory server model. Computation node zero exhausts its local memory and swaps page p to node one. Some time later, node zero attempts to access page p. A page fault occurs and node zero fetches p from node one; this node then deletes p from its local memory.

The memory server model can also reduce the average page miss penalty. First, for applications with reasonable temporal locality, most paging in the memory server model is from remote memory rather than disks. When the memory in all the nodes is exhausted, the least recently used pages in each node are swapped to disks. The LRU replacement strategy guarantees that the pages on disk are much older than those in physical memory. Therefore, with reasonable data locality, pages on disks are less likely to be fetched than those stored on remote memories. Second, fetching a page from remote memory is two orders of magnitude faster than paging from disk.

For example, transferring a 8 KB page from a remote memory takes about 100 microseconds on the Intel Paragon, whereas reading a page from a disk takes around 10 milliseconds. Consequently, the average page miss penalty is significantly less

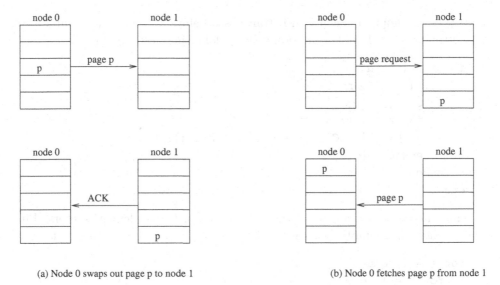

(a) Node 0 swaps out page p to node 1   (b) Node 0 fetches page p from node 1

Figure 9.2
Local and remote memory interactions.

than that for standard virtual memory.

Finally, the memory server model is very similar as the distributed shared memory model. Both manage all distributed memory as one single memory. The main difference is that the distributed shared memory model supports cache coherence, whereas the memory server model does not.

9.2 Fine-Grained Thread Scheduling

Fine-grained thread scheduling [210] was originally proposed to improve data locality for second-level caches. However, the proposed method is limited to independent threads. Here, we extend the thread scheduling approach to handle dependent threads.

9.2.1 Background and Examples

The original motivation for fine-grained thread scheduling was to decompose a program into fine-grained threads and schedule these threads to improve a program's data locality. For example, with fine-grained threads, one can substitute a thread for the innermost loop of a program that may be causing second-level cache misses.

Consider an example from [210] to illustrate the thread scheduling scheme. The example is a matrix multiply of two $n \times n$ matrices A and B with the result put in matrix C. To improve locality, A is transposed before and after the computation. One straightforward implementation uses the following nested loops.

```
for i = 1 to n
   for j = 1 to n
      C[i,j] = 0;
      for k = 1 to n
         C[i,j] = C[i,j] + A[k,i] * B[k,j];
      enddo
   enddo
enddo
```

The innermost loop computes the dot product of two n-element vectors. Fine-grained threading simply replaces the dot-product loop with a thread, as follows

```
for i = 1 to n
   for j = 1 to n
      Fork(DotProduct, i, j);
      RunThreads();

      DotProduct(i, j);

      C[i,j] = 0;
      for k = 1 to n
         C[i,j] = C[i,j] + A[k,i] * B[k,j];
      enddo
   enddo
enddo
```

where Fork creates and schedules a thread that will compute the specified dot product, and RunThreads runs each thread in some order determined by the scheduling algorithm.

Matrix multiplication is a very simple example, and no data dependency exists between any two threads. Therefore, threads can be executed in any order without yielding incorrect results. However, many applications such as matrix factorization have data dependencies between iterations. The original approach does not work with such applications since it cannot support dependencies among threads.

9.2.2 Thread Dependencies

In some applications, a thread can not start until another thread completes. For example, if a thread t needs to read the data produced by another thread t', or t will overwrite the data needed by t', then t has to be executed after t' is done.

Consider a simplified Gaussian elimination of matrix A:

```
for i = 1 to n
   for j = i+1 to n
      a[i,j] /= a[i,i];

      for k = i+1 to n
         a[j,k] = a[j,k] = a[i,j] * a[j,k];
      enddo
   enddo
enddo
```

Just as in the matrix multiplication example, we can turn inner loops become threads:

```
for i = 1 to n
   th[i,i] = Fork(Pivot, i);
   for j = i+1 to n
      th[j,i] = Fork(Compute, i, j);
   enddo

   RunThreads();

   Pivot(i):
   for j = i+1 to n
      a[i,j] /= a[i,i];

      Compute(i,j):
      for k = i+1 to n
         a[j,k] = a[j,k] - a[i,k] * a[j,k];
      enddo
   enddo
enddo
```

where Pivot() replaces the the first inner loop above and *Compute*() replaces the second one. The *Fork* interface is modified to return the identifier to the forked thread. For the purpose of easy explanation, we use th[i,j] to name the threads.

In contrast to matrix multiplication, this application has thread dependencies. For example, thread th[j,i] depends on thread th[i,i] and thread th[j,i-1] since it needs to use the *i*th and *j*th row, which are produced by thread th[i,i] and th[j,i-1] respectively. Similarly, thread th[i,i] has to execute after thread th[i,i-1]. To assume the correct execution order of threads, we need to specify dependency relations to the thread system at thread creation time. Based on these, the thread system will schedule threads without violating the dependency specifications. To achieve this goal, we must add a few parameters to the Fork interface to allow applications to specify dependencies.

```
for i = 1 to n
   th[i,i] = Fork(Pivot, i, th[i,i-1]);

   for j = i+1 to n
      th[j,i] = Fork(Compute, i, j, th[i,i], th[j,i-1]);
   enddo
enddo


RunThreads();
```

The two examples above show how such transformation can be performed manually, with or without thread dependencies. To implement the thread system to reduce the number of page misses, the total cost associated with threading must be significantly less than the cost of the page misses eliminated. To achieve this, the scheduling algorithm needs to make intelligent decisions to improve the program's locality without violating thread dependencies specified by the application.

9.2.3 Scheduling with Dependencies

To produce correct results, a thread scheduling algorithm must obey thread dependencies, and the dependencies must be correctly specified. A thread t, which depends on threads t_1, t_2, ..., t_k, cannot execute until t_1, t_2, ..., t_k complete. The challenge is to design a scheduling algorithm that obeys thread dependencies and performs efficiently for a large number of threads.

Our approach to the scheduling challenge with dependencies is to use a ready set S, which contains all ready threads. A thread is ready if and only if all threads on which it depends have been executed. Threads in the ready set can be executed in any order without violating the correctness of the program.

Each thread has a dependency counter. The dependency counter for thread t is decremented by 1 when one of its dependencies completes. Thread t will be put into the ready set when its dependency counter reaches 0.

Although the scheduler can execute threads in the ready set in any order, a poor execution sequence can cause many capacity misses and adversely affect the overall performance of the program. For example, with Gaussian elimination of a matrix whose size does not fit in the physical memory, if threads are executed in the same order as they are forked, each thread would have page misses on the row it processes. Although the row for a thread may have been brought to memory, it is evicted from the physical memory to make space for the data required for previously running threads. Therefore, a good scheduler should be locality conscious.

9.2.4   Scheduling for Locality

To schedule threads for data locality, the thread scheduler must have some information about the memory references made by the threads. Following [210], we assume each thread provides some hints about the main data structures it references during its execution. These hints are used by the scheduler to estimate the locality relationship among threads. Applications can give either omit or provide hints without affecting correctness but may have different performance. For example, in the Gaussian elimination application, each thread can give two hints about the rows it computes.

```
for i = 1 to n
   th[i,i] = Fork(Pivot, i, th[i,i-1], a[i]);

   for j = i+1 to n
      th[j,i] = Fork(Compute, i, j, th[i,i], th[j,i-1], a[i], a[j]);
   enddo
enddo

RunThreads();
```

Every time a thread completes, the scheduler selects another thread from the ready set to execute. The goal for the scheduler is to find a selection algorithm that minimizes the number of page misses.

Our scheduling algorithm extends the one described in [210]. The original idea of the algorithm is to schedule threads in "bins." When the threads in a bin are successively scheduled, they will not cause many capacity page misses.

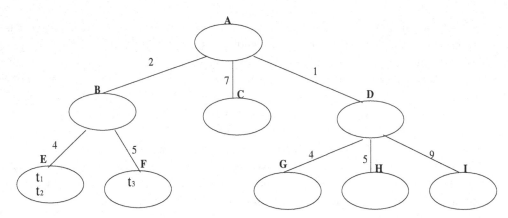

Figure 9.3
The schedule tree.

The virtual address space is first divided into large blocks. Threads referencing the same blocks belong to the same bin. For example, assume the block size is 16, the address hints for thread t_1 are 32 and 64, the address hints for thread t_2 are 40 and 72, and the hints for t_3 are 36 and 84. Threads t_1 and t_2 reference block 2 and block 4. Therefore, they belong to the same bin. t_3 accesses block 2 and 5, so it is contained in a different bin. Once we have grouped threads into bins, we just need to traverse the bins along some path. For each non-empty bin, the scheduler runs all threads it contains one after another until it becomes empty.

However, unlike the original algorithm, our scheduler uses a fat tree rather than a simple hash table as its primary data structure. The tree structure enables us to support as many hints as possible. It is also much easier to support thread dependencies. Each node n represents a bin $B(n)$. Edges represent block numbers. The path from the root to node indicates all the blocks every thread contained in $B(n)$ references. As shown in Figure 9.3, threads t_1 and t_2 reference block 2 and 4, so they all fall into the node E. t_3 accesses block 2 and 5, so it belongs to node F. However, n_1 and n_2 share the same parent since they have the same first block number.

At run time, the algorithm simply traverses the tree to move from one bin to another until all nodes in the tree are visited. After a node is visited, we then move to its siblings. For example, the bin traversal sequence for Figure 9.3 is ABEFCDGHI.

The advantage of this bin traversal scheme is that it allows more data reuse than a random scheme. The reason is that threads in sibling bins share some hints. After all threads in a bin B complete, executing threads in a sibling may have fewer page misses than executing other threads because hopefully some data may have been brought into the memory by threads in bin B.

9.3   Implementation

To evaluate the effectiveness of the combination of the memory server model with the fine-grained thread scheduling for out-of-core applications, we have implemented the memory server model and the thread system on a ten node Intel Paragon. The memory server model required a small modification to the kernel, whereas the thread system runs at user level.

9.3.1   Paragon System

The Intel Paragon multicomputer used in our experiments consists of ten computation nodes. Each node has one compute processor and a communication co-processor. Both processors are 50 MHz i860 microprocessors with 16 KB of data cache and 16 KB of instruction cache [126]. The two processors share 64 MB of local memory, with around 56 MB memory available to user applications. The memory bus provides a peak of 400 MB/s. The nodes are interconnected with a wormhole routed 2-D mesh network whose peak is 200 MB/s per link [272].

The operating system is a micro-kernel based version of OSF/1 with multicomputer extensions for a parallel programming model and the NX/2 message passing primitives. The co-processor runs exclusively in kernel mode, and it is dedicated to communication. The one-way message-passing latency of a 4-byte NX/2 message on the Paragon is about 50 microseconds [211]. The transfer bandwidth for large messages depends on data alignment. When data are aligned properly, the achievable maximal bandwidth at the user level is 175 MB/s. Without proper alignment, the peak bandwidth is about 45 MB/s

9.3.2   Memory Server Implementation

To implement the memory server model on the Intel Paragon, one straightforward approach would be to use the external memory management (EMM) mechanism in OSF 1 (derived from Mach 3.0). The advantage of this approach is that the implementation can be done at user level. However, our prototype implementation using EMM showed that this method is very inefficient because the operating system overhead, including context switch and Mach IPC overhead, is surprisingly high.

Another approach would be to change the Mach kernel to support paging to/from remote memory. However, this approach is difficult to debug and has poor portability. Therefore, we implemented the memory server model at the user level by

	Method		
	VM	EMM	MS
Time (ms)	13	6.5	1.4

Table 9.1
Average page fault time.

	Handler Invoking	Request Transfer	Context Switch	Page Transfer	Page Protection	Total
Time (ms)	0.3	0.05	0.7	0.1	0.2	1.4

Table 9.2
Distribution of times for processing a memory server page fault.

adding a new system call supporting virtual to physical page mapping. To simplify our later explanation, we use MS to represent this implementation.

The memory server manages the local memory by itself. To achieve this, the implementation needs to address three issues:

- The memory server system must catch page faults. We achieve this by using the virtual memory protection fault mechanism. When a page is swapped to remote memory or disks, its access permission is turned off. When the application references this page, an protection fault triggers the user page fault handler. The handler fetches the missing page from remote memory or disks, changes its access permission and restarts the faulting instruction.

- To avoid the Mach kernel swapping application pages to disk when the amount of free memory is below some threshold, our implementation pins all application pages.

- When local memory is exhausted, the memory sever swaps out some pages and gives the physical frames to faulted pages. This requires a mechanism to map an old virtual page's physical frame to a new virtual page. To support this efficiently, we added one system call $remap\_addr(addr1, addr2)$ to the Mach kernel. This system call maps $addr1$'s physical frame to $addr2$.

The memory server system uses NX messages to send requests and pages between nodes. Each node, except dedicated memory server nodes, runs two threads, one for application computation, one for servicing remote memory requests.

Table 9.1 compares the average page fault handling time with virtual memory management (VM), the memory server implementation using external memory management (EMM), and the memory server implementation MS. The MS implementation has the smallest average page fault handling time, 8 times less than traditonal VM and 4 times less than the implementation using EMM.

Table 9.2 shows the distribution of times for handling a page fault in the MS implementation. Transferring a page costs only 10 percent of the total page fault handling time, while operating system related overhead takes 90 percent of the handling time. This indicates the memory server performance can be improved significantly by reducing an operating system overhead.

9.3.3 Thread System Implementation

Implementation of the thread system is straightforward for sequential applications. Applications are manually modified to create small threads. The thread scheduler runs at user level. As described earier, all bins are organized as a fat scheduling tree, which is implemented using a binary tree.

Each application's virtual address space is divided into 16 MB blocks. Threads accessing the same blocks are executed one after another. To reduce the thread system memory overhead, when the number of created threads has reached some threshold, the scheduler is triggered to start running threads. When all created threads complete, all data structures in the thread system can be reused.

Our thread system also supports parallel applications using NX message passing primitives. In these applications, nodes synchronize implicitly through messages. Some reorderings of communication events in different nodes may generate incorrect results or deadlocks. Consider a case when node 0 sends a message of type 1 to node 1 and waits for a message of type 2 from node 1, while node 1 waits for the message of type 1 from node 0 and then sends a message of type 2 to node 0:

$$\text{Node 0} \qquad\qquad\qquad \text{Node 1}$$

$$send(TYPE1, 1, message0, size0); \quad recv(TYPE1, 0, buffer0, size0)$$
$$recv(TYPE2, 1, message1, size1); \quad send(TYPE2, 0, buffer1, size1)$$

The code can proceed normally. However, if the order of the *send* and *recv* are switched on node 0, and the code on node 1 remains unchanged, a deadlock will occur. This indicates that a reordering that only obeys dependencies among local threads may not work for message-passing parallel applications.

Therefore, the challenge in the thread system is to support communication among nodes but still improve data locality. One solution is to reorder threads between any two consecutive communication events. This approach is very simple. The drawback is that the number of reorderable threads is so few that any

	Fork	Run	Total
Time (ms)	0.013	0.006	0.02

Table 9.3
Intel Paragon thread overhead, with times in microseconds.

scheduling is unlikely to improve data locality. The second solution is to reorder threads on all nodes by treating a *send* and *recv* pair on two different nodes as a dependency between the *recv* and *send* thread. This method is more aggressive but requires rewriting applications.

Our solution to the scheduling challenge with communication is similar to the global reordering method. It also treats *send* and *recv* pairs on different nodes as dependencies. The *recv* thread cannot execute until the corresponding *send* thread on another node completes. Dependencies among *send*'s and *recv*'s on the same node follow the same rule as those in sequential applications.

The difference between our solution and the global reordering method is that each node only reorders its own threads. If a thread t on node 0 depends on another thread t_1 on node 1, when t_1 completes, node 1 sends a message to node 0. Node 0 decrements t's dependency counter just as when a local dependency of t completes. This method can schedule more threads than the first solution and does not require rewriting applications. The drawback of this method is that it does not consider parallelism. Sometimes, it is better to sacrifice data locality to schedule a thread which can reduce the message waiting time in another node.

Table 9.3 reports the overhead to fork (create and schedule) and run (execute and terminate) a null thread on the Intel Paragon. The thread overheads were calculated using a simple loop that created one million threads to call the null procedure and then ran them. The threads were evenly distributed across the scheduling plane. The total overhead for one thread is only 0.02 milliseconds, which is two orders of magnitude less than the average page miss penalty in the MS system. This indicates that the thread scheduling can improve applications' performance if the scheduling algorithm can reduce at least one page miss per thread.

9.4   Performance

To evaluate the performance of our implementations of the memory server system and fine-grained thread scheduler, we used three sequential applications (matrix multiply, Gaussian elimination and Cholesky factorization), the parallel versions of these three applications, and one parallel application with uneven data partition (N-body).

Applications		Problem Size	Data (MB)	Time
Sequential	Matrix multiply	4,096 x 4,096	384	162,364.4
	Gaussian elimination	4,096 x 4,096	128	58,864.8
	Cholesky factorization	4,096 x 4,096	128	28,256.7
Parallel	Matrix multiply	8,192 x 8,192	1,536	514,756.8
	Gaussian elimination	8,192 x 8,192	512	202,169.6
	Cholesky factorization	8,192 x 8,192	512	123,143.3
Irregular	N-body	80,000 bodies	300 total	19,640.1
		30 iterations	70 max,28 min	

Table 9.4
Memory server performance for selected applications. All times are in seconds.

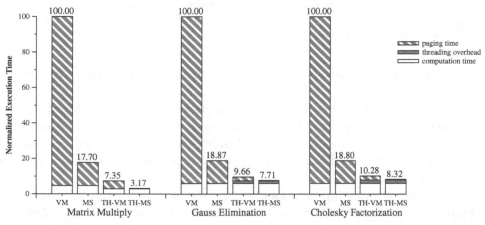

Figure 9.4
Sequential application performance. The execution times with VM and TH-VM are estimated).

Table 9.4 gives the problem sizes, data set sizes and execution time with MS for the seven applications. We choose the problem sizes large enough so that the whole data sets cannot fit in the physical memory. All applications take several hours to several days to execute with MS.

9.4.1   Sequential Applications

Figure 9.4 compares performance (on a logarithmic scale) across traditional virtual memory (VM), our memory server implementation (MS), VM with threading (TH-VM) and MS with threading (TH-MS). All times are normalized to that of VM. In these cases, the memory server uses eight dedicated server nodes. Because running applications with VM take more than 10 days to complete, we estimated

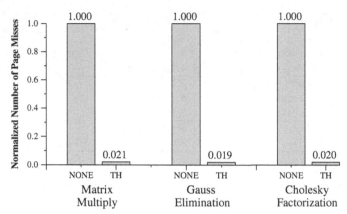

Figure 9.5
Page misses with sequential applications.

performance with VM and TH-VM using the number of page misses with MS and Th-MS, respectively.

The memory server model performs dramatically better than VM for three of the sequential applications. As shown in Figure 9.4, paging overhead consumes more than 97 percent of the time for the VM implementation. MS reduces this by a factor of 14 for three applications. As a result, MS performs an order of magnitude better than VM.

Fine-grained threading significantly improves the performance. As shown in Figure 9.5, the number of page misses with the threaded versions are only 2 percent of those with the original versions. As a result, fine-grained threading reduces paging time by a factor of 50. The overhead of the thread system is less than 25 percent of the execution time for Gaussian and Cholesky factorization.

For matrix multiply, the overhead of threading is negligible because this application has no thread dependencies. In addition, fine-grained threading also reduces the number of cache and TLB misses for matrix multiply. This is indicated by the reduced computation time with TH-VM and TH-MS. Consequently, The performance with fine-grained threading improves by 94-97 percent with respect to VM and 56-82 percent with respect to MS.

Overall, the combination of fine-grained threading and the memory server performs 22 to 60 times better than traditional VM. The paging overhead is reduced from 97 percent with VM to less than 10 percent using fine-grained threading with memory server.

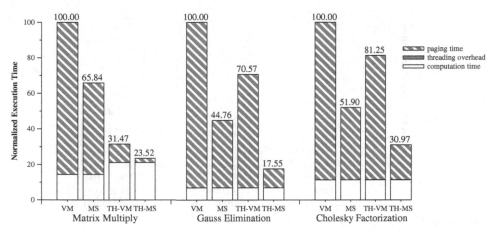

Figure 9.6
Parallel application performance. The execution times with VM and TH-VM are estimated.

9.4.2   Parallel Applications

All three of our parallel applications use message passing. The matrix multiply application is parallelized by row partitioning the result matrix. The other two applications partition the matrix in interleaved rows. Moreover, all three applications have thread dependencies. We conducted our experiments on 8 computation nodes and 2 dedicated memory server nodes.

Figures 9.6 and 9.7 show that the memory server model and fine-grained threading can also effectively improve the performance for parallel out-of-core applications. The memory server model alone reduces the paging time by a factor of 3 to 7. As a result, MS improves the performance of three parallel applications by 65-77 percent. Fine-grained threading further improves the performance with MS by reducing the number of page misses by 48-96 percent. The combination of MS and fine-grained threading reduces the execution time of the original code with VM by 91-84 percent.

The performance improvement by the memory server model and fine-grained threading is less pronounced with parallel applications than that with sequential applications. The main reason is serialization at dedicated memory servers. In our experiments, 2 dedicated memory servers must service 8 computation nodes. In addition, with parallel applications, fewer threads can be reordered by the scheduler for data locality due to dependencies among threads on different nodes.

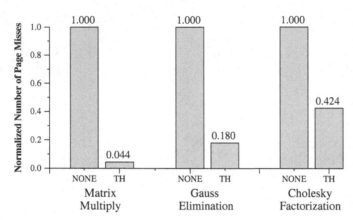

Figure 9.7
Page misses with parallel applications.

9.4.3 Irregular Applications

N-body applications are widely used in many areas of science and engineering, including astrophysics, molecular biology and even graphics. The test application simulates the interactions among a system of particles over a number of time steps, using the Barnes-Hut hierarchical N-body method [12].

Our N-body application is based on Salmon's implementation with message passing [277]. It uses an orthogonal recursive bisection partitioning technique. It is parallelized in a way that the work on each node is well balanced. If all particles have the same mass, all particles are evenly distributed among all nodes. Otherwise, an imbalance in data partition can occur. A dark hole in a galaxy is such an example. Our input simulates this scenario.

The total memory requirement is around 300 MB, and the data partition is uneven among 8 nodes, ranging from 28 MB to 70 MB. The application causes paging in nodes whose data partitions exceed the physical memory limit, while some other nodes still have more than 20 MB of free physical memory available.

Figure 9.8 shows the performance for the N-body application on 8 computation nodes with VM, the memory server with no dedicated server nodes (MS-0) and memory server with one dedicated server node (MS-1). The memory server reduces the paging time with VM by 50% without using additional nodes. As a result, the memory server with the same number of nodes performs 35 percent better than traditional VM. This indicates that paging to other computation nodes with less memory utilization is helpful to overcome the imbalance of the data partition. Using the memory server, the problem size without causing disk paging is limited

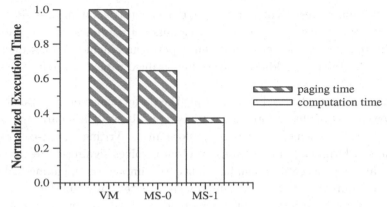

Figure 9.8
N-body application performance. In the figure, MS-0 denotes 8 computation nodes with no
dedicated memory server, and MS-1 denotes 8 computation nodes with 1 dedicated memory
servers.

by the total amount of memory on all nodes, rather than the amount of memory
on a single node.

Using one dedicated memory server node (MS-1) substantially outperforms the
memory server without dedicated server nodes (MS-0). The paging overhead is
reduced from 46 percent of the execution time in MS-0 to less than 10 percent in
MS-1. With no dedicated server nodes, paging requests to a remote node need
to interrupt the computation of this node, while in MS-1, all paging requests are
first sent to dedicated memory server nodes, which are always waiting for requests
from computation nodes. Because context switching and message notification on
the Intel Paragon are very expensive, the memory server system overhead and the
average page miss penalty with MS-0 are much greater than those with MS-1.

9.5 Related Work

Local area networking researchers have taken an approach similar to the memory
server model [56, 91, 228, 89], using the memory available on other nodes as backing stores. All these studies use a cluster of workstations and run sequential or
distributed applications, whereas our memory server model runs on a multicomputer for sequential and parallel applications. Therefore, we have different design
tradeoffs.

Memory servers for multicomputers were first proposed in [123]. They presented
the model and discussed several design issues, including compute vs. memory server
nodes, page mapping and replacement, and caching and prefetching. They also

showed preliminary results of a prototype implementation on an Intel iPSC/860 for sequential applications. Our memory server model supports both dedicated and non-dedicated memory server nodes. Our experiments include both sequential and parallel applications. In addition, we use fine-grained threads to reduce the number of page misses.

Much research has focused on improving the performance of out-of-core applications. Developers of out-of-core applications typically write a separate version with explicit I/O calls to achieve reasonable performance. Writing an out-of-core version of a code is a formidable task because it often involves significant restructuring of the code, and in some cases, it can have a negative impact on the numerical stability of the algorithm [282]. Our approach provides a potentially simpler alternative.

Compiling for out-of-core applications tends to focus on two areas: reordering computation to improve data reuse [28] and inserting explicit I/O calls or I/O prefetches into application codes [65, 145, 203, 257, 187]. Most of these compilation techniques are limited by the alias analysis problem and are only useful for array codes.

Fine-grained thread scheduling was originally proposed in [210]. It was used to reduce second level cache misses, whereas we use fine-grained threads to reduce page misses. In addition, their thread package assumes all threads are independent, whereas our thread system can support thread dependencies and therefore runs with more applications, such as matrix factorizations.

9.6 Conclusions and Limitations

This chapter has described use of fine-grained threads with a memory server to reduce the number of disk accesses for out-of-core applications. Our implementation on the Intel Paragon has shown that the memory server mechanism reduces the page miss penalty relative to traditional virtual memory (VM) by a factor of 18. The overhead of the fine-grained thread scheduling algorithm with dependencies is very small, less than the time for an average page miss in the memory server system.

Our results have also shown that the memory server system substantially outperforms traditional virtual memory for sequential applications. For parallel applications, the memory server becomes useful when the application reaches the scalability limit. Our experiments with three parallel applications showed that the memory server system performs 65-70 percent better than traditional VM. The combination of the memory server model and fine-grained threading outperforms traditional VM by 84-90 percent

The memory server model can also help parallel applications with uneven data partitions, such as N-body applications. Our experiments with this application have shown that with the same number of multicomputer nodes, the memory server system performs 35 percent better than traditional VM. With one dedicated memory server node, the memory server system can achieve 60 percent performance improvement over traditional VM.

Fine-grained threads can reduce the number of page misses for applications that have no information about memory reference patterns at compile time. Our results with six applications have shown that fine-grained threading can reduce the number of page misses by 97 percent for sequential applications and 60-80 percent for parallel applications. As a result, threading improves memory server performance by 55-80 percent for sequential applications and 40-60 percent for parallel applications. When static information is available, a good compiler may do better than the thread package.

Our study has several limitations. First, we have not compared our results with explicit I/O or compiler-inserted I/O versions for out-of-core applications. Also, we have not compared fine-grained thread scheduling with a manually tiled version. Because of test platform limitations, we were unable to investigate the effectiveness of fine-grained thread scheduling for reducing second level cache misses in addition to memory swapping. Finally, we have not studied how much thread scheduling and memory server can help shared memory applications. However, we expect that it also can reduce the number of disk accesses caused by paging.

Acknowledgments

This work benefitted greatly from discussions with Jaswinder Pal Singh, who helped us with understanding the N-body application. We are also grateful to Tracy J. Kimbrel and Sandy Irani for their help improving the thread scheduling algorithm.

This work is sponsored in part by the Scalable I/O project under DARPA contract DABT63-94-C-0049 and by NSF under grants EIA-9806751, EIA-9975011, and ANI-9906704.

10 A Scalability Study of Shared Virtual Memory Systems

YUANYUAN ZHOU, LIVIU IFTODE AND KAI LI

Shared memory is considered an attractive paradigm because it provides a simple yet effective parallel programming model. Research in the last decade shows that it is difficult to build or provide shared memory on a large-scale system. Although the hardware approach to implementing cache coherence has been shown to perform quite well, it requires a high engineering cost [171]. Shared virtual memory (SVM) [173], on the other hand, is a cost-effective method to provide the shared memory abstraction on a network of computers since it requires no special hardware support. The main problem with this approach has been its lack of scalable performance when compared with hardware cache coherence. The challenge is to reduce the overhead of software coherence protocols and to implement efficient shared virtual memory that performs well with various applications on large-scale machines.

The known software approach to reduce the overhead of shared virtual memory is to employ relaxed memory consistency models such as Release Consistency. Release Consistency improves the performance of SVM by maintaining coherence only at synchronization. Lazy Release Consistency (LRC) [42, 143] is a state-of-the-art implementation of the release consistency model. Although previous prototypes have shown reasonably good performance for some applications on small systems [142], protocol overhead becomes substantial on large-scale systems. Our own experience shows that many applications do not speedup well using standard LRC-based shared virtual memory on a 32-node machine, and that the speedup curves go down when increasing the number of nodes to 64.

Three factors limit the scalability of the traditional LRC protocol. First, it requires a large number of messages. LRC detects updates using *diffs*, which are created and merged on demand in a distributed fashion. Therefore, it may require more than one round trip message to fetch all missing diffs to satisfy a page miss. Second, the traditional LRC protocol consumes a large amount of memory for protocol overhead data. Distributed diffs can occupy a lot of memory space because they can be freed only after all the nodes have the updates. Third, performing the memory coherence protocol in software is expensive because the computation has to be interrupted to service both local and remote memory coherence protocol requests.

We have investigated three protocols to improve the scalability of the LRC protocol. The first is the Home-based LRC protocol (HLRC). The second protocol uses the communication co-processor on each node to avoid interrupting the com-

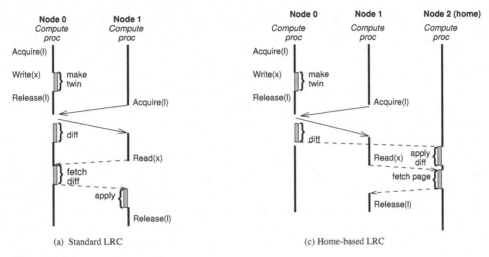

Figure 10.1
An example of LRC, AURC and home-based lazy release consistency (LRC).

putation while servicing remote memory coherence requests (OLRC). The third
protocol is the combination of the first two (OHLRC).

We have implemented all three approaches and traditional LRC on an Intel
Paragon multicomputer: HLRC, OHLRC, the standard LRC and an overlapped
LRC. We also compared the performance of the two home-based protocols with the
two homeless LRC protocols using several Splash-2 benchmark programs.

Our results show that the home-based protocols provide substantial improvements in performance and scalability over the homeless ones and that protocol
overlapping using a communication processor adds only modest improvements. By
studying detailed time breakdowns, communication traffic, and memory requirements, we show also that the home-based protocols scale better than the homeless
ones.

10.1 Protocols

In this section, we briefly describe the standard Lazy Release Consistency (LRC)
[143] protocol, the Home-based LRC (HLRC) protocol and their overlapped variations (OLRC and OHLRC).

10.1.1 Lazy Release Consistency

The standard LRC [143] is an all-software, page-based, multiple-writer protocol.
It has been implemented and evaluated in the TreadMarks system [142]. The

LRC protocol postpones updates to shared pages and uses the causal orders to obtain up-to-date versions. The main idea of the protocol is to use *timestamps*, or intervals, to establish the happen-before ordering between causal-related events. Local intervals are delimited by synchronization events. In our implementation an interval on processor P is delimited by one of the following two events: (i) processor P performs a remote acquire operation, or (ii) processor P receives a remote lock request.

Every writer locally records the changes it makes to every shared page during each interval. When a processor first writes a page within a new interval, it saves a copy of the page, called a *twin*, before writing to it. When the interval ends, the processor saves the interval and the page numbers that were updated in a record called a *write-notice*. The processor then compares the dirty copy of the page with the twin to detect updates and records these in a structure called a *diff*. The LRC protocol creates diffs either eagerly, at the end of each interval, or lazily, on demand.

On an acquire, the requesting processor invalidates all pages according to the write-notices received. The first access to an invalidated page causes a page fault. The page fault handler collects all the diffs for the page and applies them locally in the proper causal order to reconstitute the coherent page. Figure 10.1(a) shows how the protocol works with a simple example.

Such a multiple-writer protocol has several benefits. Since multiple nodes can update the same page simultaneously, the protocol can greatly reduce the protocol overhead due to false sharing. By delaying coherence actions until a synchronization point, the protocol can reduce the number of messages for protocol and data, and hence reduce software protocol overhead. Furthermore, the protocol can reduce the communication traffic due to data transfer: instead of transferring the whole page each time, the protocol transfer diffs to propagate updates.

On the other hand, diff processing can be expensive. First, the diff creations and applications all have substantial software overhead and pollute the processor's caches. Second, the acquiring processor may have to visit more than one processor to obtain diffs when multiple nodes update the same page simultaneously. Third, even when consecutive diffs of the same page (from multiple synchronization intervals) are obtained from one place, they have to be obtained as separate diffs and applied individually by the faulting processor. However, multiple diff traffic and application is avoided when the page has only one writer by transferring the whole page instead.

The data structures of this protocol can consume a substantial amount of memory. The memory required to store diffs and write notices can grow quickly since they cannot be discarded as long as there are nodes that may still need them.

When implementing the protocol on a large-scale machine, memory consumption can become a severe problem. To reduce memory consumption the shared virtual memory system must perform garbage collection frequently [142].

10.1.2 Home-based LRC Protocol

Home-based LRC (HLRC) protocol [288] is a variation of the traditional LRC. The main idea of HLRC is to have a "home" node for each shared page at which updates from writers of that page are collected. This protocol is inspired by the design of Automatic Update Release Consistency (AURC) [122]. The difference is that updates are detected in software and propagated using diffs unlike in AURC, which a special automatic update hardware is required to propagate the updates automatically.

HLRC computes diffs at the end of an interval to detect updates and to transfer the updates as diffs to their homes. The lifetime of diffs is extremely short, both on the writer nodes and the home nodes. Writers can discard their diffs as soon as they are sent. Home nodes apply arriving diffs to their copies as soon as they arrive and then discard them. Later, on a page fault following a coherence invalidation, the faulting node fetches the whole page from the home node. Figure 10.1(c) shows an example of how HLRC works.

HLRC has some advantages when compared to standard LRC: (i) accesses to pages on their home nodes cause no page faults, (ii) diffs do not need to be created when the writer is the home node, (iii) non-home nodes can always bring their shared pages up-to-date with a single round-trip message, and (iv) protocol data and control messages are much smaller than under standard LRC. The disadvantages are that whole pages are fetched in order to satisfy a page miss and good home assignment may be important.

10.1.3 Overlapped Protocols

Many parallel architectures [211, 116, 163, 168] contain dedicated communication and/or protocol processors that take over most of the overhead of performing these operations from the compute processor(s). Even though the occupancy of these processors is in general low, they cannot be used for general application computation since they are running a server polling loop in kernel mode. In addition, in most cases, the communication processor is one generation behind the compute processors.

This section describes two protocol variations, called Overlapped LRC and Overlapped Home-based LRC, that extend the use of the communication co-processors on the Paragon as protocol processors to overlap some of the SVM protocol overhead with computation.

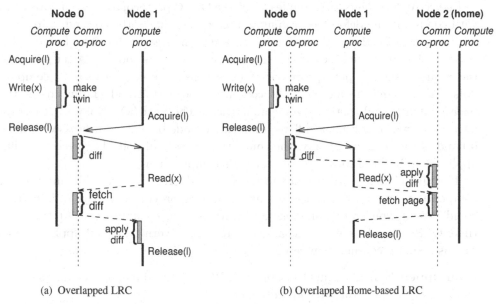

(a) Overlapped LRC   (b) Overlapped Home-based LRC

Figure 10.2
An example of overlapped LRC and overlapped home-based LRC.

Overlapped LRC The Overlapped LRC (OLRC) protocol uses the communication co-processor for two tasks: to perform diffs and to service remote fetch requests.
For the first task the compute processor asks its co-processor to compute diffs at
the end of each interval for all pages that have been updated during that interval.
Once performed, diffs are stored and propagated to remote nodes on demand.

The second task of the co-processor is to service remote requests for diffs and
pages without interrupting the compute processor. These requests are sent by
remote processors on a page access fault in order to bring their copies up-to-date
according to the information previously provided by the write-notices. The co-
processor sends the requested diffs if available. If a diff computation is in progress,
the co-processor queues the request until the diff is ready. Full-page requests are
issued only when the faulting node does not have a local copy for the page.

Other operations, like twin creation and diff application, are still performed by
the compute processor. Usually, these do not expose enough overlapping potential
to justify co-processor involvement. Also, the remote lock acquire operation, which
requires coherence control handling, is still serviced by the main processor. We

made this decision in an early stage of the implementation to keep the co-processor interface independent of any particular protocol.

Figure 10.2(a) shows an example of how the OLRC protocol overlaps its overhead with computation. Before performing `write(x)` on node 0, the compute processor creates a twin for the page holding `x`. Node 0 then releases the lock. Later, when node 1 tries to acquire lock l, it sends a lock request to node 0. After servicing the request, the compute processor of node 0 asks its co-processor to compute diffs. After acquiring the lock, the compute processor of node 1 invalidates the page holding `x` and continues its computation. The `read(x)` on node 1 causes a page fault, which triggers a diff request sent to node 0. The co-processor of node 0 handles the request. Finally, the compute processor of node 1 receives the diff, applies it to its local copy, and continues its computation.

The OLRC approach is similar to the standard LRC protocol. Moving the diff computation and fetching to the communication co-processor is easy. Applications could benefit from overlapping these operations with computation. At the same time, OLRC has the same drawbacks as LRC. The overhead of diff application as well as memory consumption can greatly affect application performance.

Overlapped HLRC   The Overlapped HLRC (OHLRC) uses the communication co-processor to perform three operations:

- Compute diffs after each interval and send them to their home node.

- Apply diffs on the local copy (at the home node).

- Service the remote requests for pages at home.

After completing a diff of a given page, the co-processor sends it to the co-processor of the home of that page. There the diff is applied and the timestamps of the corresponding page are updated. When servicing a page fetch remote request, the co-processor compares the timestamps in the request with the local timestamps of that page to ensure that the required updates are in place. If an element in the local timestamp vector is smaller than the corresponding element in the timestamp vector of the fetch request, then some diffs are still in progress and the page request is put into the pending request list attached to that page. Once all the necessary diffs have been applied, the co-processor sends the page to the faulting node.

Figure 10.2(b) shows an example of the OHLRC protocol. To service remote acquire requests on node 0, the current interval is ended, the co-processor starts to compute a diff, and a reply is sent back immediately to node 1, with the corresponding write notices. Node 1 invalidates the page holding `x` and then continues its computation. In the meantime, the co-processor of node 0 computes diffs and sends them to the appropriate home (node 2). The co-processor of node 2 receives the diffs and applies them to its local page. The `Read(x)` operation on node 1 causes a page fault that triggers a request sent to the home node (node 2). The co-processor of node 2 services the page request after checking the timestamps.

OLRC and OHLRC are both overlapped protocols, but their degrees of overlapping are different. Both protocols overlap diff computation and fetching with computation, but OHLRC also overlaps diff applications by performing them eagerly at the home. It appears that this may cause OHLRC to transfer more data than OLRC since OHLRC always fetches full pages from home nodes and OLRC fetches diffs instead. But this is not always true, as shown in our experiments on communication traffic. Our experiments show that OHLRC is the best among the four protocols.

10.2   Prototype Implementations

To evaluate the performance of the protocols we have implemented four SVM prototypes on a 64-node Intel Paragon multicomputer: the standard LRC protocol, the Home-based LRC (HLRC), the Overlapped LRC (OLRC) protocol and the Overlapped Home-based LRC (OHLRC) protocol. Standard LRC is our baseline implementation. It runs on the compute processor without any overlapping. Both OLRC and OHLRC use the communication processor to overlap some protocol tasks with computation.

10.2.1   The Paragon System

The Intel Paragon multicomputer used in our implementation consists of 64 nodes for computation. Each node has one compute processor and a communication co-processor, sharing 64 MB of local memory. Both processors are 50 MHz i860 microprocessors with 16 KB of data cache and 16 KB of instruction cache [126]. The data caches are coherent between the two processors. The memory bus provides a peak of 400 MB/s. The nodes are interconnected with a wormhole routed 2-D mesh network whose peak is 200 MB/s per link [272].

The operating system is a micro-kernel based version of OSF/1 with multicomputer extensions for a parallel programming model and the NX/2 message passing primitives. The co-processor runs exclusively in kernel mode, and it is dedicated to communication. The one-way message-passing latency of a 4-byte NX/2 message on the Paragon is about 50 μsec [211]. The transfer for large messages depends on data alignment. When data are aligned properly, the peak achievable at the user level is 175 MB/s. Without proper alignment, the peak is about 45 MB/s.

The operating system uses an 8 KB page size for its virtual memory, though the hardware virtual memory page size is 4 KB. All implementations use the vm_protect Mach system call to set access protection for shared pages. Access faults can be handled by either the external memory manager or the exception handling mechanism. We used the Mach exception handling mechanism for efficiency reasons.

In our prototypes for the overlapped protocols we extended the functionality of the communication co-processor with SVM protocol related operations. The standard LRC protocol is implemented exclusively at user-level using the NX/2 message library. For the overlapped protocols we modified the co-processor kernel to perform diff-related operations.

10.2.2   Shared Memory API

All four prototypes support the programming interface used with the Splash-2 [237] benchmark suite. This is different from the APIs supported by other software shared virtual memory systems, such as TreadMarks. The main rationale for our decision to implement the Splash-2 API is to allow programs written for a release-consistent, shared-memory multiprocessor to run on our systems without any modification.

In our implementations, all virtual address space can be shared, and global shared memory can be dynamically allocated using G_MALLOC. A typical program on P processors starts one process first that allocates and initializes global data and then spawns the other P-1 processes. All P processes perform the computation in parallel and join at the end. The only synchronization primitives used in the programs are LOCK, UNLOCK and BARRIER.

10.2.3   Co-processor Interface

The communication co-processor communicates with the compute processor via cache-coherent, shared memory. For each message passing client, which can be a kernel or user process, there is a page of memory organized as a ring buffer of request slots, called a *post page*. The client process running on the compute processor uses the post page to post requests to the co-processor and receive results back.

The code on the co-processor is a dispatch loop that runs in kernel mode with interrupts disabled. This loop inspects the next active slot in each post page. When it detects a request in one of the post pages, it uses the request number as an index in the post switch table and calls the appropriate send procedure to service the request. After the request is serviced, the co-processor puts the result or error message in some location after the message.

Within the dispatch loop, the co-processor also polls the processor status registers for incoming messages. When a packet arrives, the dispatch loop reads the packet type to index into the packet switch table, and calls the appropriate receive packet procedure.

10.2.4   Protocol Extensions

To use the co-processor to overlap some SVM protocol operations, we extended the communication co-processor code by adding one more request type and one more packet type to its interface to support the following operations:

Compute Diff. This operation is used in both overlapped protocols. The compute processor specifies the page, page size, and the address of the twin that was previously created with the clean contents of the page. After the co-processor validates the passed parameters, it flips the "done" flag to allow the computation processor to continue, and then starts computing diffs. When the diff computation is complete, the co-processor sends the diff together with the local timestamp to the home node (in the OHLRC case) or just saves the address of the diff in the corresponding write notice record (in the OLRC case).

Apply Diff. This operation is used in the OLRC protocol to receive new diffs. The receiving co-processor transfers the modifications to its local copy, updates the home's flush timestamp for that particular page and processor accordingly, and services pending page requests if they are satisfied by the current version of the page.

Fetch Diffs. This operation is used in the OLRC protocol to collect necessary diffs. The faulting processor submits fetch-diff requests to other nodes for one or multiple diffs. The co-processor of the destination node services the requests when the diff computation is complete.

Fetch Page. The fetch-page operation is used in both overlapped protocols. On a memory access miss, the faulting processor in the OHLRC protocol sends a page request to the co-processor of the home node with the vector of lock timestamps for that page, whereas in the OLRC protocol the page request is sent to a member in the approximate copyset for that page. The co-processor of the remote node either services this request if the page is ready, or simply puts it in a page request list. The page will be sent out when all the required diffs have arrived and have been applied.

10.2.5   Synchronization and Garbage Collection

Synchronization handling and related coherence checking for all four prototypes is implemented at user level using NX/2 messages. Each lock has a manager, which is assigned in a round-robin fashion among the processors. The manager keeps track of which processor has most recently requested the lock. All lock acquire requests are sent to the manager unless the node itself holds the lock. The manager forwards the lock request to the processor that last requested the lock. The request message contains the current maximal vector timestamp of the acquiring processor. When the lock arrives, it contains the releaser's knowledge of all time intervals for the requester to update its timestamp vectors.

Barriers are also implemented using a centralized manager algorithm. When a barrier is entered, each node sends the barrier manager the write notices for all intervals that the manager has not seen. The barrier manager collects the intervals from all other nodes, computes the maximal timestamp, and selectively forwards the missing write notices to each node.

For LRC and OLRC, barrier synchronizations trigger garbage collection of protocol data structures when the free memory is below a certain threshold, similar to the approach used in TreadMarks [142]. Garbage collection is quite complex because it needs to collect all "live" diffs, which are distributed on various nodes. All last writers for each individual shared page need to validate the page by requesting all the missing diffs from other nodes. The non-last writers can simply invalidate the page, and modify the copyset for that page. After this phase, the collection algorithm can clean up the heaps and data structures.

For the HLRC and OHLRC protocols, there is no need to perform garbage collection since no diffs or write notices are ever stored beyond a release or barrier.

10.3   Performance

This section presents performance results for our implementations on five benchmark programs. We begin with a description of the benchmark applications and problem sizes used. We then evaluate the overall performance of the four protocols on these benchmarks, using speedup on 8, 32, and 64 processors as the metric. We conclude by examining the experimental results in more detail, giving execution time breakdowns, communication traffic, and memory requirements.

10.3.1   Applications

To evaluate the performance of our implementations, we used two kernels (LU and SOR) and three applications (Water-Nsquared, Water-Spatial and Raytrace), four of which (LU, Water-Nsquared, Water-Spatial and Raytrace) are from the Splash-2 suite. Although the names of two of the applications (Water-Nsquared and Water-Spatial) indicate a similar problem, the algorithms and their sharing patterns are different.

Application	Problem	Execution Time (seconds)
LU	2048 × 2048	1,028
SOR	1024 × 4096	1,360
Water-Nsquared	4096 molecules	1,130
Water-Spatial	4096 molecules	1,080
Raytrace	Balls4.env(256x256)	956

Table 10.1
Benchmark applications, problem sizes, and sequential execution times.

LU performs blocked LU factorization of a dense matrix. The matrix is decomposed in contiguous blocks that are distributed to processors in contiguous chunks. Therefore this kernel exhibits coarse-grain sharing and low synchronization to computation frequency, but the computation is inherently unbalanced. The results presented in this section are for a 2048 × 2048 matrix with 32 × 32 blocks.

SOR is a kernel from the suite of programs used in TreadMarks. It corresponds to the red-black successive over-relaxation (SOR) method for solving partial differential equations. The black and red arrays are partitioned into roughly equal size bands of rows, which are distributed among the processors. Communication occurs across the boundary rows between bands and is synchronized with barriers. We ran the kernel with a 1024 × 4096 matrix for 51 iterations starting, as in Treadmarks, with all elements initialized randomly. We chose to run this kernel, in particular, to allow some extreme case comparison between the protocols.

Water-Nsquared simulates a system of water molecules in liquid state, using an $O(n^2)$ brute force method with a cutoff radius. The water molecules are allocated contiguously in an array of n molecules, and partitioned among processors into contiguous pieces of n/p molecules each. The interesting communication occurs at the end of each step when each processor updates its own n/p molecules and the following $(n/2 - n/p)$ molecules of other processors in the array, using per-partition locks to protect these updates.

Water-Spatial solves the same problem as Water-Nsquared, but uses a spatial directory rather than a brute-force method, making it more suitable for large problems. The 3-d physical space is broken up into cells, and each processor is assigned a contiguous cubical partition of cells together with the linked lists of molecules currently within those cells. A processor reads data from those processors that own cells on the boundary of its partition. Molecules migrate slowly between cells, so the irregularity of the application, although present, has little impact on performance.

Application	8 Nodes			
	LRC	**OLRC**	**HLRC**	**OHLRC**
LU	4.4	4.7	5.2	6.0
SOR	4.3	4.8	6.4	6.5
Water-Nsquared	6.7	7.0	7.0	7.1
Water-Spatial	7.4	7.5	7.4	7.7
Raytrace	6.9	7.1	7.6	7.7

Application	32 Nodes			
	LRC	**OLRC**	**HLRC**	**OHLRC**
LU	11.5	13.5	13.9	16.6
SOR	13.0	13.6	22.7	23.6
Water-Nsquared	11.7	14.0	18.9	21.0
Water-Spatial	14.1	17.1	20	23.5
Raytrace	10.6	10.6	26.8	28.0

Application	64 Nodes			
	LRC	**OLRC**	**HLRC**	**OHLRC**
LU	15.5	16.8	27.0	29.1
SOR	12.3	12.6	35.7	36.9
Water-Nsquared			19.2	20.6
Water-Spatial	10.6	11.5	22.6	26.4
Raytrace	7.4	7.4	40.6	43.0

Table 10.2
Speedups on the Intel Paragon with 8, 32, and 64 nodes.

Raytrace renders complex scenes in computer graphics using an optimized ray tracing method. The accesses to the scene data, into which rays are shot in this program, are read-only and relatively uninteresting other than the fact that they cause fragmentation. The interesting communication occurs in task stealing using distributed task queues, and in updating pixels in the image plane as part of a task. Both types of access patterns are fine-grained and cause considerable false sharing and fragmentation at the page level. The original Splash-2 application was modified to reorganize the task queues and remove unnecessary synchronization to alleviate the problems observed in [125].

Table 10.1 shows the problem sizes and their sequential execution times. For all applications we chose relatively large problem sizes, each requiring approximately 20 minutes of sequential execution. Problem sizes were determined by the capabilities of our four prototypes: although the home-based protocols can run larger problems, we chose the largest problems runnable under all protocols and all machine sizes for the sake of comparison.

10.3.2   Overall Performance: Speedups

Table 10.2 summarizes the speedups for the LRC, HLRC, OLRC and OHLRC implementations on 8, 32 and 64 nodes. There are two key observations to be made here. First, the home-based LRC protocols(HLRC and OHLRC) clearly outperform their "homeless" counterparts (LRC and OLRC) with one exception (Water-Spatial on 8 node, non-overlapped protocols), in which case the speedups are comparable. These results are consistent with those obtained through simulation in the comparison between LRC and AURC [125]. Second, the performance gap between home and homeless protocols increases dramatically for 32 and 64 processors configurations. This result, which is consistent across all applications, reveals a significant difference in scalability between the two classes of protocols. For instance, the difference in speedups between HLRC and LRC for 64 processors reaches a factor of 1.7 for LU, a factor of 2 for Water Spatial, a factor of 3 for SOR and a factor of almost 6 for Raytrace. For two of these applications (Water Spatial and Raytrace) the speedups under the LRC protocol actually drop when going from 32 to 64 processors. Obviously such insights would have been impossible to guess from the 8-processor runs, where the performance of the home-based and homeless protocols are very close.

The overlapped protocols provide modest improvements over the non-overlapped ones. The range of speedup improvements varies among applications, from as little as 2-3% to as much as 30%.

Summarizing, given the limitations of the Paragon architecture (e.g., large message latency and high interrupt cost, as explained next), all five real Splash-2 applications perform surprisingly well under the home-based protocols, with more than 50% parallel efficiency on 32 nodes, and between 30% and 66% on 64 nodes.

We now turn to a more detailed examination of these results, starting with the determination of the basic operation costs on the Paragon that provide the context in which the results can be better understood.

10.3.3   Cost of Basic Operations

Table 10.3 shows the costs of important basic operations on the Intel Paragon.

Using the basic operation costs we can determine the minimum cost (assuming no contention) for a page miss and a lock acquire. In a non-overlapped protocol, like HLRC, a page miss takes at least 290+50+690+92+50=1,172 microseconds for a full page transfer. In an overlapped protocol, such as OHLRC, the same

Operation	Time microseconds
Message Latency	50
Page Transfer	92
Receive Interrupt	690
Twin Copy	120
Diff Creation	380-560
Diff Application	0-430
Page Fault	290
Page Invalidation	200
Page Protection	50

Table 10.3
Timings for basic operations on the Intel Paragon.

page miss takes only 290+50+92+50=482 microseconds. Similarly, a page miss in LRC takes at least 290+50+690+50+50=1,130 microseconds without overlapping and 440 microseconds with overlapping for one single-word diff transfer. A remote acquire request, which is intermediated by the home of the lock, costs at least 50+690+50+690+50=1,550 microseconds. This could be reduced to only 150 microseconds if this service were moved to the co-processor.

10.3.4   Home Effect

Table 10.4 shows the frequency of page faults and diff related operations for HLRC and LRC on 8 and 64-nodes. (We do not give results for the overlapped protocols because they are similar to the non-overlapped ones.) There are several "home effects" revealed by this table. First, since the home's copy of the page is eagerly updated, page faults do not occur and diffs are not created at the home. This can lead to substantial protocol savings, particularly if there is a one writer- multiple readers sharing pattern and the writer is chosen as the home. This explains why no diffs are created for LU and SOR.

The other three applications also have reduced page faults and diffs due to the home effect. However, sometimes HLRC creates slightly more diffs than LRC, as shown in the Raytrace application, because of laziness.

Finally, the home-based protocols have fewer diff-applications than the homeless ones because home-based protocols apply diffs eagerly but only once, whereas the homeless protocols may apply diffs multiple times.

Code	Nodes	Read Misses		Diffs Created		Diffs Applied		Lock	Barr.
		LRC	HLRC	LRC	HLRC	LRC	HLRC		
LU	8	1,050	1,050	5,704	0	0	0	0	64
	64	452	452	1,396	0	0	0	0	128
SOR	8	343	343	25,088	0	171	0	0	98
	64	385	385	3136	0	342	0	0	98
Water	8	938	811	1,266	810	4,809	810	652	12
Nsquared	32	893	859	956	815	8,742	815	556	12
Water	8	1,361	1,356	466	10	74	10	11	10
Spatial	64	918	878	122	66	3,948	66	11	10
Raytrace	8	339	209	551	733	3,591	733	340	1
	64	108	87	83	103	2,368	103	94	1

Table 10.4
Average number of operations on each node.

10.3.5 Time Breakdowns

To better understand where time goes, we instrumented our systems to collect the average execution time breakdowns per node. Figure 10.3 shows the breakdowns, including the computation time, data transfer time, garbage collection time, synchronization time including locks and barriers, and protocol overhead. Protocol overhead includes diff and twin creation, diff application, write-notice handling, and remote request service.

We use Water-Nsquared (Figure 10.3(c)) as an example to introduce the time breakdown analysis. In both the 8- and 32-node cases, the speedups of HLRC are better than LRC, with the advantage more significant in the 32-node case. The time breakdowns show that the differences are due to the reduction of both lock and barrier synchronization time, of data transfer time, and of protocol overhead.

Synchronization cost dominates the total overhead. To identify the sources of the execution imbalance among processors, we instrumented all applications to collect per processor execution time breakdowns between two consecutive barriers. Figure 10.4 shows per-processor breakdowns of the execution time for Water-Nsquared between barriers 9 and 10 for both LRC and HLRC protocols on 8 and 64 processors. For 8 processors the imbalance is small and mostly due to computation imbalance. For 64 processors the computation time is evenly distributed among processors; in this case almost all the imbalance is due to lock contention and communication imbalance.

Lock waiting time is significant because page misses occur in critical sections.

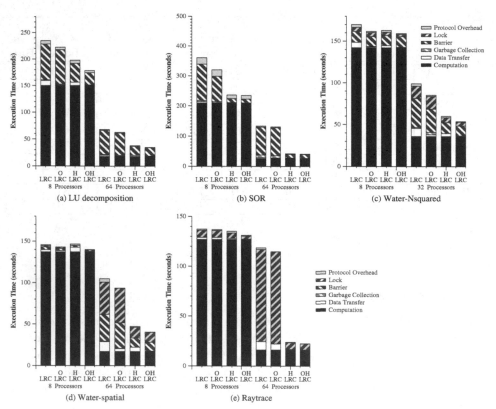

Figure 10.3
Time breakdowns of LU, SOR, Water-Nsquared,Water-Spatial and Raytrace.

Therefore variations in the data transfer time are reflected in the lock waiting time as well. For instance, in Water-Nsquared, the lock waiting time is larger under LRC than under HLRC because the data transfer time is larger as well. Lock waiting time can cause execution imbalance due to serialization of lock acquisitions when lock contention occurs. For Water-Nsquared, which is a regular application, lock contention occurs when an imbalance in data transfer time occurs. This explains why there is an imbalance in the lock waiting time for LRC but not for HLRC. For irregular applications, like Water Spatial, imbalance in the lock waiting time occurs even when data transfer time is balanced.

For regular applications data transfer time imbalance occurs as a result of serialization when multiple data requests arrive at the same processor simultaneously. We call this situation a "hot spot". Homeless protocols are likely to generate hot

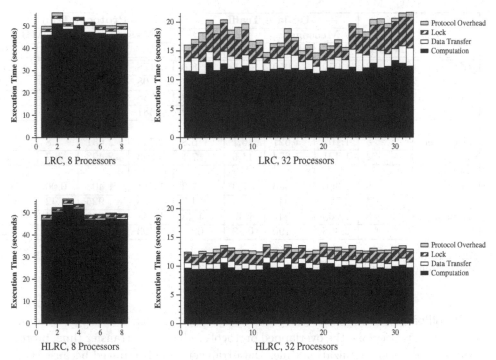

Figure 10.4
Time breakdowns of Water-Nsquared between barriers 9 and 10.

spots more frequently than home-based protocols because in the homeless protocols updates usually are collected from the last writer, whereas in the home-based protocols updates are distributed to homes. This situation occurs for instance in Water-Nsquared, which exhibits a multiple-writer multiple-reader sharing pattern with coarse-grained read and writes [125].

The second dominating overhead is data transfer time. The data transfer times of HLRC are smaller than those of LRC for three reasons. First, for regular applications with coarse-grain sharing and migratory data patterns [125], the data traffic to service page misses is higher for the homeless protocol than for the home-based protocol. This is counter-intuitive, since LRC transfers diffs whereas HLRC always transfers full pages. However, migratory data patterns can produce aggregate diff sizes in LRC significantly larger than a page. Second, LRC has to apply the diffs on the faulting page following the happen-before partial order, whereas HLRC does not require any additional processing after fetching. Third, HLRC has fewer page misses because of the home effect.

Code	Nodes	Update Traffic				Protocol Traffic			
		Messages		MB		Messages		MB	
		LRC	HLRC	LRC	HLRC	LRC	HLRC	LRC	HLRC
LU	8	1,050	1,050	8.6	8.6	1,178	1,178	0.28	0.16
	64	452	452	3.7	3.7	708	708	1.7	0.6
SOR	8	343	343	4.2	2.8	538	538	0.95	0.76
	64	385	385	6.0	3.2	581	581	2.6	0.9
Water Nsquared	8	1,102	1,621	16.1	6.8	2,784	2,531	1.8	0.8
	32	1,421	1,674	11.5	7.1	3,093	2,493	6.7	1.2
Water Spatial	8	1,360	1,366	7.3	7.3	1,411	1,403	0.06	0.03
	64	2,581	944	16.4	4.7	2,628	925	0.42	0.08
Raytrace	8	1,069	942	1.46	1.43	1,446	586	0.44	0.22
	64	2,368	190	0.10	0.61	403	313	0.52	0.20

Table 10.5
Average communication traffic on each node.

By offloading some of the protocol overhead from the critical path to the communication processors, the overlapped protocols reduce data transfer time, protocol overhead, and synchronization time. Data transfer time is reduced because the remote fetch requests are handled on the communication processor. Synchronization cost is reduced slightly because overlapping does not change the execution imbalance among the processors. Protocol time is always reduced with overlapping, but its relative contribution to the total execution time is small.

The performance analysis for Water-Nsquared holds for the other applications as well. The 8-processor run of Water-Spatial reveals a case in which HLRC performs slightly worse than LRC. Although Water-Spatial induces a multiple-writer sharing pattern at page level [125], for a small number of steps (two in our case) most pages are single-writer, so LRC and HLRC are similar in terms of data traffic. However, the message-size limitation of the Paragon, forces HLRC to send more physical messages, thus increasing the data transfer time compared to LRC.

10.3.6 Communication Traffic

Table 10.5 shows the communication traffic of the LRC and HLRC prototypes for all applications. The traffic information gives us several insights that substantiate our time breakdown analysis. Since the overlapped protocols have approximatively the same communication traffic as the non-overlapped ones, we compare only HLRC

Code, Memory, and Nodes		Protocol Data Structure Memory (MB)								
		Twins		Diffs		Page Table		Write Notes		Total	
		LRC	HLRC	LRC	HLRC	LRC	HLRC	LRC	HLRC	LRC	HLRC
LU	8	4.2	0	4.4	0	1.3	2.6	0.1	0.1	10.0	2.8
(32 MB)	64	2.5	0	2.7	0	1.3	2.6	1.3	0.2	7.8	2.8
SOR	8	4.2	0	8.4	0	1.3	2.6	0.13	0.01	14.3	2.6
(33 MB)	64	2.3	0	5.2	0	1.3	2.6	0.9	0.01	9.8	2.6
Water Nsquared (2.5 MB)	8	7.3	0.3	10.8	0	0.1	0.2	1.8	0.04	20.0	0.54
	32	3.9	0.1	4.2	0	0.1	0.2	5.4	0.15	13.6	0.45
Water Spatial (4.8 MB)	8	2.8	0.5	6.4	0	0.2	0.4	0.12	0.00	9.5	0.9
	64	0.4	0.1	12.0	0	0.2	0.4	0.4	0.01	13.0	0.5
Raytrace	8	0.4	0.4	0.6	0	0.3	0.6	0.8	0.1	2.1	1.1
(10.2 MB)	64	0.7	0.1	13	0	0.3	0.7	1.3	0.1	15.2	0.9

Table 10.6
Average memory requirements on each node.

with LRC.

For each created diff, HLRC always sends one message to update the home. In addition one message is always enough in HLRC to satisfy any page miss. On the other hand, a homeless LRC protocol requires at least one message per page miss. It requires exactly one when there is only one writer per page or when the page contains migratory data (in which case all the diffs are found at the last writer). If there is only one writer per page, as in SOR, the two protocols send about the same number of messages unless LRC is penalized by the garbage collection process, as in LU, in which case it requires additional messages to fetch pages. In a regular migratory data application, like Water-Nsquared, HLRC ends up sending more messages than LRC because of the additional messages sent to update the homes eagerly. In the common case, which corresponds to multiple reader and writer pages, as in Raytrace, LRC sends more messages than HLRC because it requires more than one diff message to satisfy a page miss.

For applications with predominantly single-writer pages, such as LU and Water-Spatial, the amount of update-related traffic in HLRC and LRC is similar because LRC can avoid diff aggregation. In SOR, which also exposes single-writer pages, LRC data traffic is affected by garbage collection. For applications with multiple-writer pages, such as Water-Nsquared or Water-Spatial, on 64 processors the data traffic under HLRC is substantially less than under LRC.

For applications with fine-grain sharing, like Raytrace, the comparison moves towards what we expected to be the typical comparison pattern between HLRC and LRC: more messages in LRC and more traffic in HLRC. This leads to a latency vs tradeoff in the comparison of the two protocols with respect to data transfer time. For instance, a system like the Paragon (as well as ATM networks), which has relatively high message latency and high bandwidth is likely to benefit more from the home-based protocols.

Finally, for the protocol traffic, the home based LRC approach is consistently cheaper than the homeless LRC protocol. The homeless protocol sends more protocol related data than a home-based one, especially for large number of processors where write notices can become substantially larger due to full vector timestamp inclusion.

In conclusion, home-based protocols scale better than the homeless protocols in terms of protocol traffic.

10.3.7 Memory Requirements

Protocol memory requirement is an important criterion for scalability. It directly affects application performance in two ways: the limitation on the problem sizes and the frequency of garbage collection of protocol related data.

Table 10.6 reveals some interesting facts. If a garbage collection is triggered only at barriers (as we actually implemented in our prototypes), then the memory requirement of homeless protocols can be even larger than the application memory (by a factor of 8 in Water-Nsquared). On the other hand, the memory used by the home-based protocols is only a small percentage of the application memory (10 percent to 25 percent). As we increase the number of processors, the memory required for protocol data doesn't change much in HLRC, but in LRC it can increase dramatically (Water-Spatial and Raytrace). Although it is possible to reorganize the data structures to reduce the memory consumption, we do not expect that the overall picture would change dramatically.

Out of the various protocol data structures, the major memory consumers are the diffs and the write notices. In HLRC, diffs are discarded almost immediately after they are created or applied, while in LRC they have to be kept for an indefinite amount of time (until the garbage collection time in most cases). Write notices can consume a large amount of memory. For instance, the LRC protocol consumes about 5 MB of memory on each of the 32 processors to store write notices in the Water-Nsquared application. Since the write-notice data structure includes the full vector timestamps in the homeless protocols, the storage requirement increases proportionally with the number of processors.

In short, home-based protocols scale much better than the homeless ones with respect to memory requirements.

10.3.8   Discussion

An interesting question is whether home-based protocols are always better than homeless ones. The performance evaluation we have conducted on the Paragon provides limited answers towards a complete understanding of the tradeoffs between home-based and homeless LRC protocols. The Paragon architecture is characterized by message latency, page fault, and interrupt times that are relatively large compared with memory and network (Table 10.3). As a consequence, a roundtrip communication for either a page or lock transfer is at best on the order of a millisecond. Current network technologies [24, 102, 26], as well as aggressive software for fast interrupts, exceptions [269] and virtual memory mapped communication [79, 92] have brought such latencies down significantly to the neighborhood of a couple of microseconds. An interesting question is to what extent our results are specific to the Paragon architecture and how they would be affected by different architectural parameters. Fast interrupts and low latency messages make the roundtrips shorter and since LRC has usually more messages than HLRC it is likely that the homeless protocols will benefit more from these architectural improvements. Therefore, the performance gap between the home-based and the homeless protocols would probably be smaller on such architectures.

Our performance evaluation shows that home-based protocols perform much better than the homeless ones for three regular applications with coarse-grain sharing and for two irregular applications with small communication to computation ratios. The traffic ratio for the two classes of protocols will probably be different if fine-grain sharing dominates. To help answer this question we ran SOR with all elements 0, except at the edges. Under this initialization, the interior elements of the matrix do not change for the first many iterations. Consequently, these pages have no updates during those intervals, and so do not produce diffs. Even when diffs are produced later in the computation, there is only a single writer per page, a single diff is produced per interval, and the diff size increases gradually. Consequently, the conditions of this experiment favor LRC over HLRC, which must transfer full pages. Despite these factors, the experimental results show that HLRC is still 10% better than LRC. This experiment suggests that HLRC is likely to have robust performance behavior for a large number of applications.

10.3.9   Limitations

In addition to the Paragon communication parameters there are several specific limitations in our experiments. The virtual memory page size used in the OSF-1 operating system is 8 KB, although the hardware allows 4 KB page size. We have not been able to modify the virtual memory system to change the page size to conduct more experiments. Asynchronous receives are not interruptible. The Paragon NX/2 message layer cannot support message packets larger than the page size. This limitation can affect both HLRC and LRC. HLRC must always send two messages in reply to a page fetch request: one with the page and the other with the timestamps of the page. In LRC when the aggregate diff size exceeds the page size, the number of actual messages sent is larger than the number of logical messages.

Several possible optimizations are still unexplored. Synchronization operations have been implemented in a straightforward way using NX/2 messages and centralized algorithms. Overlapping using the communication processor was not employed for coherence and synchronization control. Finally, we have reported the results for only five applications and for a single problem size.

10.4   Related Work

Since shared virtual memory was first proposed ten years ago [173], a lot of work has been done on it. The Release Consistency (RC) model was proposed in order to improve hardware cache coherence [99]. The model was used to implement shared virtual memory and reduce false sharing by allowing multiple writers [42]. Lazy Release Consistency (LRC) [143, 69, 3] further relaxed the RC protocol to reduce protocol overhead. TreadMarks [142] was the first SVM implementation using the LRC protocol on a network of stock computers. That implementation has achieved respectable performance on small-scale machines.

The recently proposed Automatic Update Release Consistency protocol (AURC) [122] is an LRC protocol that takes advantage of the automatic update mechanism in virtual memory-mapped communication. The idea of using a home-based approach to build an all-software protocol similar to AURC was proposed in [124]. Our home-based LRC protocols are based on the AURC protocol, but the updates are detected in software using diffs, as in the standard LRC. A degree of overlapping similar to the one the automatic update mechanism provides is achieved in our Overlapped Home-based LRC (OHLRC) protocol, where the communication co-processor is used to perform, transfer, and apply the diffs.

In a recent work [144], Keleher has shown that a simple single-writer LRC protocol perform almost as well as a more complicated multiple-writer LRC. His protocol totally eliminates diff-ing at the expense of a higher requirement for full page transfers. Our home-based protocols support multiple writers using diffs but replace most of the diff traffic with full page traffic. The home-based protocols reduce to a single-writer protocol for applications that exhibit one-writer multiple-readers sharing patterns, like SOR or LU.

Other relaxed consistency models include Entry Consistency [22] and Scope Consistency [124]. Both models take advantage of the association of data with locks, either explicitly (Entry Consistency) or implicitly (Scope Consistency), to reduce the protocol overhead. Both Orca [10] and CRL [134] are designed to implement distributed shared memory by maintaining coherence at object level instead of page level. These methods require specialized APIs, unlike the prototype systems presented in this chapter. Our systems allow programs written for a release-consistent, shared-memory multiprocessor to run without modification.

Several multicomputers use a dedicated co-processor for communication on each node. Examples include the Intel Paragon [211] and the Meiko CS-2 [116]. The Typhoon [168] system uses a special hardware board to detect access faults at fine granularity and implements distributed shared memory on a network of Hyper-Sparc workstations. It uses one of the two CPUs in the dual-processor workstation as a protocol processor. In the Flash multiprocessor [163], each node contains a programmable processor called MAGIC that performs protocol operations and handles all communications within the node and among all nodes. Neither system uses LRC-based relaxed consistency models.

Bianchini et al. [23] proposed a dedicated protocol controller to offload some of the communication and coherence overheads from the computation processor. Using simulations they show that such a protocol processor can double the performance of TreadMarks on a 16-node configuration and that diff prefetching is not always beneficial. The protocol they evaluate is similar to our overlapped homeless LRC protocol (OLRC).

A recent study [140] investigated how to build an SVM system on a network of SMPs. They studied the tradeoffs of using a dedicated processor or the spare cycles of a compute processor to execute coherence protocol. The study is limited to simulations.

10.5   Conclusions

This chapter proposes two new home-based protocols based on Lazy Release Consistency (LRC): Home-based HLRC (HLRC) and Overlapped Home-based LRC (OHLRC). Our experiments with five applications on a 64-node Intel Paragon multicomputer show that the home-based protocols perform and scale substantially better than their homeless counterparts. To our knowledge this is the first performance study of a page-based software shared memory system on such a large configuration. We have also found that protocol overlapping using the communication processor provides only modest performance improvement.

The HLRC protocol outperforms the standard LRC protocol for several reasons:

- Synchronization cost is higher for the homeless protocols. This is because the waiting time depends to a large extent on the data transfer time, which is both larger and possibly imbalanced in the homeless protocols. For all applications, the synchronization cost is the main component limiting performance for large configurations.

- Data transfer time is also larger for the homeless LRC protocols. Data traffic is usually larger in LRC because the aggregate diff size fetched on a page miss in LRC can exceed the size of a page, the fixed transfer size in HLRC. Also, the number of messages is usually larger in LRC. Finally, hot spots are likely to occur more frequently for a homeless protocol.

- A home-based protocol is simpler than a homeless one. As a consequence, HLRC produces less protocol overhead, generates less protocol traffic, and requires substantially less memory than LRC. Diff garbage collection is not required in HLRC because diffs have a very short lifetime in a home-based protocol.

An interesting question is whether home-based protocols are always better than homeless ones. While our study provides only limited answers, it suggests that home-based protocols are likely to perform robustly for a large number of applications.

Acknowledgments

This work was sponsored in part by the Scalable I/O project under DARPA contract DABT63-94-C-0049 and by NSF under grants EIA-9806751, EIA-9975011, and ANI-9906704. We would like to thank Paul Messina for loaning us a small Paragon multicomputer so that we could efficiently develop and run our experiments. We also would like to thank Sharon Brunett and Heidi Lorenz-Wirzba at Caltech for helping us run our experiments on the Caltech Paragon machine.

A Appendix: Proposal for a Common Parallel File System Programming Interface

PETER F. CORBETT, JEAN-PIERRE PROST, CHRIS DEMETRIOU, GARTH GIBSON, ERIK RIEDEL, JIM ZELENKA, YUQUN CHEN, ED FELTEN, KAI LI, JOHN HARTMAN, LARRY PETERSON, BRIAN BERSHAD, ALEC WOLMAN AND RUTH AYDT

This proposal was developed by the Scalable I/O Initiative (SIO), a consortium of universities, national laboratories, and industries studying parallel and scalable I/O systems for large parallel computers. This proposal is not a commitment on the part of any member of SIO to support these interfaces. However, it is intended that within the SIO effort several implementations of parallel file systems compliant with this interface be produced on several different platforms. We do not expect these interfaces to be finalized until implementation and user experience are obtained. SIO will foster such implementation and application development experience. The ultimate goal of this effort to produce a common parallel file system interface is two-fold: to support research in the area of parallel I/O, and to eventually recommend additions of parallel I/O interfaces to the χ/Open and POSIX standards.

This document contains a basic API plus several extensions. In §A.3–§A.14 we describe the basic API, which all conforming implementations must implement. In turn, §A.15 and §A.16 contain extensions to the API that may optionally be provided by implementations. Perhaps unavoidably, this document is more about the description of interfaces than it is about their rationalizations. We apologize in advance for your many unanswered questions.

A.1 Overview

The intent of the interfaces presented here is to add to the standard χ/Open XPG 4.2 interfaces, which were earlier defined in IEEE Standard 1003.1 (POSIX). It is widely recognized by vendors of distributed memory parallel computers and work-station clusters, such as IBM and Intel, that extensions to the χ/Open XPG 4.2 and POSIX interfaces to support high performance file I/O for parallel applications are desirable. However, there is little agreement about what these extensions should be. This results in part from vendor extensions that exclusively emphasize the capabilities of a specific machine or application class. As a result, it is not currently possible for programmers to write application programs using extended file system interfaces that are portable from one parallel computer to another.

Clearly, there is a need for a new set of standard interfaces, preferably a set of extensions to the χ/Open XPG 4.2 interfaces, if we wish users and third party software vendors to use the extended features of parallel file systems. The SIO community has chosen to divide the file system interface into two levels: a *low-level* interface which hides machine-dependent details and contains only those features needed to provide good performance, and a *high-level* interface which provides features for programmer convenience and to support particular application classes.[1] This document describes only the low-level interface.

There are portions of this API which provide functionality that is redundant with the function provided in the χ/Open interfaces. This is to enable some SIO members to develop complete experimental file systems with just this API, without the added burden of implementing a complete χ/Open compliant file systems interface. In the cases of redundant interfaces, the SIO functions can simply be implemented as wrappers over the standard functions. However, these functions should be implemented in such a way as to ensure that all libraries written to this API can run properly.

Our two-level approach arises from the conflicting goals of some aspects of different extended interfaces. For example, in a discussion of the commonalities between IBM's PIOFS and Intel's PFS in February 1995, we identified little more than the basic UNIX functions in common. Largely this is because IBM had chosen to support the concept of dynamic partitioning and subfiles, while Intel supported a set of file modes to define the semantics of parallel access. Our two-level approach moves the implementation of the special character of these parallel file systems (Intel I/O modes or IBM subfiles) to high-level libraries and proposes a low-level interface capable of efficiently supporting both of these and other specialized parallel file system function sets. The approach follows CMU's December 1994 suggestion, in that the new interfaces are low level, but are powerful for implementing high-level parallel I/O libraries.

The usage scenario is that I/O libraries can be easily and efficiently built on top of the interfaces provided by this API. Each vendor is free to implement whatever libraries they wish on top of these interfaces. Likely libraries include MPI-IO, a PIOFS subfile library, and a library which supports Intel's I/O modes.[2] It is simpler to implement or share a library at this level than to implement the function in the vendor-specific file system itself. Also, third party vendors (or groups such as SIO) can produce libraries that could compile and run on another vendor's machine. In addition, these interfaces could be a compiler target.

---

[1] MPI-IO is an example of such a high-level interface.

[2] We do not intend to prescribe the software structure of an implementation of PIOFS or PFS built with this API. Our expectation is that implementations will be efficient enough to allow libraries built entirely on the interfaces in this API to obtain high performance. For example, an application coded for an SIO-based Intel I/O-mode library should run efficiently on an IBM SP2 offering these interfaces. Of course, when this application runs on a Paragon, it is not required to use the I/O-mode library in favor of the native PFS interfaces.

Code written to this low-level API is intended to be portable. By this we mean source compatibility. In particular, each implementation of this API is free to assign different bit lengths to most types and different bit values to all constants, except as noted. Because the size of fields is implementation dependent, the range of some variables may also vary. In some cases this may limit source compatibility, so we have tried to require comfortably large limits wherever possible.

A.1.1   Independent Messaging and Minimal Synchronization

One view of a parallel application is of a set of tasks, typically executing on different nodes, communicating among themselves, possibly via shared memory. There are a variety of abstractions, toolkits, and mechanisms for communicating from which a particular parallel application may choose. One principle of this low-level API is to avoid dependence on the application's chosen method for communication. This means that a low-level parallel file system client implementation may not be aware of application-level messages and certainly cannot expect to use the same methods for communicating with its peer client agents. Of course, each client agent of the low-level parallel file system must be able to communicate with the parallel file system servers (if any). The method of this communication is implementation specific and will most likely be unavailable to the application programmer.

Another guiding principle in the design of this API is to discourage unnecessary synchronization of the client applications or of the client agents of the parallel file system. To this end, this API is designed to admit efficient low-level parallel file system implementations which restrict internal communication to a single client and the parallel file system server(s) responsible for a particular file. That is, this API does not require that client agents of the parallel file system directly communicate. This means that a compliant parallel file system implementation need not provide coherent distributed shared memory, shared file pointer synchronization, or collective I/O barrier synchronization. As described below, distributed shared memory may be avoided with application-managed weakly consistent caches and collective I/O barrier synchronization can be made implicit by requiring the application to distribute an opaque collective I/O handle defined by the parallel file system.

A.1.2   No Shared File Pointers

One of the original points of disagreement in the development of the API was support for shared file pointers. Some parallel file systems exploit shared file pointers extensively while others avoid this implicit synchronization as much as possible. The position of this API is similar to the latter: that shared file pointers can require extensive synchronization of the client agents of the parallel file system; that they implicitly synchronize the application's tasks; and that they can easily lead to excessive synchronization, slowing the application. Further, we contend that if this level of application synchronization is valuable, it should be provided by the higher level parallel file system libraries which may have access to peer-to-peer messaging systems and can be customized to specific applications' needs. For these reasons this API does not support shared file pointers; in fact, it does not support file pointers at all, requiring the offsets for all I/O operations to be explicitly provided.

A.1.3   Scatter-Gather Transfers

Batching transfers is a powerful strategy for improving performance. A parallel file system implementation can be expected to try to batch accesses to the disk, transfers between machine nodes, and buffer manipulations. Traditional UNIX read-write interfaces transfer contiguous file regions and contiguous memory regions, dramatically reducing batching opportunities for applications that manipulate large, non-contiguous data regions. Correspondingly, a principle extension for high-performance file systems is the compact representation of transfers of non-contiguous regions, commonly known as scatter-gather. In the core of this API proposal, the expressive power of scatter-gather is limited to a list of strided (vector) regions. [3]

A.1.4   Asynchronous I/O

The API provides interfaces for asynchronous reads and writes. Outstanding accesses can be polled or waited upon (either singly or as a list of accesses).

A.1.5   I/O Controls

This API allows applications to get and set file status data (such as file sizes), get and set performance-related information (such as file caching and layout), and perform various operations (such as cache consistency) via a general I/O control mechanism. Vendors can define their own control operations, allowing the API to be extended easily.

Some controls, notably data layout and capacity preallocation controls, may be performed much more efficiently as a group and/or at the time a file is created or opened. For this reason, multiple controls may be specified in the same operation, and the extended open interface in this API allows a set of controls to be executed when a file is opened. Because of the large amount of work that might be done by

---

[3] Beyond this proposal, some SIO researchers have shown an interest in nested lists of strided regions.

a set of controls, the API allows failure of I/O controls to fail the overall open or control operation immediately, and allows implementations to declare that certain controls may not be issued as a part of the same operation.

A.1.6   Client Caching

Because parallel files will experience concurrent read-write sharing, maintaining client cache consistency could become quite expensive. An implementation of this API may provide no client caching (for example, in some parallel systems the latency for fetching a file block from a server's cache may be low enough to not warrant client file caches). It may also provide strong consistency using shared memory mechanisms. However, many parallel applications will synchronize concurrent sharing at a higher level and can explicitly determine when to propagate written data from their local caches and when to refresh stale data from their local caches. This API enables these applications to improve their client cache performance by requesting weak consistency on a particular open file and to issue the appropriate propagate and refresh controls. In the case of weak consistency, an implementation may divide the file address space into fixed sized consistency units (cache lines or blocks) which are entirely present in a client cache if at all. Concurrent write sharing of a weakly consistent file within one consistency unit is not guaranteed to have reasonable semantics.

Note that this API makes no requirement that a low-level parallel file system implementation control or even detect unintentional read-write sharing, that is, read-write sharing by tasks that are parts of multiple uncoordinated parallel applications. In situations like this, which are common to many file systems, the atomicity of file creation can be used by higher level tools to provide simple advisory locks by using the existence of a file to signify a held lock.

A.1.7   File Access Pattern Hints

Allowing an application to provide hints about file accesses can substantially improve performance, particularly when a large amount of data is read non-sequentially (but predictably), or when a large number of small files are read one at a time. There are at least two distinct approaches to giving hints: explicitly listing an ordered sequence of future accesses (such as "read block 5, then block 7), and describing an access pattern with a single identifier (such as "random access," "sequential access," or "will not access"). Because it is not clear how to interpret a set of hints that intermingle these approaches, this API provides separate hint classes for each, does not specify how to interpret combinations containing both, and allows vendors to add new classes of hints as needed. To allow applications to provide information to the file system as early as possible, hints can be applied to open file descriptors or to files that have not yet been opened. In either case, hints apply only to the task that issued them, and not other tasks.

A.1.8   Extensions to this API

In discussing earlier low-level API proposals, we found that there are some features that are almost universally agreed upon, and a few features that have significant constituencies but were not supported by all members of the group. We thus chose to define the low-level API as a *basic API* plus a set of optional *extensions*. An extension is a feature that:

- has significant research value;

- impacts performance, at least on some architectures; and

- is not trivial to implement correctly;

As a part of the basic API, implementations must provide mechanisms for allowing applications to determine which extensions are supported. Those mechanisms are detailed in Section A.14.

A.1.9   Collective I/O

As mentioned in Section A.1.3, batching is a powerful mechanism for improving performance. When multiple client nodes access one file at the same time, batching can again be useful, particularly when each client's access is a complex pattern but the sum of all client accesses is a large contiguous access (e.g. the whole file). Accesses of this type are known as "collective I/O," and this API includes an extension which provides collective I/O facilities.

Current collective I/O mechanisms commonly exploit the implementation system's task identifiers or task groups to name the members of a collective I/O. In this API we avoid dependence on the systems' task naming mechanisms by dynamically defining an opaque identifier for a collective I/O that is distributed via the application's communication system and presented to the parallel file system by each participant (client involved in the collective I/O). With this mechanism we enable at least three types of batching. First, the parallel file system implementation may choose to wait for all participants to join the collective I/O before doing any of the work. Second, the application can provide a hint describing the total work to be done by the collective I/O at the time the collective I/O is defined. Third, a collective I/O may be defined to have multiple iterations, avoiding multiple defining operations and enabling earlier collective hints.

A.1.10   Checkpoints and File Versioning

Many parallel applications want the ability to create checkpoints of their files. Others want the ability to efficiently create a series of versions of a file over time. Rather than directly supporting checkpoints or file versions, this API includes an extension which offers a generic "fast copy" operation. A fast copy might be implemented as duplication of a file's metadata, with shared pointers to all data pages, each of which is marked copy-on-write. The tracking of copies is left up to the applications (or higher level parallel file system libraries).

A.1.11   File Names and Access Protection

When these interfaces are merged with POSIX it is expected that POSIX conventions will be adopted for directories and access control. However, during SIO research, compliant implementations need not deal with these (important) issues.

This API does not define directories or directory operations. Files may be named in a flat name space, though implementations may choose to offer additional name space management. A directory structure is not viewed as essential to parallel file system performance and can be provided by vendor-defined extensions as needed.

Similarly, access control checking, permission specifications, and user and group identifiers are not specified by this API. Implementations which provide access control management are expected to do so via vendor-defined extensions.

A.1.12   File Labels

An important issue for higher level library systems and application systems is interoperability. To support interoperability without inserting header data into the file's actual data, the low-level API was offers a small amount of application controlled data called a *label* for each file. A file's label is stored in its metadata.

A.2   Document Conventions

This document describes both the "basic" (or "core") API and extensions to the basic API. The basic API is described in §A.3 through §A.14, and the extensions are described in §A.15 and §A.16. Some sections of this document refer to "this document," which is meant to indicate the entirety of the basic API and the extensions described herein.

Implementations wishing to conform to this API must provide all of the types, definitions, and functions specified in the basic API, including those necessary to determine whether or not extensions are present.

A.2.1   Typesetting Conventions

Type definitions, functions definitions, and constants (including control operation identifiers) are typeset in the **bold** font.

Function names are typeset in the **bold** font and are followed by parentheses, e.g. **sio_open()**.

Variables, structure members, and function arguments are typeset in the *italic* font.

A.2.2   Definition of Terms

Throughout this document (except where explicitly noted) the phrase "file system" is used to indicate a file system which provides this API, and "implementation" is used to refer to the implementation of such a file system. Except where noted, the terms "application" and "higher-level library" are used interchangeably, and are meant to indicate the programs or libraries which are using this API to access parallel files.

Throughout this document, several words or phrases are used to indicate how given functionality must be used or implemented. For clarity, they are defined here:

"will," "shall," or "must"

> When describing functionality provided by file system implementations, these terms indicate that conforming implementations have to implement the functionality as described.

> When describing behavior of applications, these terms indicate the behavior of properly-written applications (i.e. applications behaving in other ways are considered buggy).

"should"

> When describing functionality provided by file system implementations, this term suggests that an implementation provide the functionality in the manner described, but that doing so is not necessary for conformance.

> When describing behavior of applications, this term indicates that the described behavior is the preferred behavior, but that other behavior may be correct.

"may"

> When describing functionality provided by file system implementations, this term indicates that conforming implementations can implement functionality in the manner described, but doing so may not be suggested.

When describing behavior of applications, this term indicates that the described behavior is allowed, but not necessarily encouraged.

"undefined"

Undefined behavior is not specified by this standard, and is usually a result of a programming error or similar problem. Applications must avoid invoking undefined behavior. File system implementations may produce completely arbitrary results when undefined behavior is invoked, including producing random data, on disk or in memory buffers provided, or generating an exception.

"unspecified"

Unspecified behavior is not specified by this standard, but is usually the result of a correct programming practice. Behavior is left unspecified to give file system implementations freedom to implement functionality in different ways. Unspecified behavior must not have harmful permanent effects on the application or its data, and should be documented in individual implementations' documentation. Portable applications must not rely on unspecified behavior causing the same results on multiple file system implementations.

A.2.3   How to Read this Document

It is recommended that you read sections 6,8,9,10,11,12, and 13 before sections 3,4, and 5. The reason for this is that sections 3,4, and 5 provide definitions which refer to functions explained in later sections.

A.3   The sio_fs.h Include File

File system implementations must provide a C include file named **sio_fs.h** which contains the data type definitions, constants, and function declarations and/or prototypes for all functions defined in this document. Implementations which provide extensions not defined in this document may require additional files be included to use those extensions. Implementations which do so must still define the extension support constants and extension identifiers (see Section A.14.1) for the extensions in **sio_fs.h**.

Applications or higher-level libraries must include **sio_fs.h** in their source files before referencing any of the types, constants, or functions described in this API.

A.4   Data Types

This section defines the data types which are referenced in the basic API, and gives brief explanations of the rationale behind them. Types used exclusively by extensions are not defined here–they are defined with the extensions.

All of the types defined in this section must be provided by conforming implementations. Vendors may provide additional types with names of the form **sio_vend_***vendordefinedname***_t**, where *vendordefinedname* can be a name of the vendor's choosing. All other type names beginning with **sio_** and ending with **_t** are reserved for future use by this API.

Except where otherwise noted, the sizes of all non-structure data types are fixed on a per-implementation basis and those data types must be fully copyable (i.e. they must not contain any pointers to other objects).

A.4.1   File Descriptor

All file descriptors are described as being of type **int**, primarily for compatibility with other systems (including UNIX) which use **int**s as file descriptors. A task may have up to **SIO_MAX_OPEN** parallel files open at any given time.

A.4.2   File Name

All file names are character strings terminated by a byte with the value zero, and are described being of type **const char ***. (They must never be modified by the system, and thus are **const**.) File names must not be longer than **SIO_MAX_NAME_LEN** characters, including the terminating zero byte.

A.4.3   Memory Address

Memory addresses are described as being of type **void ***. Each task must only access its own or a shared address space. Attempting to access memory for which the task does not have access permission produces undefined results.

A.4.4   sio_async_flags_t

This is an unsigned integral type used as a set of bits. Currently it can contain one of **SIO_ASYNC_BLOCKING** or **SIO_ASYNC_NONBLOCKING**. These flags indicate whether or not **sio_async_status_any()** will block waiting for an asynchronous I/O to complete. The use of these flags is described in Section A.10.2.

A.4.5   sio_async_handle_t

This is an opaque type used to identify asynchronous I/Os.

A.4.6   sio_async_status_t

```
typedef struct {
    sio_transfer_len_t count;
```

```
        sio_return_t status;
    } sio_async_status_t;
```

This structure is used to return the status of an asynchronous I/O. For a successful operation, *count* is set to the number of bytes transferred, and *status* is set to **SIO_SUCCESS**. For an unsuccessful operation, *status* is set to a value which indicates the nature of the error, and count is set to the number of bytes guaranteed to have been transferred correctly (see Section A.10.2).

A.4.7   sio_caching_mode_t

This is an unsigned integral type used by the client cache control interfaces, and is defined in Section A.12.

A.4.8   sio_control_t

```
    typedef struct {
        sio_control_flags_t flags;
        sio_control_op_t op_code;
        void *op_data;
        sio_return_t result;
    } sio_control_t;
```

This type is used to store the information associated with a control operation (see Section A.13). Control operations are specified by providing the appropriate operation code in *op_code*, an indication in *flags* of what to do if the control cannot be performed, and a pointer to a data buffer (if necessary) in *op_data*.

The *result* field is set by the function performing the control operation to indicate success or failure.

A.4.9   sio_control_flags_t

This is an unsigned integral type used as a set of bits. Currently it can contain one of **SIO_CONTROL_MANDATORY** or **SIO_CONTROL_OPTIONAL**. These flags indicate whether failure of this control operation will cause the entire set of control operations to fail, with semantics as described in Section A.8.1.

A.4.10   sio_control_op_t

This is an unsigned integral type used to indicate a control operation code. Control operations codes which are part of the basic API are defined in Section A.13.

A.4.11   sio_count_t

This is an unsigned integral type with the range $[0 \ldots \textbf{SIO\_MAX\_COUNT}]$. It is used to represent a quantity of objects.

A.4.12   sio_extension_id_t

This is an unsigned integral type used to contain extension identifiers. See Section A.14.1 for more details about its use.

A.4.13   sio_file_io_list_t

```
typedef struct {
    sio_offset_t offset;
    sio_size_t size;
    sio_size_t stride;
    sio_count_t element_cnt;
} sio_file_io_list_t;
```

This structure is used to describe a collection of regions within a file that is involved in a parallel file system operation. Its purpose is to encapsulate the description of many simple transfers into one larger and more complex transfer to enable the file system to be more efficient in the execution of the total transfer. Each **sio_file_io_list_t** structure describes a sequence of equally-sized and evenly-spaced contiguous byte regions within a file; this is sometimes called a "strided" access pattern. Common matrix decompositions can be described with such data structures.

The structure describes a set of *element_cnt* contiguous regions, each of size *size*, with the first region beginning at offset *offset* from the beginning of the file, and the beginning of each subsequent region starting *stride* bytes after the start of its predecessor. These contiguous byte regions may overlap; see Section A.9 for details.

A.4.14   sio_hint_t

```
typedef struct {
    sio_hint_flags_t flag;
    sio_file_io_list_t *io_list;
    sio_count_t list_len;
    void *arg;
    sio_size_t arg_len;
} sio_hint_t;
```

This structure is used to store hint information (see Section A.11). The *flag* field describes the access patterns being hinted, and the *io_list* and *list_len* fields describe the regions of the file to which the hint applies. The *arg* and *arg_len* fields contain a pointer to a hint-specific argument and the (non-negative) length of the argument, respectively. These fields allow different types of hints to require different types of arguments, while using the same hint interfaces.

A.4.15 sio_hint_class_t

This is an unsigned integral type which contains the class identifier of hints passed with the **sio_hint()** and **sio_hint_by_name()** functions. Each class of hints contains one or more hint types whose interaction is specified. Interactions between hint types of different classes are unspecified. This document defines the **SIO_HINT_CLASS_ORDERED** and **SIO_HINT_CLASS_UNORDERED** constants to describe mandatory hint classes, and reserves constants whose names begin with with **SIO_HINT_CLASS_VEND_** for use by vendors. See Section A.11 for more details about hints and hint classes.

A.4.16 sio_hint_flags_t

This is an unsigned integral type used as a set of bits. It is used to describe the hint information stored in a **sio_hint_t**. See Section A.11 for a list of possible values for this type and explanations of their use.

A.4.17 sio_label_t

```
typedef struct {
    sio_size_t size;
    void *data;
} sio_label_t;
```

This type is used to store a file label, which can contain application-managed descriptive information about its associated file. The *data* field points to a memory buffer *size* bytes long. The **SIO_CTL_GetLabel** and **SIO_CTL_SetLabel** control operations use this structure in different manners; see Section A.13.9 for more information about this structure's use.

A.4.18 sio_layout_t

```
typedef struct {
    sio_layout_flags_t flags;
    sio_count_t stripe_width;
```

```
        sio_size_t stripe_depth;
        sio_layout_algorithm_t algorithm;
        void * algorithm_data;
    } sio_layout_t;
```

The number of parallel storage devices over which the file's data are striped is contained in the *stripe_width* field, while the (non-negative) number of contiguous bytes stored on each device (the unit of striping) is contained in *stripe_depth*. The *stripe_width* does not include any devices containing redundancy information, such as ECC codes or duplicate copies of the data. The *algorithm* field indicates the style of layout used for the file to provide guidance in the interpretation of the *stripe_width* and *stripe_depth* fields. The *algorithm_data* field is used to store algorithm-specific information about the layout.

The *flags* field indicates which portions of the **sio_layout_t** structure are being provided to the system or should be filled in by the system as described in Section A.13.8.

A.4.19   sio_layout_algorithm_t

This is an unsigned integral type whose value indicates the style of layout used for an SIO file. The layout algorithm describing a simple round-robin striping across all storage devices used for a file is **SIO_LAYOUT_ALGORITHM_SIMPLE_STRIPING**. This must be defined, though not necessarily supported, by all implementations. Implementations may choose to support additional layout algorithms that describe layouts in more detail or provide for more complex storage system architectures. The *algorithm_data* field in the **sio_layout_t** structure can be used to store additional information about the layout algorithm.

Layout algorithm names beginning with **SIO_LAYOUT_ALGORITHM_VEND_** are reserved for use by vendors. All other names beginning with **SIO_LAYOUT_ALGORITHM_** are reserved for future use by this API.

A.4.20   sio_layout_flags_t

This is an unsigned integral type used as a set of bits. It may contain zero or more of **SIO_LAYOUT_WIDTH**, **SIO_LAYOUT_DEPTH**, or **SIO_LAYOUT_ALGORITHM**, bitwise ORed to specify the fields of an **sio_layout_t** structure are to be returned or set.

A.4.21   sio_mem_io_list_t

```
typedef struct {
    void *addr;
    sio_size_t size;
    sio_size_t stride;
    sio_count_t element_cnt;
} sio_mem_io_list_t;
```

This type is similar to **sio_file_io_list_t** except that it describes a collection of regions within one memory space that is involved in a parallel file system operation, rather than a collection of file regions. Its purpose is to encapsulate the description of many simple transfers into one larger and more complex transfer in order to enable the file system to be more efficient in the execution of the total transfer. Each **sio_mem_io_list_t** structure describes a sequence of equally-sized and evenly-spaced contiguous byte regions within the memory space.

The structure describes a set of *element_cnt* contiguous regions, each of size *size*, with the first region beginning at address *addr*, and the beginning of each subsequent region starting *stride* bytes after the start of its predecessor. These contiguous byte regions may overlap; see Section A.9 for details.

A.4.22   sio_mode_t

This is an unsigned integral type used as a set of bits to specify the mode of a file operation. For example, the mode flags **SIO_MODE_READ** and **SIO_MODE_WRITE** can be specified together or separately to open the file for reading and/or writing, or to indicate what operation is being hinted. Other flags are documented in Section A.8.2.

A.4.23   sio_offset_t

This is a signed integral type whose absolute value is in the range $[0 \dots \mathbf{SIO\_MAX\_OFFSET}]$.[4] This type is signed to allow an offset variable to be decremented in a loop, and have the loop terminate when the variable becomes negative.

---

[4]We do not take advantage of the defined behavior of C, which allows the effect of negative signed numbers to be achieved by using large unsigned numbers that are congruent modulo 2^n. $2^{63} - 1$ is a sufficiently large offset that the extra factor of 2 possible by using unsigned offsets is not expected to be important before machines with 128 bit word sizes become widely used for high performance computing.

A.4.24   sio_return_t

This is an unsigned integral type used by functions in this API to return a result code.[5] The constant **SIO_SUCCESS**, whose value must be 0, denotes success.

Other values indicate specific errors which have been encountered in processing this request (the enumeration of standard error codes is included in §A.17). Error code names beginning with **SIO_ERR_VEND_** may be used by vendors for vendor-specific error codes. All other error code names, beginning with **SIO_ERR** are reserved for future use by this API. At least 16384 error codes (including 0, for **SIO_SUCCESS**) must be available for use by this API.

A.4.25   sio_size_t

This type is used to describe sizes of file and memory regions. It is a signed integral type whose absolute value is in the range $[0 \ldots \textbf{SIO\_MAX\_SIZE}]$. It is signed to allow expression of reverse strides for operations such as **sio_sg_read()**.

A.4.26   sio_transfer_len_t

This   is   an   unsigned   integral   type   in   the   range $[0 \ldots \textbf{SIO\_MAX\_TRANSFER\_LEN}]$.   It is used to count the total number of bytes transferred in I/O operations. This type differs from **sio_size_t** in that a single I/O operation may transfer many buffers whose length is represented by **sio_size_t**, hence **sio_transfer_len_t** is needed.

A.5   Range Constants

This section describes the constants used in this basic API to specify the ranges of data types. These constants are implementation-specific. However, for each of them, both a minimum value and a recommended value are given.

A.5.1   SIO_MAX_ASYNC_OUTSTANDING

This constant specifies the maximum number of outstanding asynchronous I/O requests that one task can have at one time. The minimum value is 1, and the recommended value is 512.

---

[5]An earlier version of this document used UNIX-style returns, where 0 indicated success, and -1 indicated failure, with specific UNIX error codes being set in the global error register. This was deemed inappropriate for two reasons. One is that the values of UNIX error numbers vary from platform to platform, as does the specific list of errors available. Another more serious problem is that it is difficult for multi-threaded applications to express different errors to different callers using a single global error register. Some systems, such as **pthreads**, provide a thread-specific error register for this reason. This was also deemed unacceptable, because it would require the parallel file system to be aware of the threading mechanism.

A.5.2   SIO_MAX_COUNT

This constant specifies the maximum number of items that can be defined by an **sio_count_t**. The minimum value is $2^{16} - 1$, and the recommended value is $2^{32} - 1$.

A.5.3   SIO_MAX_LABEL_LEN

This constant specifies the maximum length of a file label. The minimum value is **SIO_MAX_NAME_LEN** (whose minimum value is 256 bytes). The recommended value is the maximum of 1024 and the implementation's value of **SIO_MAX_NAME_LEN**.

A.5.4   SIO_MAX_NAME_LEN

This constant specifies the maximum length of a file name. The minimum value is 256, and the recommended value is 1024.

A.5.5   SIO_MAX_OFFSET

This constant specifies the maximum value for a file offset. The minimum value is $2^{63} - 1$, and the recommended value is $2^{63} - 1$.

A.5.6   SIO_MAX_OPEN

This constant specifies the maximum number of open files that a task can have at one time. The minimum value is 256, and the recommended value is 512. Note that a task may still fail to open a file before reaching this number because of system resource exhaustion.

A.5.7   SIO_MAX_SIZE

This constant specifies the maximum size in bytes of a variety of objects in the API. The minimum value is $2^{31} - 1$, and the recommended value is $2^{63} - 1$.

A.5.8   SIO_MAX_TRANSFER_LEN

This constant specifies the maximum number of bytes that can be transferred by a single I/O operation. The minimum value is **SIO_MAX_SIZE**, and the recommended value is $2^{63} - 1$. Since several components of a scatter-gather I/O list can be transferred at once, **SIO_MAX_TRANSFER_LEN** must be greater than or equal to **SIO_MAX_SIZE**.

A.6   File Attributes

This section describes the attributes associated with an SIO file. The file attributes are unique to each SIO file and visible to all tasks opening the file. These attributes include the logical, physical, and preallocation sizes of the file, file label, and file layout information. Extended controls may define additional file attributes.

A.6.1   File Sizes

The **logical size** of an SIO file is the number of bytes from the beginning of the file (offset zero) to the end of the file (the largest offset from which data can be read successfully). The file may contain regions which have not yet been written (referred to as "holes"), which are read as zeros. The logical size can be increased or decreased with the control operation **SIO_CTL_SetSize** (see Section A.13). Decreasing the logical size via **SIO_CTL_SetSize** corresponds to truncating the file, and increasing it creates a hole extending from the previous end of file to the new end of file. A file's logical size can also be increased by writing data past the current end of file.

The **physical size** of an SIO file is the amount of physical storage in bytes allocated to store the file data (excluding metadata). It may be different from the logical size of the file because of fixed size allocation blocks and because each implementation has the freedom to store data in any appropriate manner, including not storing the content of holes and the use of data compression techniques. The user has no direct control over the file's physical size.

The **preallocation size** of an open SIO file is the minimum logical size to which the file system guarantees the file may grow without running out of space. When a file is opened (created), its preallocation size defaults to its physical size (zero) unless a **SIO_CTL_SetPreallocation** control operation (see Section A.13) is specified in the **sio_open()** call. Preallocation size is not affected by any operation defined by this API other than **SIO_CTL_SetPreallocation** control operation and **sio_close()**.

A.6.2   File Label

The **file label** of an SIO file is a part of the file's metadata that is accessible to the user for storing descriptive information about the file without keeping a header in the file itself. Labels are intended to support interoperability by associating information about a file's representation (including file type, version, writing application, etc) with the file itself. Labels are not necessarily the same length in all implementations, but must always be long enough to record a maximum length file name for that implementation. This allows representation information too large to fit in a file label to be stored in a separate file named in the file label. The size of a label is given in the **sio_label_t** containing the label. This size is at least as large as an implementation's longest name which must be at least 256 bytes. The maximum size of a label in any specific implementation is given by the constant **SIO_MAX_LABEL_LENGTH** and is recommended to be at least 1024 bytes.

A.6.3   File Layout

The file layout of an SIO file expresses the placement of the file bytes on the parallel storage devices. Some implementations may allow the user to specify the file layout when the file is created with the **SIO_CTL_SetLayout** control operation. Other implementations may allow the user to query the file layout parameters with the **SIO_CTL_GetLayout** control operation, but not to set the layout. Still others may choose not to reveal anything about the underlying file layout and will support neither of the layout control operations.

A given file layout consists of the number of parallel storage devices over which the file data are striped, the number of contiguous bytes constituting each striping unit, and the algorithm which specifies the striping pattern of the striping units. For example, a simple striping pattern on four storage devices using a striping unit of 1024 bytes would look like the following (the starting byte number of each striping unit is shown):

Storage Unit 0	Storage Unit 1	Storage Unit 2	Storage Unit 3
0	1024	2048	3072
4096	5120	6144	7168
8192	9216	10240	11264
12288	13312	14336	15360
16384	17408	18432	19456
20480	21504	22528	23552
24576	25600	26624	27648
28672	29696	30720	31744
⋮	⋮	⋮	⋮

Note to implementor. The underlying implementation may employ advanced redundancy encodings or dynamic data representation (compressed and uncompressed or mirrored and parity protected). In cases like these, these layout parameters may be insufficient. In these cases the width of a stripe should be interpreted as the parallelism of accesses of at most an aligned striping unit.

A.7 Error Reporting

To make it easier for applications to deal with SIO error codes, the function **sio_error_string()** is provided. This function takes a **sio_return_t** value and returns a **const char ***. The sio_error_string function maps error codes to meaningful error strings. When passed an error code that is not defined by the implementation, **sio_error_string()** must return a string indicating the error number and noting that the error code is unrecognized.

A.7.1 sio_error_string

Purpose

> Translate a **sio_return_t** into a string.

Syntax

> **#include <sio_fs.h>**
>
> **const char *sio_error_string(sio_return_t** *Result*);

Parameters

> *Result* The return code to translate.

Description

> This function translates a return code to a string. The string pointed to must not be modified by the program, and may be overwritten by subsequent calls to **sio_error_string()**. If the implementation supports NLS (the suite of internationalization functions mandated by χ/Open XPG 4.2), the contents of the returned error message string should be determined by the setting of the **LC_MESSAGES** category in the locale.

A.8 Basic Operations

This section defines the basic operations that can be performed on parallel files. Interfaces are provided to open and close parallel files, to remove files from a parallel file system, and to perform control operations on parallel files.

This section defines some operations that appear to be similar to functions already supported in the POSIX standard. These operations exist so that implementations of this interface can be written without having to implement the entire

POSIX interface. Implementations that do support complete POSIX interfaces must still support the functions in this section, although their implementation may use the POSIX functions.

Three of the functions defined in this section, **sio_open()**, **sio_control()**, and **sio_test()**, allow the application to specify a set of controls to be applied to a file. Because **sio_control()** provides the simplest introduction to the use of controls, it is described first.

A.8.1   sio_control

Purpose

Perform a set of control operations on a given file.

Syntax

#include <sio_fs.h>

sio_return_t sio_control(int *FileDescriptor*, **sio_control_t** *Ops,
sio_count_t *OpCount*);

Parameters

FileDescriptor The file descriptor of the open parallel file on which to perform the control operations.

Ops An array of control operations to be performed.

OpCount The number of control operations in the array referenced by *Ops*.

Description

This function performs the set of control operations specified by the *Ops* argument on the open file specified by the *FileDescriptor* argument. Each control operation is either mandatory or optional, depending on the bits set in its *flags* field. If any of the mandatory operations would fail, the **sio_control()** operation fails and returns **SIO_ERR_CONTROL_FAILED**. In contrast, the failure of an optional control does *not* cause **sio_control()** to fail. The status of the individual controls can be checked after **sio_control()** returns, via the *result* field in the **sio_control_t** structures.

The application must not assume any ordering on the execution of the controls in *Ops*; the implementation is free to examine and/or execute the *Ops* in any order. Those control operations that succeed may take effect in any order.

If the **sio_control()** operation succeeds, then all of the mandatory controls take effect and have their result codes set to **SIO_SUCCESS**. With regard to the optional controls, one of two situations can occur:

- all of the optional controls take effect and have their result codes set to **SIO_SUCCESS**; or

- at least one of the optional controls fails and has its result code set to a control-specific error value. The remainder of the optional controls may individually 1) fail and have their result code set to a control-specific error value, 2) take effect and have their result code set to **SIO_SUCCESS**, 3) not be attempted and have their result code set to **SIO_ERR_CONTROL_NOT_ATTEMPTED**.

If the **sio_control()** operation fails for any reason, then all of the control operations in *Ops* are annulled, that is, they have no permanent effect on the file system. If **sio_control()** fails, none of the controls will have their *result* field set to **SIO_SUCCESS**. In this case, the implementation may set the result field of a particular control to a control-specific error code if that control would have failed or if the control caused the **sio_control()** to fail, or to **SIO_ERR_CONTROL_WOULD_HAVE_SUCCEEDED** if that control would have succeeded had the **sio_control()** operation not failed, or to **SIO_ERR_CONTROL_NOT_ATTEMPTED** if the **sio_control()** failed before the implementation checked whether or not that control would have succeeded.

Section A.13 defines the control operations included in the basic API.

Return Values

SIO_SUCCESS
> All mandatory control operations succeeded.

SIO_ERR_CONTROL_FAILED
> At least one of the mandatory control operations failed.

SIO_ERR_CONTROLS_CLASH
> Some of the mandatory control operations are incompatible with each other and cannot be performed together by this implementation. If a control operation fails with this error, then at least two of the individual control operations must also have their result fields set to **SIO_ERR_CONTROLS_CLASH**.

SIO_ERR_INVALID_DESCRIPTOR
> The *FileDescriptor* parameter is not a valid file descriptor.

A.8.2   sio_open

Purpose

Open a file for reading and/or writing.

Syntax

#include <sio_fs.h>

sio_return_t sio_open(int *FileDescriptorPtr, const char *Name,
                      sio_mode_t Mode, sio_control_t *ControlOps,
                      sio_count_t ControlOpCount);

Parameters

FileDescriptorPtr On success, this will contain the file descriptor of the newly opened file.

Name The name of the file to open. The name must be at most **SIO_MAX_NAME_LEN** characters in length.

Mode The mode used to open the file. Must include at least one of **SIO_MODE_READ** and **SIO_MODE_WRITE**, or both ORed together. May also include **SIO_MODE_CREATE**.

ControlOps An array of control operations to be performed on the file during the open.

ControlOpCount The number of operations in the array specified by *ControlOps*.

Description

This function takes a logical file name, and produces a file descriptor which supports reading and/or writing, depending on the value of *Mode*. If the named file does not exist and *Mode* has the **SIO_MODE_CREATE** bit set, then the file will be created; if the bit is not set then **SIO_ERR_FILE_NOT_FOUND** will be returned. If **SIO_MODE_CREATE** is set and the file already exists, **SIO_ERR_ALREADY_EXISTS** will be returned.

As part of the operation of opening the file, **sio_open()** performs the control operations described by *ControlOps* and *ControlOpCount*. The control operations have the same meaning and are treated in the same way as in the **sio_control()** function.

If the **sio_open()** operation fails for any reason, then all of the control operations are annulled and have their result codes set in the same way **sio_control()** sets the result codes when it fails.

Note that the semantics of **sio_open()** do not require any permission or security checks. Implementations not embedded in a POSIX file system that wish to provide file permissions can check those permissions on open and can allow those permissions to be set via implementation-specific control operations.

Return Codes

SIO_SUCCESS

The open succeeded.

SIO_ERR_ALREADY_EXISTS

SIO_MODE_CREATE was specified and the file already exists.

SIO_ERR_CONTROL_FAILED

At least one of the mandatory control operations would have failed.

SIO_ERR_CONTROLS_CLASH

Some of the mandatory control operations specified are incompatible with each other and cannot be performed together by this implementation.

SIO_ERR_FILE_NOT_FOUND

The file did not exist and **SIO_MODE_CREATE** was not specified.

SIO_ERR_INVALID_FILENAME

The *Name* parameter is not a legal file name.

SIO_ERR_IO_FAILED

A physical I/O error caused the open to fail.

SIO_ERR_MAX_OPEN_EXCEEDED

Opening the file would result in the task having more than **SIO_MAX_OPEN** open file descriptors.

A.8.3   sio_close

Purpose

Close a previously opened file.

Syntax

#include <sio_fs.h>

sio_return_t sio_close(int *FileDescriptor*);

Parameters

FileDescriptor The file descriptor of the open parallel file to close.

Description

This function closes an open file. All resources associated with having the file open will be deallocated. Cached pending writes are made visible to other nodes before **sio_close()** returns (see Section A.12 for details). The results of any asynchronous I/Os in progress at the time **sio_close()** is called are unspecified, and the handles for those I/Os may be invalidated by the system. Applications may ensure that all asynchronous I/Os are complete by calling **sio_async_status_any()** prior to calling **sio_close()** (see Section A.10.2). Pre-allocated space, unnecessary for the physical file associated with the open file, may be released.

Note to implementors: Implementations should close all of a task's open parallel file descriptors when the task terminates.

Return Codes

SIO_SUCCESS

The close succeeded.

SIO_ERR_INVALID_DESCRIPTOR

The *FileDescriptor* parameter does not refer to a valid file descriptor previously returned by **sio_open()**.

SIO_ERR_IO_FAILED

A physical I/O error caused the close to fail.

A.8.4   sio_unlink

Purpose

Remove a file from the parallel file system.

Syntax

#include <sio_fs.h>

sio_return_t sio_unlink(const char *Name);

Parameters

Name The name of the file to remove.

Description

This function removes a file from the parallel file system, deallocating any space that was allocated for the file. The semantics of unlinking an open file are implementation-specific; possibilities include (but are not limited to) allowing tasks which have this file open to continue to use their open file descriptors, allowing subsequent I/O operations on the file to fail, and allowing **sio_unlink()** itself to fail if the file is open.

Return Codes

SIO_SUCCESS

The unlink succeeded.

SIO_ERR_FILE_NOT_FOUND

The file did not exist.

SIO_ERR_FILE_OPEN

The file *Name* is open and the implementation does not allow open files to be unlinked.

SIO_ERR_INVALID_FILENAME

The *Name* parameter is not a legal file name.

SIO_ERR_IO_FAILED

A physical I/O error caused the unlink to fail.

A.8.5   sio_test

Purpose

Use mode and control operations to determine attributes of a file by name, without opening the file.

Syntax

#include <sio_fs.h>

sio_return_t sio_test(const char *Name, sio_mode_t Mode,
                        sio_control_t *ControlOps,
                        sio_count_t ControlOpCount);

Parameters

Name The name of the target file.

Mode The access mode to be tested. May include one or more of **SIO_MODE_READ**, **SIO_MODE_WRITE**, and **SIO_MODE_CREATE**, ORed together.

ControlOps An array of control operations to be performed on the file.

ControlOpCount The number of operations in the array specified by *ControlOps*.

Description

This function allows an application to test for the existence of a file or test whether a file can be created, and get the attributes of the file, without opening or creating the file.

This function is similar to **sio_open()**, except for two differences:

- It does not actually open or create the specified file.

- It is not allowed to perform any control operations that change the permanent state of the file system.

This function may only use controls that do not change the permanent state of the file system.   Of the controls defined in this document, only the following may be performed by **sio_test()**:   **SIO_CTL_GetSize   SIO_CTL_GetAllocation SIO_CTL_GetPreallocation   SIO_CTL_GetLayout SIO_CTL_GetLabel SIO_CTL_GetConsistencyUnit**.

Controls that change file state will return **SIO_ERR_CONTROL_NOT_ON_TEST**.   If implementation-specific controls are defined, the implementation must specify whether or not each additional control modifies file state.

Provided a disallowed control is not specified, this function succeeds if a call to **sio_open()** with the same parameters would have succeeded.

If this function fails for any reason, then the result codes of the individual *Ops* are set in the same manner that **sio_open()** sets the result codes of its *Ops*.

Return Codes

SIO_SUCCESS
  The test succeeded.

SIO_ERR_ALREADY_EXISTS
  SIO_MODE_CREATE was specified and the file already exists.

SIO_ERR_CONTROL_FAILED
  At least one of the mandatory control operations would have failed.

SIO_ERR_CONTROL_NOT_ON_TEST

At least one of the control operations changes the file state and may not be used with **sio_test()**.

SIO_ERR_CONTROLS_CLASH

Some of the mandatory control operations specified are incompatible with each other and cannot be performed together by this implementation.

SIO_ERR_FILE_NOT_FOUND

The file did not exist and **SIO_MODE_CREATE** was not specified.

SIO_ERR_INVALID_FILENAME

The *Name* parameter is not a legal file name.

SIO_ERR_IO_FAILED

A physical I/O error caused the function to fail.

SIO_ERR_MAX_OPEN_EXCEEDED

Opening the file would result in the task having more than **SIO_MAX_OPEN** open file descriptors.

A.8.6   sio_rename

Purpose

Rename a file.

Syntax

#include <sio_fs.h>

sio_return_t sio_rename(const char *OldName,
                        const char *NewName);

Parameters

OldName The current name of the file.

NewName The new name of the file.

Description

This function changes the name of the file *OldName* to *NewName*. The semantics of renaming an open file are implementation-specific; possibilities include (but are not limited to) allowing tasks which have this file open to continue to use their open file descriptors, allowing subsequent I/O operations on the file to fail, and allowing the rename itself to fail if the file is open.

Return Codes

SIO_SUCCESS

The rename succeeded.

SIO_ERR_ALREADY_EXISTS

NewName already exists.

SIO_ERR_FILE_NOT_FOUND

OldName did not exist.

SIO_ERR_FILE_OPEN

The file *OldName* is open and the implementation does not allow open files
to be renamed.

SIO_ERR_INVALID_FILENAME

One of the file names is not a valid name for a file.

SIO_ERR_IO_FAILED

A physical I/O error caused the function to fail.

A.9   Synchronous File I/O

This section introduces new functions for file read and write operations. These
provide file system functions previously unavailable in UNIX systems, as they allow
strided scatter and gather of data in memory and also in a file.

One of the primary performance-limiting problems for file systems and parallel
programs arises when the data-moving interfaces are restricted to moving single
contiguous regions of bytes. This restriction causes applications to ask too frequently for small amounts of work and it denies the system the ability to obtain
performance benefits from grouping (batching, scheduling, coalescing). Our first
step toward removing this limitation is to offer interfaces that allow the transfer
of multiple ranges in a file to or from multiple ranges in memory. We call this
capability *scatter-gather*.

The read and write operations introduced in this section are not like traditional
read/write operations. Rather than describing file and memory addresses as linear
buffers, these calls describe them as lists of strided accesses. Each element of the
list specifies a single strided access, consisting of a starting address (offset), size of
each contiguous region, stride between the contiguous regions, and the total number
of regions in the strided access (see Section A.4 for the formats of these elements).
Data are copied from the source buffer to the destination in *canonical order*. The
canonical order of an individual strided access is the sequence of contiguous byte
regions specified by the access. The canonical order for a list of strided accesses is

simply the concatenation of the canonical orders for the strided accesses. Intuitively, all byte regions specified by the canonical ordering in a file are concatenated into a contiguous zero-address based virtual window. The byte regions specified in memory are also concatenated in canonical order into this virtual window. Each byte of the virtual window corresponds to one byte of the file and also to one byte of memory. The number of bytes specified in the two lists must be equal.

We place no restrictions on the values of addresses occurring in the canonical ordering of the data structure from the file or memory. This mapping may be increasing, decreasing or non-monotonic in the file or memory, and may cover a given byte more than once.

Note that the file system need not access the file or memory in canonical order. Data can be accessed in the file or memory in any sequence as preferred by the file system to optimize performance. The canonical sequence of file regions is used only to compute the association of the file data with memory regions.

If the source list (i.e. the memory buffer during a write or the file buffer during a read) contains the same region more than once then its data will be copied into the destination buffer multiple times. If the destination list contains the same region more than once then the resulting contents of the duplicated region are undefined.[6]

Applications must not access an I/O operation's memory buffer while the operation is in progress. For example, a thread in a multi-threaded application must not read or write a buffer while another thread has an I/O in progress using the same buffer. Failure to avoid such accesses may corrupt the task and/or file in undefined ways, including leaving the contents of the file corrupted or causing the task to fault. Applications that wish to share I/O buffers between threads must explicitly synchronize the threads' accesses to those buffers.

It is expected that many users of this API will desire simpler interfaces to this functionality. In addition to the basic POSIX interfaces, the interfaces in §A.18 are easily built on the interfaces provided in this API. These, or similar simplified interfaces, could easily be provided by a high-level library, and are not defined by this API.

A.9.1   sio_sg_read, sio_sg_write

Purpose

Transfer data between a file and memory.

Syntax

---

[6]No function to check for duplicate regions in the destination list is provided. However, such a function could be implemented as part of a higher-level library built on top of this API.

#include <sio_fs.h>

sio_return_t sio_sg_read(int *FileDescriptor*,
                         const sio_file_io_list_t *FileList*,
                         sio_count_t *FileListLength*,
                         const sio_mem_io_list_t *MemoryList*,
                         sio_count_t *MemoryListLength*,
                         sio_transfer_len_t *TotalTransferred*);

sio_return_t sio_sg_write(int *FileDescriptor*,
                          const sio_file_io_list_t *FileList*,
                          sio_count_t *FileListLength*,
                          const sio_mem_io_list_t *MemoryList*,
                          sio_count_t *MemoryListLength*,
                          sio_transfer_len_t *TotalTransferred*);

Parameters

FileDescriptor The file descriptor of an open file.

FileList Specification of file data to be read or written.

FileListLength Number of elements in *FileList*.

MemoryList Specification of the memory buffer containing data to be read or written.

MemoryListLength Number of elements in *MemoryList*.

TotalTransferred Used to return the total number of bytes read or written.

Description

These functions move data between a list of file locations and a list of memory locations. All I/O must be done to a single file, in the *FileDescriptor* argument.

The mapping between the collection of file regions specified by *FileList* and the collection of memory byte regions specified by *MemoryList* is in matching indices in the canonical ordering of the corresponding sio_file_io_list_t and sio_mem_io_list_t.

If the total transfer cannot be completed because a file address is not valid (i.e. reading beyond the end of the file), these interfaces will complete successfully, and return in *TotalTransferred* the index of the first byte in the canonical ordering that could not be transferred (following the UNIX example);

bytes preceding this index in the canonical ordering have been transferred successfully and bytes following (and including) it may or may not have been transferred successfully.

Implementations may return a value less than the actual amount transferred if the operation was not successful; in particular, an implementation may indicate that zero bytes were transferred successfully on all failures.

Return Codes

SIO_SUCCESS

The function succeeded.

SIO_ERR_INCORRECT_MODE

The mode of the file descriptor does not permit the I/O.

SIO_ERR_INVALID_DESCRIPTOR

FileDescriptor does not refer to a valid file descriptor.

SIO_ERR_INVALID_FILE_LIST

The file regions described by *FileList* are invalid, e.g. they contain illegal addresses.

SIO_ERR_INVALID_MEMORY_LIST

The memory regions described by *MemoryList* are invalid, e.g. they contain illegal addresses.

SIO_ERR_IO_FAILED

A physical I/O error caused the function to fail.

SIO_ERR_NO_SPACE

The file system ran out of space while trying to extend the file.

SIO_ERR_UNEQUAL_LISTS

The number of bytes in *MemoryList* and *FileList* are not equal.

A.10   Asynchronous File I/O

Asynchronous I/O allows a single-threaded task to issue concurrent I/O requests. The parallel file system supports up to **SIO_MAX_ASYNC_OUTSTANDING** (see Section A.5.1) asynchronous I/Os at a time for each task. Asynchronous I/O functions merely initiate an I/O, returning to the task a handle that may be used by the task to wait for the I/O to complete, to check its status of the I/O, or to cancel the I/O.

These handles are of type **sio_async_handle_t**, which is an opaque type defined by the system. Only the task that issued the asynchronous I/O is able to use the sio_async_handle_t associated with the I/O to retrieve the status of or cancel the I/O. Other tasks that wish to retrieve the status of or cancel an I/O must contact the task that initiated the I/O.

A.10.1   sio_async_sg_read, sio_async_sg_write

Purpose

Asynchronously transfer data between a file and memory.

Syntax

#include <sio_fs.h>

sio_return_t sio_async_sg_read(int *FileDescriptor*,
                        const sio_file_io_list_t *FileList*,
                        sio_count_t *FileListLength*,
                        const sio_mem_io_list_t *MemoryList*,
                        sio_count_t *MemoryListLength*,
                        sio_async_handle_t *Handle*);

sio_return_t sio_async_sg_write(int *FileDescriptor*,
                        const sio_file_io_list_t *FileList*,
                        sio_count_t *FileListLength*,
                        const sio_mem_io_list_t *MemoryList*,
                        sio_count_t *MemoryListLength*,
                        sio_async_handle_t *Handle*);

Parameters

FileDescriptor The file descriptor of an open file.

FileList Specification of file data to be read or written.

FileListLength Number of elements in *FileList*.

MemoryList Specification of the memory buffer containing data to be read or written.

MemoryListLength Number of elements in *MemoryList*.

Handle Handle returned by the operation, which can be used later to determine the status of the I/O, to wait for its completion, or to cancel it.

Description

These functions behave similarly to **sio_sg_read()** and **sio_sg_write()**. A successful return, however, indicates only that the I/O has been queued for processing by the parallel file system.

Handle is a task-specific value which may be used to poll for completion, block until the I/O completes, or cancel the I/O. The handle remains valid until either the task completes, or **sio_async_status_any()** indicates that the I/O transfer associated with *Handle* is no longer in progress. While a handle is valid it counts towards the **SIO_MAX_ASYNC_OUTSTANDING** asynchronous I/Os that a task may have.

As in synchronous I/O, applications must neither access nor modify the contents of a memory buffer while an asynchronous I/O is in progress on that buffer. Doing so may leave the buffer and/or the file in an undefined state, and may cause the task to fault. See Section A.9 for details.

Return Codes

SIO_SUCCESS
The function succeeded.

SIO_ERR_INCORRECT_MODE
The mode of the file descriptor does not allow the I/O.

SIO_ERR_INVALID_DESCRIPTOR
FileDescriptor does not refer to a valid file descriptor.

SIO_ERR_INVALID_FILE_LIST
The file regions described by *FileList* are invalid, e.g. they contain illegal addresses. Implementations may defer returning this error until **sio_async_status_any()** is invoked on the I/O.

SIO_ERR_INVALID_MEMORY_LIST
The memory regions described by *MemoryList* are invalid, e.g. they contain illegal addresses. Implementations may defer returning this error until **sio_async_status_any()** is invoked on the I/O.

SIO_ERR_IO_FAILED
A physical I/O error caused the function to fail.

SIO_ERR_MAX_ASYNC_OUTSTANDING_EXCEEDED
The I/O request could not be initiated because doing so would cause the calling task's number of outstanding asynchronous I/Os to exceed the limit.

SIO_ERR_NO_SPACE
The file system ran out of space while trying to extend the file. Implementations may defer returning this error until **sio_async_status_any()** is invoked on the I/O.

SIO_ERR_UNEQUAL_LISTS
The number of bytes in *MemoryList* and *FileList* are not equal. Implementations may defer returning this error until **sio_async_status_any()** is invoked on the I/O.

A.10.2   sio_async_status_any

Purpose

Get the status of asynchronous I/Os.

Syntax

#include <sio_fs.h>

sio_return_t sio_async_status_any(sio_async_handle_t *HandleList,
                          sio_count_t *HandleListLength*,
                          sio_count_t *Index*,
                          sio_async_status_t *Status*,
                          sio_async_flags_t *Flags*);

Parameters

HandleList An array of **sio_async_handle_t**s identifying the asynchronous I/Os for which status is desired.

HandleListLength The number of elements in *HandleList*.

Index Used to return the index of handle within *HandleList* for which status is returned.

Status Pointer to an **sio_async_status_t** to be filled in.

Flags Determines whether or not the operation blocks or returns immediately.

Description

This function retrieves the status of one of the asynchronous I/Os specified by *HandleList*. The index of the handle within *HandleList* for which the status is returned is stored in *Index*. The system may return the status for any of the handles, provided that if any of the I/Os are complete or canceled, then the status for one of these I/Os is returned and not the status of an I/O that is still in progress.

It is important to note that once the status for an I/O indicates that the I/O is no longer in progress (i.e. it completed or was canceled) the handle for the I/O is no longer valid. If it is subsequently passed to **sio_async_status_any()**

the value **SIO_ERR_INVALID_HANDLE** will be returned if the handle is still invalid, otherwise the status of the new asynchronous I/O will be returned if the handle has been reused.

The task may place a dummy handle in the **HandleList** by setting the entry to **SIO_ASYNC_DUMMY_HANDLE**. The system ignores a handle with this value, allowing the task to retrieve the status for a set of handles using the same *HandleList* array, by replacing the handle for the I/O just finished with the dummy value.

If the *Flags* parameter includes **SIO_ASYNC_BLOCKING**, this function will not return until at least one of the I/Os has completed. If it includes **SIO_ASYNC_NONBLOCKING**, this function returns immediately, regardless of whether or not one of the I/Os has completed.

Note to implementors: When an I/O is canceled the *count* field in *Status* will contain the number of bytes guaranteed to have been transferred prior to the cancellation. Implementations may always set this value to zero, indicating that none of the bytes are guaranteed to have been transferred.

Status Results

The following values are returned in the *result* field of the *Status* structure, indicating the status of the I/O:

SIO_SUCCESS
The I/O has completed or been canceled. The *count* field contains the number of bytes transferred.

SIO_ERR_INVALID_FILE_LIST
The file regions described by the *FileList* parameter passed to the function that initiated the I/O are invalid, e.g. they contain illegal addresses.

SIO_ERR_INVALID_MEMORY_LIST
The memory regions described by the *MemoryList* parameter passed to the function that initiated the I/O are invalid, e.g. they contain illegal addresses.

SIO_ERR_IO_CANCELED
The I/O was canceled without completing. The *count* field contains the number of bytes *guaranteed* to have been transferred successfully prior to the cancellation. Implementations may set *count* to zero.

SIO_ERR_IO_FAILED
A physical I/O error caused the function to fail.

SIO_ERR_IO_IN_PROGRESS
The I/O is still in progress.

SIO_ERR_MIXED_COLL_AND_ASYNC
The implementation does not support mixing of asynchronous and collective I/O handles, and a mix of handle types was supplied.

SIO_ERR_NO_SPACE
The file system ran out of space while trying to extend the file.

SIO_ERR_UNEQUAL_LISTS
The size of the memory buffer doesn't match size of the file regions to be accessed.

Return Values

SIO_SUCCESS
An I/O has completed or been canceled, the index and result of which are stored in *Index* and *Status*, respectively.

SIO_ERR_INVALID_HANDLE
At least one of the elements of *HandleList* is neither a valid handle for an asynchronous I/O nor a dummy handle. *Index* will contain the index of one of the invalid handles.

SIO_ERR_IO_IN_PROGRESS
All I/Os are still in progress.

A.10.3   sio_async_cancel_all

Purpose

Request that a collection of asynchronous I/Os be canceled.

Syntax

#include <sio_fs.h>

sio_return_t sio_async_cancel_all(sio_async_handle_t **HandleList,*
                    sio_count_t *HandleListLength***);**

Parameters

HandleList An array of **sio_async_handle_t**s identifying the asynchronous I/Os to be canceled.

HandleListLength The number of elements in *HandleList*.

Description

This function is used to request that asynchronous I/Os be canceled. It is not guaranteed that the I/O will not complete in full or in part; an implementation may ignore cancel requests. A canceled read leaves the contents of the I/O's memory buffer undefined. Likewise, if a write is canceled, the contents of the regions of the file regions being written are undefined.

The status of a canceled request remains available until an **sio_async_status_any()** reports its completion. An application should test for this status or its maximum outstanding asynchronous I/Os will appear to diminish.

Note to implementors:

An implementation may ignore cancellation requests altogether. In this case a call to **sio_async_status_any()** on an I/O that whose cancellation was requested should return the normal, uncanceled completion status of the I/O.

Note to implementors: Implementations are encouraged to avoid reusing the same handles for different asynchronous I/Os within the same task. A handle becomes invalid once the I/O is no longer in progress and its status has been retrieved, but bugs may cause a task to use such an invalid handle. If the system has reassigned the handle to a new I/O the task will end up affecting the new I/O, instead of getting an invalid handle error. Although this behavior is caused by a bug in the application, avoiding reuse of handles will help track the problem.

Return Values

SIO_SUCCESS

The request for cancellation was accepted. This does not mean that the I/Os were actually canceled.

SIO_ERR_INVALID_HANDLE

One of the elements in *HandleList* is not a valid handle for an asynchronous I/O.

A.11   File Access Pattern Hints

File access pattern hints provide a useful mechanism for users and libraries to disclose the intended use of file regions to the file system. The hints, if properly given, allow file systems to implement significant performance optimizations. Many parallel scientific programs, for example, have access patterns that are anathemic to some file system architectures. These applications could benefit if the file system accepted access hints that protected the application from the performance consequences of the default file system behavior. For example, access hints can be used by the file system to choose caching and pre-fetching policies.

Hints are issued with the **sio_hint()** and **sio_hint_by_name()** interfaces described in Section A.11.3. These interfaces indicate a file, a hint class, and a list of hints. Hints apply only to the future accesses of the task passing in the hints, they are not associated with the accesses of other tasks. There are two hint classes specified in this API: ordered and unordered. Vendors are encouraged to extend this API with vendor-defined hint classes, which must have names beginning with **SIO_HINT_CLASS_VEND_**. Within any class of hints, the interaction of all hint types must be specified, but the interaction of hint types from different classes need not be specified. In particular, two calls issuing hints with different hint classes for the same open file may not be meaningful to an implementation. However, since the information in these hints are not commands, the file system implementation has broad freedom not to act where hint combinations are not meaningful.

The intent of hints is to allow the application to precisely specify what its future access patterns will be. The hint interface does not provide specific guarantees of how implementations will interpret these hints. Different implementations are free to choose different strategies for responding to hints (including ignoring them completely), but the application's description of its future accesses must conform to this interface.

System performance may be degraded due to inaccurate hints. Implementations should attempt to protect against such performance degradation, but are not required to. Similarly, applications should not assume that the file system can always limit the performance impacts of inaccurate hints (accesses that have been hinted, but will not actually be performed) and should make use of the cancel options to minimize these effects.

A.11.1   Ordered Hints

In a set of ordered hints, each hint indicates a particular future access to be issued by the calling task, and the sequence of issued hints indicates the order of these accesses. The total order of future accesses expressed by multiple invocations of the hint interfaces is determined by concatenating the hint array in each invocation onto the end of the hint array built by previously issued hints. This allows access to different files to be ordered. The accesses to different files predicted by one hint are expected to occur after the accesses predicted by all hints preceding it, and before the accesses predicted by all hints following it in the total order.

The *flag* field of each **sio_hint_t** in the class of ordered hints can contain the following flags that can be ORed with each other:

SIO_HINT_READ or SIO_HINT_WRITE

SIO_HINT_READ indicates the hint describes a read access. **SIO_HINT_WRITE** indicates the hint describes a write access.

Exactly one of these flags must be specified for each hint. When used to cancel a hint the flags in the cancel request must match the hint's flags.

SIO_HINT_CANCEL_ALL or SIO_HINT_CANCEL_NEXT

Regardless of the file specified by the hint interface call and the regions specified by the *io_list* fields in the **sio_hint_t** structures, **SIO_HINT_CANCEL_ALL** indicates that all previously issued hints should be ignored.

SIO_HINT_CANCEL_NEXT indicates that the previously issued hint matching the file and region specified with this **SIO_HINT_CANCEL_NEXT** whose predicted access is next to occur should be ignored. A hint is considered "outstanding" if the data transfer request predicted by the hint has not yet occurred. It is expected the data transfer requests will take place in the sequence given by the total ordered list of hints for the task, with the possibility that not all transfer requests will have corresponding hints. The "next outstanding hint" will be the first matching hint in the set of ordered hints previously issued by this task for which no corresponding for transfer request has occurred.

A previously issued hint's profile "matches" the current hint's profile if the hints pertain to the same file, and the regions specified by the *io_list* entry in the **sio_hint_t** structures are the same and the **SIO_HINT_READ** or **SIO_HINT_WRITE** flag matches.

No more than one of these flags may be specified for each hint.

Note to implementors: Implementations are not required to keep track of "outstanding" hints. The concept of "outstanding" only describes the application's intent in issuing the hint, and does not describe the implementation's behavior. In implementations that do not keep track of "outstanding" hints the **SIO_HINT_CANCEL_NEXT** hint may not be useful.

A.11.2   Unordered Hints

In an unordered set of hints, each hint independently specifies information about some set of future accesses. There is no explicit ordering among the accesses predicted by unordered hints. These predictions remain in effect until explicitly canceled.

The flag field of each **sio_hint_t** in the class of unordered hints can contain the following flags:

SIO_HINT_READ and/or SIO_HINT_WRITE

SIO_HINT_READ indicates that the hint describes read accesses. **SIO_HINT_WRITE** indicates that the hint describes write accesses. If **SIO_HINT_READ** and **SIO_HINT_WRITE** are given together, they indicate that the hint describes a read-write access.

At least one of these flags must be specified for each hint.

SIO_HINT_CANCEL_ALL or SIO_HINT_CANCEL_MATCHING

SIO_HINT_CANCEL_ALL suggests that the file system ignore all previously issued unordered hints from this task, regardless of the file and file regions given in any of these hints. **SIO_HINT_CANCEL_MATCHING** suggests that the file system ignore all previously issued unordered hints from this task which match the given **sio_hint_t**.

No more than one of these flags may be specified for each hint.

SIO_HINT_SEQUENTIAL, SIO_HINT_REVERSE, SIO_HINT_RANDOM_PARTIAL, SIO_HINT_RANDOM_COMPLETE, SIO_HINT_NO_FURTHER_USE, or SIO_HINT_WILL_USE

Each hint expresses an access pattern predicted for the file region given by the hint. When changing a predicted access pattern on a region, a **SIO_HINT_CANCEL_MATCHING** hint should be issued to cancel the old hint before the new access hint is issued. The interpretation of multiple predicted access patterns on the same region or partial (overlapping) region is unspecified. These patterns are:

SIO_HINT_SEQUENTIAL

The entire region will be accessed in non-overlapping blocks whose starting offsets increase monotonically.

SIO_HINT_REVERSE

The entire region will be accessed in non-overlapping blocks whose starting offsets decrease monotonically.

SIO_HINT_RANDOM_COMPLETE

Accesses in the region will have starting addresses and sizes that vary without pattern but the entire region will be accessed.

SIO_HINT_RANDOM_PARTIAL

Accesses in the region will have starting addresses and sizes that vary without pattern and the entire region may not be accessed.

SIO_HINT_NO_FURTHER_USE

No further accesses are expected in the region.

SIO_HINT_WILL_USE

All data in the region will be accessed although no explicit pattern can be predicted or excluded.[7]

Exactly one of these flags must be specified for each hint.

A.11.3   sio_hint, sio_hint_by_name

Purpose

Issue a set of predictions about the future accesses of this task.

Syntax

#include <sio_fs.h>

sio_return_t sio_hint(int *FileDescriptor*, sio_hint_class_t *HintClass*,
                            const sio_hint_t **Hints*, sio_count_t *HintCount*);

sio_return_t sio_hint_by_name(const char **FileName*,
                            sio_hint_class_t *HintClass*,
                            const sio_hint_t **Hints*,
                            sio_count_t *HintCount*);

Parameters

FileDescriptor The file descriptor of an open file to which these hints apply.

FileName The name of a file, not necessarily an open file, to which these hints apply.

HintClass The class of the hints being issued.

Hints An array of file access pattern hints.

---

[7]This pattern should be used in cases where **SIO_HINT_RANDOM_COMPLETE** cannot because the access pattern might not be random.

HintCount The number of entries in the *Hints* array.

Description

This function reports the application's knowledge of future access patterns to the file system. The purpose of issuing this information is to enable optimizations in the dynamic behavior of the parallel file system. This knowledge is expressed as a set of hints, all from the same hint class. The interpretation of mixtures of hint types from different hint classes is unspecified. Hints can be applied to an open file using **sio_hint()**, or to a named file (which may not be open) using **sio_hint_by_name()**. Each **sio_hint_t** structure in the *Hints* array describes a hint type applied to a list of file regions and optionally hint-specific arguments.

If the *size*, *stride*, and *element_cnt* fields for a particular **sio_file_io_list_t** in a hint are all zero, then the region being specified begins at the offset given by the *offset* field of that **sio_file_io_list_t** and continues until the end of the file. The entire contents of a file are specified as the region whenever an **sio_file_io_list_t** contains zero in the four fields: *offset*, *size*, *stride* and *element_cnt*.

The implementation may not act on any specific hint or on any hints at all.

Return Codes

SIO_SUCCESS
The function succeeded.

SIO_ERR_FILE_NOT_FOUND
The specified file did not exist.

SIO_ERR_HINT_TYPES_CLASH
The class of this hint differs from the class of another hint previously issued for the same file region.[8]

SIO_ERR_INVALID_CLASS
The hint class given in *HintClass* is not a valid hint class.

SIO_ERR_INVALID_DESCRIPTOR
FileDescriptor does not refer to a valid file descriptor created by **sio_open()**.

---

[8]As mentioned above, the effects of mixing hints of different classes for the same file region are undefined. This error code is provided for implementations that attempt to resolve hints from different classes.

SIO_ERR_INVALID_FILENAME

The name given by *FileName* is invalid.

A.12   Client Cache Control

The basic API includes facilities to control caching of data in client memory. The caching interfaces are specified such that it is a valid implementation strategy to simply ignore all cache control calls. The only requirement of an implementation that ignores these calls is that it must provide strongly consistent semantics.

The client caching mode of an SIO file may be specified by including the **SIO_CTL_SetCachingMode** control operation when making **sio_open()** or **sio_control()** calls.

This API specifies client caching modes with the type **sio_caching_mode_t**, which can have the following values:

SIO_CACHING_NONE

Completely disable client caching.

SIO_CACHING_STRONG

Allow strongly-consistent client caching. The file system may choose to provide caching with strong sequential consistency, or provide no caching at all.

SIO_CACHING_WEAK

Allow weakly-consistent client caching. The file system may provide no client caching, strongly-consistent client caching, or weakly-consistent client caching.

Caching mode names beginning with **SIO_CACHING_** are reserved for future use by this API. Vendors may define their own caching modes by naming them with the prefix **SIO_CACHING_VEND_**.

An SIO parallel file system implementation's default client caching mode must provide sequential consistency. That is, it must be either **SIO_CACHING_NONE**, **SIO_CACHING_STRONG**, or a vendor-defined mode that provides strong sequential consistency.

If client caching is not disabled by using a caching mode of **SIO_CACHING_NONE**, the file system on a client node is free to maintain local copies of file data for both read and write operations.

In a system with strongly-consistent caching, every write forces the client node to immediately make the file system aware that the file has changed. This also requires that client nodes either check the validity of cached data before providing them to applications to satisfy a read, or be notified whenever cached or potentially cached data have changed.

On the other hand, weakly-consistent client caching allows the file system to avoid the messaging and bookkeeping which a sequentially consistent caching mode mandates, while providing the application with the benefits of caching. With this form of caching, client nodes may defer exposing all or part of a set of changes to a file until instructed otherwise by the application. Likewise, a client node need not confirm the validity of cached data with the server unless explicitly instructed to do so by the application.

An application informs the file system that data written on a file descriptor should become visible to other readers via the **SIO_CTL_Propagate** control operation. If the changed data have not already been exposed to the rest of the file system, this is done so immediately. Note that all, none, or part of this changed data may already have been exposed to the rest of the file system.

Likewise, an application informs the file system that locally cached data may be stale using the **SIO_CTL_Refresh** control operation. Reads of refreshed regions of a file are guaranteed to yield either the most current available data, or data that were not stale at the time of the most recent refresh operation. That is to say, if the data returned by the read are stale, it was made so *after* the refresh.

It is assumed that applications using weakly-consistent client caching either do not share data between nodes, or provide their own internal synchronization to coordinate when nodes must propagate and refresh data.

Thus, the way in which a node **A** would write data which are then read by a node **B** is:

A writes data to region **R**

A propagates data in region **R**

(Implicit:) **A** and **B** synchronize; **B** becomes aware that new data in region **R** are available

B refreshes data in region **R**

B reads data in region **R**

The granularity of caching is known as the *consistency unit*. This defines both the size and the alignment of the blocks of data within the file for which the file system insures that all non-conflicting writes are merged into the file. Tasks on different nodes cannot use weak consistency and achieve consistent parallel updates

within a single consistency unit. Any conflicting writes within a single consistency
unit will be resolved by an arbitrary selection of a winning writer when the data
arrive at a server. The size of the consistency unit is implementation specific, and
is represented by the constant **SIO_CACHE_CONSISTENCY_UNIT**. Additionally, the control operation **SIO_CTL_GetConsistencyUnit** can be used to
retrieve the consistency unit for a file descriptor.[9] Applications should not make
any assumptions about the size of the consistency unit; it may vary between individual bytes, cache lines, pages, and file blocks depending upon the implementation
of the file system.

The motivation for providing weakly-consistent client caching as an option within
the parallel file system is to allow parallel applications that could benefit from a
decrease in the total amount of data being transferred between clients and servers
to exercise relatively fine-grained control over the consistency of their local caches.
SIO_CTL_Propagate and **SIO_CTL_Refresh** operations can be piggy-backed
onto synchronization steps that already exist in parallel applications. These primitives allow application programmers and toolkit developers the mechanisms necessary to ensure consistency of the local parallel file system cache, without requiring
the parallel file system to enforce any consistency model itself.

This implementation of weakly-consistent caching is only intended to cope with
sharing among the tasks of a parallel application. To avoid unintended sharing
among independent applications, traditional methods based on detecting conflicts
at open time and disabling caching or resorting to strongly-consistent caching may
be used.

Some   implementations   may   choose   not   to   provide   weak   client
cache   consistency   by   ignoring   a   **SIO_CTL_SetCachingMode**   operation   that   specifies   the   **SIO_CACHING_WEAK**   mode,   as   well   as
the   **SIO_CTL_Propagate**   and   **SIO_CTL_Refresh**   operations.   In
this   case,   the   **SIO_CTL_GetCachingMode**   should   return   a   value   of
SIO_CACHING_NONE,   **SIO_CACHING_STRONG**,   or   a   sequentially-
consistent vendor-defined caching mode as appropriate, and **SIO_CTL_Propagate**
and **SIO_CTL_Refresh** should always return success. (This way, an application
which can tolerate weakly-consistent caching will not see extraneous errors in its
absence.[10]

---

[9]Currently, this should always yield **SIO_CACHE_CONSISTENCY_UNIT**. This is intended to allow for future extensions, which may provide different consistency units within the
same implementation.

[10]Since weak caching mode can be implemented using strong caching, it is possible that an
application running on one node may see data modifications that have not yet been propagated

Note that client caching is controlled on a per-file descriptor basis, so it is possible to have a file opened with one client caching mode on one file descriptor and with a different mode on another file descriptor.

Descriptions of the **SIO_CTL_GetCachingMode**, **SIO_CTL_SetCachingMode**, **SIO_CTL_Propagate**, **SIO_CTL_Refresh**, and **SIO_CTL_GetConsistencyUnit** control operations are given in Section A.13.

Note to implementors: The routine **sio_close()** implicitly performs a **SIO_CTL_Propagate** on the file descriptor. This causes all cached writes to be exposed to the file system at the time the file is closed, if they have not been already.

A.13   Control Operations

This section describes the file control operations that can be performed using the functions **sio_control()**, **sio_open()**, **sio_test()**.

These control operations allow properties of files, file descriptors, and the file system to be set and retrieved.

Control operations are performed by invoking **sio_open()**, **sio_control()**, or **sio_test()** with the list of operations to be performed. Each operation description, an **sio_control_t**, includes the code of the operation to be performed, a pointer to the data to be manipulated by that operation, and space for a result code. In the following sections, information is provided about the various operation codes that must be implemented by file systems that conform to this API.

Operation names beginning with **SIO_CTL_** are reserved for use by this API. Operation names beginning with **SIO_CTL_VEND_** may be used by vendors to define vendor-specific operations.

A.13.1   SIO_CTL_GetSize, SIO_CTL_SetSize

Purpose

Get or set the file's logical size.

Affects

Open file

Parameter Type

Pointer to a **sio_offset_t**.

---

on a remote node. This is normal, since a weakly-consistent caching policy may expose the results of writes soon after or immediately as they occur.

Description

Applications may query and adjust the logical size (see Section A.6.1) of a file using these control operations. The **SIO_CTL_SetSize** operation causes the logical size of the file to be set to the value in the **sio_offset_t** pointed to by the *op_data* field of the **sio_control_t**. Setting a file's logical size may change the amount of storage that the file uses, but is not guaranteed to do so. An application wishing to preallocate storage for a file should use the **SIO_CTL_SetPreallocation** control operation.

The **SIO_CTL_GetSize** operation causes the logical size of the file being operated on to be placed in the **sio_offset_t** pointed to by the *op_data* member of the **sio_control_t**.

Result Values

SIO_SUCCESS

The operation succeeded.

SIO_ERR_INCORRECT_MODE

The mode of the file descriptor does not permit the operation.

SIO_ERR_IO_FAILED

A physical I/O error caused the operation to fail.

SIO_ERR_NO_SPACE

The system needs to increase the amount of storage used by the file but cannot.

A.13.2   SIO_CTL_GetAllocation

Purpose

Get the file's physical size.

Affects

Underlying file.

Parameter Type

Pointer to a **sio_offset_t**.

Description

The **SIO_CTL_GetAllocation** operation causes file's physical size (see Section A.6.1) to be placed in the **sio_offset_t** pointed to by the *op_data* field of the **sio_control_t**.

Result Values

SIO_SUCCESS
The operation succeeded.

SIO_ERR_INCORRECT_MODE
The mode of the file descriptor does not permit the operation.

SIO_ERR_IO_FAILED
A physical I/O error caused the operation to fail.

A.13.3   SIO_CTL_GetPreallocation, SIO_CTL_SetPreallocation

Purpose

Get or set amount of space preallocated for the file.

Affects

Underlying file.

Parameter Type

Pointer to a **sio_offset_t**.

Description

The **SIO_CTL_GetPreallocation** operation causes the amount of space preallocated (see Section A.6.1) for the file being operated on to be placed in the **sio_offset_t** pointed to by the *op_data* field of the **sio_control_t**.

The **SIO_CTL_SetPreallocation** operation causes the amount of space preallocated for the file being operated on to be set to the value in the **sio_offset_t** pointed to by the *op_data* field of the **sio_control_t**. A preallocation applies to an open file and will be reset to zero when the file is closed. While open, writes by other tasks that extend the physical size of the file may reduce the unconsumed preallocation.

If either the **SIO_CTL_GetPreallocation** operation or the **SIO_CTL_SetPreallocation** operation is supported, both must be supported.

Result Values

SIO_SUCCESS
The operation succeeded.

SIO_ERR_INCORRECT_MODE

> The mode of the file descriptor does not permit the operation.

SIO_ERR_IO_FAILED

> A physical I/O error caused the operation to fail.

SIO_ERR_NO_SPACE

> There isn't enough free space in the system to satisfy the request.

SIO_ERR_OP_UNSUPPORTED

> The operation is not supported by the system.

A.13.4   SIO_CTL_GetCachingMode, SIO_CTL_SetCachingMode

Purpose

> Get or set the file's caching mode.

Affects

> File descriptor.

Parameter Type

> Pointer to a **sio_caching_mode_t**.

Description

> The **SIO_CTL_GetCachingMode** operation causes the caching mode of the file descriptor to be placed in the **sio_caching_mode_t** pointed to by the *op_data* field of the **sio_control_t**.

> The **SIO_CTL_SetCachingMode** operation causes the caching mode of the file descriptor to be set to the value of the **sio_caching_mode_t** pointed to by the *op_data* field ¡of the **sio_control_t**. SIO implementations which provide support for multiple caching modes may elect not to provide support for changing the caching mode of an open file.

Result Values

SIO_SUCCESS

> The operation succeeded.

SIO_ERR_INCORRECT_MODE

> The mode of the file descriptor does not permit the operation.

SIO_ERR_ONLY_AT_OPEN

> The system does not allow the caching mode of an open file to be changed. Caching modes can only be changed as part of **sio_open()**.

SIO_ERR_OP_UNSUPPORTED

The system does not support **SIO_CTL_SetCachingMode**.

A.13.5   SIO_CTL_Propagate

Purpose

Force locally cached writes to be made visible to other nodes.

Affects

Cached writes associated with file descriptor.

Parameter Type

Pointer to a **sio_file_io_list_t**.

Description

This operation allows a task to force the parallel file system to make any data associated with a particular set of byte ranges visible to other nodes in the system (see Section A.12 for information about why this might be necessary), as specified by the **sio_file_io_list_t** pointed to by the *op_data* field of the control request. If *op_data* is **NULL**, the propagation will apply to all bytes in the file. If the *size, stride* , and *element_cnt* fields of the **sio_file_io_list_t** pointed to by the op_data field are all zero, then the set of bytes to be propagated begins at the offset specified in the *offset* field of the **sio_file_io_list_t** and continues until the end of the file.

This operation only affects those bytes written via the given file descriptor; if an application writes to a file using more than one file descriptor, it must perform a propagate operation on each of them to guarantee the dirty data become visible to other nodes. While it is guaranteed after a propagate operation completes that all locally cached writes for the specified file regions have been exposed to the rest of the file system, it is *not* guaranteed that some or all the changed data was not visible to the rest of the file system *prior to* the propagate. That is, weakly-consistent client caching implies only that cached writes will be exposed to the rest of the file system *no later than* the completion of the propagate operation.

Result Values

SIO_SUCCESS

The results of all writes on this file descriptor in the specified region(s) have been exposed to the rest of the file system.

SIO_ERR_INVALID_FILE_LIST

op_data is not **NULL** nor a pointer to a valid **sio_file_io_list_t**.

A.13.6   SIO_CTL_Refresh

Purpose

Inform the file system that locally cached data may be invalid.

Affects

Blocks in client's cache containing data for this file.

Parameter Type

Pointer to a **sio_file_io_list_t**.

Description

This operation informs the parallel file system that data cached for a file may be stale, that is, superseded by more recent writes (see Section A.12 for information about why this might be necessary). Future reads to the specified client region(s) are guaranteed to not yield data that were stale at the time the refresh operation began.[11] File region(s) are specified by the **sio_file_io_list_t** pointed to by the *op_data* field of the control request. If *op_data* is NULL, the operation will apply to all bytes in the file. If the *size*, *stride*, and *element_cnt* fields of the **sio_file_io_list_t** pointed to by the op_data field are all zero then the operation applies to the set of bytes beginning at the offset specified in the *offset* field of the **sio_file_io_list_t** and ending at the end of the file.

Result Values

SIO_SUCCESS

The regions have been refreshed.

SIO_ERR_INVALID_FILE_LIST

op_data is not **NULL** or a pointer to a valid **sio_file_io_list_t**.

A.13.7   SIO_CTL_Sync

Purpose

Force dirty data to stable storage.

---

[11]The file system may satisfy this requirement by explicitly validating all cached data in the specified region(s) with the server, or by ejecting the specified blocks from the cache entirely.

Affects

Blocks written via the file descriptor.

Parameter Type

None

Description

This operation causes all dirty blocks associated with the file descriptor to be written to stable storage. The meaning of "stable storage" is implementation specific – it may be the disk, non-volatile memory, or another mechanism that provides greater reliability than the volatile memory in the node caching the blocks. **SIO_CTL_Sync** performs a superset the operations performed by **SIO_CTL_Propagate**.

Result Values

SIO_SUCCESS

The operation succeeded.

SIO_ERR_IO_FAILED

A physical I/O error caused the operation to fail.

A.13.8   SIO_CTL_GetLayout, SIO_CTL_SetLayout

Purpose

Get or set the layout of the file data on the storage system.

Affects

Underlying file.

Parameter Type

Pointer to a **sio_layout_t**.

Description

These operations allow the layout of a file's data on the underlying storage system to be queried and modified.

The control **SIO_CTL_GetLayout** will return the layout for the underlying file, while **SIO_CTL_SetLayout** will set the layout, if possible. Implementations may choose to ignore **SIO_CTL_SetLayout** entirely, returning **SIO_ERR_OP_UNSUPPORTED**.

Result Values

> **SIO_SUCCESS**
>> The operation succeeded.
>
> **SIO_ERR_OP_ONLY_AT_CREATE**
>> The implementation only supports **SIO_CTL_SetLayout** when a file is being created.
>
> **SIO_ERR_INCORRECT_MODE**
>> The mode of the file descriptor does not permit the operation.
>
> **SIO_ERR_OP_UNSUPPORTED**
>> The operation is not supported by the system.

A.13.9   SIO_CTL_GetLabel, SIO_CTL_SetLabel

Purpose

> Get or set the file's label.

Affects

> Underlying file.

Parameter Type

> Pointer to a **sio_label_t**.

Description

> These operations allow the label associated with a file to be set and retrieved. A file's label is not interpreted by the file system. The intent is for applications to store descriptive information about a file in the a file's label, rather than in the file itself. That removes the need for file headers and the inefficiencies that go with them.
>
> The maximum size of a file's label is **SIO_MAX_LABEL_LEN**, the value of which is implementation-specific. It is guaranteed, however, to be at least as big as **SIO_MAX_NAME_LEN**, allowing any legal file name to fit in a label. This allows descriptive information that is too large to fit in a label to be stored in an auxiliary file whose name can be stored in the label of the file being described.
>
> For descriptive labels to be portable across implementations they must be no larger than the minimum allowed value for **SIO_MAX_LABEL_LEN**.

When performing **SIO_CTL_SetLabel**, the *data* field of the **sio_label_t** must contain a pointer to a buffer, the *length* field must contain the length of that buffer. If the length given is greater than **SIO_MAX_LABEL_LEN**, **SIO_ERR_INVALID_LABEL** will be returned and the operation will fail. After a **SIO_CTL_SetLabel** operation successfully completes, the length of the file's label will be equal to *length*, and the file's label data will be the same as the contents of the buffer.

When performing **SIO_CTL_GetLabel**, the *data* field of the **sio_label_t** must contain a pointer to a buffer to be filled in with the file's current label data, and the *length* field must contain the size of that buffer. If the buffer is too small to contain the label, the **SIO_ERR_INVALID_LABEL** error code will be returned, *length* will be set to the actual length of the label, and the contents of the data buffer will be unspecified. If the buffer is at least as large as the current file label, **SIO_SUCCESS** will be returned, *length* will be set to the actual length of the label (as set by a previous call to **SIO_CTL_SetLabel**, or to zero if the file's label has never been set), and the data buffer will be filled with that many bytes of label data. If the buffer is larger than the label, the contents of the bytes in the buffer following the label are unspecified.

Result Values

SIO_SUCCESS

The operation succeeded.

SIO_ERR_INCORRECT_MODE

The mode of the file descriptor does not permit the operation.

SIO_ERR_INVALID_LABEL

The length of the new label being set exceeds **SIO_MAX_LABEL_LEN**, or the length of the label being retrieved exceeds the size of the application-provided buffer.

SIO_ERR_IO_FAILED

A physical I/O error caused the operation to fail.

SIO_ERR_NO_SPACE

The system needs to increase the amount of storage used by the file but cannot.

A.13.10   SIO_CTL_GetConsistencyUnit

Purpose

Get the size of the cache consistency unit.

Affects

File system.

Parameter Type

Pointer to a **sio_size_t**.

Description

This operation returns the size of the cache consistency unit. The consistency unit defines the granularity of cache consistency under weak caching, as described in Section A.12.

Result Values

SIO_SUCCESS

The operation succeeded.

A.14 Extension Support

Support for querying the presence of extensions is part of the basic API, and must be implemented by all conforming implementations, even if no extensions are supported by an implementation. Applications may determine either statically (described in Section A.14.1) or dynamically (via the **sio_query_extension()** function, described in Section A.14.2) whether or not an extension is supported by the implementation of the API. Sample code indicating the proper way to check for the presence of extensions is included in SectionA.14.3.

A.14.1 Static Constants

Extension Support Constants   Applications may statically determine via constants which extensions are supported by a given implementation. For each extension that an implementation is capable of supporting, the implementation should define a constant which indicates that the extension is supported, that it is not, or that the support status cannot be determined during compilation. These constants are of the form **SIO_EXT_*NAME*_SUPPORTED**, where *NAME* is the name of the extension. Each of these constants must be set to one of the following values:

SIO_EXT_ABSENT (equal to 0) The extension is not supported.

SIO_EXT_PRESENT The extension is supported.

SIO_EXT_MAYBE The extension might be supported. A dynamic check must be used to make a final determination.

The **SIO_EXT_ABSENT** constant must be zero so that existence of extensions which the implementation is completely unaware of can be checked.[12] The values of the other constants are unspecified.

If the static constant for an extension is equal to **SIO_EXT_ABSENT**, then the application cannot depend on any of the functions or definitions that are a part of the extension (including the extension ID) being present. If the static constant is **SIO_EXT_PRESENT** or **SIO_EXT_MAYBE**, then the functions and definitions that are a part of the extension will be present. In the case of **SIO_EXT_MAYBE**, the functions and definitions may be usable only if the extension is determined to be available at run-time.

The definition of **SIO_EXT_ABSENT** allows for implementations to conform to this API without requiring updates for any new extensions which may be added in the future. The **SIO_EXT_MAYBE** value allows for binary compatibility across different versions of an implementation that support different sets of extensions.

Extension Identifiers Extension identifiers are constants of the form **SIO_EXT_***NAME*, where *NAME* is the name of the extension. Extension identifiers with names of the form **SIO_EXT_VEND_***NAME* are reserved for use by vendors, and all other extension names are reserved for future use by this API.

An implementation must define an extension identifier for each extension which is supported or may be supported by that implementation as determined by the value of the extension's **SIO_EXT_***NAME***_SUPPORTED** constant described in Section A.14.1. Extension identifiers can be given to **sio_query_extension()** to check whether or not the extensions in question are actually available. [13]

A.14.2   sio_query_extension

Purpose

Determine whether or not an extension is supported.

Syntax

#include <sio_fs.h>

---

[12]The C preprocessor will expand an unknown definition as zero when used in preprocessor directives, and this allows undefined extension support macros to match **SIO_EXT_ABSENT**.

[13]It is not necessary to call **sio_query_extension()** for extensions whose extension support constants indicate that they are present, but it is safe to do so and **sio_query_extension()** must indicate that those extensions are supported.

sio_return_t sio_query_extension(sio_extension_id_t *ExtID*);

Parameters

ExtID Extension identifier of extension being queried.

Description

This function takes an extension identifier and returns **SIO_SUCCESS** if the extension is supported by this implementation, or **SIO_ERR_INVALID_EXTENSION** if the extension is not supported, or if the identifier is not recognized as valid.

Return Codes

SIO_SUCCESS

The extension is supported by the implementation.

SIO_ERR_INVALID_EXTENSION

ExtID contains an invalid or unsupported extension ID.

A.14.3   Sample Code to Check for Extension Presence

A code fragment which queries the presence of an extension might look like:

```
    int fooext_is_present;
    sio_return_t rc;

#if SIO_EXT_FOO_SUPPORTED == SIO_EXT_ABSENT
    fooext_is_present = 0;
#elif SIO_EXT_FOO_SUPPORTED == SIO_EXT_PRESENT
    fooext_is_present = 1;
#else /* SIO_EXT_FOO_SUPPORTED == SIO_EXT_MAYBE */
    rc = sio_query_extension(SIO_EXT_FOO);
    switch(rc) {
      case SIO_SUCCESS:
        fooext_is_present = 1;
        break;
      case SIO_ERR_INVALID_EXTENSION:
        fooext_is_present = 0;
        break;
      default:
        fooext_is_present = 0;
```

```
        printf("can't determine if extension foo is present (%s)\n",
          sio_error_string(rc));
    }
#endif /* SIO_EXT_FOO_SUPPORTED == SIO_EXT_ABSENT */
```

A.15   Extension: Collective I/O

Static Constant: SIO_EXT_COLLECTIVE_SUPPORTED

Extension ID: SIO_EXT_COLLECTIVE

A.15.1   Motivation

As demonstrated by Kotz et al., collective I/O allows for a distributed batching process which can greatly enhance I/O performance in a parallel file system. Semantically, by declaring an I/O or set of I/Os to be part of a single, collective I/O, an application is indicating to the file system that the relative ordering of the components of the collective I/O is irrelevant, since no portion of the application awaiting a component of the collective I/O can make any progress until the entirety of the collective I/O completes. File systems can take advantage of this to drastically reorder I/O components to reduce overall latency, at the potential cost of increasing the latency of component I/Os (the constraint which prevents this optimization from occurring in the standard case).

A.15.2   High Level Look

To initiate a collective I/O one task of the application requests that a new collective I/O handle be created. This is what we refer to as "defining" the collective I/O. At this time, the application indicates the number of participants, whether the collective I/O is a read or write operation (we do not allow collective mixed read/writes), the number of iterations of the collective I/O, and optionally indicates what portions of the file will be operated on. Specification of file regions at define time provides (ordered) file access hints which, if properly given, allow the file system to implement performance optimizations.

Each participant "joins" an iteration of the collective I/O by providing the handle created by the define operation, the file descriptor, the portions of the file they wish to read or write, the source/destination memory locations, their participant identifier, and a sequence number indicating which iteration of the collective I/O they are joining.

Note that the application will generally need to pass the handle from the task that defined the collective I/O to any other tasks that participate in the I/O. A single task may participate multiple times in a given collective I/O iteration by joining that iteration multiple times using different participant numbers. Prior to joining a collective I/O operation, a task must open the file being accessed so a file descriptor for the file is available for use with the join call.

A.15.3   New Data Types

sio_coll_handle_t   This is a 64-bit integral type used as an abstract handle to represent a collective I/O. We explicitly define the format and size of this datatype because applications will need to use their own communications mechanisms to pass these among tasks on different nodes, and therefore need to be aware of size and network ordering issues.

sio_coll_participant_t   This is an unsigned integral type with the range $[0 \ldots$ **SIO_MAX_COLL_PARTICIPANTS**$]$ which is used in the definition of a collective I/O operation to specify the number of participants, and in the collective I/O join to identify the participant joining the collective I/O iteration.

These values have no meaning or permanence beyond the collective I/O in which they are used.

sio_coll_iteration_t   This is an unsigned integral type with the range $[0 \ldots$ **SIO_MAX_COLL_ITERATIONS**$]$ which is used in the definition of a collective I/O operation to specify the number of iterations, and in the collective I/O join to identify the iteration being joined.

A.15.4   New Range Constants

SIO_MAX_COLL_ITERATIONS   This constant specifies the maximum number of iterations that a collective I/O can describe. The minimum value is 1, and the recommended value is 128.

SIO_MAX_COLL_PARTICIPANTS   This constant specifies the maximum number of participants that can take part in a collective I/O. The minimum value is 16, but the recommended value is at least 256.

SIO_MAX_COLL_OUTSTANDING   This constant specifies the maximum number of outstanding collective I/O requests that one task can have at any given time. The minimum value is 1, and the recommended value is at least 512.

A.15.5   New Functions

Two new functions are added by the collective I/O extension: **sio_coll_define()** and **sio_coll_join()**, which are described in §A.15.5 and §A.15.5, respectively.

sio_coll_define

Purpose

Define a new collective I/O and get a handle to refer to it.

Syntax

#include <sio_fs.h>

sio_return_t sio_coll_define(int *FileDescriptor,*
              sio_coll_iteration_t *NumIterations,*
              const sio_file_io_list_t **FileList,*
              sio_count_t *FileListLength,*
              sio_size_t *IterationStride,*
              sio_mode_t *ReadWrite,*
              sio_coll_participant_t *NumParticipants,*
              sio_coll_handle_t **Handle);*

Parameters

FileDescriptor The file descriptor of an open file.

NumIterations The number of times the collective I/O will be repeated.

FileList Specification of file data to be read or written.

FileListLength Number of elements in *FileList*. This may be zero.

IterationStride A value that modifies the location of the file data to be read or written as specified in *FileList* based on the iteration in progress.

ReadWrite One of **SIO_MODE_READ** or **SIO_MODE_WRITE**.

NumParticipants The number of participants in each iteration of the collective I/O.

Handle On success, returns the handle of the newly-defined collective I/O.

Description

This interface creates a new handle for a collective I/O, and returns it in *Handle*. The *NumIterations* parameter indicates the number of times the collective I/O will be performed. The application programmer may choose to disclose the portions of the file which will be affected in *FileList*, or *FileListLength* may be zero in which case the file system must wait for a participant to call **sio_coll_join()** before its workload is known.

In cases where the collective I/O will be performed more than once and the application programmer indicates what portions of the file will be operated on, it is often true that the access patterns for each iteration are identical except for their offsets from the beginning of the file, and that the offsets are based on the iteration being performed. The *IterationStride* parameter lets the programmer express these common cases without having to separate them into individual collective I/O operations. If i is the iteration number (starting at iteration 0), the *offset* field in each **sio_file_io_list_t** structure of the *FileList* parameter would have the value:

$$offset_i = offset_0 + (i \times IterationStride)$$

For example, if *FileList* has two entries with the values (*offset*=0, *size*=2, *stride*=3, *element_cnt*=4) and (*offset*=100, *size*=5, *stride*=0, *element_cnt*=1), the programmer is hinting that the first iteration will access bytes (0, 1, 3, 4, 6, 7, 9, 10, 100, 101, 103, 104, 105) in the file. If *IterationStride* is zero, the second iteration will access the same bytes. However, if *IterationStride* is 50, the second iteration will access bytes (50, 51, 53, 54, 56, 57, 59, 60, 150, 151, 153, 154, 155) – the *offset* components of the *FileList* structures are adjusted based on the iteration (1) and the *IterationStride* (50).

Note that **sio_coll_join()** must always be called by each participant and must provide a *FileList* for that participant's portion of the collective I/O, whether or not *FileListLength* is zero in **sio_coll_define()**. Providing a description of the entire operation in *FileList* simply provides a way for the file system to optimize scheduling of the transfer.

Return Codes

SIO_SUCCESS
The function succeeded.

SIO_ERR_INCORRECT_MODE
The mode of the file descriptor does not permit the I/O.

SIO_ERR_INVALID_DESCRIPTOR
FileDescriptor does not refer to a valid file descriptor created by **sio_open()**.

SIO_ERR_INVALID_FILE_LIST
The file regions described by *FileList* are invalid, e.g. they contain illegal offsets.

SIO_ERR_MAX_COLL_ITERATIONS_EXCEEDED

The number of iterations described by *NumIterations* exceeds the maximum allowed as defined by **SIO_MAX_COLL_ITERATIONS**.

SIO_ERR_MAX_COLL_PARTICIPANTS_EXCEEDED

The number of participants described by *NumParticipants* exceeds the maximum allowed as defined by **SIO_MAX_COLL_PARTICIPANTS**.

sio_coll_join

Purpose

Initiate an asynchronous transfer as part of a collective I/O.

Syntax

#include <sio_fs.h>

sio_return_t sio_coll_join(int *FileDescriptor*, **sio_coll_handle_t** *Handle*,
　　　　　　　sio_coll_participant_t *Participant*,
　　　　　　　sio_coll_iteration_t *Iteration*,
　　　　　　　const sio_file_io_list_t **FileList*,
　　　　　　　sio_count_t *FileListLength*,
　　　　　　　const sio_mem_io_list_t **MemoryList*,
　　　　　　　sio_count_t *MemoryListLength*,
　　　　　　　sio_async_handle_t **AsyncHandle*);

Parameters

FileDescriptor The file descriptor of the open file where the collective I/O is being performed.

Handle The handle provided by **sio_coll_define()** for this collective operation.

Participant The identifier for this participant. This is a number in the range [0...(*NumParticipants* − 1)], where *NumParticipants* is the number of participants that was provided to **sio_coll_define()**.

Iteration Which iteration of the collective I/O the participant is joining.

FileList Specification of file data to be read or written by this participant.

FileListLength Number of elements in *FileList*.

MemoryList Memory locations read or written by this I/O component.

MemoryListLength Number of elements in *MemoryList*.

AsyncHandle Handle returned by the operation, which can be used later to determine the status of the I/O, to wait for its completion, or to cancel it.

Description

This interface initiates a component of a collective I/O. At this point, the file system may immediately begin transferring data to or from these memory locations, or it may choose to wait for other participants to join the collective I/O. The number of participants in each iteration of the collective I/O must equal the *NumParticipants* specified to **sio_coll_define()**, i.e. **sio_coll_join()** must be called *NumParticipants* times for each iteration. **sio_coll_join()** returns immediately and **sio_async_status_any()** or **sio_async_cancel_all()** must be called with the *AsyncHandle* to complete or cancel the operation.

Note that calls to **sio_async_status_any()** or **sio_async_cancel_all()** reflect only this participant's portion of this iteration of the collective I/O, as identified by the value of *AsyncHandle*. Also, calls to the **sio_async_status_any()** and **sio_async_cancel_all()** may contain multiple *AsyncHandles*, but the *AsyncHandles* returned by the **sio_coll_join()** may not be mixed with *AsyncHandles* returned by **sio_async_sg_read()** or **sio_async_sg_write()** functions in the same call.

To clarify some of the parameters a bit further, the *FileDescriptor* parameter must refer to the same file as was specified by the *FileDescriptor* in the **sio_coll_define()** for this collective operation. However, the actual *FileDescriptor* value may differ from the one in the **sio_coll_define()** because the task making the join call may be different from the task that defined the collective operation.

If the **sio_coll_define()** for this collective operation contained information about the bytes that would be accessed in its *FileList* parameter, then to realize performance gains the *FileList* parameter in this **sio_coll_join()** call should contain bytes that appeared in the original **sio_coll_define()** *FileList* parameter. If this is not the case, or if the **sio_coll_define()** did not contain file region information, the bytes specified in the **sio_coll_join()** *FileList* parameter will still be read or written, but potentially with poorer performance.

Finally, note that there is no parameter in the **sio_coll_join()** call corresponding to the **sio_coll_define()** parameter *IterationStride*. In the join, it is the responsibility of the application programmer to adjust the *FileList* offset values as appropriate for the iteration being joined.

Return Codes

SIO_SUCCESS
The function succeeded.

SIO_ERR_INCORRECT_MODE
The mode of the file descriptor does not permit the I/O.

SIO_ERR_INVALID_DESCRIPTOR
FileDescriptor does not refer to a valid file descriptor created by **sio_open()**, or does not refer to the file specified to **sio_call_define()** when the collective I/O was created.

SIO_ERR_INVALID_FILE_LIST
The file regions described by *FileList* are invalid, e.g. they contain illegal offsets. Implementations may defer returning this error until **sio_async_status_any()** is invoked on the I/O.

SIO_ERR_INVALID_HANDLE
Handle is not the handle for a collective I/O.

SIO_ERR_INVALID_ITERATION
Iteration is not valid, either because it is greater than the number of iterations specified when the collective I/O was created or between the task already joined that iteration of the I/O.

SIO_ERR_INVALID_MEMORY_LIST
The memory regions described by *MemoryList* are invalid, e.g. they contain illegal addresses. Implementations may defer returning this error until **sio_async_status_any()** is invoked on the I/O.

SIO_ERR_INVALID_PARTICIPANT
Participant is not valid because it is greater than the number of participants specified when the collective I/O was created.

SIO_ERR_MAX_ASYNC_OUTSTANDING_EXCEEDED
The I/O request could not be initiated because doing so would cause the calling task's number of outstanding asynchronous I/Os to exceed the limit.

SIO_ERR_UNEQUAL_LISTS
The number of bytes in *MemoryList* and *FileList* are not equal. Implementations may defer returning this error until **sio_async_status_any()** is invoked on the I/O.

A.16 Extension: Fast Copy

Static Constant: SIO_EXT_FAST_COPY_SUPPORTED

Extension ID: SIO_EXT_FAST_COPY

This extension provides a low-level versioning mechanism by allowing an efficient "snapshot" of a file's current contents to be created. This is done via the **sio_control()** operation **SIO_CTL_FastCopy**.

The **SIO_CTL_FastCopy** control operation creates snapshots by replacing the contents of a parallel file (created and opened with **sio_open()**), with the contents of the file being duplicated. Since snapshots are normal parallel files, they can be accessed in all of the ways that parallel files can be accessed. That is, snapshots created by **SIO_CTL_FastCopy** can be read, written, operated on by controls, etc.

If a higher-level file system library is using **SIO_CTL_FastCopy** to provide versioning support, that library is responsible for managing the translation between its notion of versions and that provided by the **SIO_CTL_FastCopy** mechanism. For instance, the higher-level library must translate between the file name and version number that the application supplies and the actual parallel name for that snapshot. The higher-level library must also enforce its own version reference semantics (perhaps preventing write access to old versions of the file, or taking other actions as necessary).

A.16.1 SIO_CTL_FastCopy

Purpose

Efficiently copy the contents of one file into another.

Affects

Underlying file.

Parameter Type

Pointer to an **int** which is a file descriptor for the open parallel file to be used as the source of the efficient copy operation.

Description

This operation performs an efficient copy of the contents of one parallel file into another. The source file descriptor is specified by the **int** pointed to by the *op_data* member of the **sio_control_t**. The destination file is specified by the *Name* argument to **sio_open()** or by the *FileDescriptor* argument to **sio_control()**.

The implementation of the efficient copy operation performed by this function is intended to use copy-on-write or similar techniques to minimize data duplication.

If the **SIO_CTL_FastCopy** operation fails or is not supported, an error will be returned and the source and destination files will be unmodified.

Effects of Successful Operation on the Source File

The source file's data are unmodified by the **SIO_CTL_FastCopy** operation.

The source file's physical size at the conclusion of the **SIO_CTL_FastCopy** operation is unspecified.

None of the source file's other file or file descriptor attributes (as defined by this API) are modified by the **SIO_CTL_FastCopy** operation.

If vendors define new attributes, the effect of **SIO_CTL_FastCopy** on the source file with respect to those attributes should be specified.

Hints about expected use of the source file are unmodified by the **SIO_CTL_FastCopy** operation.

Effects of Successful Operation on the Destination File

The destination file's logical size is set to the source file's logical size, and the destination file's contents are made to appear identical (e.g. if accessed with **sio_sg_read()**) to those of the source file. If **SIO_CTL_SetSize** is specified in the same set of control operations as **SIO_CTL_FastCopy**, the resulting size of the destination file is undefined.

The destination file's physical size at the conclusion of the **SIO_CTL_FastCopy** operation is unspecified.

The destination file's label is made identical to the source file's label.

The destination file's other file attributes (preallocation and layout) are not affected.

None of the destination's file descriptor attributes (caching mode and consistency unit) are affected. Note that if a weak client caching mode is in use on the destination file, the destination file's new contents may need to be propagated (with **SIO_CTL_Propagate**) before they can be used by other clients.

If vendors define new attributes, the effect of **SIO_CTL_FastCopy** on the destination file with respect to those attributes should be specified.

The effect of the **SIO_CTL_FastCopy** operation on hints about expected use of the destination file is unspecified. Portable applications or libraries that wish to hint about future accesses to the destination file should cancel all outstanding hints on the destination file after performing a **SIO_CTL_FastCopy** operation and then reissue hints as appropriate.

Result Values

> **SIO_SUCCESS**
>
>> The function succeeded.
>
> **SIO_ERR_INVALID_DESCRIPTOR**
>
>> The file descriptor for the source file is invalid.
>
> **SIO_ERR_NO_SPACE**
>
>> There isn't enough free space to perform a fast copy.
>
> **SIO_ERR_OP_UNSUPPORTED**
>
>> Fast copy is not supported by the implementation for files with the attributes of the source file and/or destination file.

A.17   Result Codes for sio_return_t

This section describes some error and return codes that the parallel file system may wish to return. As discussed in the Data Types section, implementors should feel free to add whatever additional codes they see fit, and should make **sio_error_string()** aware of them.

SIO_SUCCESS

> The operation completed successfully. The value of **SIO_SUCCESS** must always be 0.

SIO_ERR_ALREADY_EXISTS

> The file name to be created already exists.

SIO_ERR_CONTROL_FAILED

> One or more of the control operations requested by **sio_control()**, **sio_open()**, or **sio_test()** was unsuccessful.

SIO_ERR_CONTROL_NOT_ATTEMPTED

> A control operation requested by **sio_control()**, **sio_open()**, or **sio_test()** was not attempted.

SIO_ERR_CONTROL_NOT_ON_TEST

The control operation cannot be used with **sio_test()**.

SIO_ERR_CONTROL_WOULD_HAVE_SUCCEEDED

The control operation would have succeeded but the function performing the control failed.

SIO_ERR_CONTROLS_CLASH

The list of controls contains combinations of operations that are incompatible.

SIO_ERR_FILE_NOT_FOUND

The specified file did not exist.

SIO_ERR_FILE_OPEN

The operation failed because the file was open.

SIO_ERR_INCORRECT_MODE

The mode of the file descriptor does not permit the operation or function.

SIO_ERR_INVALID_CLASS

The hint class is not valid.

SIO_ERR_INVALID_DESCRIPTOR

A file descriptor argument was not a valid parallel file descriptor.

SIO_ERR_INVALID_EXTENSION

An invalid extension identifier was given, or the indicated extension is not supported.

SIO_ERR_INVALID_FILE_LIST

The file list argument is invalid (e.g contains illegal offsets).

SIO_ERR_INVALID_FILENAME

A file name argument did not contain a legal file name (e.g. it was too long).

SIO_ERR_INVALID_HANDLE

A handle argument does not contain a valid handle.

SIO_ERR_INVALID_ITERATION

The iteration argument is invalid.

SIO_ERR_INVALID_MEMORY_LIST

The memory list argument is invalid (e.g. contains an illegal address).

SIO_ERR_INVALID_PARTICIPANT

The participant number provided is not valid because it is greater than the number of participants specified when the collective I/O was created.

SIO_ERR_IO_CANCELED

An asynchronous I/O did not complete because it was canceled while in progress.

SIO_ERR_IO_FAILED

A physical I/O error occurred.

SIO_ERR_IO_IN_PROGRESS

An asynchronous I/O has not yet completed.

SIO_ERR_MAX_ASYNC_OUTSTANDING_EXCEEDED

The I/O request could not be initiated because doing so would cause the calling task's number of outstanding asynchronous I/Os to exceed the limit.

SIO_ERR_MAX_COLL_ITERATIONS_EXCEEDED

The number of iterations specified for a collective I/O exceeds the limit.

SIO_ERR_MAX_COLL_OUTSTANDING_EXCEEDED

The I/O request could not be initiated because doing so would cause the calling task's number of outstanding collective I/O's to exceed the limit.

SIO_ERR_MAX_COLL_PARTICIPANTS_EXCEEDED

The number of participants specified for a collective I/O exceeds the limit.

SIO_ERR_MAX_OPEN_EXCEEDED

The file could not be opened because doing so would cause the calling task's number of open files to exceed the limit.

SIO_ERR_MIXED_COLL_AND_ASYNC

The implementation does allow asynchronous I/O handles created by **sio_coll_define()** to be passed to functions in the same list as handles from **sio_async_sg_read()** and **sio_async_sg_write()**.

SIO_ERR_NO_SPACE

An operation that would allocate more storage to a file failed because no storage could be allocated.

SIO_ERR_ONLY_AT_CREATE

The control operation may only be specified during a call to **sio_open()** which is creating a file.

SIO_ERR_ONLY_AT_OPEN

The control operation may only be specified during a call to **sio_open()**.

SIO_ERR_OP_UNSUPPORTED

The parallel file system has elected to not support this interface. Note that some interfaces may not be supported, but implementations can choose to return **SIO_SUCCESS** for all cases instead.

SIO_ERR_UNEQUAL_LISTS

The number of bytes in the memory and file lists arguments to an I/O operation are not the same.

A.18 Sample Derived Interfaces

This section describes some simple interfaces which could easily be created using the interfaces provided by this API. These derived interfaces are *not* a part of this API, and are intended only as examples of interfaces which could be provided by high level libraries.

If a high level library provides interfaces similar (or identical) to the sample interfaces presented here, those interfaces should be named in accordance with the rest of the interfaces provided by that library. In other words, *use of the names given here is strongly discouraged.*

A.18.1 Synchronous I/O

Routines

> sio_return_t sample_read(int *FileDescriptor*, sio_addr_t *BufferPointer*,
> sio_offset_t *Offset*, sio_size_t *Count*,
> sio_transfer_len_t **BytesRead*);

> sio_return_t sample_write(int *FileDescriptor*, sio_addr_t *BufferPointer*,
> sio_offset_t *Offset*, sio_size_t *Count*,
> sio_transfer_len_t **BytesWritten*);

> sio_return_t sample_read_io_list(int *FileDescriptor*,
> sio_addr_t *BufferPointer*,
> sio_file_io_list_t **FileList*,

sio_count_t *FileListLength*,
sio_transfer_len_t *BytesRead);

sio_return_t sample_write_io_list(int *FileDescriptor*,
sio_addr_t *BufferPointer*,
sio_file_io_list_t *FileList,
sio_count_t *FileListLength*,
sio_transfer_len_t *BytesWritten);

sio_return_t sample_read_mem_list(int *FileDescriptor*,
sio_mem_io_list_t *MemoryList,
sio_count_t *MemoryListLength*
sio_offset_t *Offset*,
sio_transfer_len_t *BytesRead);

sio_return_t sample_write_mem_list(int *FileDescriptor*,
sio_mem_io_list_t *MemoryList,
sio_count_t *MemoryListLength*
sio_offset_t *Offset*,
sio_transfer_len_t *BytesWritten);

Parameters

FileDescriptor The file descriptor of an open parallel file.

BufferPointer Memory address of contiguous buffer containing data to be written or to contain data being read.

Offset Starting file offset from which to read or at which to write.

Count Number of bytes to read or write.

BytesRead Number of bytes actually read.

BytesWritten Number of bytes actually written.

FileList Description of strided regions within the file.

FileListLength Number of valid elements to use in *FileList*.

MemoryList Description of strided regions within the memory buffer.

MemoryListLength Number of valid elements to use in *MemoryList*.

Description

These functions would provide a simplified synchronous I/O interface. They may be implemented as wrappers which would convert the given arguments into **sio_mem_io_list_t** and **sio_file_io_list_t** structures (as necessary) and invoke **sio_sg_read()** or **sio_sg_write()**.

The functions **sample_read()** and **sample_write()** would transfer data between a single contiguous memory buffer and a single contiguous region of the file. The functions **sample_read_io_list()** and **sample_write_io_list()** would use a single contiguous memory buffer, but a strided region within the file. Similarly, **sample_read_mem_list()** and **sample_write_mem_list()** would use a contiguous file region, but a strided region within the memory buffer.

A.18.2   Asynchronous I/O

Routines

> **sio_return_t sample_async_read(int** *FileDescriptor,*
> > **sio_addr_t** *BufferPointer,*
> > **sio_offset_t** *Offset,* **sio_size_t** *Count,*
> > **sio_async_handle_t** *Handle);

> **sio_return_t sample_async_write(int** *FileDescriptor,*
> > **sio_addr_t** *BufferPointer,*
> > **sio_offset_t** *Offset,* **sio_size_t** *Count,*
> > **sio_async_handle_t** *Handle);

> **sio_return_t sample_async_read_io_list(int** *FileDescriptor,*
> > **sio_addr_t** *BufferPointer,*
> > **sio_file_io_list_t** **FileList,*
> > **sio_count_t** *FileListLength*
> > **sio_async_handle_t** *Handle);

> **sio_return_t sample_async_write_io_list(int** *FileDescriptor,*
> > **sio_addr_t** *BufferPointer,*
> > **sio_file_io_list_t** **FileList,*
> > **sio_count_t** *FileListLength*
> > **sio_async_handle_t** *Handle);

> **sio_return_t sample_async_read_mem_list(int** *FileDescriptor,*
> > **sio_mem_io_list_t** **MemoryList,*
> > **sio_count_t** *MemoryListLength*
> > **sio_offset_t** *Offset,*
> > **sio_async_handle_t** *Handle);

> **sio_return_t sample_async_write_mem_list(int** *FileDescriptor,*
> **sio_mem_io_list_t** **MemoryList,*
> **sio_count_t** *MemoryListLength*
> **sio_offset_t** *Offset,*
> **sio_async_handle_t** *Handle);

Parameters

FileDescriptor The file descriptor of an open parallel file.

BufferPointer Memory address of contiguous buffer containing data to be written or to contain data being read.

Offset Starting file offset from which to read or at which to write.

Count Number of bytes to read or write.

BytesRead Number of bytes actually read.

BytesWritten Number of bytes actually written.

FileList Description of strided regions within the file.

FileListLength Number of valid elements to use in *FileList*.

MemoryList Description of strided regions within the memory buffer.

MemoryListLength Number of valid elements to use in *MemoryList*.

Handle Handle for asynchronous I/O that can later be used to test its status.

Description

These routines would provide a simplified asynchronous I/O interface. They may be implemented as wrappers which would convert the given arguments into **sio_mem_io_list_t** and **sio_file_io_list_t** structures (as necessary) and invoke **sio_async_sg_read()** or **sio_async_sg_write()**.

These functions would take arguments similar to those given to the simplified synchronous functions, and perform similar actions.

A.18.3   Cache Consistency

Functions

> **sio_return_t sample_propagate(int** *FileDescriptor,* **sio_offset_t** *Offset,*
> **sio_size_t** *Length*);

> **sio_return_t sample_refresh(int** *FileDescriptor,* **sio_offset_t** *Offset,*
> **sio_size_t** *Length*);

Parameters

FileDescriptor File descriptor to which cache consistency action applies.

Offset Starting file offset affected by consistency action.

Length Number of bytes affected by consistency action.

Description

These functions would perform cache consistency actions on the specified region of the file associated with the given file descriptor. It may be implemented as wrappers which would invoke **sio_control()** to perform the appropriate **SIO_CTL_Propagate** or **SIO_CTL_Refresh** operation.

Acknowledgments

Many of the ideas presented in the 0.1 draft were developed in discussions with many different people. Among these are Dror Feitelson, Yarsun Hsu, and Marc Snir of IBM Research, Bob Curran, Joe Kavaky, and Jeff Lucash of IBM Power Parallel Division, and Daniel Stodolsky of CMU, David Kotz of Dartmouth, and David Payne and Brad Rullman of Intel SSD. Also contributing were members of the SIO community as a whole who participated in the discussions we had in the first half of 1995.

The second draft, version 0.2, reflected comments made by Dror Feitelson, Marc Snir, Jeff Lucash, and Bob Curran of IBM.

The third draft, version 0.3, incorporating asynchronous and return-by-reference interface variants and client caching control, reflects comments from Adam Beguelin, Dave O'Halleron, Jaspal Subhlok, and Thomas Stricker of CMU, December 1995.

The fourth draft, version 0.41, was presented to the SIO Operating Systems Working Group at Princeton on 8 February 1996.

The fifth draft, version 0.52, was presented to the SIO technical committee meeting at Chicago on 2 April 1996. It incorporates comments and results of discussion from the Princeton workshop and specific detailed comments from Tom Cormen of Dartmouth.

The sixth draft, version 0.54, was presented at the SIO technical meeting held at Argonne National Laboratory on May 13-14, 1996.

The seventh draft, version 0.60, was presented at the meeting of the SIO Operating Systems Working Group, held at Carnegie Mellon University on July 2, 1996.

The eighth and ninth drafts, 0.62 and 0.63 were presented and discussed at the meeting of the SIO Operating Systems Working Group at Princeton University on August 8-9, 1996.

Version .66 was reviewed by e-mail, August 21-31, 1996.

Members of the SIO Performance Evaluation working group at UIUC reviewed and commented on the API beginning with the fifth draft. In particular, Ruth Aydt, Andrew Chien, Chris Elford, Tara Madhyastha, Dan Reed, Huseyin Simitci, and Evgenia Smirni contributed to the discussions and suggestions put forth by the UIUC group.

References

[1] ABU-SUFAH, W. *Improving the Performance of Virtual Memory Computers.* PhD thesis, Department of Computer Science, University of Illinois at Urbana-Champaign, 1979.

[2] ACHARYA, A., UYSAL, M., BENNETT, R., MENDELSON, A., BEYNON, M., HOLLINGSWORTH, J., SALTZ, J., AND SUSSMAN, A. Tuning the Performance of I/O-Intensive Parallel Applications. In *Proceedings of the Fourth ACM Workshop on I/O in Parallel and Distributed Systems* (May 1996).

[3] ADVE, S. V., COX, A. L., DWARKADAS, S., RAJAMONY, R., AND ZWAENEPOEL, W. A Comparison of Entry Consistency and Lazy Release Consistency Implementation. In *Proceedings of the 2nd IEEE Symposium on High-Performance Computer Architecture* (February 1996).

[4] ADVE, V., AND MELLOR-CRUMMEY, J. Using Integer Sets for Data-Parallel pProgram Analysis and Optimization. In *Proceedings of the SIGPLAN'98 Conference on Programming Language Design and Implementation (PLDI)* (Montreal, CA, June 1998).

[5] AFEWORK, A., BEYNON, M. D., BUSTAMANTE, F., DEMARZO, A., FERREIRA, R., MILLER, R., SILBERMAN, M., SALTZ, J., SUSSMAN, A., AND TSANG, H. Digital Dynamic Telepathology - the Virtual Microscope. In *Proceedings of the 1998 AMIA Annual Fall Symposium* (November 1998), American Medical Informatics Association.

[6] AGBARIA, A., AND FRIEDMAN, R. Starfish: Fault-Tolerant Dynamic MPI Programs on Clusters of Workstations. In *8th IEEE International Symposium on High Performance Distributed Computing* (1999).

[7] AGRAWAL, G. A General Interprocedural Framework for Placement of Split-Phase Large Latency Operations. *IEEE Transactions on Parallel and Distributed Systems 10*, 4 (April 1999), 394–413.

[8] ALLEN, J. R., AND KENNEDY, K. Vector Register Allocation. *IEEE Transactions on Computers 41*, 10 (October 1992), 1290–1317.

[9] BAILEY, D. The NAS Parallel Benchmarks 2.0. Tech. Rep. Technical Report NAS-95-020, NASA Ames Research Center, December 1995.

[10] BAL, H. E., KAASHOEK, M. F., AND TANENBAUM, A. S. A Distributed Implementation of the Shared Data-Object Model. In *USENIX Workshop on Experiences with Building Distributed and Multiprocessor Systems* (October 1989), pp. 1–19.

[11] BARATLOO, A., DASGUPTA, P., AND KEDEM, Z. M. Calypso: A Novel Software System for Fault-Tolerant Parallel Processing on Distributed Platforms. In *4th IEEE International Symposium on High Performance Distributed Computing* (August 1995).

[12] BARNES, J., AND HUT, P. A Hierarchical $O(N \log N)$ Force Calculation Algorithm. *Nature* *324:446–449* (December 1986).

[13] BARU, C., FROST, R., LOPEZ, J., MARCIANO, R., MOORE, R., RAJASEKAR, A., AND WAN, M. Metadata Design for a Massive Data Analysis System. In *Proceedings of CASCON'96 Conference* (November, 1996).

[14] BARU, C., MOORE, R., RAJASEKAR, A., AND WAN, M. The SDSC Storage Resource Broker. In *Proceedings of the CASCON'98 Conference* (Toronto, Canada, December 1998).

[15] BATORY, D., BARNETT, J., GARZA, J., SMITH, K., TSUKUDA, K., TWICHELL, B., AND WISE, T. GENESIS: An Extensible Database Management System. *IEEE Transactions on Software Engineering 14*, 11 (November 1988), 1711–1730.

[16] BAUMANN, P., FURTADO, P., RITSCH, R., AND WIDMANN, N. Geo/Environmental and Medical Data Management in the RasDaMan System. In *Proceedings of the 23rd International Conference on Very Large Data Bases (VLDB97)* (Athens, Greece, August 1997), pp. 548–552.

[17] BECKMANN, N., KRIEGEL, H.-P., SCHNEIDER, R., AND SEEGER, B. The R^*-tree: An Efficient and Robust Access Method for Points and Rectangles. In *Proceedings of the 1990 ACM-SIGMOD Conference* (Atlantic City, NJ, May 1990), pp. 322–331.

[18] BEGUELIN, A., SELIGMAN, E., AND STEPHAN, P. Application Level Fault Tolerance in Heterogeneous Networks of Workstations. Tech. Rep. Technical Report CMU-CS-96-157, Carnegie Mellon University, August 1996.

[19] BENNETT, R., BRYANT, K., SUSSMAN, A., DAS, R., AND SALTZ, J. Jovian: A Framework for Optimizing Parallel I/O. In *Proceedings of the Scalable Parallel Libraries Conference* (Mississippi State, MS, October 1994), IEEE Computer Society Press, pp. 10–20.

[20] BERGER, M. J., AND BOKHARI, S. H. A Partitioning Strategy for Nonuniform Problems on Multiprocessors. *IEEE Transactions on Computers C-36*, 5 (May 1987), 570–580.

[21] BERRENDORF, R., BURG, H., AND DETERT, U. Performance Characteristics of Parallel Computers: Intel Paragon Case Study. *IT+TI Informationstechnik und Technische Informatik 37*, 2 (April 1995), 37–45. (In German).

[22] BERSHAD, B. N., ZEKAUSKAS, M. J., AND SAWDON, W. The Midway Distributed Shared Memory System. In *Proceedings of the IEEE COMPCON '93 Conference* (February 1993).

[23] BIANCHINI, R., KONTOTHANASSIS, L. I., PINTO, R., MARIA, M. D., ABUD, M., AND AMORIM, C. L. Hiding Communication Latency and Coherence Overhead in Software DSMs. In *Proceedings of the 7th International Conference on Architectural Support for Programming Languages and Operating Systems* (October 1996).

[24] BLUMRICH, M., DUBNICK, C., FELTEN, E., AND LI, K. Protected, User-Level DMA for the SHRIMP Network Interface. In *Proceedings of the 2nd IEEE Symposium on High-Performance Computer Architecture* (February 1996).

[25] BLUMRICH, M., LI, K., ALPERT, R., DUBNICKI, C., FELTEN, E., AND SANDBERG, J. A Virtual Memory Mapped Network Interface for the SHRIMP Multicomputer. In *Proceedings of the 21st Annual Symposium on Computer Architecture* (April 1994), pp. 142–153.

[26] BODEN, N. J., COHEN, D., FELDERMAN, R. E., KULAWIK, A. E., SEITZ, C. L., SEIZOVIC, J. N., AND SU, W.-K. Myrinet: A Gigabit-per-Second Local Area Network. *IEEE Micro 15(1):29–36* (February 1995).

[27] BORDAWEKAR, R., CHOUDHARY, A., KENNEDY, K., KOELBEL, C., AND PALECZNY, M. A Model and Compilation Strategy for Out-of-Core Data Parallel Programs. In *Proceedings of the Fifth ACM SIGPLAN Symposium on Principles and Practice of Parallel Programming* (Santa Barbara, CA, July 1995), ACM Press, pp. 1–10. Also available as the following technical reports: NPAC Technical Report SCCS-0696, CRPC Technical Report CRPC-TR94507-S, SIO Technical Report CACR SIO-104.

[28] BORDAWEKAR, R., CHOUDHARY, A., AND RAMANUJAM, J. Automatic Optimization of Communication in Compiling Out-of-Core Stencil Codes. In *Proceedings of the 10th ACM International Conference on Supercomputing* (Philadelphia, PA, May 1996), ACM Press, pp. 366–373.

[29] BORDAWEKAR, R., CHOUDHARY, A., AND RAMANUJAM, J. Compilation and Communication Strategies for Out-of-Core Programs on Distributed-Memory Machines. *Journal of Parallel and Distributed Computing 38*, 2 (November 1996), 277–288.

[30] BORDAWEKAR, R., DEL ROSARIO, J. M., AND CHOUDHARY, A. Design and Evaluation of Primitives for Parallel I/O. In *Proceedings of Supercomputing '93* (1993), pp. 452–461.

[31] BORDAWEKAR, R., THAKUR, R., AND CHOUDHARY, A. Efficient Compilation of Out-of-Core Data Parallel Programs. Tech. Rep. SCCS-622, NPAC, April 1994.

[32] BREZANY, P. *Input/Output Intensive Massively Parallel Computing*. Lecture Notes in Computer Science. Springer-Verlag, Berlin, Germany, 1997.

[33] BREZANY, P., AND CHOUDHARY, A. Techniques and Optimizations for Developing Irregular Out-of-Core Applications on Distributed Memory Systems. Tech. rep., Institute for Software Technology and Parallel Systems, University of Vienna, November 1996.

[34] BREZANY, P., CHOUDHARY, A., AND DANG, M. Parallelization of Irregular Out-of-Core Applications for Distributed Memory Systems. *High-Performance Computing and Networking 1225* (1997), 811–820.

[35] BROWN, P., TROY, R., FISHER, D., LOUIS, S., MCGRAW, J. R., AND MUSICK, R. Metadata Sharing for Balanced Performance. In *Proceedings of the First IEEE Metadata Conference* (Silver Spring, Maryland, 1996).

[36] CAO, P., FELTEN, E., AND LI, K. Application-Controlled File Caching Policies. In *Proceedings of the 1994 Summer USENIX Technical Conference* (June, 1994), pp. 171–182.

[37] CARDENAS, A. Analysis and Performance of Inverted Data Base Structures. *CACM 18*, 5 (May 1975), 253–263.

[38] CAREY, M., DEWITT, D., FRANKLIN, M., HALL, N., MCAULIFFE, M., NAUGHTON, J., SCHUH, D., SOLOMON, M., TAN, C., TSATALOS, O., WHITE, S., AND ZWILLING, M. Shoring Up Persistent Applications. In *Proceedings of the ACM SIGMOD International Conference on Management of Data* (1994), pp. 383–394.

[39] CAREY, M. J., DEWITT, D. J., GRAEFE, G., HAIGHT, D. M., RICHARDSON, J. R., SCHUH, D. T., SHEKITA, E. J., AND VANDENBERG, S. L. The EXODUS Extensible DBMS Project: An Overview. In *Readings on Object-Oriented Database Systems*, D. Zdonik, Ed. Morgan Kaufman, San Mateo, CA, 1990, pp. 474–499.

[40] CARR, S., AND KENNEDY, K. Compiler Blockability of Numerical Algorithms. In *Proceedings of Supercomputing '92* (Minneapolis, MN, November 1992).

[41] CARRETERO, J., NO, J., PARK, S., CHOUDHARY, A., AND CHEN, P. COMPASSION: A Parallel I/O Runtime System Including Chunking and Compression for Irregular Applications. In *Proceedings of the International Conference on High-Performance Computing and Networking* (April 1998).

[42] CARTER, J. B., BENNETT, J. K., , AND ZWAENEPOEL, W. Implementation and Performance of Munin. In *Proceedings of the Thirteenth Symposium on Operating Systems Principles* (October 1991), pp. 152–164.

[43] CASAS, J., CLARK, D. L., GALBIATI, P. S., KONURU, R., OTTO, S. W., PROUTY, R. M., AND WALPOLE, J. MIST: PVM with Transparent Migration and Checkpointing. Tech. rep., 3rd Annual PVM Users' Group Meeting, Pittsburgh, PA, May 1995.

[44] CERCO, C. F., AND COLE, T. User's Guide to the CE-QUAL-ICM Three-Dimensional Eutrophication Model, Release Version 1.0. Tech. Rep. EL-95-15, US Army Corps of Engineers Water Experiment Station, Vicksburg, MS, 1995.

[45] CHANG, C., MOON, B., ACHARYA, A., SHOCK, C., SUSSMAN, A., AND SALTZ, J. Titan: A High-Performance Remote-Sensing Database. In *Proceedings of the Thirteenth International Conference on Data Engineering* (Birmingham, U.K., April 1997).

[46] CHARNIAK, E. *Statistical Language Learning.* The MIT Press, 1993.

[47] CHEN, P., LEE, E., GIBSON, G., KATZ, R., AND PATTERSON, D. RAID: High-Performance, Reliable Secondary Storage. *ACM Computing Surveys 26* (June 1994), 145–185.

[48] CHEN, Y., FOSTER, I., NIEPLOCHA, J., AND WINSLETT, M. Optimizing Collective I/O Performance on Parallel Computers: A Multisystem Study. In *Proceedings of the 11th ACM International Conference on Supercomputing* (July 1997), ACM Press, pp. 28–35.

[49] CHIEN, A., CRANDALL, P., AYDT, R., AND REED, D. A. Input/Output Characteristics of Scalable Parallel Applications. In *Proceedings of SuperComputing 95* (1995).

[50] CHIPPADA, S., DAWSON, C. N., MARTÍNEZ, M. L., AND WHEELER, M. F. A Godunov-Type Finite Volume Method for the System of Shallow Water Equations. *Computer Methods in Applied Mechanics and Engineering* (1997). Also a TICAM Report 96-57, University of Texas, Austin.

[51] CHIPPADA, S., DAWSON, C. N., MARTÍNEZ, M. L., AND WHEELER, M. F. A Projection Method for Constructing a Mass Conservative Velocity Field. *Computer Methods in Applied Mechanics and Engineering* (1997). Also a TICAM Report 97-09, University of Texas, Austin.

[52] CHIUEH, T., AND DENG, P. Efficient Checkpoint Mechanisms for Massively Parallel Machines. In *26th International Symposium on Fault-Tolerant Computing* (June 1996).

[53] CHOUDHARY, A., BORDAWEKAR, R., HARRY, M., KRISHNAIYER, R., PONNUSAMY, R., SINGH, T., AND THAKUR, R. PASSION: Parallel and Scalable Software for Input-Output. Tech. Rep. NPAC Technical Report SCCS-636, Northeast Parallel Architectures Center, Syracuse University, September, 1994.

[54] CHOUDHARY, A., AND KANDEMIR, M. System-Level Metadata for High Performance Data Management. In *Proceedings of the Third IEEE Meta-Data Conference* (Bethesda, Maryland, April, 6–7, 1999).

[55] COLVIN, A., AND CORMEN, T. H. ViC*: A Compiler for Virtual-Memory C*. Tech. Rep. PCS-TR97-323, Dartmouth College, Computer Science, Hanover, NH, November 1997.

[56] COMER, D., AND GRIFFOEN, J. A New Design for Distributed Systems: The Remote Memory Model. In *Proceedings of the USENIX Summer Conference* (June 1990), pp. 127–135.

[57] CORBETT, P., FEITELSON, D., HSU, Y., PROST, J., SNIR, M., FINEBERG, S., NITZBERG, B., TRAVERSAT, B., AND WONG, P. MPI-IO: A Parallel I/O Interface for MPI, Version 0.2. Tech. Rep. IBM Research Report RC 19841(87784), IBM T. J. Watson Research Center, November 1994.

[58] CORBETT, P., FEITELSON, D., PROST, J.-P., ALMASI, G., BAYLOR, S. J., BOLMARCICH, A., HSU, Y., SATRAN, J., SNIR, M., COLAO, R., HERR, B., KAVAKY, J., MORGAN, T., AND ZLOTEK, A. Parallel File Systems for the IBM SP Computers. *IBM Systems Journal 34*, No. 2 (January 1995), 222–248.

[59] CORBETT, P., FIETELSON, D., FINEBERG, S., HSU, Y., NITZBERG, B., PROST, J., SNIR, M., TRAVERSAT, B., AND WONG, P. Overview of the MPI-IO Parallel I/O Interface. In *Procdings of the Third Workshop on I/O in Parallel and Distributed Systems, IPPS'95* (Santa Barbara, CA, April 1995).

[60] CORBETT, P., PROST, J.-P., DEMETRIOU, C., GIBSON, G., RIEDEL, E., ZELENKA, J., CHEN, Y., FELTEN, E., LI, K., HARTMAN, J., PETERSON, L., BERSHAD, B., WOLMAN, A., AND AYDT, R. Proposal for a Common Parallel File System Programming Interface Version 1.0, September 1996.

[61] CORBETT, P. F., BAYLOR, S. J., AND FEITELSON, D. G. Overview of the Vesta Parallel File System. In *Proceedings of the IPPS '93 Workshop on Input/Output in Parallel Computer Systems* (Newport Beach, CA, 1993), pp. 1–16. Also published in Computer Architecture News 21(5), December 1993, pages 7–14.

[62] CORBETT, P. F., AND FEITELSON, D. G. The Vesta Parallel File System. *ACM Transactions on Computer Systems 14*, 3 (August 1996), 225–264.

[63] CORBETT, P. F., FEITELSON, D. G., PROST, J.-P., AND BAYLOR, S. J. Parallel Access to Files in the Vesta File System. In *Proceedings of Supercomputing'93* (November 1993), pp. 472–481.

[64] CORMEN, T. H. *Virtual Memory for Data-Parallel Computing*. PhD thesis, Department of Electrical Engineering and Computer Science, Massachusetts Institute of Technology, 1992.

[65] CORMEN, T. H., AND COLVIN, A. ViC*: A Preprocessor for Virtual-Memory C*. Tech. Rep. PCS-TR94-243, Department of Computer Science, Dartmouth College, November 1994.

[66] CORMEN, T. H., AND HIRSCHL, M. Early Experiences in Evaluating the Parallel Disk Model with the ViC* Implementation. *Parallel Computing 23*, 4 (June 1997), 571–600.

[67] CORMEN, T. H., AND NICOL, D. M. Performing Out-of-Core FFTs on Parallel Disk Systems. *Parallel Computing 24*, 1 (January 1998), 5–20.

[68] COSTA, M., GUEDES, P., SEQUEIRA, M., NEVES, N., AND CASTRO, M. Lightweight Logging for Lazy Release Consistent Distributed Shared Memory. In *2nd Symposium on Operating Systems Design and Implementation* (October 1996).

[69] COX, A. L., DWARKADAS, S., KELEHER, P., LU, H., RAJAMONY, R., AND ZWAENEPOEL, W. Software Versus Hardware Shared-Memory Implementation: A Case Study. In *Proceedings of the 21st Annual Symposium on Computer Architecture* (April 1994), pp. 106–117.

[70] COYNE, R. A., HULEN, H., AND WATSON, R. The High Performance Storage System. In *Proceedings of Supercomputing 93* (Portland, OR, November 1993).

[71] CRANDALL, P. E., AYDT, R. A., CHIEN, A. A., AND REED, D. A. Characterization of a Suite of Input/Output Intensive Applications. In *Proceedings of Supercomputing '95* (December 1995).

[72] DAVIS, J. R. Datalinks: Managing External Data with DB2 Universal Database. IBM Corporation White Paper, August, 1997.

[73] DEL ROSARIO, J., AND CHOUDHARY, A. High Performance I/O for Parallel Computers: Problems and Prospects. *IEEE Computer* (March 1994).

[74] DEL ROSARIO, J. M., BORDAWEKAR, R., AND CHOUDHARY, A. Improved Parallel I/O via a Two-Phase Run-time Access Strategy. In *IPPS '93 Workshop on Input/Output in Parallel Computer Systems* (1993), pp. 56–70.

[75] DEWITT, D. J., KABRA, N., LUO, J., PATEL, J. M., AND YU, J.-B. Client–Server Paradise. In *Proceedings of the 20th International Conference on Very Large Data Bases (VLDB94)* (1994), Morgan Kaufmann Publishers, Incorporated, pp. 558–569.

[76] DONGARRA, J., CROZ, J. D., HAMMARLING, S., AND DUFF, I. S. A Set of Level 3 Basic Linear Algebra Subprograms. *ACM Transactions on Mathematical Software 16*, 1 (March 1990), 1–17.

[77] DREWRY, M., CONOVER, H., McCOY, S., AND GRAVES, S. Metadata: Quality vs. Quantity. In *Proceedings of the Second IEEE Metadata Conference* (1997).

[78] DU, H. C., AND SOBOLEWSKI, J. S. Disk Allocation for Cartesian Product Files on Multiple-Disk Systems. *ACM Transactions on Database Systems 7*, 1 (March 1982), 82–101.

[79] DUBNICKI, C., IFTODE, L., FELTEN, E. W., AND LI, K. Software Support for Virtual Memory-Mapped Communication. In *Proceedings of the 10th International Parallel Processing Symposium* (April 1996).

[80] DUZETT, B., AND BUCK, R. An Overview of the nCUBE 3 Supercomputer. In *Proceedings of the Fourth Symposium on the Frontiers of Massively Parallel Computation* (1992), pp. 458–464.

[81] EDJLALI, G., SUSSMAN, A., AND SALTZ, J. Interoperability of Data Parallel Runtime Libraries. In *Proceedings of the Eleventh International Parallel Processing Symposium* (April 1997), IEEE Computer Society Press.

[82] ELLIS, C. S., AND KOTZ, D. Prefetching in File Systems for MIMD Multiprocessors. In *Proceedings of the 1989 International Conference on Parallel Processing* (St. Charles, IL, August 1989), Pennsylvania State University Press, pp. I:306–314.

[83] ELNOZAHY, E. N., ALVISI, L., WANG, Y.-M., AND JOHNSON, D. B. A Survey of Rollback-Recovery Protocols in Message-Passing Systems. Tech. Rep. Technical Report CMU-CS-99-148, Carnegie Mellon University, June 1999.

[84] ELNOZAHY, E. N., JOHNSON, D. B., AND WANG, Y. M. A Survey of Rollback-Recovery Protocols in Message-Passing Systems. Tech. Rep. Technical Report CMU-CS-96-181, Carnegie Mellon University, October 1996.

[85] ELNOZAHY, E. N., JOHNSON, D. B., AND ZWAENEPOEL, W. The Performance of Consistent Checkpointing. In *11th Symposium on Reliable Distributed Systems* (October 1992), pp. 39–47.

[86] ELNOZAHY, E. N., AND ZWAENEPOEL, W. On the Use and Implementation of Message Logging. In *24th International Symposium on Fault-Tolerant Computing* (Austin, TX, June 1994), pp. 298–307.

[87] FALOUTSOS, C., AND BHAGWAT, P. Declustering Using Fractals. In *Proceedings of the 2nd International Conference on Parallel and Distributed Information Systems* (January 1993), pp. 18–25.

[88] FANG, M. T., LEE, R. C. T., AND CHANG, C. C. The Idea of De-clustering and Its Applications. In *Proceedings of the 12th International Conference on Very Large Data Bases (VLDB86)* (1986), pp. 181–188.

[89] FEELEY, M. J., MORGAN, W. E., PIGHIN, F. H., KARLIN, A. R., AND LEVY, H. M. Implementing Global Memory Management in a Workstation Cluster. In *Proc. of the 15th ACM Symp. on Operating Systems Principles (SOSP-15)* (December 1995), pp. 201–212.

[90] FELDMAN, S. I., AND BROWN, C. B. Igor: A System for Program Debugging via Reversible Execution. In *ACM SIGPLAN Notices, Workshop on Parallel and Distributed Debugging* (1989), vol. 24(1):112–123.

[91] FELTEN, E., AND ZAHORJAN, J. Issues in the Implementation of a Remote Memory Paging System. Tech. Rep. Technical Report 91-03-09, University of Washington, March 1991.

[92] FELTEN, E. W., ALPERT, R. D., BILAS, A., BLUMRICH, M. A., CLARK, D. W., DAMIANAKIS, S., DUBNICKI, C., IFTODE, L., AND LI, K. Early Experience with Message Passing on the SHRIMP Multicomputer. In *Proceedings of the 23rd Annual Symposium on Computer Architecture* (May 1996).

[93] FERREIRA, R., MOON, B., HUMPHRIES, J., SUSSMAN, A., SALTZ, J., MILLER, R., AND DEMARZO, A. The Virtual Microscope. In *Proceedings of the 1997 AMIA Annual Fall Symposium* (October 1997), American Medical Informatics Association, Hanley and Belfus, Incorporated, pp. 449–453.

[94] FINKEL, R. A., AND BENTLEY, J. L. Quad-Trees - A Data Structure for Retrieval on Composite Keys. *Acta Informatica 4* (1974), 1–9.

[95] FOSTER, I. *Designing and Building Parallel Programs.* Addison-Wesley Publishing Company, Reading, MA, 1995.

[96] FRENCH, J. C. Characterizing the Balance of Parallel I/O Systems. In *Sixth Annual Distributed Memory Computer Conference* (1991), pp. 724–727.

[97] G. E. HINTON, G. E. Connectionist Learning Procedures. *Artificial Intelligence 40* (1989).

[98] GALBREATH, N., GROPP, W., AND LEVINE, D. Applications-Driven Parallel I/O. In *Proceedings of Supercomputing '93* (November 1993), IEEE Computer Society Press, pp. 462–471.

[99] GHARACHORLOO, K., LENOSKI, D., LAUDON, J., GIBBONS, P., GUPTA, A., AND HENNESSY, J. Memory Consistency and Event Ordering in Scalable Shared-Memory Multiprocessors. In *Proceedings of the 17th Annual Symposium on Computer Architecture* (May 1990), pp. 15–26.

[100] GIBSON, G., STODOLSKY, D., CHANG, P., COURTWRIGHT II, W., DEMETRIOU, C., GINTING, E., HOLLAND, M., MA, Q., NEAL, L., PATTERSON, R., SU, J., YOUSSEF, R., AND ZELENKA, J. The Scotch Parallel Storage System. In *Proceedings of 40th IEEE Computer Society International Conference (COMPCON 95)* (Spring 1995), IEEE Computer Society Press, pp. 403–410.

[101] GIBSON, G. A., NAGLE, D. F., AMIRI, K., BUTLER, J., CHANG, F. W., GOBIOFF, H., HARDIN, C., RIEDEL, E., ROCHBERG, D., AND ZELENKA, J. A Cost-Effective, High-Bandwidth Storage Architecture. In *Proceedings of the Eighth Conference on Architectural Support for Programming Languages and Operating Systems* (1998), ACM Press.

[102] GILLETT, R., COLLINS, M., , AND PIMM, D. Overview of Network Memory Channel for PCI. In *Proceedings of the IEEE Spring COMPCON '96* (February 1996).

[103] NSF/ARPA Grand Challenge Project at the University of Maryland for Land Cover Dynamics, 1995. *http://www.umiacs.umd.edu:80/research/GC/*.

[104] GRAY, J., BOSWORTH, A., LAYMAN, A., AND PIRAHESH, H. Data Cube: A Relational Aggregation Operator Generalizing Group-By, Cross-Tab, and Sub-Totals. In *Proceedings of the 1996 International Conference on Data Engineering* (1996), IEEE Computer Society Press, pp. 152–159.

[105] GRIFFIOE, J., AND APPLETON, R. Reducing File System Latency Using a Predictive Approach. In *Proceedings of USENIX Summer Technical Conference* (June 1994), pp. 197–207.

[106] GRIMSHAW, A. S., AND LOYOT, JR., E. C. ELFS: Object-oriented Extensible File Systems. In *Proceedings of the First International Conference on Parallel and Distributed Information Systems* (1991), p. 177.

[107] GROPP, W., LUSK, E., DOSS, N., AND SKJELLUM, A. A High-Performance, Portable Implementation of the MPI Message-Passing Interface Standard. *Parallel Computing 22*, 6 (September 1996), 789–828.

[108] GROSSMAN, R., AND QIN, X. Ptool: A Scalable Persistent Object Manager. In *Proceedings of ACM SIGMOD 94* (1994).

[109] GUTTMAN, A. R-Trees: A Dynamic Index Structure for Spatial Searching. In *Proceedings of the 1984 ACM-SIGMOD Conference* (June 1984), pp. 47–57.

[110] HAAS, L. M., FREYTAG, J., LOHMAN, G., AND PIRAHESH, H. Extensible Query Processing in Starburst. In *Proceedings of the 1989 ACM-SIGMOD Conference* (Portland, OR, June 1989), pp. 377–388.

[111] HAVLAK, P., AND KENNEDY, K. An Implementation of Interprocedural Bounded Regular Section Analysis. *IEEE Transactions on Parallel and Distributed Systems 2*, 3 (July 1991), 350–360.

[112] HENDERSON, R. D. *Unstructured Spectral Element Methods: Parallel Algorithms and Simulations*. PhD thesis, Princeton University, June 1994.

[113] HENDERSON, R. D., AND KARNIADAKIS, G. E. Unstructured Spectral Element Methods for Simulation of Turbulent flows. *Journal of Computation Physics 122(2):191–217* (December 1995).

[114] HERRARTE, V., AND LUSK, E. Studying Parallel Program Behavior with Upshot. Tech. Rep. ANL–91/15, Mathematics and Computer Science Division, Argonne National Laboratory, August 1991.

[115] HILLIS, W. D., AND TUCKER, L. W. The CM-5 Connection Machine: A Scalable Supercomputer. *Communications of the ACM 36, 11:31–40* (1993).

[116] HOMEWOOD, M., AND McLAREN, M. Meiko CS-2 Interconnect Elan-Elite Design. In *Proceedings of Hot Interconnects* (August 1993).

[117] HUANG, Y., AND KINTALA, C. Software Implemented Fault Tolerance: Technologies and Experience. In *23rd International Symposium on Fault-Tolerant Computing* (July 1993), pp. 2–9.

[118] HUBER, JR., J. V. PPFS: An Experimental File System for High Performance Parallel Input/Output. Master's thesis, Department of Computer Science, University of Illinois at Urbana-Champaign, February 1995.

[119] HUBER, JR., J. V., ELFORD, C. L., REED, D. A., CHIEN, A. A., AND BLUMENTHAL, D. S. PPFS: A High Performance Portable Parallel File System. In *Proceedings of the International Conference on Supercomputing* (July 1995).

[120] IBM CORPORATION. IBM AIX Parallel I/O File System: Installation, Administration, and Use. Document Number SH34-6065-01, August 1995.

[121] HPSS: The High Performance Storage System. *http://www.sdsc.edu/hpss/hpss1.html.*

[122] IFTODE, L., DUBNICKI, C., FELTEN, E. W., AND LI, K. Improving Release-Consistent Shared Virtual Memory using Automatic Update. In *Proceedings of the 2nd IEEE Symposium on High-Performance Computer Architecture* (February 1996).

[123] IFTODE, L., PETERSEN, K., AND LI, K. Memory Servers for Multicomputers. In *Proceedings of the IEEE Spring COMPCON '93* (February 1993), pp. 538–547.

[124] IFTODE, L., SINGH, J., AND LI, K. Scope Consistency: A Bridge Between Release Consistency and Entry Consistency. In *Proceedings of the 8th Annual ACM Symposium on Parallel Algorithms and Architectures* (June 1996). Also in Theory of Computing Systems Journal 31, 451-473 (1998).

[125] IFTODE, L., SINGH, J. P., AND LI, K. Understanding Application Performance on Shared Virtual Memory. In *Proceedings of the 23rd Annual Symposium on Computer Architecture* (May 1996).

[126] INTEL. $i860^{TM}$ XP Microprocessor, 1991.

[127] Paragon XP/S Product Overview. Intel Corporation, 1991.

[128] INTEL SCALABLE SYSTEMS DIVISION. Paragon System User's Guide. Order Number 312489-004, May 1995.

[129] IOANNIDIS, Y., LIVNY, M., GUPTA, S., AND PONNEKANTI, N. ZOO: A Desktop Experiment Management Environment. In *Proceedings of the 22nd International Conference on Very Large Data Bases (VLDB96)* (1996), pp. 274–285.

[130] JAIN, R., WERTH, J., AND BROWNE, J. C., Eds. *Input/Output in Parallel and Distributed Computer Systems*, vol. 362 of *The Kluwer International Series in Engineering and Computer Science*. Kluwer Academic Publishers, 1996.

[131] JANAKIRAMAN, G., AND TAMIR, Y. Coordinated Checkpointing-Rollback Error Recovery for Distributed Shared Memory Multicomputers. In *13th Symposium on Reliable Distributed Systems* (October 1994), pp. 42–51.

[132] JENSEN, D. W. *Disk I/O In High-Performance Computing Systems.* PhD thesis, Univ. Illinois, Urbana-Champagne, 1993.

[133] JENSEN, D. W., AND REED, D. A. File Archive Activity in a Supercomputing Environment. In *Proceedings of the 1993 ACM International Conference on Supercomputing* (July 1993).

[134] JOHNSON, K. L., KAASHOEK, M. F., AND WALLACH, D. A. CRL: High-Performance All-Software Distributed Shared Memory. In *Proceedings of the Fifteenth Symposium on Operating Systems Principles* (December 1995), pp. 213–228.

[135] JUSTICE, C. O., TOWNSHEND, J. R. G., HOLBEN, B. N., AND TUCKER, C. J. Analysis of the Phenology of Global Vegetation Using Meteorological Satellite Data. *International Journal of Remote Sensing* (1985), 1271–1318.

[136] KANDEMIR, M., BORDAWEKAR, R., AND CHOUDHARY, A. Data Access Reorganizations in Compiling Out-of-Core Data Parallel Programs on Distributed Memory Machines. In *Proceedings of the Eleventh International Parallel Processing Symposium* (April 1997), pp. 559–564.

[137] KANDEMIR, M., CHOUDHARY, A., AND BORDAWEKAR, R. I/O Optimizations for Compiling Out-of-Core programs on Distributed-Memory Machines. In *Proceedings of the Eighth SIAM Conference on Parallel Processing for Scientific Computing* (March 1997), Society for Industrial and Applied Mathematics.

[138] KANDEMIR, M., CHOUDHARY, A., RAMANUJAM, J., AND BORDAWEKAR, R. Compilation Techniques for Out-of-Core Parallel Computations. *Parallel Computing 24*, 3 (May 1998), 597–628.

[139] KANDEMIR, M., CHOUDHARY, A., RAMANUJAM, J., AND KANDASWAMY, M. A Unified Compiler Algorithm for Optimizing Locality, Parallelism, and Communication in Out-of-Core Computations. In *Proceedings of the Fifth Workshop on Input/Output in Parallel and Distributed Systems* (San Jose, CA, November 1997), ACM Press, pp. 79–92.

[140] KARLSSON, M., AND STENSTROM, P. Performance Evaluation of Cluster-Based Multiprocessor Built from ATM Switches and Bus-Based Multiprocessor Servers. In *Proceedings of the 2nd IEEE Symposium on High-Performance Computer Architecture* (February 1996).

[141] KARPOVICH, J., GRIMSHAW, A., AND FRENCH, J. Extensible File Systems (ELFS): An Object-Oriented Approach to High Performance File I/O. In *Proceedings of the Ninth Annual Conference on Object-Oriented Programming Systems, Languages, and Applications* (October 1994), pp. 191–204.

[142] KELEHER, P., COX, A. L., DWARKADAS, S., AND ZWAENEPOEL, W. TreadMarks: Distributed Shared Memory on Standard Workstations and Operating Systems. In *Proceedings of the Winter USENIX Conference* (January 1994), pp. 115–132.

[143] KELEHER, P., COX, A. L., AND ZWAENEPOEL, W. Lazy Consistency for Software Distributed Shared Memory. In *Proceedings of the 19th Annual Symposium on Computer Architecture* (May 1992), pp. 13–21.

[144] KELEHER, P. J. The Relative Importance of Concurrent Writers and Weak Consistency Models. In *Proceedings of the 16th International Conference on Distributed Computing Systems* (May 1996).

[145] KENNEDY, K., KOELBEL, C., AND PALECZNY, M. Scalable I/O for Out-of-Core Structures. Tech. Rep. CRPC-TR93357-S, Center for Research on Parallel Computation, Rice University, November 1993. Updated August, 1994.

[146] KERMARREC, A.-M., CABILLIC, G., GEFFLAUT, A., MORIN, C., AND PUAUT, I. Recoverable Distributed Shared Memory Integrating Coherence and Recoverability. In *25th International Symposium on Fault-Tolerant Computing* (June 1995), pp. 289–298.

[147] KIM, M.-H., AND PRAMANIK, S. Optimal File Distribution for Partial Match Retrieval. In *Proceedings of the 1988 ACM-SIGMOD Conference* (Chicago, IL, June 1988), pp. 173–182.

[148] KIM, W., GARZA, J. F., BALLOU, N., AND WOELK, D. Architecture of the ORION Next-Generation Database System. In *Readings in Database Systems*, M. Stonebraker, Ed. Morgan Kaufmann, 1994, pp. 857–872.

[149] KIMBREL, T., TOMKINS, A., PATTERSON, R. H., BERSHAD, B., CAO, P., FELTEN, E. W., GIBSON, G. A., KARLIN, A. R., AND LI, K. A Trace-Driven Comparison of Algorithms for Parallel Prefetching and Caching. In *Proceedings of the USENIX Association Second Symposium on Operating Systems Design and Implementation* (1996), pp. 19–34.

[150] KINGSBURY, B. A., AND KLINE, J. T. Job and Process Recovery in a UNIX-based Operating System. In *Usenix Winter 1989 Technical Conference* (San Diego, CA, January 1989), pp. 355–364.

[151] KLEINROCK, L. *Queueing Systems, Vol. 1, Theory.* John Wiley, 1975.

[152] KODUKULA, I., AHMED, N., AND PINGALI, K. Data-Centric Multi-Level Blocking. In *Proceedings of the SIGPLAN '97 Conference on Programming Language Design and Implementation* (June 1997), ACM Press, pp. 346–357. ACM SIGPLAN Notices, Vol. 32, No. 5.

[153] KORNER, K. Intelligent Caching for Remote File Service. In *Proceedings of the 10th International Conference on Distributed Computing Systems* (1990), pp. 220–226.

[154] KOTZ, D. Multiprocessor File System Interfaces. In *Proceedings of the Second International Conference on Parallel and Distributed Information Systems* (1993), IEEE Computer Society Press, pp. 194–201.

[155] KOTZ, D. Disk-directed I/O for MIMD Multiprocessors. In *Proceedings of the 1994 Symposium on Operating Systems Design and Implementation* (November 1994), pp. 61–74.

[156] KOTZ, D. Disk-Directed I/O for MIMD Multiprocessors. *ACM Transactions on Computer Systems 15*, 1 (February 1997), 41–74.

[157] KOTZ, D., AND ELLIS, C. S. Practical Prefetching Techniques for Multiprocessor File Systems. *Journal of Distributed and Parallel Databases 1*, 1 (January 1993), 33–51.

[158] KOTZ, D., AND NIEUWEJAAR, N. Dynamic File-Access Characteristics of a Production Parallel Scientific Workload. In *Proceedings of Supercomputing '94* (Washington, DC, November 1994), IEEE Computer Society Press, pp. 640–649.

[159] KOTZ, D., TOH, S. B., AND RADHAKRISHNAN, S. A Detailed Simulation Model of the HP 97560 Disk Drive. Tech. Rep. PCS-TR94-220, Dept. of Computer Science, Dartmouth College, July 1994.

[160] KRIEGER, O., AND STUMM, M. HFS: A performance-oriented flexible file system based on building-block compositions. In *Proceedings of Fourth Workshop on Input/Output in Parallel and Distributed Systems* (May 1996), ACM Press, pp. 95–108.

[161] KROEGER, T. M., AND LONG, D. D. E. Predicting File System Actions from Prior Events. In *Proceedings of the USENIX 1996 Annual Technical Conference* (January 1996), pp. 319–328.

[162] KURC, T. M., SUSSMAN, A., AND SALTZ, J. Coupling Multiple Simulations via a High Performance Customizable Database System. In *Proceedings of the Ninth SIAM Conference on Parallel Processing for Scientific Computing* (March 1999), SIAM.

[163] KUSKIN, J., OFELT, D., HEINRICH, M., HEINLEIN, J., SIMONI, R., GHARACHORLOO, K., CHAPIN, J., NAKAHIRA, D., BAXTER, J., HOROWITZ, M., GUPTA, A., ROSENBLUM, M., AND HENNESSY, J. The Stanford Flash Multiprocessor. In *Proceedings of the 21st Annual Symposium on Computer Architecture* (April 1994), pp. 302–313.

[164] KWAN, T. T., AND REED, D. A. Performance of the CM-5 Scalable File System. In *Proceedings of the 1994 ACM International Conference on Supercomputing* (July 1994).

[165] LAM, M., ROTHBERG, E., AND WOLF, M. The Cache Performance and Optimizations of Blocked Algorithms. In *ASPLOS92* (April 1991).

[166] Land Satellite Thematic Mapper (TM). *http://edcwww.cr.usgs.gov/nsdi/html/landsat_tm/landsat_tm*.

[167] LANDAU, C. R. The Checkpoint Mechanism in Keykos. In *Proceedings of the 2nd International Workshop on Object Orientation in Operating Systems* (September 1992), IEEE, pp. 86–91.

[168] LARUS, J. R., REINHARDT, S. K., AND WOOD, D. A. Tempest and Typhoon: User-level Shared Memory. In *Proceedings of the 21st Annual International Symposium on Computer Architecture* (April 1994), pp. 325–337.

[169] LAWRIE, D. H., RANDAL, J. M., AND BARTON, R. R. Experiments with Automatic File Migration. *IEEE Computer* (July 1982), 45–55.

[170] LEI, H., AND DUCHAMP, D. An Analytical Approach to File Prefetching. In *Proceedings of the USENIX 1997 Annual Technical Conference* (January 1997), pp. 275–288.

[171] LENOSKI, D., LAUDON, J., JOE, T., NAKAHIRA, D., STEVENS, L., GUPTA, A., AND HENNESSY, J. The Stanford DASH Prototype: Logic Overhead and Performance. In *Proceedings of the 19th Annual Symposium on Computer Architecture* (May 1992).

[172] LEÓN, J., FISHER, A. L., AND STEENKISTE, P. Fail-safe PVM: A Portable Package for Distributed Programming with Transparent Recovery. Tech. Rep. Technical Report CMU-CS-93-124, Carnegie Mellon University, February 1993.

[173] LI, K., AND HUDAK, P. Memory Coherence in Shared Virtual Memory Systems. In *Proceedings of the 5th Annual ACM Symposium on Principles of Distributed Computing* (August 1986), pp. 229–239.

[174] LIANG, S., DAVIS, L., TOWNSHEND, J., CHELLAPPA, R., DUBAYAH, R., GOWARD, S., JAJA, J., KRISHNAMACHARI, S., ROUSSOPOULOS, N., SALTZ, J., SAMET, H., SHOCK, T., AND SRINIVASAN, M. Land Cover Dynamics Investigation Using Parallel Computers. In *Proceedings of the 1995 International Geoscience and Remote Sensing Symposium, Quantitative Remote Sensing for Science and Applications.* (July 1995), pp. 332–334.

[175] LIVNY, M., RAMAKRISHNAN, R., BEYER, K., CHEN, G., DONJERKOVIC, D., LAWANDE, S., MYLLYMAKI, J., AND WENGER, K. DEVise: Integrated Querying and Visual Exploration of Large Datasets. In *Proceedings of the ACM SIGMOD International Conference on Management of Data (SIGMOD97)* (1997), pp. 301–312.

[176] LoVERSO, S. J., ISMAN, M., NANOPOULOS, A., NESHEIM, W., MILNE, E. D., AND WHEELER, R. *sfs*: A Parallel File System for the CM-5. In *Proceedings of the 1993 Summer USENIX Technical Conference* (1993), pp. 291–305.

[177] LUETTICH, R. A., WESTERINK, J. J., AND SCHEFFNER, N. W. ADCIRC: An Advanced Three-Dimensional Circulation Model for Shelves, Coasts, and Estuaries. Tech. Rep. 1, Department of the Army, U.S. Army Corps of Engineers, Washington, D.C., December 1991.

[178] MA, K.-L., AND ZHENG, Z. 3D Visualization of Unsteady 2D Airplane Wake Vortices. In *Proceedings of Visualization'94* (October 1994), pp. 124–31.

[179] MADHYASTHA, T. M. *Automatic Classification of Input/Output Access Patterns*. PhD thesis, University of Illinois at Urbana-Champaign, Department of Computer Science, August 1997.

[180] MESSAGE PASSING INTERFACE FORUM. MPI-2: Extensions to the Message-Passing Interface, July 1997. On the World-Wide Web at http://www.mpi-forum.org/docs/docs.html.

[181] MESSAGE PASSING INTERFACE FORUM. *MPI: A Message-Passing Interface Standard.* Version 1.1, June 1995. On the World-Wide Web at http://www.mpi-forum.org/docs/docs.html.

[182] MILLER, E. L., AND KATZ, R. H. Input/Output Behavior of Supercomputing Applications. In *Proceedings of Supercomputing '91* (November 1991), pp. 567–576.

[183] The Moderate Resolution Imaging Spectrometer. *http://ltpwww.gsfc.nasa.gov/MODIS/MODIS.html.*

[184] MOON, B., ACHARYA, A., AND SALTZ, J. Study of Scalable Declustering Algorithms for Parallel Grid Files. In *Proceedings of the Tenth International Parallel Processing Symposium* (April 1996), IEEE Computer Society Press, pp. 434–440.

[185] MOON, B., AND SALTZ, J. H. Scalability Analysis of Declustering Methods for Multidimensional Range Queries. *IEEE Transactions on Knowledge and Data Engineering 10*, 2 (March/April 1998), 310–327.

[186] MOWRY, T. C. *Tolerating Latency Through Software-Controlled Data Prefetching*. PhD thesis, Department of Electrical Engineering, Stanford University, March 1994.

[187] MOWRY, T. C., DEMKE, A. K., AND KRIEGER, O. Automatic Compiler-Inserted I/O Prefetching for Out-of-Core Applications. In *Proceedings of the 1996 Symposium on Operating Systems Design and Implementation* (October 1996), USENIX Association, pp. 3–17.

[188] MOWRY, T. C., LAM, M. S., AND GUPTA, A. Design and Evaluation of a Compiler Algorithm for Prefetching. In *Proceedings of the Fifth International Conference on Architectural Support for Programming Languages and Operating Systems (ASPLOS V)* (October 1992), ACM Press, pp. 62–73.

[189] MOYER, S., AND SUNDERAM, V. PIOUS: A Scalable Parallel I/O System for Distributed Computing Environments. In *Proceedings of the Scalable High-Performance Computing Conference* (1994), pp. 71–78.

[190] MOYER, S. A., AND SUNDARAM, V. S. PIOUS: A Scalable Parallel I/O System for Distributed Computing Environments. In *1994 Scalable High Performance Computing Conference* (May 1994), pp. 71–78.

[191] NAIK, V. K., MIDKIFF, S. P., AND MOREIRA, J. E. A Checkpointing Strategy for Scalable Recovery on Distributed Parallel Systems. In *SC97: High Performance Networking and Computing* (San Jose, November 1997).

[192] NASA GODDARD DISTRIBUTED ACTIVE ARCHIVE CENTER (DAAC). Advanced very high resolution radiometer global area coverage (AVHRR GAC) data. *http://daac.gsfc.nasa.gov/CAMPAIGN_DOCS/ LAND_BIO/origins.html.*

[193] NATIONAL CENTER FOR SUPERCOMPUTING APPLICATIONS. HDF Reference Manual, Version 4.1. Tech. rep., University of Illinois, 1997.

[194] NEEDLEMAN, S. B., AND WUNSCH, C. D. An Efficient Method Applicable to the Search for Similarities in the Amino Acid Sequences of Two Proteins. *Journal of Molecular Biology 48* (1970), 444–453.

[195] NIEPLOCHA, J., AND FOSTER, I. Disk Resident Arrays: An Array-Oriented I/O Library for Out-of-Core Computations. In *Proceedings of the Sixth Symposium on the Frontiers of Massively Parallel Computation* (October 1996), IEEE Computer Society Press, pp. 196–204.

[196] NIEUWEJAAR, N., AND KOTZ, D. The Galley Parallel File System. In *Proceedings of the 10th ACM International Conference on Supercomputing* (May 1996).

[197] NIEUWEJAAR, N., AND KOTZ, D. Low-Level Interfaces for High-level Parallel I/O. In *Proceedings of the Third Annual Workshop on I/O in Parallel and Distributed Systems* (April 1995), pp. 47–62.

[198] NITZBERG, B. Performance of the iPSC/860 Concurrent File System. Tech. Rep. RND-92-020, NAS Systems Division, NASA Ames, December 1992.

[199] NO, J., PARK, S., CARRETERO, J., CHOUDHARY, A., , AND CHEN, P. Design and Implementation of a Parallel I/O Runtime System for Irregular Applications. In *Proceedings of the 12th International Parallel Processing Symposium* (March 1998).

[200] OLSSON, S., AND BUSCH, C. A National Telepathology Trial in Sweden: Feasibility and Assessment. *Arch Anat Cytol Pathol 43* (1995), 234–241.

[201] The Oracle 8 Spatial Data Cartridge, 1997. *http://www.oracle.com/st/cartridges/spatial/.*

[202] OUSTERHOUT, J., *et al.* A Trace-Driven Analysis of the UNIX 4.2 BSD File System. In *Proceedings of the Tenth Symposium on Operating System Principles* (Dec. 1985).

[203] PALECZNY, M., KENNEDY, K., AND KOELBEL, C. Compiler Support for Out-of-Core Arrays on Data Parallel Machines. In *Proceedings of the Fifth Symposium on the Frontiers of Massively Parallel Computation* (McLean, VA, February 1995), pp. 110–118.

[204] PALMER, M., AND ZDONIK, S. B. Fido: A Cache That Learns to Fetch. In *Proceedings of the 17th International Conference on Very Large Data Bases* (September 1991), pp. 255–262.

[205] PASQUALE, B. K., AND POLYZOS, G. Dynamic I/O Characterization of I/O Intensive Scientific Applications. In *Proceedings of Supercomputing '94* (Novermber 1994), pp. 660–669.

[206] PASQUALE, B. K., AND POLYZOS, G. C. Dynamic I/O Characterization of I/O Intensive Scientific Applications. In *Proceedings of Supercomputing '94* (1994), pp. 660–669.

[207] PATEL, J., YU, J., KABRA, N., TUFTE, K., NAG, B., BURGER, J., HALL, N., RAMASAMY, K., LUEDER, R., ELLMANN, C., KUPSCH, J., GUO, S., LARSON, J., DEWITT, D., AND NAUGHTON, J. Building a Scalable Geo-spatial DBMS: Technology, Implementation, and Evaluation. In *SIGMOD97* (1997), pp. 336–347.

[208] PATNAIK, G., KAILASNATH, K., AND ORAN, E. Effect of Gravity on Flame Instabilities in Premixed Gases. *AIAA Journal 29*, 12 (December 1991), 2141–8.

[209] PATTERSON, R. H., GIBSON, G. A., GINTING, E., STODOLSKY, D., AND ZELENKA, J. Informed prefetching and caching. In *Proceedings of the Fifteenth ACM Symposium on Operating Systems Principles* (Copper Mountain, CO, December 1995), ACM Press, pp. 79–95.

[210] PHILBIN, J. Thread Scheduling for Cache Locality. In *Seventh International Conference on Architectural Support for Programming Languages and Operating Systems* (October 1996), ACM Press, pp. 60–71.

[211] PIERCE, R., AND REGNIER, G. The Paragon Implementation of the NX Message Passing Interface. In *Proceedings of the Scalable High-Performance Computing Conference* (May 1994).

[212] PLANK, J. S. *Program Diagnostics*, vol. 17. John Wiley & Sons, Inc., New York, 1999.

[213] PLANK, J. S., BECK, M., AND KINGSLEY, G. Compiler-Assisted Memory Exclusion for Fast Checkpointing. In *IEEE Technical Committee on Operating Systems and Application Environments* (1995), vol. 7(4):10–14, Winter.

[214] PLANK, J. S., BECK, M., KINGSLEY, G., AND LI, K. **Libckpt**: Transparent checkpointing under UNIX. In *Usenix Winter 1995 Technical Conference* (January 1995), pp. 213–223.

[215] PLANK, J. S., CHEN, Y., LI, K., BECK, M., AND KINGSLEY, G. Memory Exclusion: Optimizing the Performance of Checkpointing Systems. *Software – Practice & Experience 29(2):125–142* (1999).

[216] PLANK, J. S., AND LI, K. Ickp — A Consistent Checkpointer for Multicomputers. *IEEE Parallel & Distributed Technology 2(2):62–67, Summer* (1994).

[217] PONNUSAMY, R., HWANG, Y. S., DAS, R., SALTZ, J., CHOUDHARY, A., AND FOX, G. Supporting Irregular Distributions in FORTRAN 90D/HPF Compliers. Tech. rep., University of Maryland, Syracuse University, 1995.

[218] POOL, J. Scalable I/O Initiative. Tech. rep., California Institute of Technology, 1996.

[219] POOLE, J. T. Preliminary Survey of I/O Intensive Applications. Tech. Rep. CCSF-38, Scalable I/O Initiative, Caltech Concurrent Supercomputing Facilities, Caltech, 1994.

[220] PROST, J.-P., SNIR, M., CORBETT, P., AND FEITELSON, D. MPI-IO, A Message-Passing Interface for Concurrent I/O. Tech. Rep. RC 19712 (87394), IBM T.J. Watson Research Center, August 1994.

[221] PURAKAYASTHA, A., ELLIS, C. S., KOTZ, D., NIEUWEJAAR, N., AND BEST, M. Characterizing Parallel File-Access Patterns on a Large-Scale Multiprocessor. In *Proceedings of the Ninth International Parallel Processing Symposium* (April 1995). To appear.

[222] RABINER, L. R. A Tutorial on Hidden Markov Models and Selected Applications in Speech Recognition. In *Proceedings of the IEEE 77* (1989).

[223] REED, D. A. Experimental Performance Analysis of Parallel Systems: Techniques and Open Problems. In *Proceedings of the 7th International Conference on Modelling Techniques and Tools for Computer Performance Evaluation* (May 1994), pp. 25–51.

[224] REED, D. A., AYDT, R. A., NOE, R. J., ROTH, P. C., SHIELDS, K. A., SCHWARTZ, B. W., AND TAVERA, L. F. Scalable Performance Analysis: The Pablo Performance Analysis Environment. In *Proceedings of the Scalable Parallel Libraries Conference*, A. Skjellum, Ed. IEEE Computer Society, 1993, pp. 104–113.

[225] RUEMMLER, C., AND WILKES, J. Modelling Disks. Tech. Rep. HPL-93-68, Hewlett Packard Laboratories, July 1993.

[226] RULLMAN, B. *Paragon Parallel File System*. Intel Supercomputer Systems Division. External Product Specification.

[227] RUSSINOVICH, M., AND SEGALL, Z. Fault-Tolerance for Off-the-Shelf Applications and Hardware. In *25th International Symposium on Fault-Tolerant Computing* (Pasadena, CA, June 1995), pp. 67–71.

[228] SCHILIT, B. N., AND DUCHAMP, D. Adaptive Remote Paging for Mobile Computers. Tech. rep., Department of Computer Science, Columbia University, 1991.

[229] SEAMONS, K. E., CHEN, Y., CHO, Y., KUO, S., AND SUBRAMANIAM, M. Persistent Array Access Using Server-Directed I/O. In *Proceedings of the 8th International Working Conference on Scientific and Statistical Database Management* (Stockholm, Sweden, June, 1996).

[230] SEAMONS, K. E., CHEN, Y., JONES, P., JOZWIAK, J., AND WINSLETT, M. Server-Directed Collective I/O in Panda. In *Proceedings of Supercomputing '95* (San Diego, CA, December 1995), IEEE Computer Society Press.

[231] SEAMONS, K. E., AND WINSLETT, M. A Data Management Approach for Handling Large Compressed Arrays in High Performance Computing. In *Proceedings of the Fifth Symposium on the Frontiers of Massively Parallel Computation* (February 1995), pp. 119–128.

[232] SEAMONS, K. E., AND WINSLETT, M. An Efficient Abstract Interface for Multidimensional Array I/O. In *Proceedings of Supercomputing '94* (November, 1994), pp. 650–659.

[233] SESHADRI, P., LIVNY, M., AND RAMAKRISHNAN, R. The Case for Enhanced Abstract Data Types. In *Proceedings of the 23rd International Conference on Very Large Data Bases (VLDB97)* (Athens, Greece, August 1997).

[234] SHOCK, C. T., CHANG, C., MOON, B., ACHARYA, A., DAVIS, L., SALTZ, J., AND SUSSMAN, A. The Design and Evaluation of a High-Performance Earth Science Database. *Parallel Computing 24*, 1 (January 1998), 65–90.

[235] SILVA, L. M., SILVA, J. G., CHAPPLE, S., AND CLARKE, L. Portable Checkpointing and Recovery. In *Proceedings of the HPDC-4, High-Performance Distributed Computing* (August 1995), pp. 188–195.

[236] SILVA, L. M., VEER, B., AND SILVA, J. G. Checkpointing SPMD Applications on Transputer Networks. In *Scalable High Performance Computing Conference* (Knoxville, TN, May 1994), pp. 694–701.

[237] SINGH, J. P., WEBER, W.-D., AND GUPTA, A. SPLASH: Stanford Parallel Applications for Shared Memory. *Computer Architecture News 20(1):5-44* (1992).

[238] SMIRNI, E., AYDT, R. A., CHIEN, A. A., AND REED, D. A. I/O Requirements of Scientific Applications: An Evolutionary View. In *Fifth International Symposium on High Performance Distributed Computing* (1996), pp. 49-59.

[239] SMITH, A. J. Analysis of Long Term File Reference Patterns for Application to File Migration Algorithms. *IEEE Transactions on Software Engineering SE-7*, 4 (July 1981), 403-417.

[240] SNIR, M., OTTO, S. W., HUSS-LEDERMAN, S., WALKER, D. W., AND DONGARRA, J. *MPI: The Complete Reference*. Scientific and Engineering Computation Series. MIT Press, 1996.

[241] SpatialWare DataBlade Module (from MapInfo) Corp, 1997. *http://www.informix.com/informix/ bussol/iusdb/databld/dbtech/sheets/spware.htm.*

[242] STEERE, D. C. Using Dynamic Sets to Speed Search in World Wide Information Systems. Tech. Rep. CMU-CS-95-174, School of Computer Science, Carnegie Mellon University, March 1995.

[243] STEINWAND, D. R. Mapping Raster Imagery to the Interrupted Goodes Homolosine Projection. *http://edcwww.cr.usgs.gov/landdaac/1KM/goodesarticle.html.*

[244] STELLNER, G. CoCheck: Checkpointing and Process Migration for MPI. In *10th International Parallel Processing Symposium* (April 1996).

[245] STERN, H. *Managing NFS and NIS*. O'Reilly & Associates, Incorporated, 1991.

[246] STONEBRAKER, M. An Overview of the Sequoia 2000 Project. In *Proceedings of the 1992 COMPCON Conference* (San Francisco, CA, 1992), pp. 383-388.

[247] STONEBRAKER, M. *Object-Relational DBMSs: Tracking the Next Great Wave*. Morgan Kaufman Publishers, 1998.

[248] STONEBRAKER, M., ROWE, L., AND HIROHAMA, M. The Implementation of POSTGRES. *IEEE Transactions on Knowledge and Data Engineering 2*, 1 (March 1990), 125-142.

[249] STONEBRAKER, M., AND ROWE, L. A. The Design of POSTGRES. In *Proceedings of the ACM SIGMOD'86 International Conference on Management of Data* (Washington, DC, May, 1986), pp. 340-355.

[250] STRITTER, T. R. *File Migration*. PhD thesis, Stanford University, Department of Computer Science, Jan. 1977.

[251] SURI, G., JANSSENS, B., AND FUCHS, W. K. Reduced Overhead Logging for Rollback Recovery in Distributed Shared Memory. In *25th International Symposium on Fault-Tolerant Computing* (June 1995), pp. 279-288.

[252] TANAKA, T. Configurations of the Solar Wind Flow and Magnetic Field Around the Planets with no Nagnetic Field: Calculation by a New MHD. *Jounal of Geophysical Research 98*, A10 (October 1993), 17251-62.

[253] TANNENBAUM, T., AND LITZKOW, M. The Condor Distributed Processing System. *Dr. Dobb's Journal #227:40-48* (February 1995).

[254] THAKUR, R. *Runtime Support for In-Core and Out-of-Core Data-Parallel Programs*. PhD thesis, Department of Electrical and Computer Engineering, Syracuse University, May 1995.

[255] THAKUR, R., BORDAWEKAR, R., AND CHOUDHARY, A. Compilation of Out-Of-Core Data Parallel Programs for Distributed Memory Machines. In *Proceedings of the IPPS '94 Workshop on Input/Output in Parallel Computer Systems* (April 1994), Syracuse University, pp. 54–72. Also appeared in Computer Architecture News 22(4).

[256] THAKUR, R., BORDAWEKAR, R., AND CHOUDHARY, A. Compiler and Runtime Support for Out-of-Core HPF Programs. In *Proceedings of the 8th ACM International Conference on Supercomputing* (Manchester, UK, July 1994), ACM Press, pp. 382–391.

[257] THAKUR, R., BORDAWEKAR, R., CHOUDHARY, A., PONNUSAMY, R., AND SINGH, T. PASSION Runtime Library for Parallel I/O. In *Proceedings of the Scalable Parallel Libraries Conference* (October 1994), pp. 119–128.

[258] THAKUR, R., AND CHOUDHARY, A. Runtime Support for Out-of-Core Parallel Programs. In Jain et al. [130], ch. 6, pp. 147–165.

[259] THAKUR, R., AND CHOUDHARY, A. An extended two-phase method for accessing sections of out-of-core arrays. Tech. Rep. CACR–103, Scalable I/O Initiative, Center for Advanced Computing Research, Caltech, Revised May 1996. (Also appeared in *Scientific Programming* 5,4 (Winter 1996), 301-317).

[260] THAKUR, R., CHOUDHARY, A., BORDAWEKAR, R., MORE, S., AND KUDITIPUDI, S. PASSION: Optimized I/O for Parallel Applications. *IEEE Computer 29*, 6 (June 1996), 70–78.

[261] THAKUR, R., GROPP, W., AND LUSK, E. An Abstract-Device Interface for Implementing Portable Parallel-I/O Interfaces. In *Proceedings of the 6th Symposium on the Frontiers of Massively Parallel Computation* (October 1996), IEEE Computer Society Press, pp. 180–187.

[262] THAKUR, R., GROPP, W., AND LUSK, E. An Experimental Evaluation of the Parallel I/O Systems of the IBM SP and Intel Paragon Using a Production Application. In *Proceedings of the 3rd International Conference of the Austrian Center for Parallel Computation (ACPC) with Special Emphasis on Parallel Databases and Parallel I/O* (September 1996), Lecture Notes in Computer Science 1127. Springer-Verlag, pp. 24–35.

[263] THAKUR, R., GROPP, W., AND LUSK, E. Data Sieving and Collective I/O in ROMIO. In *Proceedings of the 7th Symposium on the Frontiers of Massively Parallel Computation* (February 1999), IEEE Computer Society Press, pp. 182–189.

[264] THAKUR, R., GROPP, W., AND LUSK, E. A case for using MPI's derived data types to improve I/O performance. In *Proceedings of SC98: High Performance Networking and Computing* (November 1998).

[265] THAKUR, R., GROPP, W., AND LUSK, E. On implementing MPI-IO portably and with high performance. Tech. Rep. ANL/MCS-P732-1098, Mathematics and Computer Science Division, Argonne National Laboratory, October, 1998.

[266] THAKUR, R., LUSK, E., AND GROPP, W. I/O in Parallel Applications: The Weakest Link. *International Journal of Supercomputer Applications and High Performance Computing* (1998).

[267] THAKUR, R., LUSK, E., AND GROPP, W. Users Guide for ROMIO: A High-Performance, Portable MPI-IO Implementation. Tech. Rep. ANL/MCS-TM-234, Mathematics and Computer Science Division, Argonne National Laboratory, July 1998.

[268] THE MPI-IO COMMITTEE. MPI-IO: A Parallel File I/O Interface for MPI, Version 0.5. On the World-Wide Web at http://parallel.nas.nasa.gov/MPI-IO, April 1996.

[269] THEKKATH, C. A., AND LEVY, H. Hardware and Software Support for Efficient Exception Handling. In *Proceedings of the 6th International Conference on Architectural Support for Programming Languages and Operating Systems* (October 1994), pp. 110–121.

[270] TOLEDO, S., AND GUSTAVSON, F. G. The Design and Implementation of SOLAR, A Portable Library for Scalable Out-of-Core Linear Algebra Computations. In *Proceedings of the Fourth Annual Workshop on I/O in Parallel and Distributed Systems* (May, 1996).

[271] TOMKINS, A., PATTERSON, R. H., AND GIBSON, G. Informed Multi-Process Prefetching and Caching. In *Proceedings of the ACM International Conference on Measurement and Modeling of Computer Systems* (June 1997).

[272] TRAYLOR, R., AND DUNNING, D. Routing Chip Set for Intel Paragon Parallel Supercomputer. In *Proceedings of Hot Chips '92 Symposium* (August 1992).

[273] TRIVEDI, K. S. Prepaging and Applications to the STAR-100 Computer. In *Proceedings of the Symposium on High Speed Computer and Algorithm Organization* (April 1977), pp. 435–446.

[274] TRIVEDI, K. S. On the Paging Performance of Array Algorithms. *IEEE Transactions on Computers C-26*, 10 (October 1977), 938–947.

[275] UNITREE SOFTWARE, INCORPORATED. *UniTree User Guide*, 1998.

[276] The USGS General Cartographic Transformation Package, version 2.0.2. *ftp://mapping.usgs.gov/ pub/software/current_software/gctp/*, 1997.

[277] WARREN, M. S., AND SALMON, J. K. Astrophysical N-Body Simulations Using Hierarchical Data Structures. In *Proceedings Supercomputing '92* (Minn., MN, November 1992), IEEE, pp. 570–576.

[278] WEINSTEIN, M., AND EPSTEIN, J. I. Telepathology Diagnosis of Prostate Needle Biopsies. *Human Pathology 28*, 1 (January 1997), 22–29.

[279] WEINSTEIN, R. S., BHATTACHARYYA, A., GRAHAM, A. R., AND DAVIS, J. R. Telepathology: A Ten-Year Progress Report. *Human Pathology 28*, 1 (January 1997), 1–7.

[280] WELCH, T. A. A Technique for High Performance Data Compression. *IEEE Computer 17(6):8–19* (June 1984).

[281] WINSTEAD, C., AND MCKOY, V. Studies of Electron-Molecule Collisions on Massively Parallel Computers. In *Modern Electronic Structure Theory*, D. R. Yarkony, Ed., vol. 2. World Scientific, 1994.

[282] WOMBLE, D., GREENBERG, D., RIESEN, R., AND WHEAT, S. Out of Core, Out of Mind: Practical Parallel I/O. In *Proceedings of the Scalable Parallel Libraries Conference* (Mississippi State University, October 1993), pp. 10–16.

[283] WOMBLE, D., GREENBERG, D., WHEAT, S., AND RIESSEN, R. Beyond Core: Making Parallel Computer I/O Practical. In *DAGS93* (Hanover, NH, June 1993).

[284] WOMBLE, D. E. Sandia National Laboratories, July 1993. Private communication.

[285] WORLEY, P., AND FOSTER, I. T. Parallel Spectral Transform Shallow Water Model: A Runtime-Tunable Parallel Benchmark Code. In *Proceedings of Scalable High-Performance Computing Conference (SHPCC) 94* (1994).

[286] WU, Y. S. M., CUCCARO, S. A., HIPES, P. G., AND KUPPERMANN, A. Quantum Chemical Reaction Dynamics on a Highly Parallel Supercomputer. *Theoretica Chimica Acta 79* (1991).

[287] WU, Y. S. M., AND KUPPERMANN, A. The Quantitative Prediction and Lifetime of a Pronounced Reactive Scattering Resonance. *Chemical Physics Letters 241* (1995).

[288] ZHOU, Y., IFTODE, L., AND LI, K. Performance Evaluation of Two Home-Based Lazy Release Consistency Protocols for Shared Virtual Memory Systems. In *Proceedings of the Operating Systems Design and Implementation Symposium* (October 1996).

About the Editor

Dan Reed holds an Edward William and Jane Marr Gutgsell Professorship at the University of Illinois at Urbana-Champaign. He also serves as director of the National Computational Science Alliance (Alliance) and the National Center for Supercomputing Applications (NCSA) at the University of Illinois. In this dual directorship role, Reed provides strategic direction and leadership to the Alliance and NCSA and is the principal investigator for the Alliance cooperative agreement with the National Science Foundation. He is one of two principal investigators and the Chief Architect for the NSF TeraGrid project to create a national infrastructure for Grid computing.

Professor Reed was head of the University of Illinois computer science department from 1996 to 2001. He is currently a member of several national collaborations, including the NSF Center for Grid Application Development Software, the Department of Energy (DOE) Scientific Discovery through Advanced Computing program, and the Los Alamos Computer Science Institute. He is co-chair of the NSF Grid Physics Network (GriPhyN) Advisory Committee and is a member of the board of directors of the Computing Research Association.